적중 100

영어 기출 문제집

중**2**

시사 | 박준언

Best Collection

구성과 특징

교과서의 주요 학습 내용을 중심으로 학습 영역별 특성에 맞춰 단계별로 다양한 학습 기회를 제공하여
단원별 학습능력 평가는 물론 중간 및 기말고사 시험 등에 완벽하게 대비할 수 있도록 내용을 구성

Words & Expressions

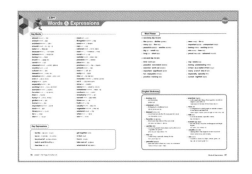

Step1 Key Words 단원별 핵심 단어 설명 및 풀이
Key Expression 단원별 핵심 숙어 및 관용어 설명
Word Power 반대 또는 비슷한 뜻 단어 배우기
English Dictionary 영어로 배우는 영어 단어

Step2 실력평가 단원별 수시평가 대비 주관식, 객관식 문제풀이

Step3 서술형 대비 학업성취도 및 수행능력평가 대비 서술형 문제풀이

Conversation

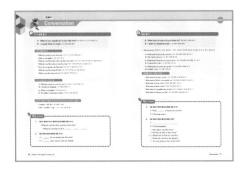

Step1 핵심 의사소통 소통에 필요한 주요 표현 방법 요약
핵심 Check 기본적인 표현 방법 및 활용능력 확인

Step2 대화문 익히기 교과서 대화문 심층 분석 및 확인

Step3 교과서 확인학습 빈칸 채우기를 통한 문장 완성 능력 확인

Step4 기본평가 시험대비 기초 학습 능력 평가

Step5 실력평가 단원별 수시평가 대비 주관식, 객관식 문제풀이

Step6 서술형 대비 학업성취도 및 수행능력평가 대비 서술형 문제풀이

Grammar

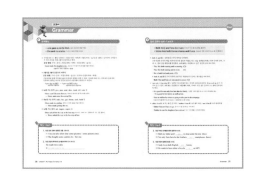

Step1 주요 문법 단원별 주요 문법 사항과 예문을 알기 쉽게 설명
핵심 Check 기본 문법사항에 대한 이해 여부 확인

Step2 기본평가 시험대비 기초 학습 능력 평가

Step3 실력평가 단원별 수시평가 대비 주관식, 객관식 문제풀이

Step4 서술형 대비 학업성취도 및 수행능력평가 대비 서술형 문제풀이

Reading

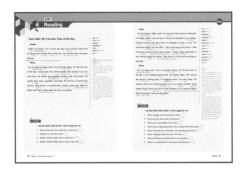

Step1 구문 분석 단원별로 제시된 문장에 대한 구문별 분석과 내용 설명
확인문제 문장에 대한 기본적인 이해와 인지능력 확인

Step2 확인학습A 빈칸 채우기를 통한 문장 완성 능력 확인

Step3 확인학습B 제시된 우리말을 영어로 완성하여 작문 능력 키우기

Step4 실력평가 단원별 수시평가 대비 주관식, 객관식 문제풀이

Step5 서술형 대비 학업성취도 및 수행능력평가 대비 서술형 문제풀이
교과서 구석구석 교과서에 나오는 기타 문장까지 완벽 학습

Composition

|영역별 핵심문제|

단어 및 어휘, 대화문, 문법, 독해 등 각 영역별 기출문제의 출제 유형을 분석하여 실전에 대비하고 연습할 수 있도록 문제를 배열

|단원별 예상문제|

기출문제를 분석한 후 새로운 시험 출제 경향을 더하여 새롭게 출제될 수 있는 문제를 포함하여 시험에 완벽하게 대비할 수 있도록 준비

|서술형 실전 및 창의사고력 문제|

학교 시험에서 점차 늘어나는 서술형 시험에 집중 대비하고 고득점을 취득하는데 만전을 기하기 위한 학습 코너

|단원별 모의고사|

영역별, 단계별 학습을 모두 마친 후 실전 연습을 위한 모의고사

교과서 파헤치기

- **단어Test1~3** 영어 단어 우리말 쓰기, 우리말을 영어 단어로 쓰기, 영영풀이에 해당하는 단어와 우리말 쓰기
- **대화문Test1~2** 대화문 빈칸 완성 및 전체 대화문 쓰기
- **본문Test1~5** 빈칸 완성, 우리말 쓰기, 문장 배열연습, 영어 작문하기 복습 등 단계별 반복 학습을 통해 교과서 지문에 대한 완벽한 습득
- **구석구석지문Test1~2** 지문 빈칸 완성 및 전문 영어로 쓰기

이책의 차례

Contents

Lesson	5	Different Countries, Different Cultures	05~56
Lesson	6	Wonders of Nature	57~108
Lesson	7	Work on Your Dreams	109~160

〈Insight on the textbook〉 교과서 파헤치기   01~58

〈책 속의 책〉 정답 및 해설   01~43

Lesson 5

Different Countries, Different Cultures

 의사소통 기능

- 길 알려 주기
  Go straight one block and turn right. It's on your left.

- 선호 묻기
  Which do you prefer, the London Eye or the Sky Garden?

 언어 형식

- 수동태
  Spain **is loved by** lots of tourists.

- so ~ that ... 구문
  It was **so** delicious **that** we all enjoyed it.

Words & Expressions

Key Words

- □ **abroad** [əbrɔ́ːd] 부 외국으로, 외국에서
- □ **artist** [ɑ́ːrtist] 명 화가, 예술가
- □ **capital** [kǽpətl] 명 수도
- □ **care** [kɛər] 명 돌봄, 보살핌
- □ **careful** [kɛ́ərfəl] 형 조심하는, 주의 깊은
- □ **ceiling** [síːliŋ] 명 천장
- □ **cheer** [tʃiər] 동 환호하다, 갈채하다 명 환호
- □ **coaster** [kóustər] 명 (롤러) 코스터
- □ **column** [kɑ́ləm] 명 기둥
- □ **curry** [kə́ːri] 명 카레
- □ **design** [dizáin] 동 설계하다, 디자인하다
- □ **dish** [diʃ] 명 음식, 접시
- □ **excuse** [ikskjúːz] 동 ~을 용서하다, 너그러이 봐주다
- □ **experience** [ikspíəriəns] 명 경험 동 경험하다
- □ **fan** [fæn] 명 팬, 부채
- □ **Ferris wheel** 대관람차
- □ **flamenco** [flɑːméŋkou] 명 플라멩코 (스페인 남부 **Andalusia** 지방 집시의 춤)
- □ **hamburger** [hǽmbəːrgər] 명 햄버거
- □ **helpful** [hélpfəl] 형 도움이 되는
- □ **historic** [histɔ́ːrik] 형 역사적인, 역사상 중요한
- □ **island** [áilənd] 명 섬
- □ **language** [lǽŋgwidʒ] 명 언어
- □ **lizard** [lízərd] 명 도마뱀
- □ **match** [mætʃ] 명 경기, 시합 동 어울리다

- □ **movement** [múːvmənt] 명 동작
- □ **near** [niər] 부 근처에
- □ **paella** [pɑːéijilə] 명 파에야
- □ **prefer** [prifə́ːr] 동 선호하다
- □ **purple** [pə́ːrpl] 명 보라색
- □ **right** [rait] 형 옳은, 오른쪽의
- □ **roll** [roul] 동 구르다, 굴리다
- □ **shine** [ʃain] 동 빛나다
- □ **slide** [slaid] 동 미끄러지다, 활주하다
- □ **Spain** [spein] 명 스페인
- □ **Spanish** [spǽniʃ] 형 스페인의 명 스페인어
- □ **stadium** [stéidiəm] 명 경기장
- □ **stop** [stɑp] 명 정거장 동 멈추다, 정지하다
- □ **tea** [tiː] 명 차
- □ **theater** [θíːətər] 명 극장
- □ **title** [táitl] 명 제목
- □ **tour** [tuər] 명 여행 동 관광하다
- □ **tourist** [túərist] 명 여행객
- □ **traditional** [trədíʃənl] 형 전통적인
- □ **unique** [juːníːk] 형 독특한
- □ **Vietnamese** [viètnɑːmíːz] 명 베트남어 형 베트남의
- □ **view** [vjuː] 명 전망, 경치
- □ **wave** [weiv] 동 흔들다 명 파도
- □ **work** [wəːrk] 동 일하다 명 작품

Key Expressions

- □ **across from**: ~의 맞은편에
- □ **be famous for**: ~로 유명하다
- □ **be full of**: ~으로 가득 차다
- □ **be known for**: ~로 알려져 있다
- □ **by+교통수단**: 교통수단으로 → **by bus**: 버스로, **by subway**: 지하철로, **by taxi**: 택시로
- □ **cheer for**: ~을 응원하다
- □ **far from**: ~로부터 멀리
- □ **get on**: ~에 타다
- □ **get to** 장소 명사, **get** 장소 부사: ~에 도착하다
- □ **go on**: (어떤 일이) 계속되다

- □ **How can I get there**?: 그곳에 어떻게 가니?
- □ **on foot**: 걸어서
- □ **on top of**: ~의 위에, ~의 꼭대기에
- □ **put off**: (시간, 날짜를) 미루다, 연기하다
- □ **so** 형용사/부사 **that** 주어 동사: 너무 ~해서 그 결과 …하다
- □ **take a tour**: 관광하다, 여행을 가다
- □ **try on**: 입어 보다
- □ **turn off**: (전기, 가스, 수도 등을) 끄다
- □ **turn on**: 켜다
- □ **Which do you prefer, A or B**?: A와 B 중 어느 것을 선호하니?

Word Power

※ 접미사 '-ful'이 붙어서 형용사가 되는 명사
□ **pain**(고통) → **painful**(고통스러운)
□ **color**(색깔) → **colorful**(다채로운)
□ **hope**(희망, 기대) → **hopeful**(희망에 찬, 기대하는)
□ **wonder**(놀라움) → **wonderful**(놀랄 만한, 멋진)

□ **use**(사용) → **useful**(유용한)
□ **peace**(평화) → **peaceful**(평화로운)
□ **help**(도움) → **helpful**(도움이 되는)
□ **care**(조심) → **careful**(조심하는)

※ 'take'를 사용한 다양한 표현들
□ **take a rest**(쉬다)
□ **take a walk**(산책하다)
□ **take a seat**(자리에 앉다)
□ **take a class**(수업을 받다)
□ **take a shower**(샤워를 하다)

□ **take a look (at)**((~을) (한 번) 보다)
□ **take a chance**((모험삼아) 해 보다)
□ **take a tour**(여행하다)
□ **take a picture**(사진을 찍다)

English Dictionary

□ **abroad**: 외국으로[에서]
→ in or to a foreign country
외국에서 또는 외국으로

□ **capital**: 수도
→ the main city of a country where its government is
정부가 있는 한 나라의 주요 도시

□ **ceiling**: 천장
→ the upper inside surface of a room
방의 위쪽 내부 표면

□ **cheer**: 환호하다, 갈채하다
→ to give a shout out of pleasure, praise, or support
기쁨, 칭찬 또는 지지를 위해 소리를 지르다

□ **curry**: 카레
→ a spicy Indian food with meat and vegetables in sauce
소스 안에 고기와 야채가 있는 매운 인도 음식

□ **excuse**: ~을 용서하다, 너그러이 봐주다
→ to forgive someone for something bad that they have done, especially something that is not very serious
어떤 나쁜 일, 특히 매우 심각하지 않은 어떤 일을 한 사람을 용서하다

□ **flamenco**: 플라멩코
→ a vigorous rhythmic dance style of the Andalusian Gypsies
안달루시아 집시의 격렬한 리듬을 가진 춤

□ **lizard**: 도마뱀
→ a reptile that has a rough skin and a long tail
거친 피부와 긴 꼬리를 가진 파충류

□ **prefer**: 선호하다
→ to like something or someone better than another
다른 것보다 어떤 것이나 어떤 사람을 더 좋아하다

□ **purple**: 보라색
→ a mixture of blue and red color
파란색과 빨간색을 섞은 색

□ **shine**: 빛나다
→ to produce bright light
밝은 빛을 만들어 내다

□ **slide**: 미끄러지다, 활주하다
→ to move along smoothly
부드럽게 움직이다

□ **Spanish**: 스페인의
→ relating to the language, people or culture of Spain
스페인의 언어, 사람 또는 문화와 관련된

□ **theater**: 극장
→ a building with a big screen or stage where many people watch movies or plays
많은 사람들이 영화나 연극을 보는 큰 스크린이나 무대를 가진 건물

□ **tour**: 여행
→ a journey for pleasure during which various places of interest are visited
흥미 있는 다양한 장소를 방문하는 즐거움을 위한 여행

□ **Vietnamese**: 베트남의
→ relating to the language, people or culture of Vietnam
베트남의 언어, 사람 또는 문화와 관련된

□ **view**: 전망, 경치
→ an outlook onto, or picture of a scene
어떤 경치의 전망이나 풍경

01 다음 밑줄 친 부분과 의미가 가장 가까운 것을 고르시오.

Each character has a unique personality.

① various   ② only   ③ unusual
④ common   ⑤ useful

02 다음 빈칸에 들어갈 말로 적절한 것은?

_____ me, which way is the closest subway station?

① Forgive   ② Accuse
③ Watch   ④ Exercise
⑤ Excuse

[03~04] 다음 영영 풀이에 해당하는 단어를 고르시오.

03
the upper inside surface of a room

① wall   ② floor   ③ roof
④ closet   ⑤ ceiling

04
to produce bright light

① shine   ② shut   ③ rise
④ tear   ⑤ shake

05 다음 주어진 우리말에 맞게 빈칸을 채우시오.

(1) 파리는 프랑스의 수도이다.
➡ Paris is the _____ of France.
(2) 그녀는 스페인 친구가 있다.
➡ She has a _____ friend.

06 다음 제시된 단어를 사용하여 자연스러운 문장을 만들 수 없는 것은?

┌─── 보기 ───┐
coaster   column   curry   lizard

① The man is riding a roller _____.
② A _____ has four legs and a long tail.
③ The _____ is too spicy for me.
④ I'd like to have a room with a great _____.
⑤ The _____ was made of white marble.

07 다음 밑줄 친 부분과 의미가 가장 가까운 것을 주어진 철자로 시작하여 쓰시오.

(1) What do you think the most typical Korean food is?
(2) Rachel loves the distinctive smell of a rose.

➡ (1) d_____, (2) u_____

08 주어진 단어 뒤에 -ful을 붙여 형용사로 만들 수 없는 것을 고르시오.

① help   ② care
③ wonder   ④ friend
⑤ peace

01 다음 〈보기〉처럼 짝지어진 두 단어의 관계와 같도록 빈칸에 알맞은 단어를 쓰시오.

┌── 보기 ┐
use – useful
└────────┘

(1) tradition : _____
(2) history : _____

02 〈보기〉에서 두 문장에 공통으로 들어갈 수 있는 단어를 찾아 쓰시오.

┌── 보기 ┐
cheers   match   experience   waves
works
└────────┘

(1)
• My mom always _____ me up when I am about to give up.
• The _____ of the fans filled the stadium.

(2)
• If you like tennis, let's go to watch a tennis _____.
• Her pants _____ the blouse perfectly.

(3)
• He _____ for the company which sells smartphones.
• His paintings are beautiful _____ of art.

(4)
• Surfers are riding the huge _____.
• She _____ her hands to him when she leaves home.

(5)
• We can learn from _____.
• I can _____ different cultures when I travel to other countries.

03 다음 우리말에 맞게 주어진 단어를 바르게 배열하시오.

(1) 너는 매일 얼마나 많은 여행객들이 Boston을 방문하는지 아니?
(tourists, every, do, know, how, visit, day, Boston, you, many, ?)
➡ _____

(2) 태양은 빛나고 나무는 자란다.
(grows, the, the, tree, and, shines, sun)
➡ _____

(3) 군중은 그 희소식을 듣고 기운이 났다.
(the, news, the, cheered, at, crowd, good, up)
➡ _____

(4) 나는 외국에서 공부하고 싶다.
(study, I, abroad, to, want)
➡ _____

04 다음 빈칸에 알맞은 단어를 〈보기〉에서 골라 쓰시오. (한 단어는 한 번 밖에 사용할 수 없음)

┌── 보기 ┐
put   take   try   turn
└────────┘

(1) Do you want to _____ a tour?
(2) Please _____ off the TV. It's past your bedtime.
(3) Is it possible to _____ off my trip until the 25th?
(4) Can I _____ on this jacket?

Conversation

① 길 알려 주기

> **Go straight one block and turn right. It's on your left.** 한 블록 직진한 후 우회전하세요. 왼편에 있어요.

■ 'Where is ~?'는 '~가 어디에 있나요?'라는 의미로 길이나 위치를 물어볼 때 사용하는 표현이다. 같은 의미를 가진 표현으로 'How can I get to ~?', 'How do I get to ~?', 또는 'Is there ~ around here?' 등이 있다. 이에 대한 대답으로 'Go straight.', 'Turn left.', 'It's on your right.' 등의 표현을 이용해서 길을 알려줄 수 있다.

길 묻기

- Where is ~? (~가 어디에 있나요?)
- How can/do I get to ~? (~에 어떻게 가나요?)
- Is there ~ around here? (근처에 ~가 있나요?)
- Do you know how to get to ~? (~에 어떻게 가는지 아나요?)
- Can/Could you tell me where ~ is? (어디에 ~가 있는지 말해 줄 수 있나요?)
- Can/Could you tell me how to get to ~? (~에 어떻게 가는지 말해 줄 수 있나요?)

길 알려 주기

- Go straight. (직진하세요.)
- Turn left/right. (좌회전/우회전 하세요.)
- It is across from ~. (~ 맞은편에 있어요.)
- It is on your left/right. (왼편/오른편에 있어요.)
- You'll see ~ on your left/right. (왼편에/오른편에 ~이 보일 거예요.)
- It is around the corner. (모퉁이 지나서 있어요.)
- Walk to the end of this block. (이 블록 끝까지 가세요.)
- Go straight until you see ~. (~가 보일 때까지 직진하세요.)
- It takes ten minutes on foot. (걸어서 10분 걸려요.)
- You can't miss it. (꼭 찾을 거예요.)

장소나 위치를 나타내는 표현

- around(~ 근처에)
- across from(~ 맞은편에)
- before(~ 전에)
- in front of(~ 앞에)
- near(근처에)
- next to(~ 옆에)
- on the corner(모퉁이에)
- around the corner(모퉁이를 돌아서)

핵심 Check

1. 다음 우리말과 일치하도록 빈칸에 알맞은 말을 쓰시오.

   A: Excuse me. _____ is the _____? (실례합니다. 은행이 어디에 있나요?)

   B: _____ until you see a crosswalk. (횡단보도가 보일 때까지 직진하세요.)

   A: And then? Should I cross the street? (그 다음엔? 길을 건너야 해요?)

   B: Yes. Then, you'll see the bank. It is _____ the school.
   (네. 그러면 은행이 보일 거예요. 학교 옆에 있어요.)

② 선호 묻기

Which do you prefer, the London Eye or the Sky Garden? 런던 아이와 스카이 가든 중 어느 곳을 선호하나요?

■ A와 B 둘 중에 어느 것을 더 좋아하는지 물을 때 'Which do you prefer, A or B?'라는 표현을 사용한다. prefer는 like better[more]로도 바꾸어 쓸 수 있으므로 'Which do you like better[more], A or B?'라고도 할 수 있다. which가 뒤에 나오는 명사를 수식하는 의문형용사로도 쓰일 수 있으므로 'Which place do you prefer, the London Eye or the Sky Garden?'이라고도 할 수 있다.

선호 묻기

- Which do you prefer, A or B? (A와 B 중 어느 것을 선호하니?)
- Do you prefer A to B? (너는 B보다 A를 더 좋아하니?)

■ 두 가지 중에서 어느 것을 더 선호하는지 말할 때 'I prefer A to B.', 'I think A is better than B.'로 말할 수 있다. 이때 비교 대상이 되는 than B나 to B는 생략할 수 있다. prefer A to B에서 to가 전치사이므로 뒤에 명사나 동명사가 오는 것에 유의해야 한다.

선호 표현하기

- I prefer A (to B). (나는 A를 (B보다) 선호한다.)
- I like A more than B.
- I think A is better than B.
- I think A is preferable to B.

핵심 Check

2. 다음 우리말과 일치하도록 빈칸에 알맞은 말을 쓰시오. (철자가 주어진 것도 있음)

(1) **A:** _____ do you p_____, baseball or tennis? (야구와 테니스 중에 어느 것을 더 좋아하니?)

   B: I _____ baseball _____ tennis. (나는 테니스보다 야구가 더 좋아.)

(2) **A:** Which do you _____ _____, meat or fish?

   (너는 고기와 생선 중에 어느 것을 더 좋아하니?)

   B: I _____ meat to fish. (나는 생선보다 고기를 더 좋아해.)

Listen & Speak 1 A-1

B: Excuse me. Is the Picasso Museum ❶near here?

G: Yes. It's not ❷far from here.

B: ❸How can I get there?

G: ❹Go straight one block and turn left. It's on your right.

B: 실례할게. 이 근처에 피카소 박물관이 있니?
G: 응, 여기서 멀지 않아.
B: 그곳에 어떻게 가니?
G: 한 블록 직진한 후 좌회전해. 오른편에 있어.

❶ near: ~ 근처에
❷ far from: ~에서 먼
❸ 'How can I get to 장소 ~?'는 '~에 어떻게 가니?'란 의미로 길을 물어보는 표현이다. 여기서 there는 위에서 언급된 the Picasso Museum을 의미한다. How can I get there? (= Do you know how to get there?)
❹ Go straight.: 직진하세요. Turn left/righ.t: 좌회전/우회전 하세요. It is on your left/right.: 왼편/오른편에 있어요.

Check(√) True or False

(1) The Picasso Museum is near here.　　T ☐ F ☐

(2) The girl knows how to get to the Picasso Museum.　　T ☐ F ☐

(3) The Picasso Museum is far from here.　　T ☐ F ☐

Listen & Speak 2 A-1

B: ❶It's really hot here in Thailand. ❷Let's go to the night market and have some fresh fruit juice.

G: ❸Sounds good. ❹How do we get there?

B: ❺We can go on foot or by bus. ❻Which do you prefer?

G: I ❼prefer the bus.

B: 태국은 정말 더워. 야시장에 가서 신선한 과일 주스를 마시자.
G: 좋아. 우리는 그곳에 어떻게 가지?
B: 우리는 걸어가거나 버스를 탈 수 있어. 어느 것을 선호하니?
G: 나는 버스를 선호해.

❶ 특정한 주어가 없이 날씨, 계절, 시간 등을 나타내는 문장에서는 주어의 자리에 It을 쓸 수 있다. Thailand: 태국
❷ '~하자'라는 제안을 하고자 할 때 'Let's ~'의 표현을 쓸 수 있다. have(먹다, 마시다)는 접속사 and로 go와 연결되어 있다. night market: 야시장
❸ sound+형용사: ~하게 들리다
❹ get to 장소 명사, get 장소 부사: ~에 도착하다
❺ on foot: 걸어서, by+교통수단: 교통수단으로 → by bus: 버스로, by subway: 지하철로, by taxi: 택시로
❻ 'Which do you prefer'의 뒤에 'on foot or by bus'가 생략되어 있다. A와 B 둘 중에 어느 것을 더 좋아하는지 물을 때 'Which do you prefer, A or B?'라는 표현을 사용한다.
❼ prefer: 선호하다

Check(√) True or False

(4) They are going to walk to the night market.　　T ☐ F ☐

(5) They are in Thailand.　　T ☐ F ☐

(6) They are going to the night market to have fruit juice.　　T ☐ F ☐

Listen & Speak 1 A-2

B: Sally, I ❶need to buy some candies for Halloween. Where can I buy ❷them?

G: You ❸can buy them at Wendy's Candy Shop.

B: ❹Where is it?

G: ❺Go straight two blocks and turn right. It's across from the library.

❶ need: ～이 필요하다, need는 뒤에 to부정사(to+동사원형)를 목적어로 취할 수 있다.
❷ them = some candies
❸ can+동사원형: ～할 수 있다. at+장소: ～에서
❹ Where is ～?'는 '～가 어디에 있나요?'라는 의미로 길이나 위치를 물어볼 때 사용하는 표현이다.
❺ Go straight: 직진하세요. Turn left/right: 좌회전/우회전 하세요. across from: ～ 맞은편에

Listen & Speak 2 A-2

G: ❶What is this long dress called?

M: ❷It is an Ao dai, a type of traditional clothing from Vietnam.

G: Can I ❸try one on?

M: Sure. ❹Which do you prefer, the purple one or the yellow one?

G: The purple one, please.

❶ 이름을 모르는 물건에 대해 어떻게 말하는지 물어볼 때 'How do you say ～?', 'What is ～ called?', 'What do you call ～?' 등으로 질문할 수 있다.
❷ an Ao dai와 a type of traditional clothing from Vietnam은 동격 관계이다. traditional: 전통적인 clothing: 옷, 의복
❸ try on: 입어 보다
❹ Which do you prefer, A or B?: A와 B 중 어느 것을 선호하니? one은 an Ao dai를 의미한다.

Conversation A

M: Welcome to London City Tour. ❶Today, we'll visit famous places in London. Can you see the London Eye? ❷It's on your right. ❸It's a Ferris wheel near the River Thames. ❹The view from the London Eye is amazing. Many people visit it every year.

❶ we'll = we will (우리는 ～할 것이다) famous: 유명한 place: 장소
❷ It is on your left/right: 왼편/오른편에 있어요.
❸ Ferris wheel: 대관람차 near: ～ 근처에
❹ view: 전망, 경치 amazing: 놀라운

Conversation B

Staff: ❶How may I help you?

Hana's mom: We ❷want to enjoy a good view of London.

Hana: Where is the best place ❸to go to?

Staff: We have two great places. ❹The London Eye is a Ferris wheel and the Sky Garden is a glass garden on top of a tall building. ❺Which do you prefer?

Hana's mom: Hmm... I ❻prefer the London Eye.

Hana: Me, too.

Staff: Good choice. You can ❼get there by bus.

Hana's mom: ❽Where is the nearest stop?

Staff: Go straight one block and turn right. It's on your left. ❾Have a good trip!

Hana: Wow, I can see all of London. Look! There is a big clock.

Hana's mom: I think that's Big Ben. ❿Why don't we go and visit it later?

Hana: That sounds great.

❶ 'May I help you?(도와드릴까요?)'에 의문사 How를 붙인 'How may I help you?'는 '무엇을 도와드릴까요?' 또는 '어떻게 도와드릴까요?'의 의미를 지닌다.
❷ want는 뒤에 to부정사(to+동사원형)를 목적어로 취할 수 있지만 동명사는 목적어로 취할 수 없다. view: 전망, 경치
❸ to부정사의 형용사적 용법으로 앞의 the best place를 수식하고 있다. the best place to go to: 가기에 가장 좋은 장소
❹ Ferris wheel: 대관람차 glass: 유리 on top of: ～의 위에, ～의 꼭대기에
❺ 문장 뒤에 'the London Eye or the Sky Garden'이 생략되어 있다. Which do you prefer, A or B?: A와 B 중 어느 것을 선호하니?
❻ prefer: 선호하다
❼ get 장소 부사: ～에 도착하다 by+교통수단: 교통수단으로 → by bus: 버스로
❽ Where is ～?: ～가 어디에 있나요? nearest: near(가까운)의 최상급, 가장 가까운 stop: 정거장
❾ Have a good trip!: 좋은 여행 하세요!
❿ 상대방에게 '함께 ～하자'는 표현으로 'Why don't we ～?'를 사용할 수 있다.

● 다음 우리말과 일치하도록 빈칸에 알맞은 말을 쓰시오.

Listen & Speak 1 A

1. B: Excuse me. _____ the Picasso Museum _____ here?

   G: Yes. It's not _____ _____ here.

   B: _____ can I get there?

   G: _____ _____ one block and turn _____. It's _____ your right.

2. B: Sally, I need _____ _____ some candies for Halloween. _____ _____ I buy them?

   G: You can buy _____ _____ Wendy's Candy Shop.

   B: _____ _____ _____?

   G: _____ _____ two _____ and turn right. It's _____ _____ the library.

Listen & Speak 1 B

1. A: Excuse me. _____ _____ the park?

   B: _____ _____ _____ _____ and turn left. It's _____ your right.

2. A: Excuse me. _____ _____ the school?

   B: Go _____ one block and turn left. _____ _____ your right. _____ _____ _____ the restaurant.

Listen & Talk 2 A

1. B: _____ really hot here in Thailand. _____ _____ to the night market and have some fresh fruit juice.

   G: Sounds _____. _____ do we _____ _____?

   B: We can go _____ _____ _____ _____ _____ _____. _____ _____ _____ _____?

   G: I _____ the bus.

2. G: _____ _____ this long dress _____?

   M: It is an Ao dai, a _____ of _____ _____ from Vietnam.

   G: Can I _____ _____ _____?

   M: Sure. _____ _____ _____ _____, the purple one or the yellow one?

   G: The purple one, please.

1. B: 실례할게. 이 근처에 피카소 박물관이 있니?
   G: 응, 여기서 멀지 않아.
   B: 그곳에 어떻게 가니?
   G: 한 블록 직진한 후 좌회전해. 오른편에 있어.

2. B: Sally야, 나는 할로윈에 필요한 사탕을 사야 해. 그것들을 어디서 살 수 있니?
   G: 넌 그것들을 Wendy's 사탕 가게에서 살 수 있어.
   B: 그곳은 어디에 있니?
   G: 두 블록 직진한 후 우회전해. 도서관 맞은편에 있어.

1. A: 실례합니다. 공원이 어디에 있나요?
   B: 두 블록 직진한 후 좌회전하세요. 오른편에 있어요.

2. A: 실례합니다. 학교가 어디에 있나요?
   B: 한 블록 직진한 후 좌회전하세요. 오른편에 있어요. 식당 맞은편에 있어요.

1. B: 태국은 정말 더워. 야시장에 가서 신선한 과일 주스를 마시자.
   G: 좋아. 우리는 그곳에 어떻게 가지?
   B: 우리는 걸어가거나 버스를 탈 수 있어. 어떤 것을 선호하니?
   G: 나는 버스를 선호해.

2. G: 이 긴 드레스를 뭐라고 부르나요?
   M: 그것은 베트남 전통 의상의 한 종류인 아오자이야.
   G: 제가 한 번 입어볼 수 있나요?
   M: 물론이지. 너는 보라색과 노란색 중 어떤 것을 선호하니?
   G: 보라색이요.

Listen & Talk 2 B

1. **A:** _____ _____ _____ _____, hamburgers or spaghetti?

   B: I prefer hamburgers.

2. **A:** _____ _____ _____ _____ , curry _____ paella?

   B: I prefer paella.

Conversation A

M: Welcome to London City Tour. Today, _____ _____ famous places in London. Can you _____ the London Eye? It's _____ _____ _____. It's a Ferris wheel near the River Thames. The _____ _____ the London Eye is amazing. Many people visit it every year.

Conversation B

Staff: _____ may I _____ you?

Hana's mom: We _____ _____ _____ a good view of London.

Hana: Where is the best place _____ _____ _____?

Staff: We have two great places. The London Eye is a Ferris wheel and the Sky Garden is a glass garden _____ _____ _____ a tall building. _____ do you prefer?

Hana's mom: Hmm... I _____ the London Eye.

Hana: Me, too.

Staff: Good choice. You can _____ there _____ _____.

Hana's mom: _____ is the _____ _____?

Staff: Go _____ one block and _____ _____. It's on your left. Have a good trip!

Hana: Wow, I can see all of London. Look! _____ _____ a big clock.

Hana's mom: I think that's Big Ben. _____ _____ _____ go and visit it later?

Hana: That sounds great.

해석

1. **A:** 햄버거와 스파게티 중 어느 것을 선호하니?
   B: 나는 햄버거를 선호해.

2. **A:** 카레와 파에야 중 어느 것을 선호하니?
   B: 나는 파에야를 선호해.

M: 런던 시티 투어에 오신 걸 환영합니다. 오늘 우리는 런던에서 유명한 장소들을 방문할 거예요. 런던 아이가 보이죠? 오른편에 있어요. 그것은 템스강 근처에 있는 대관람차예요. 런던 아이에서의 전망은 놀라워요. 매년 많은 사람들이 그곳을 방문해요.

직원: 무엇을 도와드릴까요?
엄마: 우리는 런던의 멋진 경치를 즐기고 싶어요.
하나: 가기에 가장 좋은 장소는 어디인가요?
직원: 두 곳이 있습니다. 런던 아이는 대관람차이고 스카이 가든은 높은 건물 꼭대기에 있는 유리 정원이에요. 어느 것을 선호하시나요?
엄마: 흠... 저는 런던 아이가 좋아요.
하나: 저도요.
직원: 좋은 선택이에요. 그곳에 버스로 갈 수 있답니다.
엄마: 가장 가까운 버스 정거장은 어디에 있나요?
직원: 여기서 한 블록 직진한 후 오른쪽으로 도세요. 왼편에 있어요. 좋은 여행하세요!
하나: 와, 런던 전체를 다 볼 수 있어요. 보세요! 커다란 시계가 있어요.
엄마: 내 생각에 저것은 빅벤 같아. 우리 나중에 가서 그곳을 방문해 볼래?
하나: 좋아요.

01 다음 대화의 빈칸에 알맞은 말은?

> A: Excuse me. _____ is the park?
> B: Go straight two blocks and turn left. It's on your right.

① When   ② Where   ③ Who
④ What   ⑤ How

02 다음 대화의 밑줄 친 부분과 바꾸어 쓸 수 <u>없는</u> 것을 고르시오.

> A: Which do you prefer, hamburgers or spaghetti?
> B: <u>I like hamburgers more than spaghetti.</u>

① I prefer hamburgers.
② I prefer hamburgers to spaghetti.
③ I think hamburgers are better than spaghetti.
④ I think I prefer hamburgers to spaghetti.
⑤ I think hamburgers are less preferable to spaghetti.

03 다음 대화의 밑줄 친 부분과 바꾸어 쓸 수 있는 것을 <u>모두</u> 고르시오.

> A: Excuse me. <u>Where is the school?</u>
> B: Go straight one block and turn left. It's on your right. It's across from the restaurant.

① How can I get to the school?
② Do you know when to go to the school?
③ How do I get to the school?
④ Could I tell you where the school is?
⑤ Is there the school around here?

04 자연스러운 대화가 되도록 순서대로 배열하시오.

> (A) How can I get there?
> (B) Go straight one block and turn left. It's on your right.
> (C) Excuse me. Is the Picasso Museum near here?
> (D) Yes. It's not far from here.

➡ _____

[01~02] 다음 대화를 읽고 물음에 답하시오.

> B: Excuse me. Is the Picasso Museum near here?
> G: Yes. It's not far (A)_____ here.
> B: (B)_____ can I get there?
> G: Go straight one block and turn left. It's on your right.

01 빈칸 (A)에 알맞은 말을 고르시오.

① for ② from ③ to
④ in ⑤ into

02 빈칸 (B)에 알맞은 의문사를 고르시오.

① Where ② How ③ What
④ When ⑤ Who

[03~05] 다음 대화를 읽고 물음에 답하시오.

> B: ⓐIt's really hot here in Thailand. (①) ⓑ Let's go to the night market and have some fresh fruit juice. (②)
> G: Sounds good. (③)
> B: ⓒWe can go on foot or by bus. (④) ⓓ What do you prefer?
> G: ⓔI prefer the bus. (⑤)

03 위 대화의 ①~⑤ 중 다음 주어진 말이 들어갈 알맞은 곳은?

> How do we get there?

① ② ③ ④ ⑤

04 ⓐ~ⓔ 중 어법상 어색한 것을 고르시오.

① ⓐ ② ⓑ ③ ⓒ ④ ⓓ ⑤ ⓔ

05 위 대화의 내용과 일치하지 않는 것을 고르시오.

① The boy wants to drink some fresh fruit juice.
② They are going to go to the night market.
③ They are in Thailand.
④ They are going to take a bus to go to the night market.
⑤ The girl knows how they get to the night market.

06 다음 중 짝지어진 대화가 어색한 것은?

① A: Which do you like better, Korean movies or foreign movies?
   B: I think Korean movies are better than foreign movies.
② A: Can you tell me how to get to the hospital?
   B: Of course. Go straight and turn left.
③ A: I prefer the park to the beach.
   B: OK. Let's go to the park.
④ A: Do you know how to get to the library?
   B: I'm a stranger, too. Go straight and turn left. It's next to the bookstore.
⑤ A: Which shirt do you prefer, the red one or the yellow one?
   B: I'd prefer the red one.

[07~09] 다음 대화를 읽고 물음에 답하시오.

> B: Jisu, (A)[why / how] don't we watch the movie *Best Friends* on Saturday? (①)
>
> G: Sounds good. (②)
>
> B: (③) On Saturday there are two showings, one at five and the other at seven. Which do you prefer?
>
> G: I prefer the seven showing. (④)
>
> B: Okay. Then (B)[how about / let's] meet at six. (⑤)
>
> G: Sounds good.

07 위 대화의 ①~⑤ 중 다음 주어진 말이 들어갈 알맞은 곳은?

> What time does it begin?

①   ②   ③   ④   ⑤

서답형

08 괄호 (A)와 (B)에서 알맞은 말을 골라 쓰시오.

➡ (A) _____, (B) _____

09 위 대화를 읽고 대답할 수 <u>없는</u> 질문을 고르시오.

① What time does the movie *Best Friends* begin on Saturday?

② Where are they going to meet on Saturday?

③ What time does the girl prefer, five or seven?

④ What time are they going to meet on Saturday?

⑤ What movie are they going to watch on Saturday?

[10~12] 그림을 참고하여 다음 대화를 읽고 물음에 답하시오.

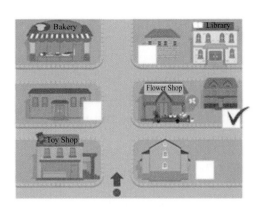

> B: Sally, I need to buy some candies for Halloween. (A)_____ can I buy them?
>
> G: You can buy them at Wendy's Candy Shop.
>
> B: (B)_____ is it?
>
> G: (C)_____ It's (D)_____ the library.

서답형

10 (A)와 (B)에 공통으로 들어갈 의문사를 쓰시오.

➡ _____

11 그림에 표시가 되어 있는 곳을 찾아 갈 때 빈칸 (C)에 알맞을 말을 고르시오.

① Go straight one block and turn left.

② Go straight one block and turn right. It's on your right.

③ Go straight two blocks and turn right.

④ Go straight two blocks and turn right. It's on your left.

⑤ Go straight two blocks and turn left.

서답형

12 그림을 참고하여 (D)에 들어갈 단어를 쓰시오. (2 단어)

➡ _____

01 다음 대화에서 어색한 부분을 찾아 고치시오.

> A: Which do you prefer, cookies or pie?
> B: Yes, I do. I prefer cookies

➡ _____

[02~03] 그림을 참고하여 다음 대화를 읽고 물음에 답하시오.

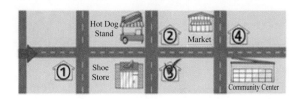

> B: Excuse me. 나에게 아프리카 박물관에 가는 방법을 말해 줄 수 있니? (how, to, to, African, the, can, me, Museum, you, tell, get, ?)
> G: Sure. Go straight two blocks and turn (A) _____.
> B: Go straight and turn (A) _____. And then?
> G: It's on your (B) _____. It's (C) _____ the shoe store.
> B: I got it. Thank you very much.

02 밑줄 친 우리말에 맞게 괄호 안에 주어진 단어를 배열하여 영작하시오.

➡ _____

03 그림에 표시된 아프리카 박물관(③번)에 갈 때 (A)~(C)에 알맞은 말을 쓰시오.

➡ (A) _____, (B) _____, (C) _____

[04~05] 다음 대화를 읽고 물음에 답하시오.

> B: It's really hot here in Thailand. Let's go to the night market and have some fresh fruit juice.
> G: Sounds good. (a)How do we get there?
> B: We can go (A) _____ foot or (B) _____ bus. Which do you prefer?
> G: I prefer the bus.

04 빈칸 (A)와 (B)에 알맞은 전치사를 쓰시오.

➡ (A) _____, (B) _____

05 밑줄 친 (a)와 같은 의미가 되도록 주어진 단어를 이용해서 문장을 만드시오.

➡ _____ (can, how)

_____
(how, know)

_____
(how, tell, can)

[06~07] 다음 대화를 읽고 물음에 답하시오.

> A: Which do you prefer, curry (A) _____ paella?
> B: (B)I prefer paella.

06 빈칸 (A)에 알맞은 접속사를 쓰시오.

➡ _____

07 위 대화의 밑줄 친 (B)에서 생략된 것을 쓰시오.

➡ _____

Grammar

① 수동태

> Leonardo da Vinci **painted** *Mona Lisa*. 〈능동태〉 Leonardo da Vinci는 모나리자를 그렸다.
> *Mona Lisa* **was painted** by Leonardo da Vinci. 〈수동태〉 모나리자는 Leonardo da Vinci에 의해 그려졌다.

■ 수동태는 '주어+be동사+동사의 과거분사+by+행위자'의 형식을 가지며 '…에 의해 ~되다[당하다, 받다]'라는 뜻이며, 주어가 동사가 나타내는 행위를 당하거나 행동의 영향을 받는 것을 나타낸다. 수동태 문장의 주어 자리에는 능동태 문장의 목적어가 오고, by 다음에는 능동태 문장의 주어를 쓴다. 이때 능동태 문장의 주어가 일반인이면 'by + 행위자'는 생략할 수 있다. 누가 그 동작을 했는지 중요하지 않거나 잘 모를 때, 수동태 문장으로 표현한다. 수동태는 현재, 과거, 미래 시제로 쓸 수 있고, 'be동사+동사의 과거분사'에서 be동사로 시제를 표현한다.

  • This place **was used** for cooking. 이곳은 요리를 위해 사용되었다.

■ 4형식 문장의 수동태는 간접목적어와 직접목적어 각각을 주어로 하는 수동태가 가능하며 직접목적어를 주어로 한 수동태에서는 간접목적어 앞에 특정한 전치사를 써야 한다. 전치사 to를 쓰는 동사에는 'give, send, tell, teach, show, bring' 등이 있고, 전치사 for를 쓰는 동사에는 'buy, make, choose, cook, get' 등이 있으며, 전치사 of를 쓰는 동사는 'ask' 등이 있다. 또한 make, buy, read, write 등은 직접목적어를 주어로 하는 수동태만 가능하다.

  • A book **was given** to Sam by Harry. 책 한 권이 Harry에 의해 Sam에게 주어졌다.

■ 조동사가 있는 문장의 수동태는 '조동사+be+p.p.' 형식을 갖는다.

  • A dress **will be bought** for Jennifer by her mom. 옷이 그녀의 엄마에 의해 Jennifer에게 사주어질 것이다.

■ 목적격보어가 원형부정사인 경우, 수동태 문장에서는 to부정사로 바뀐다.

  • Jack **was made** to wash the dishes by his mom. Jack은 그의 엄마에 의해 설거지하도록 시켜졌다.

■ by 이외의 전치사를 사용하는 수동태에 유의한다.

  • be interested in: ~에 흥미가 있다   • be filled with: ~로 가득 차다
  • be covered with: ~로 덮여 있다   • be surprised at: ~에 놀라다
  • be made of: ~로 만들어지다(물리적 변화)   • be made from: ~로 만들어지다(화학적 변화)
  • be satisfied with: ~에 만족하다   • be pleased with: ~에 기뻐하다

핵심 Check

1. 다음 괄호 안에서 알맞은 말을 고르시오.

(1) The building was (build / built) last year.

(2) The book (will / will be) written by Andy.

② so ~ that ... 구문

It was **so** delicious **that** we all enjoyed it. 너무 맛있어서 우리 모두는 그것을 즐겼다.

The movie was **so** funny **that** I laughed a lot. 그 영화는 너무 재밌어서 나는 많이 웃었다.

■ 'so+형용사[부사]+that+주어+동사' 구문은 '너무 ~해서 …하다'라는 뜻으로 원인과 결과를 나타낸다. so 뒤에 나오는 내용이 원인을 뜻하고, that 이하가 결과를 나타낸다. 이때 so는 뒤에 나오는 형용사나 부사를 강조한다.

• I was **so** tired **that** I couldn't go out. 나는 너무 피곤해서 나갈 수 없었다.

■ 'so ... that' 구문에서 that 앞에 형용사나 부사 대신 명사가 오면 so 대신 such를 쓴다.

• There was **such** a crowd **that** we could hardly move. 사람이 아주 많아서 우리는 거의 움직이지 못했다.

■ 'so that+주어+동사'는 목적을 나타내어 '~하기 위해서' 혹은 '~하도록'이라는 의미로 쓰인다. 'so ~ that ...'과 혼동하지 않도록 유의한다.

• Record this meeting **so that** people can replay it later. 이 회의를 기록하여 나중에 재생할 수 있도록 하십시오.

■ 'so+형용사[부사]+that+주어+can ~'은 '형용사[부사]+enough+to 동사원형'으로 바꿔 쓸 수 있으며, 'so+형용사[부사]+that+주어+can't ~'는 'too+형용사[부사]+to 동사원형'으로 바꿔 쓸 수 있다.

• She was **so** kind **that** she invited me.
= She was kind **enough to** invite me. 그녀는 너무 친절해서 나를 초대했다.

• Emma was **so** sick **that** she couldn't lift a finger.
= Emma was **too** sick **to** lift a finger. Emma는 너무 아파서 손가락도 까딱할 수 없었다.

핵심 Check

2. 다음 우리말에 맞게 괄호 안의 어구를 바르게 배열하시오.

(1) 물이 맑아서 밑바닥까지 보였다.

(you, the water, the bottom, could, was, see, clear, so, that)

➡ _____

(2) 그는 매우 열심히 공부해서 변호사가 되었다.

(he, he, a lawyer, became, worked, hard, that, so)

➡ _____

(3) 당신이 그곳에 제시간에 도착할 수 있게 빨리 몰겠습니다.

(you, I'll, there, time, get, drive, can, so, in, fast, that)

➡ _____

Grammar 시험대비 기본평가

01 다음 문장에서 어법상 <u>어색한</u> 부분을 바르게 고쳐 쓰시오.

(1) The room cleans by him every day.

_____ ➡ _____

(2) *The Kiss* is painted by Gustav Klimt in 1908.

_____ ➡ _____

(3) Mike felt very happy that he danced.

_____ ➡ _____

(4) She exercises hard so that may stay healthy.

_____ ➡ _____

02 다음 중 어법상 바르지 <u>않은</u> 것은?

① The pictures were taken by my sister.
② The bridge was built about 50 years ago.
③ Jessica is loved by everybody.
④ The letter is sent tomorrow.
⑤ *Harry Potter* was written by J.K. Rowling.

03 다음 문장의 밑줄 친 부분 중에서 어법상 <u>잘못된</u> 곳을 고르시오.

①It was ②<u>too</u> ③<u>delicious</u> ④<u>that we</u> ⑤<u>all</u> enjoyed it.

04 다음 우리말에 맞게 주어진 어구를 바르게 배열하시오. (필요하면 어형을 바꿀 것)

(1) 그 물은 너무 깨끗해서 우리는 그것을 마실 수 있었다. (we, the water, was, drink, could, that, it, clean, so)

➡ _____

(2) 그는 축구 시합 중에 부상을 입었다. (he, injure, during, the soccer match)

➡ _____

01 다음 빈칸에 알맞은 것은?

> English _____ all around the world.

① speaks ② spoke
③ spoken ④ is spoken
⑤ to speak

02 다음 빈칸에 알맞은 말이 순서대로 바르게 짝지어진 것은?

> • The car _____ by him every Sunday.
> • The cap was _____ small that I couldn't wear it.

① washes – so
② is washed – too
③ is washed – so
④ was washed – too
⑤ was washed – very

03 다음 중 수동태로의 전환이 <u>어색한</u> 것은?

① Soccer fans filled the stadium.
  → The stadium was filled with soccer fans.
② They make a lot of cars in Korea.
  → A lot of cars are made in Korea.
③ Mom made me a delicious spaghetti last night.
  → A delicious spaghetti was made for me by Mom last night.
④ King Sejong invented Hangeul.
  → Hangeul was invented by King Sejong.
⑤ Jenny sent me the pictures drawn in France.
  → The pictures sent to me were drawn in France by Jenny.

04 다음 문장에서 어법상 <u>틀린</u> 부분을 찾아 바르게 고치시오.

> He is weak so that he can't swim across the river.

_____ ➡ _____

05 다음 괄호 안에서 알맞은 것을 고르시오.

(1) I was (excited / exciting) because we could watch some of the world's most famous soccer players.
(2) We (consider / are considered) blue whales to be the biggest animals.
(3) English was taught (to / for) us by Ms Green.
(4) Some interesting books were chosen (to / for) me by her.
(5) The way to the station was asked (to / of) me by the old lady.
(6) Angelina is (so / very) shy that she can't speak in front of many people.
(7) Clark was so hungry (that / what) he ate all the food.

06 다음 빈칸에 알맞은 말이 바르게 짝지어진 것을 고르시오.

> • I worked _____ hard _____ I passed the test.

① so – that ② that – so
③ too – that ④ that – too
⑤ too – to

07 다음 빈칸에 공통으로 들어갈 말로 가장 적절한 것은?

> • Does that mean that you're pleased
> _____ it?
> • I am not satisfied _____ the service.

① with   ② for   ③ in

④ at   ⑤ of

08 다음 우리말에 맞게 영작한 것을 고르시오.

> • 그녀는 너무 화가 나서 얼굴이 빨개졌다.

① She was too angry to turn red.

② She was enough angry to turn red.

③ She was angry so that her face turned red.

④ She was so angry that her face turned red.

⑤ She was angry in order that her face turned red.

09 다음 우리말을 영어로 바르게 옮기지 않은 것은?

> Steve는 충분한 수면을 취하려고 어제 일찍 잤다.

① Steve went to bed early yesterday so that he could get plenty of sleep.

② Steve went to bed so early yesterday that he could get plenty of sleep.

③ Steve went to bed early yesterday to get plenty of sleep.

④ Steve went to bed early yesterday in order to get plenty of sleep.

⑤ Steve went to bed early yesterday so as to get plenty of sleep.

10 다음 문장을 수동태로 바르게 바꾼 것은?

> Jenny turned off the TV.

① The TV turned off Jenny.

② The TV turned off by Jenny.

③ The TV was turned off Jenny.

④ The TV was turned by Jenny.

⑤ The TV was turned off by Jenny.

11 다음 문장을 수동태는 능동태로, 능동태는 수동태로 고치시오.

(1) Both were designed by Antoni Gaudi.

➡ _____

(2) This photo was taken by James.

➡ _____

(3) Her mom made her a beautiful dress.

➡ _____

(4) The book fair will be held in Seoul.

➡ _____

(5) By whom is it considered to be dangerous?

➡ _____

12 다음 괄호 안에서 알맞은 말을 고르시오.

(1) Vietnam is (so / such) beautiful that you should come someday.

(2) I was in (so / such) a hurry that I could not pay you a visit.

(3) The park was so noisy that I (shouldn't / couldn't) rest.

➡ (1) _____ (2) _____ (3) _____

13 다음 중 두 문장을 서로 바꿔 쓸 수 없는 것은?

① *Romeo and Juliet* was written by Shakespeare.
→ Shakespeare wrote *Romeo and Juliet*.

② Morris bought his son a new suit last week.
→ A new suit was bought for his son by Morris last week.

③ They showed the public the photos taken by him.
→ The photos taken by him were shown to the public.

④ The thief forced Judy to hand over the money.
→ Judy was forced to hand over the money by the thief.

⑤ Our teacher made us do our homework.
→ We were made do our homework by our teacher.

14 다음 중 어법상 올바른 문장을 모두 고르시오.

① He was seen put the bag on the table by Ann.

② He was read the storybook every night by his mom.

③ Melbourne is well known for its beautiful ocean roads.

④ It was so a nice day that we went for a walk.

⑤ Julie is so kind that everybody likes her.

서답형

15 다음 문장에서 어법상 어색한 부분을 바르게 고쳐 다시 쓰시오.

(1) The World Wide Web(www) invented by Tim Berners-Lee in 1989.
_____ ➡ _____

(2) The car accident was happened last night.
_____ ➡ _____

(3) I was too careless to trust such a man.
_____ ➡ _____

[16~18] 다음 두 문장이 같은 의미가 되도록 빈칸에 알맞은 말을 고르시오.

16

> Harry chose Christine some books.
> = Some books _____ Christine by Harry.

① chose
② were choosing
③ were chosen
④ were chosen to
⑤ were chosen for

17 (중요)

> I heard him sing.
> = He _____ by me.

① heard singing
② was singing
③ was heard sing
④ heard sing
⑤ was heard to sing

18

> Because she is very sick, she can't move.
> = She is _____ she can't move.

① too sick that
② to sick too
③ so sick that
④ sick so that
⑤ very sick that

01 다음 문장을 수동태는 능동태로, 능동태는 수동태로 고치시오.

(1) The painting was stolen by someone last week.

➡ _____

(2) Its size and unique design impressed me.

➡ _____

(3) Eva heard Peter open the window.

➡ _____

(4) Angie will give me a present on my birthday.

➡ _____

(5) Cathy took care of the baby.

➡ _____

02 주어진 두 문장을 한 문장으로 만들 때, 빈칸에 알맞은 말을 3단어로 쓰시오.

(1) • I was very stupid.
  • I made the mistake.
  ➡ I was _____ I made the mistake.

(2) • He is very tall.
  • He can touch the ceiling.
  ➡ He is _____ touch the ceiling.

(3) • Alice was really shocked.
  • She couldn't say even a word.
  ➡ Alice was _____ say even a word.

03 다음 우리말을 so와 that을 이용하여 영어로 쓸 때 빈칸에 알맞은 말을 쓰시오.

(1) Robert는 시험에 합격하기 위해서 열심히 공부했다.
  ➡ Robert studied _____ he could pass the exam.

(2) Robert는 열심히 공부해서 시험에 합격할 수 있었다.
  ➡ Robert studied _____ he could pass the exam.

04 다음 문장에서 어법상 어색한 부분을 바르게 고쳐 다시 쓰시오.

(1) Cake is made of flour, milk, eggs and sugar.

➡ _____

(2) The shirts are ironed by John tomorrow morning.

➡ _____

(3) Mike was seen be hit by a car by Ms. Brown.

➡ _____

(4) Our dog was ran over by a truck.

➡ _____

(5) The matter will discussed by us tomorrow.

➡ _____

05 다음 문장을 같은 뜻을 갖는 문장으로 바꿔 쓸 때 빈칸을 알맞게 채우시오.

(1) The test was so easy that I could pass it.
→ The test was _____ pass.

(2) Andrew speaks _____ I can't understand him.
→ Andrew speaks too fast for me to understand.

06 다음 우리말을 괄호 안에 주어진 어휘를 이용하여 영작하시오.

(1) 그 소설은 Ernest Hemingway에 의해 씌여졌다. (novel, write)
➡ _____

(2) 최초의 월드컵은 1930년 우루과이에서 열렸다. (Uruguay, the first World Cup, take place)
➡ _____

(3) Laura는 그녀의 딸에게 동화책을 읽어 주었다. (read, a fairy tale book) (수동태로 쓸 것.)
➡ _____

(4) Kimberly는 그 소식을 듣고 낙담했다. (disappointed, the news)
➡ _____

(5) 너는 Allie가 노래하는 것을 들었니? (hear, sing) (수동태로 쓸 것.)
➡ _____

(6) 너무나도 추워서 그는 감기에 걸렸다. (cold, catch a cold)
➡ _____

07 괄호 안의 어휘를 사용하여 주어진 문장을 같은 의미가 되도록 다시 쓰시오.

(1) Claire got up so late that she couldn't get on the train. (too)
➡ _____

(2) Chuck spoke too low for me to hear. (so, can)
➡ _____

(3) Bill was so smart that he could solve the difficult math problems. (enough)
➡ _____

(4) Juliet is rich enough to buy the house. (so, can)
➡ _____

08 다음 문장을 주어진 어휘로 시작하여 다시 쓰시오.

(1) My grandmother made the sweater for me. (the sweater)
➡ _____

(2) Does she clean these rooms every day? (are)
➡ _____

(3) Mariel made Dan prepare dinner. (Dan)
➡ _____

(4) Your recent success pleased Joakim a lot. (Joakim)
➡ _____

My Happy Days in Spain

by Park Jinwoo

My family traveled to Spain this summer. Spain is loved by lots of
tourists. We visited many interesting places.

Our trip started in Madrid. Madrid is the capital and is famous for
soccer. We went to a stadium to watch a soccer match. My sister and I
were excited because we could watch some of the world's most famous
soccer players.

The stadium was full of soccer fans. As we watched the match, we
cheered by singing songs, waving our hands, and shouting with the
other fans.

After we toured Madrid, we went to Seville. While we walked around
the city, we saw many historic buildings. We visited a flamenco
museum and watched a flamenco dance. A woman in a red dress was
dancing the flamenco with wonderful movements.

travel 여행하다
tourist 여행객, 관광객
capital 수도
stadium 경기장
match 경기, 시합
be famous for ~으로 유명하다
be full of ~으로 가득 차다
cheer 응원하다
historic 역사적인
flamenco 플라멩코(격정적인 스페인 춤)
movement 동작

📎 확인문제

● 다음 문장이 본문의 내용과 일치하면 T, 일치하지 않으면 F를 쓰시오.

1 Jinwoo's family traveled to Spain last summer. ☐

2 Jinwoo's family trip started in Madrid. ☐

3 Jinwoo's family went to a stadium to watch a soccer match. ☐

4 The stadium was full of the world's most famous soccer players. ☐

5 Jinwoo's family went to Seville after they toured Madrid. ☐

6 Jinwoo's family watched a flamenco dance on the street. ☐

For dinner, we ate paella. It is a traditional Spanish dish with rice, 저녁 식사로 ~이 있는(전치사)

vegetables, meat, and seafood. It tasted like fried rice in Korea. It was
taste like+명사: ~와 같은 맛이 나다

so delicious that we all enjoyed it.
so+형용사/부사+that+주어+동사: '너무 ~해서 …하다'라는 원인과 결과를 나타냄

In Barcelona, we took a tour of Park Guell and Sagrada Familia.
~을 관광했다

Both were designed by Antoni Gaudi. In Park Guell, we saw some of
Park Guell과 Sagrada Familia. be동사+과거분사+by ~(수동태)

Gaudi's creative works like a colorful lizard.
작품 ~와 같은

After Park Guell, we visited Sagrada Familia. Work on the building
일, 작업 Sagrada Familia

started in 1883 and is still going on today. I was impressed by its size
아직도 진행되고 있다 ~에 감명을 받았다(수동태)

and unique design. The ceiling inside Sagrada Familia shone like the
~처럼

night sky with bright stars. Its stone columns stood like big trees. At
~이 있는 Sagrada Familia

Park Guell and Sagrada Familia I could feel Gaudi's creativity and his

love of nature.

Traveling in Spain was a wonderful experience. While I was there, I
주어 역할을 하는 동명사

learned a lot about Spain. I want to visit the country again.
많이 Spain

traditional 전통적인
paella 파에야
Spanish 스페인의
lizard 도마뱀
take a tour 여행하다, 관광하다
still 여전히
unique 특별한
ceiling 천장
shine 빛나다
column 기둥
go on 계속하다
impress 감명을 주다
experience 경험

확인문제

• 다음 문장이 본문의 내용과 일치하면 T, 일치하지 않으면 F를 쓰시오.

1 For dinner, Jinwoo's family ate paella. ☐

2 Paella tasted like kimchi pancake in Korea. ☐

3 Park Guell and Sagrada Familia were designed by Antoni Gaudi. ☐

4 Jinwoo's family visited Park Guell after Sagrada Familia. ☐

5 Jinwoo was impressed by the size and unique design of Sagrada Familia. ☐

6 The ceiling inside Sagrada Familia stood like big trees. ☐

● 우리말을 참고하여 빈칸에 알맞은 말을 쓰시오.

1 My _____ _____ in Spain – _____ Park Jinwoo

2 My family _____ _____ Spain this summer.

3 Spain _____ _____ _____ lots of tourists.

4 We _____ many _____ places.

5 _____ _____ started in Madrid.

6 Madrid is the capital and _____ _____ _____ soccer.

7 We went to a stadium _____ _____ a soccer match.

8 My sister and I _____ _____ because we could watch some of _____ _____ _____ _____ _____ _____.

9 The stadium _____ _____ _____ soccer fans.

10 As we watched the match, we cheered _____ _____ songs, waving our hands, and _____ with the other fans.

11 _____ we toured Madrid, we went to Seville.

12 _____ we _____ _____ the city, we saw many historic buildings.

13 We _____ a flamenco museum and _____ a flamenco dance.

14 A woman _____ _____ was dancing the flamenco _____ _____ _____.

---

1 스페인에서의 행복한 날들 – 박진우

2 나의 가족은 이번 여름에 스페인을 여행했다.

3 스페인은 수많은 관광객들에게 사랑받는다.

4 우리는 여러 흥미로운 장소를 방문했다.

5 우리의 여행은 마드리드에서 시작했다.

6 마드리드는 수도이며 축구로 유명하다.

7 우리는 축구 경기를 보기 위해서 경기장으로 갔다.

8 나의 여동생과 나는 세계에서 가장 유명한 축구 선수 몇몇을 볼 수 있었기 때문에 신이 났다.

9 경기장은 축구 팬들로 가득 차 있었다.

10 우리는 경기를 보는 동안 노래를 부르고, 손을 흔들고, 다른 팬들과 함께 소리를 치며 응원을 했다.

11 마드리드를 여행하고 난 후, 우리는 세비야로 갔다.

12 우리는 도시를 걸어다니는 동안, 역사상 중요한 많은 건물들을 보았다.

13 우리는 플라멩코 박물관을 방문해서 플라멩코 춤을 보았다.

14 빨간 드레스를 입은 여자가 멋진 동작으로 플라멩코를 추고 있었다.

15 _____ dinner, we ate paella.

16 It is a _____ _____ _____ _____ rice, vegetables, meat, and seafood.

17 It _____ _____ fried rice in Korea.

18 It was _____ delicious _____ we all enjoyed it.

19 In Barcelona, we _____ _____ _____ _____ Park Guell and Sagrada Familia.

20 Both _____ _____ _____ Antoni Gaudi.

21 In Park Guell, we saw some of Gaudi's _____ _____ _____ a colorful lizard.

22 _____ Park Guell, we visited Sagrada Familia.

23 Work on the building started in 1883 and _____ _____ _____ _____ today.

24 I _____ _____ _____ its size and unique design.

25 The ceiling inside Sagrada Familia _____ _____ the night sky with bright stars.

26 Its stone columns _____ _____ big trees.

27 At Park Guell and Sagrada Familia I could feel Gaudi's _____ and _____ _____ _____ _____ .

28 _____ in Spain was _____ _____ _____ .

29 _____ I was there, I learned _____ _____ about Spain.

30 I want _____ _____ the country again.

15 저녁 식사로 우리는 파에야를 먹었다.

16 그것은 쌀과 채소, 고기, 해산물이 들어간 전통적인 스페인 요리이다.

17 그것은 한국의 볶음밥과 같은 맛이 났다.

18 너무 맛있어서 우리 모두는 그것을 즐겼다.

19 바르셀로나에서 우리는 구엘 공원과 사그라다 파밀리아를 둘러보았다.

20 두 곳 모두 Antoni Gaudi에 의해 설계되었다.

21 구엘 공원에서 우리는 형형색색의 도마뱀과 같은 몇몇 Gaudi의 창의적인 작품들을 보았다.

22 구엘 공원을 본 다음, 우리는 사그라다 파밀리아를 방문했다.

23 건물 공사는 1883년에 시작되었고 오늘날까지도 여전히 진행 중이다.

24 나는 건물의 크기와 독특한 디자인에 감명 받았다.

25 사그라다 파밀리아 안의 천장은 밝은 별이 있는 밤하늘처럼 빛났다.

26 돌기둥은 큰 나무처럼 서 있었다.

27 구엘 공원과 사그라다 파밀리아에서 나는 Gaudi의 창의성과 자연에 대한 사랑을 느낄 수 있었다.

28 스페인 여행은 훌륭한 경험이었다.

29 나는 그곳에서 스페인에 대해 많은 것을 배웠다.

30 나는 그 나라를 다시 방문하고 싶다.

• 우리말을 참고하여 본문을 영작하시오.

1 스페인에서의 행복한 날들 – 박진우

➡ _____

2 나의 가족은 이번 여름에 스페인을 여행했다.

➡ _____

3 스페인은 수많은 관광객들에게 사랑받는다.

➡ _____

4 우리는 여러 흥미로운 장소를 방문했다.

➡ _____

5 우리의 여행은 마드리드에서 시작했다.

➡ _____

6 마드리드는 수도이며 축구로 유명하다.

➡ _____

7 우리는 축구 경기를 보기 위해서 경기장으로 갔다.

➡ _____

8 나의 여동생과 나는 세계에서 가장 유명한 축구 선수 몇몇을 볼 수 있었기 때문에 신이 났다.

➡ _____

9 경기장은 축구 팬들로 가득 차 있었다.

➡ _____

10 우리는 경기를 보는 동안 노래를 부르고, 손을 흔들고, 다른 팬들과 함께 소리를 치며 응원을 했다.

➡ _____

11 마드리드를 여행하고 난 후, 우리는 세비야로 갔다.

➡ _____

12 우리는 도시를 걸어다니는 동안, 역사상 중요한 많은 건물들을 보았다.

➡ _____

13 우리는 플라멩코 박물관을 방문해서 플라멩코 춤을 보았다.

➡ _____

14 빨간 드레스를 입은 여자가 멋진 동작으로 플라멩코를 추고 있었다.

➡ _____

15 저녁 식사로 우리는 파에야를 먹었다.

➡ _____

16 그것은 쌀과 채소, 고기, 해산물이 들어간 전통적인 스페인 요리이다.

➡ _____

17 그것은 한국의 볶음밥과 같은 맛이 났다.

➡ _____

18 너무 맛있어서 우리 모두는 그것을 즐겼다.

➡ _____

19 바르셀로나에서 우리는 구엘 공원과 사그라다 파밀리아를 둘러보았다.

➡ _____

20 두 곳 모두 Antoni Gaudi에 의해 설계되었다.

➡ _____

21 구엘 공원에서 우리는 형형색색의 도마뱀과 같은 몇몇 Gaudi의 창의적인 작품들을 보았다.

➡ _____

22 구엘 공원을 본 다음, 우리는 사그라다 파밀리아를 방문했다.

➡ _____

23 건물 공사는 1883년에 시작되었고 오늘날까지도 여전히 진행 중이다.

➡ _____

24 나는 건물의 크기와 독특한 디자인에 감명 받았다.

➡ _____

25 사그라다 파밀라아 안의 천장은 밝은 별이 있는 밤하늘처럼 빛났다.

➡ _____

26 돌기둥은 큰 나무처럼 서 있었다.

➡ _____

27 구엘 공원과 사그라다 파밀리아에서 나는 Gaudi의 창의성과 자연에 대한 사랑을 느낄 수 있었다.

➡ _____

28 스페인 여행은 훌륭한 경험이었다.

➡ _____

29 나는 그곳에서 스페인에 대해 많은 것을 배웠다.

➡ _____

30 나는 그 나라를 다시 방문하고 싶다.

➡ _____

[01~03] 다음 글을 읽고 물음에 답하시오.

My family traveled to Spain this summer. Spain is loved by ⓐlots of tourists. We visited many interesting places.

Our trip started in Madrid. Madrid is the capital and is famous for soccer. We went to a stadium to watch a soccer match. My sister and I were excited because we could watch some of the world's most famous soccer players. <I = Park Jinwoo>

 위 글의 종류로 알맞은 것을 고르시오.

① review　　② essay
③ traveler's journal　④ biography
⑤ article

02 위 글의 밑줄 친 ⓐlots of와 바꿔 쓸 수 없는 말을 모두 고르시오.

① a few　　② many
③ plenty of　④ a number of
⑤ much

03 위 글의 내용과 일치하지 않는 것은?

① 진우의 가족은 이번 여름에 스페인을 여행했다.
② 수많은 관광객들이 스페인을 사랑한다.
③ 진우의 가족 여행은 마드리드에서 끝났다.
④ 마드리드는 스페인의 수도이다.
⑤ 진우와 여동생은 세계에서 가장 유명한 축구 선수 몇몇을 볼 수 있었다.

[04~06] 다음 글을 읽고 물음에 답하시오.

After we toured Madrid, we went to Seville. ⓐWhile we walked around the city, we saw many historic buildings. We visited a flamenco museum and watched a flamenco dance. A woman in a red dress was ⓑdancing the flamenco with wonderful movements.

<we = Jinwoo's family>

서답형
04 Where did Jinwoo's family see many historic buildings? Fill in the blanks with the suitable words.

➡ They ＿＿＿＿＿＿＿＿＿＿＿＿.

05 위 글의 밑줄 친 ⓐWhile과 같은 의미로 쓰인 것을 고르시오.

① While Tom is very good at science, his brother is hopeless.
② While I was waiting at the bus stop, three buses went by.
③ I've read fifty pages, while he's read only twenty.
④ They chatted for a while.
⑤ The walls are green, while the ceiling is white.

06 아래 <보기>에서 위 글의 밑줄 친 ⓑdancing과 문법적 쓰임이 같은 것의 개수를 고르시오.

┌─ 보기 ├─
① His hobby is collecting stamps.
② They aren't playing tennis.
③ She heard someone calling her name.
④ I like baking cookies.
⑤ The girl standing at the door is my sister.

① 1개　② 2개　③ 3개　④ 4개　⑤ 5개

[07~10] 다음 글을 읽고 물음에 답하시오.

For dinner, we ate paella. It is a traditional Spanish dish with rice, vegetables, meat, and seafood. It tasted like fried rice in Korea. ⓐ 너무 맛있어서 우리 모두는 그것을 즐겼다.

In Barcelona, we took a tour of Park Guell and Sagrada Familia. Both were designed by Antoni Gaudi. In Park Guell, we saw some of Gaudi's creative ⓑworks like a colorful lizard.   <we = Jinwoo's family>

서답형

07 위 글의 밑줄 친 ⓐ의 우리말에 맞게 주어진 어휘를 이용하여 9단어로 영작하시오.

It, so, delicious

➡ _____

08 위 글의 밑줄 친 ⓑworks와 같은 의미로 쓰인 것을 고르시오.

① He works at a small shop.

② She collected Beethoven's piano works.

③ They started engineering works there.

④ This pill works on me.

⑤ The machine works 24 hours a day.

중요

09 위 글의 주제로 알맞은 것을 고르시오.

① how to make a traditional Spanish dish

② the difference of paella and fried rice

③ the introduction of the dish and places Jinwoo's family enjoyed

④ the historical importance of Park Guell and Sagrada Familia

⑤ the reason why Gaudi designed Park Guell and Sagrada Familia

서답형

10 다음 빈칸 (A)와 (B)에 알맞은 단어를 넣어 구엘 공원에 대한 소개를 완성하시오.

It is in (A)_____ and was designed by Antoni Gaudi. Jinwoo's family saw some of Gaudi's creative works such as (B)_____ _____ _____ there.

[11~13] 다음 인터뷰를 읽고 물음에 답하시오.

How much do you know about Vietnam?

The capital of Vietnam is Hanoi. ⓐ Vietnamese is spoken there. Pho and banh mi are popular dishes in Vietnam. Every year lots of tourists visit Halong Bay and Nha Trang. Halong Bay has 1,969 islands and Nha Trang is well known ⓑ its beautiful beaches. Vietnam is so beautiful that you should come someday.

서답형

11 위 글의 밑줄 친 ⓐ를 능동태로 바꾸시오.

➡ _____

12 위 글의 빈칸 ⓑ에 들어갈 알맞은 전치사를 고르시오.

① to   ② for   ③ by

④ as   ⑤ in

중요

13 위 글의 내용과 일치하지 않는 것은?

① 베트남의 수도는 하노이이다.

② 베트남에서는 주로 영어를 사용한다.

③ pho와 banh mi가 인기 있는 요리이다.

④ 하롱베이는 1,969개의 섬을 가지고 있다.

⑤ 나트랑은 아름다운 해변으로 잘 알려져 있다.

[14~17] 다음 글을 읽고 물음에 답하시오.

After Park Guell, we visited Sagrada Familia. Work on the building started in 1883 and is still going on today. I was impressed by its size and unique design. The (A)[ceiling / sealing] inside Sagrada Familia shone like the night sky with bright stars. Its stone columns stood like big trees. At Park Guell and Sagrada Familia I could feel Gaudi's creativity and his love of nature. ⓐTraveling in Spain was a wonderful experience. While I was (B)[there / in there], I learned a lot (C)[about / of] Spain. I want to visit the country again.   <I = Park Jinwoo>

서답형

14 위 글의 괄호 (A)~(C)에서 문맥이나 어법상 알맞은 낱말을 골라 쓰시오.

➡ (A)_____ (B)_____ (C)_____

15 위 글의 밑줄 친 ⓐ와 바꿔 쓸 수 있는 문장을 모두 고르시오.

① It was a wonderful experience to travel in Spain.
② That was a wonderful experience to travel in Spain.
③ To traveling in Spain was a wonderful experience.
④ To travel in Spain was a wonderful experience.
⑤ That was a wonderful experience traveling in Spain.

서답형

16 본문의 내용과 일치하도록 다음 빈칸 ⓐ와 ⓑ에 알맞은 단어를 쓰시오.

To Jinwoo, the ⓐ_____ and ⓑ_____ _____ of Sagrada Familia were impressive.

17 위 글을 읽고 답할 수 없는 질문은?

① Where did Jinwoo's family visit before they visited Sagrada Familia?
② When did work on Sagrada Familia start?
③ Why is work on Sagrada Familia still going on today?
④ What were the columns of Sagrada Familia made of?
⑤ Where could Jinwoo feel Gaudi's creativity and his love of nature?

[18~19] 다음 글을 읽고 물음에 답하시오.

For dinner, we ate paella. It is a traditional Spanish dish with rice, vegetables, meat, and seafood. (①) It tasted like fried rice in Korea. (②) It was so delicious that we all enjoyed it. (③) In Barcelona, we took a tour of Park Guell and Sagrada Familia. (④) In Park Guell, we saw some of Gaudi's creative works like a colorful lizard. (⑤)   <we = Jinwoo's family>

중요

18 위 글의 흐름으로 보아, 주어진 문장이 들어가기에 가장 적절한 곳은?

Both were designed by Antoni Gaudi.

①   ②   ③   ④   ⑤

19 위 글을 읽고 대답할 수 없는 질문은?

① What are the ingredients of paella?
② What's the recipe of paella?
③ In Barcelona, what did Jinwoo's family do?
④ By whom were Park Guell and Sagrada Familia designed?
⑤ In Park Guell, what did Jinwoo's family see?

[20~23] 다음 글을 읽고 물음에 답하시오.

After Park Guell, we visited Sagrada Familia. Work on the building started in 1883 and is still ⓐgoing on today. I was impressed by its size and unique design. The ceiling inside Sagrada Familia shone like the night sky with bright stars. Its stone columns stood like big trees. At Park Guell and Sagrada Familia I could feel Gaudi's __ⓑ__ and his love of nature.

Traveling in Spain was a wonderful experience. While I was there, I learned a lot about Spain. I want to visit the country again.

<I = Park Jinwoo>

20 위 글의 밑줄 친 ⓐgoing on과 바꿔 쓸 수 있는 말을 고르시오.

① stopping   ② remaining
③ increasing   ④ continuing
⑤ staying

서답형
21 위 글의 빈칸 ⓑ에 create를 알맞은 형태로 쓰시오.

➡ _____

22 위 글의 마지막 부분에서 알 수 있는 진우의 심경으로 가장 알맞은 것을 고르시오.

① satisfied   ② frightened
③ bored   ④ ashamed
⑤ disappointed

23 위 글의 내용과 일치하지 않는 것은?

① 진우의 가족은 사그라다 파밀리아 보다 구엘 공원을 먼저 보았다.
② 사그라다 파밀리아의 건물 공사는 1883년에 시작되었다.

③ 사그라다 파밀리아 안의 천장은 밝은 별이 있는 밤하늘처럼 빛났다.
④ 진우는 구엘 공원에서 Gaudi의 창의성과 자연에 대한 사랑을 느낄 수 있었다.
⑤ 진우는 스페인 여행 중에 스페인에 대해 많은 것을 배웠다.

[24~26] 다음 글을 읽고 물음에 답하시오.

How much do you know about Australia?
The capital of Australia is Canberra. English __ⓐ__ there. Meat pie and lamington are popular dishes in Australia. Every year lots of tourists visit Sydney and Melbourne. Sydney has the Sydney Opera House and Melbourne is well known for its beautiful ocean roads. ⓑ오스트레일리아는 너무 멋져서 당신은 언젠가 그곳을 꼭 방문해야 합니다.

서답형
24 위 글의 빈칸 ⓐ에 speak를 알맞은 형태로 쓰시오.

➡ _____

서답형
25 위 글의 밑줄 친 ⓑ의 우리말에 맞게 한 단어를 보충하여, 주어진 어휘를 알맞게 배열하시오.

is / you / that / visit / Australia / someday
/ wonderful / it / should

➡ _____

서답형
26 위 글을 참조하여 다음 빈칸 (A)와 (B)에 들어갈 알맞은 말을 쓰시오.

The tourist attraction of Sydney is
(A)_____ _____ _____ _____
and Melbourne is famous for its beautiful
(B)_____ _____ .

*tourist attraction: 관광명소

[01~03] 다음 글을 읽고 물음에 답하시오.

My family traveled to Spain this summer. ⓐ Spain is loved by lots of tourists. We (A)[visited / visited to] many interesting places.

Our trip started in Madrid. ⓑMadrid is the capital and is famous for soccer. We went to a stadium (B)[watching / to watch] a soccer match. My sister and I (C)[was / were] excited because we could watch some of the world's most famous soccer players.

01 위 글의 밑줄 친 ⓐ를 능동태로 고치시오.

➡ _____

02 위 글의 괄호 (A)~(C)에서 어법상 알맞은 낱말을 골라 쓰시오.

➡ (A)_____ (B)_____ (C)_____

03 위 글의 밑줄 친 ⓑ를 다음과 같이 바꿔 쓸 때 빈칸에 들어갈 알맞은 말을 쓰시오.

➡ Madrid is the capital and is _____
_____ for soccer.

[04~06] 다음 글을 읽고 물음에 답하시오.

The stadium was full of soccer fans. As we watched the match, we cheered by ⓐsing songs, ⓑwave our hands, and ⓒshout with the other fans.

ⓓ _____ we toured Madrid, we went to Seville. While we walked around ⓔthe city, we saw many historic buildings. We visited a flamenco museum and watched a flamenco dance. A woman in a red dress was dancing the flamenco with wonderful movements.

<we = Jinwoo's family>

04 위 글의 밑줄 친 ⓐ~ⓒ를 각각 알맞은 형태로 쓰시오.

➡ ⓐ _____ ⓑ _____ ⓒ _____

05 다음과 같은 뜻이 되도록 위 글의 빈칸 ⓓ에 들어갈 알맞은 말을 쓰시오.

We toured Madrid before we went to Seville.

➡ _____

06 위 글의 밑줄 친 ⓔthe city가 가리키는 것을 본문에서 찾아 쓰시오.

➡ _____

[07~09] 다음 글을 읽고 물음에 답하시오.

For dinner, we ate paella. It is a traditional ⓐ _____ dish with rice, vegetables, meat, and seafood. ⓑIt felt like fried rice in Korea. It was so delicious that we all enjoyed it.

In Barcelona, we ⓒtook a tour of Park Guell and Sagrada Familia. Both were designed by Antoni Gaudi. In Park Guell, we saw some of Gaudi's creative works like a colorful lizard.

<we = Jinwoo's family>

07 위 글의 빈칸 ⓐ에 Spain을 알맞은 형태로 쓰시오.

➡ _____

08 위 글의 밑줄 친 ⓑ에서 흐름상 어색한 부분을 찾아 고치시오.

➡ _____

09 위 글의 밑줄 친 ⓒtook a tour of를 한 단어로 고치시오.

➡ _____

[10~12] 다음 글을 읽고 물음에 답하시오.

For dinner, we ate paella. It is a traditional Spanish dish with rice, vegetables, meat, and seafood. ⓐ한국의 볶음밥과 같은 맛이 났다. ⓑIt was so delicious that we all enjoyed it.

In Barcelona, we took a tour of Park Guell and Sagrada Familia. Both were designed by Antoni Gaudi. In Park Guell, we saw some of Gaudi's creative works ⓒlike a colorful lizard.

10 위 글의 밑줄 친 ⓐ의 우리말에 맞게 한 단어를 보충하여, 주어진 어휘를 알맞게 배열하시오.

Korea / rice / it / fried / in / tasted

➡ _____

11 위 글의 밑줄 친 ⓑ이 가리키는 것을 본문에서 찾아 쓰시오.

➡ _____

12 위 글의 밑줄 친 ⓒlike를 두 단어로 바꿔 쓰시오.

➡ _____

[13~14] 다음 글을 읽고 물음에 답하시오.

ⓐAfter Park Guell, we visited Sagrada Familia. Work on the building started in 1883 and is still going on today. I was (A)[impressing / impressed] by its size and unique design. The ceiling inside Sagrada Familia (B)[shone / shined] like the night sky with bright stars. Its stone columns (C)[were stood / stood] like big trees. At Park Guell and Sagrada Familia I could feel Gaudi's creativity and his love of nature.

13 위 글의 밑줄 친 ⓐ를 before[Before]를 사용하여 고치시오.

➡ _____
_____

14 위 글의 괄호 (A)~(C)에서 문맥이나 어법상 알맞은 낱말을 골라 쓰시오.

➡ (A) _____ (B) _____ (C) _____

[15~17] 다음 글을 읽고 물음에 답하시오.

The stadium was full of soccer fans. As we watched the match, we cheered by singing songs, waving our hands, and shouting with the other fans.

After we toured Madrid, we went to Seville. While we walked around the city, we saw many ⓐ_____ buildings. We visited a flamenco museum and watched a flamenco dance. ⓑ A woman in a red dress was dancing the flamenco with wonderful movements.

<we = Jinwoo's family>

15 위 글의 빈칸 ⓐ에 history를 알맞은 형태로 쓰시오.

➡ _____

16 위 글의 밑줄 친 ⓑ를 다음과 같이 고칠 때 빈칸에 들어갈 알맞은 관계대명사를 쓰시오.

➡ A woman _____ was wearing a red dress

17 위 글을 읽고 진우의 가족이 마드리드와 세비야에서 한 일을 각각 우리말로 쓰시오.

➡ 마드리드: _____
세비야: _____

해석

Enjoy Writing

How much do you know about Vietnam?

The capital of Vietnam is Hanoi. <u>Vietnamese is spoken there</u>. Pho and banh
→ 능동태: They speak Vietnamese there.

mi are popular <u>dishes</u> in Vietnam.
요리

Every year <u>lots of</u> tourists visit Halong Bay and Nha Trang.
= a lot of. many

Halong Bay has 1,969 islands and Nha Trang <u>is well known for</u> its beautiful
be well known for: ~으로 잘 알려져 있다

beaches. Vietnam is <u>so</u> beautiful <u>that</u> you should come someday.
so ~ that ...: 너무 ~해서 ...하다

구문해설 · **capital**: 수도 · **Vietnamese**: 베트남어 · **popular**: 인기 있는 · **island**: 섬
· **someday**: 언젠가

당신은 베트남에 대해서 얼마나 많이 알고 있나요? 베트남의 수도는 하노이입니다. 그곳에서는 베트남어가 사용됩니다. 베트남에서는 pho(퍼, 베트남 쌀국수)와 banh mi(반미, 바게트 빵으로 만든 샌드위치)가 인기 있는 요리입니다. 매년 많은 관광객들이 하롱베이와 나트랑을 방문합니다. 하롱베이는 1,969개의 섬을 가지고 있고 나트랑은 아름다운 해변으로 잘 알려져 있습니다. 베트남은 너무 아름다워서 당신은 언젠가 꼭 오셔야 합니다.

Project Step 3

My group <u>chose</u> Hong Kong for a trip. Hong Kong <u>is loved by</u> many people
choose의 과거형   love의 수동태 be loved by: ~에 의해서 사랑받다

who want to do fun activities. We'll have great experiences at Mong Kok
주격 관계대명사 want는 to부정사를 목적어로 취한다.

Market, Victoria Peak, and Ocean Park.

구문해설 · **choose** 선택하다 · **activity** 활동 · **experience** 경험

우리 모둠은 여행 장소로 홍콩을 선택했다. 홍콩은 재밌는 활동을 하고 싶어 하는 많은 사람들에게 사랑받는다. 우리는 몽콕 시장, 빅토리아 피크 그리고 오션 파크에서 멋진 경험을 할 것이다.

Wrap Up

I was <u>moved by</u> a book. The title of the book is *The Old Man and the Sea*. It
수동태(= A book moved me.)

was written by Ernest Hemingway.
수동태(= Ernest Hemingway wrote it.)

The story was <u>so</u> great <u>that</u> I read it many times.
'so+형용사[부사]+that+주어+동사'의 형태로 원인과 결과를 나타낸다.(= Because the story was very great. I read it many times.)

구문해설 · **title** 제목 · **many times** 여러 번

나는 어떤 책에 감동을 받았다. 그 책의 제목은 '노인과 바다'이다. 그것은 Ernest Hemingway에 의해 씌여졌다. 그 이야기는 너무도 대단해서 나는 그것을 여러 번 읽었다.

영역별 핵심문제

Words & Expressions

01 다음 중 밑줄 친 부분의 뜻풀이가 바르지 <u>않은</u> 것은?

① Let's <u>cheer for</u> our national team! (응원하다)
② How can I <u>get</u> there? (얻다, 획득하다)
③ I <u>designed</u> my house. (설계했다)
④ The tea has a wonderful <u>flavor</u>. (차)
⑤ What's the <u>title</u> of this song? (제목)

02 다음 제시된 단어를 사용하여 자연스러운 문장을 만들 수 없는 것은? (형태 변화 가능)

┌─── 보기 ───┐
prefer roll slide wave
└─────────────┘

① The children are _____ over the frozen lake.
② The baby _____ to her mom.
③ They are _____ a big ball.
④ How about _____ a tour of the city then?
⑤ I _____ tea to coffee.

[03~04] 두 문장에 공통으로 들어갈 수 있는 단어를 쓰시오.

03

• Most people want to be famous _____ something.
• He is well known _____ his cool dancing and great music.

04

• Aren't there any ways I can get _____ the next flight to Sydney?
• It takes about ten minutes _____ foot.

05 다음 주어진 우리말에 맞게 빈칸을 채우시오.

(1) King Sejong is a _____ figure. (세종대왕은 역사상 중요한 인물이다.)
(2) They went to the _____ last night. (그들은 어젯밤 극장에 갔다.)
(3) He looked up at the _____. (그는 천장을 올려다봤다.)
(4) They _____ _____ the players and shake hands with the _____. (그들은 선수들을 응원하고 팬들과 악수합니다.)

Conversation

[06~07] 다음 대화를 읽고 물음에 답하시오.

B: Sally, I need to buy some candies for Halloween. (A)_____
G: You can buy them at Wendy's Candy Shop.
B: (B)_____
G: Go straight two blocks and turn right. It's across from the library.

06 빈칸 (A)와 (B)에 알맞은 것끼리 짝지어진 것을 고르시오.

　　　　(A)　/　　(B)
① What can I buy? / Where is it?
② What can I buy? / Is there a candy shop near here?
③ How can I buy them? / What can I buy?
④ Where can I buy them? / What can I buy?
⑤ Where can I buy them? / Where is it?

07 위 대화의 내용과 일치하지 <u>않는</u> 것을 고르시오.

① Sally knows where Wendy's Candy Shop is.

② To get to Wendy's Candy Shop, the boy should go straight 2 blocks and turn right.

③ They are going to buy candies at Wendy's Candy Shop.

④ The boy wants to buy some candies for Halloween.

⑤ Wendy's Candy Shop is across from the library.

08 다음 그림과 일치하지 <u>않는</u> 대화를 고르시오.

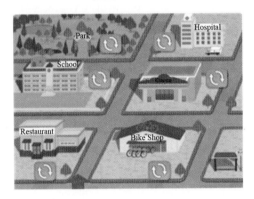

① A: Excuse me. Where is the bike shop?

B: Go straight. It's on your right.

② A: Excuse me. Where is the school?

B: Go straight one block and turn left. It's on your right. It's across from the restaurant.

③ A: Excuse me. Where is the hospital?

B: Go straight two blocks and turn right. It's on your left. It's across from the school.

④ A: Excuse me. Where is the park?

B: Go straight two blocks and turn left. It's on your right.

⑤ A: Excuse me. Where is the cinema?

B: Go straight one block and turn right. It's on your left. It's across from the bike shop.

[09~11] 다음 대화를 읽고 물음에 답하시오.

Staff: How may I help you?

Hana's mom: We want to enjoy a good view of London. (①)

Hana: Where is the best place to go to?

Staff: We have two great places. (②) Which do you prefer? (③)

Hana's mom: Hmm... (④) I prefer the London Eye.

Hana: Me, too.

Staff: Good choice. You can get there by bus.

Hana's mom: 가장 가까운 버스 정거장은 어디 있나요?

Staff: (⑤) Go straight one block and turn right. It's on your left. Have a good trip!

Hana: Wow, I can see all of London. Look! There is a big clock.

Hana's mom: I think that's Big Ben. Why don't we go and visit it later?

Hana: That sounds great.

09 다음 영영풀이에 해당하는 단어를 대화에서 찾아 쓰시오.

what you can see from a particular place or position, especially beautiful countryside

➡ _____

10 위 대화의 ①~⑤ 중 주어진 문장이 들어갈 알맞은 곳은?

The London Eye is a Ferris wheel and the Sky Garden is a glass garden on top of a tall building.

①   ②   ③   ④   ⑤

11 밑줄 친 우리말을 주어진 단어를 이용하여 영작하시오. (5단어)

➡ _____ (stop, near)

12 주어진 문장 다음에 이어질 대화의 순서를 바르게 배열하시오.

> Let's go on a trip abroad.

> (A) I prefer Bangkok. The city is so colorful that we should go there.
> (B) Okay. Let's go there.
> (C) Which city do you prefer, Bangkok or Taiwan?

➡ _____

Grammar

13 다음 중 어법상 올바르지 <u>않은</u> 것은?

① The beautiful song was written by my friend.
② The plane stopped flying and turned into a restaurant.
③ Mary wasn't made to clean her room by her sister.
④ It rained so hard that we put off the picnic.
⑤ It was so noisy in the hall that I couldn't hear him speak.

14 다음 우리말을 주어진 어휘를 이용하여 영작했을 때 빈칸에 적절한 말을 쓰시오.

> • 그 문제들은 너무 어려워서 우리는 풀 수 없었다. (difficult, solve)
> = (1) The problems were _____
>   _____ .
> = (2) The problems were _____
>   _____ .

15 다음 빈칸에 알맞은 말이 바르게 짝지어진 것은?

> • The students were made _____ their homework by the teacher.
> • John started _____ early that he didn't need to hurry up.

① to do – so
② to do – very
③ did – too
④ doing – so
⑤ doing – very

16 Which is grammatically correct?

① The room was too cold that David turned on the heater.
② This story was so funny which I laughed a lot.
③ Arnold got up so late that he didn't miss the train.
④ The movie was so sad that Rachel cried a lot.
⑤ John is kind so that everyone likes him.

17 다음 두 문장의 의미가 같도록 빈칸에 들어갈 알맞은 말을 쓰시오.

> Because the city's night view is so beautiful, we should see it.
> = The city's night view is _____ we should see it.

18 다음 그림을 보고 괄호 안에 주어진 단어를 이용하여 빈칸을 채우시오.

(1) (*The Old Man and the Sea*, write)

→ *The Old Man and the Sea*
_____ Ernest Hemingway.

(2) (The pyramids, build)

→ The pyramids _____ the ancient Egyptians.

19 다음 중 밑줄 친 부분의 쓰임이 어색한 것은?

① The ball was <u>caught by</u> Jenny.
② Nha Trang is <u>well known for</u> its beautiful beaches.
③ I <u>was written</u> a long letter by my girl friend.
④ The animals in the cage were <u>looked after</u> by Aybek.
⑤ At first, I <u>was surprised at</u> the number of side dishes.

20 괄호 안에 주어진 단어를 이용하여 다음을 영작하시오.

(1) 전화는 누구에 의해 발명되었니? (the telephone, invent, 6 단어)

➡ _____

(2) 그 집의 지붕은 눈으로 덮여 있었다. (the house, the roof, cover, 9 단어)

➡ _____

(3) 너무 어두워서 아무 것도 보이지 않았다. (nothing, see, could, dark, that, 9 단어)

➡ _____

(4) 그 달리기 선수는 너무 빨리 달려서 아무도 그를 따라잡을 수 없었다. (the runner, that, nobody, catch, 12 단어)

➡ _____

Reading

[21~23] 다음 글을 읽고 물음에 답하시오.

My family traveled to Spain this summer. Spain is loved by lots of tourists. We visited many interesting places.

Our ⓐtrip started in Madrid. Madrid is the capital and is famous for soccer. We went to a stadium ⓑ<u>to watch</u> a soccer match. My sister and I were excited because we could watch some of the world's most famous soccer players. <I = Park Jinwoo>

21 위 글의 밑줄 친 ⓐtrip과 바꿔 쓸 수 있는 단어를 본문에서 찾아 알맞은 형태로 쓰시오. (2개)

➡ _____, _____

22 위 글의 밑줄 친 ⓑto watch와 to부정사의 용법이 다른 것을 모두 고르시오.

① There's no plan to build a new office.

② He cannot be a gentleman to do such a thing.

③ She lived long to see her son come back.

④ I have lots of homework to do today.

⑤ He promised me to do the dishes.

23 위 글의 내용과 일치하도록 다음 빈칸 (A)와 (B)에 알맞은 단어를 쓰시오.

During their trip to Spain, Jinwoo's family went to (A)_____ _____ in Madrid and watched (B)_____ _____ _____.

[24~25] 다음 글을 읽고 물음에 답하시오.

The stadium was full of soccer fans. ⓐAs we watched the match, we cheered by singing songs, waving our hands, and shouting with the other fans.

After we toured Madrid, we went to Seville. While we walked around the city, we saw many historic buildings. We visited a flamenco museum and watched a flamenco dance. A woman in a red dress was dancing the flamenco with wonderful movements.

<we = Jinwoo's family>

24 위 글의 밑줄 친 ⓐAs와 같은 의미로 쓰인 것을 고르시오.

① As he is honest, everyone liked him.

② Leave the papers as they are.

③ He came up to me as I was speaking.

④ I respect him as a teacher.

⑤ As she grew older, she became more beautiful.

25 위 글의 내용과 일치하지 않는 것은?

① Jinwoo's family watched a soccer match in Madrid.

② Jinwoo's family walked around the soccer stadium.

③ Jinwoo's family saw many historic buildings.

④ Jinwoo's family watched a flamenco dance.

⑤ A woman wearing a red dress was dancing the flamenco.

[26~27] 다음 글을 읽고 물음에 답하시오.

For dinner, we ate paella. It is a traditional Spanish dish with rice, vegetables, meat, and seafood. It tasted like (A)[frying / fried] rice in Korea. It was so delicious that we all enjoyed it.

In Barcelona, we took a tour of Park Guell and Sagrada Familia. ⓐBoth (B)[was / were] designed by Antoni Gaudi. In Park Guell, we saw some of Gaudi's (C)[common / creative] works like a colorful lizard.

26 위 글의 괄호 (A)~(C)에서 문맥이나 어법상 알맞은 낱말을 골라 쓰시오.

➡ (A)_____ (B)_____ (C)_____

27 위 글의 밑줄 친 ⓐBoth가 가리키는 것을 본문에서 찾아 쓰시오.

➡ _____

[01~02] 다음 빈칸에 공통으로 들어갈 수 있는 단어를 쓰시오.

출제율 95%

01

> • I'd like to _____ a walk with my dog.
> • You can _____ a class or join a club together after school.
> • They liked to _____ a tour of the castle.

출제율 90%

02

> • The 'Mona Lisa' was painted _____ Leonardo Da Vinci.
> • It took about 5 hours _____ bus.

출제율 95%

03 다음 우리말 해석에 맞게 빈칸을 완성하시오. (철자가 주어진 경우 그 철자로 시작할 것)

(1) All the people in the concert hall stood and _____ loudly. (콘서트홀에 있던 모든 사람이 일어나 크게 환호했다.)

(2) Would you like to _____ _____ this? (이걸 입어 보시겠습니까?)

(3) India is f_____ _____ curry. (인도는 카레로 유명하다.)

(4) Can I _____ there _____ _____? (거기까지 걸어서 갈 수 있나요?)

출제율 90%

04 다음 영영풀이에 해당하는 말을 주어진 철자로 시작하여 쓰고, 알맞은 것을 골라 문장을 완성하시오.

> • f_____ : a vigorous rhythmic dance style of the Andalusian Gypsies
> • p_____ : a mixture of blue and red color
> • V_____ : relating to the language, people or culture of Vietnam

(1) He enjoys dancing the _____.

(2) She learned _____ to get a job in Vietnam.

(3) She wore a dress of dark _____.

[05~06] 다음 대화를 읽고 물음에 답하시오.

> **B:** It's really hot here in Thailand. (①)
> **G:** Sounds good. (②) How do we get there? (③)
> **B:** We can go on foot or by bus. (④) Which do you prefer? (⑤)
> **G:** I prefer the bus.

출제율 100%

05 위 대화의 ①~⑤ 중 주어진 문장이 들어갈 알맞은 곳은?

> Let's go to the night market and have some fresh fruit juice.

①   ②   ③   ④   ⑤

출제율 85%

06 위 대화를 읽고 대답할 수 <u>없는</u> 질문을 고르시오.

① How will they go to the night market?
② Which does the boy prefer, bus or taxi?
③ Where are they?
④ Where are they going to go?
⑤ What are they going to drink?

[07~10] 그림을 참고하여 다음 대화를 읽고 물음에 답하시오.

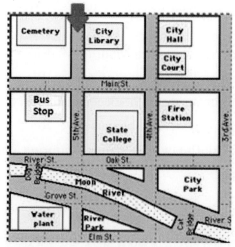

Staff: (A)_____ may I help you?

Hana's mom: We want to enjoy a good view of London. (①)

Hana: 가기에 가장 좋은 장소는 어디인가요?

Staff: We have two great places. The London Eye is a Ferris wheel and the Sky Garden is a glass garden on top of a tall building. (B)_____ do you prefer?

Hana's mom: Hmm... (②) I prefer the London Eye.

Hana: Me, too. (③)

Staff: Good choice. You can get there by bus. (④)

Hana's mom: (C)_____ is the nearest stop?

Staff: (D) _____ Have a good trip!

Hana: Wow, I can see all of London. Look! There is a big clock.

Hana's mom: I think that's Big Ben. (⑤)

Hana: That sounds great.

07 위 대화의 ①~⑤ 중 주어진 문장이 들어갈 알맞은 곳은?

Why don't we go and visit it later?

① ② ③ ④ ⑤

08 빈칸 (A)~(C)에 알맞은 의문사를 쓰시오.

➡ (A)_____ (B)_____ (C)_____

09 밑줄 친 우리말과 의미가 같도록 영작하시오. (8단어)

➡ _____

10 그림을 보고 빈칸 (D)에 들어갈 말을 주어진 단어를 이용해 두 문장으로 쓰시오.

➡ _____

(block, go, your, turn, it)

11 주어진 문장 다음에 이어질 대화의 순서를 바르게 배열하시오.

Excuse me. Can you tell me how to get to the Africa Museum?

(A) Go straight and turn right. And then?

(B) It's on your left. It's across from the shoe store.

(C) Sure. Go straight two blocks and turn right.

(D) I got it. Thank you very much.

➡ _____

12 다음 중 태의 전환이 <u>잘못된</u> 것은?

① Those pictures were not painted by the artist.
 → The artist did not paint those pictures.

② Frank showed her the album.
 → The album was shown for her by Frank.

③ Edvard Munch painted *The Scream* in 1893.
 → *The Scream* was painted by Edvard Munch in 1893.

④ They saw Marianne dance on the stage.
 → Marianne was seen to dance on the stage by them.

⑤ Teresa took good care of the little babies.
 → Good care was taken of the little babies by Teresa.

13 다음 두 문장을 'so ~ that' 구문을 사용하여 한 문장으로 연결하시오.

(1) • The shoes look really great.
 • Sandra wants to buy them.
 ➡ _____

(2) • The stereo was very loud.
 • It was impossible to sleep.
 ➡ _____

14 다음 괄호 안의 어휘를 이용하여 빈칸에 알맞은 말을 쓰시오.

(1) The story was _____ I read it many times. (great)

(2) Many soldiers _____ in the war. (kill)

[15~17] 다음 글을 읽고 물음에 답하시오.

My family traveled to Spain this summer. Spain is loved by lots of tourists. We visited many interesting places.

 Our trip started in Madrid. Madrid is the ⓐ capital and is famous for soccer. We went to a stadium to watch a soccer match. My sister and I were __(A)__ because we could watch some of the world's most famous soccer players.

15 위 글의 빈칸 (A)에 들어갈 알맞은 말을 고르시오.

① interesting ② disappointed
③ upset ④ excited
⑤ amusing

16 위 글의 밑줄 친 ⓐcapital과 같은 의미로 쓰인 것을 고르시오.

① The cause of business failure is lack of capital.
② Paris is the fashion capital of the world.
③ He set up a business with a starting capital of £100,000.
④ I want to invest my capital in your business.
⑤ Please write in capital letters.

17 What is Madrid well known for? Answer in English in a full sentence. (6 words)

 ➡ _____

[18~20] 다음 글을 읽고 물음에 답하시오.

The stadium was full of soccer fans. As we watched the match, we cheered by ⓐsinging songs, waving our hands, and shouting with the other fans.

ⓑAfter we toured of Madrid, we went to Seville. While we walked around the city, we saw many historic buildings. We visited a flamenco museum and watched a flamenco dance. A woman in a red dress was dancing the flamenco with wonderful movements.

<we = Jinwoo's family>

출제율 90%

18 위 글의 밑줄 친 ⓐsinging과 문법적 쓰임이 다른 것을 모두 고르시오.

① My son is singing songs on the musical stage.

② She is good at singing songs.

③ Do you know the boy singing songs there?

④ My dream is singing songs on the musical stage.

⑤ They always enjoy singing songs together.

출제율 90%

19 위 글의 밑줄 친 ⓑ에서 어법상 틀린 부분을 찾아 고치시오.

➡ _____

출제율 95%

20 위 글을 읽고 대답할 수 없는 질문은?

① Where did Jinwoo's family cheer?

② What did Jinwoo's family do when they cheered?

③ What did Jinwoo's family see while they walked around Seville?

④ How long did Jinwoo's family watch a flamenco dance?

⑤ What was the flamenco dancer wearing?

[21~24] 다음 글을 읽고 물음에 답하시오.

ⓐ dinner, we ate paella. It is a traditional Spanish dish ⓑ rice, vegetables, meat, and seafood. It tasted like fried rice in Korea. It was so delicious that we all enjoyed it.

In Barcelona, we took a tour of Park Guell and Sagrada Familia. Both were designed by Antoni Gaudi. In Park Guell, we saw some of Gaudi's ⓒ works like a colorful lizard.

출제율 100%

21 위 글의 빈칸 ⓐ와 ⓑ에 들어갈 전치사가 바르게 짝지어진 것은?

① To – with   ② For – by

③ In – from   ④ To – by

⑤ For – with

출제율 90%

22 다음 중 paella의 재료가 아닌 것을 고르시오.

① 쌀   ② 채소

③ 고기   ④ 국수

⑤ 해산물

출제율 95%

23 위 글의 빈칸 ⓒ에 create를 알맞은 형태로 쓰시오.

➡ _____

출제율 90%

24 By whom were Park Guell and Sagrada Familia designed? Answer in English.

➡ _____

서술형 실전문제

01 밑줄 친 부분에서 어법상 어색한 부분을 찾아 고치시오.

> M: Welcome to London City Tour. Today, we'll visit famous places in London. Can you see the London Eye? <u>It's on your right. It's a Ferris wheel near the River Thames. The view from the London Eye are amazing.</u> Many people visit it every year.

➡ _____

_____

02 그림을 보고 (A)와 (B)에 공통으로 들어갈 문장을 쓰시오. (목적지는 표시된 ③) (총 7 단어)

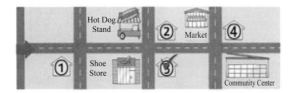

> B: Excuse me. Can you tell me how to get to the Africa Museum?
> G: Sure. (A)_____
> B: (B)_____ And then?
> G: It's on your left. It's across from the shoe store.
> B: I got it. Thank you very much.

➡ _____

03 주어진 문장 다음에 이어질 대화의 순서를 바르게 배열하시오.

> Jisu, why don't we watch the movie *Best Friends* on Saturday?

> (A) Sounds good. What time does it begin?
> (B) I prefer the seven showing.

> (C) On Saturday there are two showings, one at five and the other at seven. Which do you prefer?
> (D) Okay. Then let's meet at six.

➡ _____

04 그림을 참고하여 어떤 것을 더 선호하는지 묻는 질문을 완성하시오.

> A: _____
> _____
> B: I prefer the Scary House.

05 주어진 문장이 같은 뜻이 되도록 빈칸에 알맞은 말을 쓰시오.

(1) Because the city is so colorful, we should go there.
= The city is _____ we should go there.

(2) Emily was very tired. So, she couldn't do the dishes.
= Emily was _____ she couldn't do the dishes.
= Emily was _____ do the dishes.

06 다음 주어진 문장을 능동태는 수동태로, 수동태는 능동태로 바꾸시오.

(1) Hong Kong is loved by many people who want to do fun activities.

➡ _____

_____

(2) What did she promise to do last weekend?

➡ _____

(3) Ms. Grace taught us physics last year.

➡ _____

_____

[07~09] 다음 글을 읽고 물음에 답하시오.

ⓐThe stadium was full of soccer fans. As we watched the match, we cheered by singing songs, waving our hands, and shouting with the other fans.

After we toured Madrid, we went to Seville. While we walked around the city, we saw many historic buildings. We visited a flamenco museum and watched a flamenco dance. ⓑ빨간 드레스를 입은 여자가 멋진 동작으로 플라멩코를 추고 있었다.

<we = Jinwoo's family>

07 위 글의 밑줄 친 ⓐ를 다음과 같이 바꿔 쓸 때 빈칸에 들어갈 알맞은 말을 쓰시오.

➡ The stadium _____ _____

_____ soccer fans.

08 위 글의 밑줄 친 ⓑ의 우리말에 맞게 한 단어를 보충하여, 주어진 어휘를 알맞게 배열하시오.

movements / the flamenco / was / wonderful / dancing / a red dress / with / a woman

➡ _____

_____

09 본문의 내용과 일치하도록 다음 빈칸 (A)와 (B)에 알맞은 단어를 쓰시오.

Jinwoo's family went to (A)_____ after they toured Madrid and they saw (B) _____ _____ _____ while they walked around the city.

[10~12] 다음 글을 읽고 물음에 답하시오.

For dinner, we ate paella. It is a traditional Spanish dish with rice, vegetables, meat, and seafood. It tasted ⓐ fried rice in Korea. It was so delicious that we all enjoyed it.

In Barcelona, we took a tour of Park Guell and Sagrada Familia. ⓑBoth were designed by Antoni Gaudi. In Park Guell, we saw some of Gaudi's creative works ⓒ a colorful lizard.

10 위 글의 빈칸 ⓐ와 ⓒ에 공통으로 들어갈 알맞은 말을 쓰시오.

➡ _____

11 다음 빈칸 (A)~(D)에 알맞은 단어를 넣어 paella에 대한 소개를 완성하시오.

Paella which is a traditional (A)_____ dish tastes like fried rice in (B)_____ and its ingredients are (C)_____, _____, _____ and (D)_____ .

12 위 글의 밑줄 친 ⓑ를 능동태로 고치시오.

➡ _____

01 주어진 정보와 그림을 이용해 빈칸에 알맞은 말을 쓰시오..

<조건>
1. A는 은행을 가고 싶어 한다.
2. 'next'나 'across' 둘 중에서 하나의 단어가 반드시 들어가야 한다.
3. 'know'를 이용해 길을 물어보는 문장을 만든다.

A: Excuse me. _____
B: Of course. _____ It's on your left.
_____ / _____

02 주어진 정보를 이용해 호주를 소개하는 글을 쓰시오.

country: Australia
capital: Canberra
language: English
dish: meat pie, lamington
place • Sydney has the Sydney Opera House.
　　　• Melbourne has beautiful ocean roads.

How much do you know about Australia?
The (A)_____ of Australia is Canberra. (B)_____ is spoken there.
(C)_____ are popular dishes in Australia. Every year lots of tourists visit
Sydney and Melbourne. Sydney has (D)_____ and Melbourne is well
known for its (E)_____. Australia is so wonderful that you should visit it
someday.

03 <보기>에 주어진 어휘와 so와 that을 이용하여 3 문장 이상 쓰시오.

　보기

| practice dancing hard | thief | cartoon/interesting |
| become a B-boy dancer | run away/find | keep reading |

(1) _____
(2) _____
(3) _____

단원별 모의고사

01 다음 〈보기〉에 짝지어진 두 단어의 관계와 같도록 빈칸에 알맞은 단어를 쓰시오.

┌─ 보기 ┤

nation – national

(1) use – _____

(2) hope – _____

(3) color – _____

02 〈보기〉의 주어진 단어를 이용해 빈칸을 채우시오.

┌─ 보기 ┤

at   from   in   on   of   to

(1) The department store was full _____ customers.

(2) It's not very far _____ your home.

(3) The lamp is _____ top _____ the television.

(4) Turn _____ that fan.

03 다음 우리말 해석에 맞게 빈칸을 완성하시오. (철자가 주어진 경우 그 철자로 시작할 것)

(1) May I _____ _____ this shirt? (제가 이 셔츠를 입어 봐도 될까요?)

(2) The spring sale will g_____ _____ for a week. (봄 세일은 일주일 동안 계속될 것이다.)

(3) The museum is _____ _____ the park. (박물관은 공원 맞은편에 있습니다.)

(4) Melbourne _____ _____ _____ _____ its beautiful ocean roads. (멜버른은 아름다운 해안 도로로 잘 알려져 있다.)

04 다음 〈보기〉의 단어를 사용하여 자연스러운 문장을 만들 수 없는 것은?

┌─ 보기 ┤

hamburger   match   movement   tour

① They are playing an important _____ .

② The animal moved with quick _____ s.

③ I can speak three _____ s, English, Japanese and Korean.

④ On today's _____ , we will see many rare animals.

⑤ They had _____ s for lunch yesterday.

05 그림을 보고 대화의 빈칸을 완성하시오.

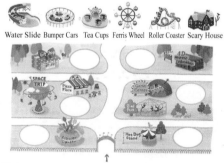

Water Slide Bumper Cars Tea Cups Ferris Wheel Roller Coaster Scary House

(1)
A: _____ is the Roller Coaster?
B: Go straight two blocks and turn _____ . It's on _____ _____ . _____ _____ _____ the 4D Movie Theater.

(2)
A: _____ _____ the Water Slide?
B: Go straight _____ _____ and _____ _____ . It's _____ _____ . It's _____ from _____ _____ .

[06~08] 다음 대화를 읽고 물음에 답하시오.

A: Let's go on a trip abroad.
B: (A)(do, Bangkok, city, prefer, which, or, Taiwan, you?)
A: I prefer Bangkok. The city is (B)[such / so] colorful (C)[what / that] we should go there.
B: Okay. Let's go there.

06 다음 영영풀이에 해당하는 단어를 대화에서 찾아 쓰시오.

in or to a foreign country

➡ _____

07 괄호 (A) 안의 단어를 배열하여 알맞은 문장을 만드시오.

➡ _____

08 괄호 (B)와 (C)에서 알맞은 단어를 골라 쓰시오.

➡ (B)_____, (C)_____

[09~10] 다음 대화를 읽고 물음에 답하시오.

B: Jisu, why don't we (A)[watch / watching] the movie *Best Friends* on Saturday?
G: Sounds good. (B)[What time / Where] does it begin?
B: On Saturday there (C)[is / are] two showings, ⓐ_____ at five and ⓑ_____ at seven. Which do you prefer?
G: I prefer the seven showing.
B: Okay. Then let's meet at six.
G: Sounds good.

09 (A)~(C)에 알맞은 단어를 골라 쓰시오.

➡ (A)_____ (B)_____ (C)_____

10 빈칸 ⓐ와 ⓑ에 들어갈 말로 적절한 것끼리 짝지어진 것을 고르시오.

	ⓐ	ⓑ
①	one	another
②	one	the other
③	one	other
④	another	the other
⑤	another	some

[11~13] 다음 대화를 읽고 물음에 답하시오.

G: What is this long dress (A)_____ (call)?
M: It is an Ao dai, a type of traditional clothing from Vietnam.
G: Can I try one (B)_____?
M: Sure. (C)너는 보라색과 노란색 중 어느 것을 선호하니?
G: The purple one, please.

11 빈칸 (A)에 주어진 단어를 어법에 맞게 쓰시오.

➡ _____

12 빈칸 (B)에 알맞은 전치사를 쓰시오.

➡ _____

13 밑줄 친 (C)의 우리말을 주어진 단어를 이용해 영작하시오.

➡ _____
_____ (one, prefer, which)

14 같은 의미가 되도록 빈칸에 알맞은 말을 쓰시오.

(1) I heard Jenny lock the door.

= Jenny _____.

(2) Because Australia is very wonderful, you should visit it someday.

= Australia is _____ you should visit it someday.

15 다음 중 어법상 어색한 것을 고르시오.

① The cake was so delicious that we all enjoyed it.

② This chair was made to Diana by my grandpa.

③ Vietnamese is spoken there.

④ The room was cleaned by Jenny.

⑤ Alex studied so hard that he could enter the university.

16 다음 두 문장을 한 문장으로 바르게 연결한 것은?

- Benjamin became very angry.
- His blood was boiling.

① Benjamin became very angry that his blood was boiling.

② Benjamin became angry enough to boil his blood.

③ Benjamin became too angry to boil his blood.

④ Benjamin became angry so that his blood was boiling.

⑤ Benjamin became so angry that his blood was boiling.

17 우리말과 일치하도록 괄호 안의 어구를 바르게 배열하시오.

(1) Sharon은 성공하기 위해 열심히 일했다. (Sharon, she, so, succeed, worked, might, hard, that)

➡ _____

(2) 상자가 너무 무거워서 아무도 움직일 수 없었다. (one, the box, it, that, no, heavy, could, was, move, so)

➡ _____

(3) 그 기계는 Kim 선생님에 의해 수리될 것이다. (Mr. Kim, the machine, repaired, will, be, by)

➡ _____

18 다음 밑줄 친 부분 중 생략할 수 있는 것은?

① Jessica is loved by everybody.

② I was moved by a book.

③ English is spoken there by them.

④ The apples were eaten by Jenny.

⑤ The room was cleaned by the students.

[19~20] 다음 글을 읽고 물음에 답하시오.

My family traveled to Spain (A)[this summer / in this summer]. Spain is loved by lots of tourists. We visited many (B)[interesting / interested] places.

Our trip started in Madrid. Madrid is the capital and is famous for soccer. We went to a stadium to watch a soccer match. My sister and I were (C)[exciting / excited] because we could watch some of the world's most famous soccer players.   <I = Park Jinwoo>

19 위 글의 괄호 (A)~(C)에서 어법상 알맞은 낱말을 골라 쓰시오.

➡ (A)_____ (B)_____ (C)_____

20 위 글을 읽고 대답할 수 <u>없는</u> 질문은?

① When did Jinwoo's family travel to Spain?

② Why did Jinwoo's family trip start in Madrid?

③ What is the capital of Spain?

④ Why did Jinwoo's family go to a stadium?

⑤ How did Jinwoo and his sister feel in the stadium?

[21~22] 다음 글을 읽고 물음에 답하시오.

The stadium was full of soccer fans. (①) As we watched the match, we cheered by singing songs, waving our hands, and shouting ⓐ the other fans. (②)
After we toured Madrid, we went to Seville. (③) We visited a flamenco museum and watched a flamenco dance. (④) A woman ⓑ a red dress was dancing the flamenco ⓐ wonderful movements. (⑤)

<we = Jinwoo's family>

21 위 글의 흐름으로 보아, 주어진 문장이 들어가기에 가장 적절한 곳은?

While we walked around the city, we saw many historic buildings.

①   ②   ③   ④   ⑤

22 위 글의 빈칸 ⓐ와 ⓑ에 들어갈 전치사가 바르게 짝지어진 것은?

① with – from   ② for – in
③ in – to   ④ for – to
⑤ with – in

[23~25] 다음 글을 읽고 물음에 답하시오.

For dinner, we ate paella. It is a ⓐtradition Spanish dish with rice, vegetables, meat, and seafood. ⓑIt tasted fried rice in Korea. It was so delicious that we all enjoyed it.
In Barcelona, we took a tour of Park Guell and Sagrada Familia. Both were designed by Antoni Gaudi. In Park Guell, we saw some of Gaudi's creative works like a colorful lizard.

<we = Jinwoo's family>

23 위 글의 밑줄 친 ⓐ를 알맞은 어형으로 고치시오.

➡ _____

24 위 글의 밑줄 친 ⓑ에서 어법상 <u>틀린</u> 부분을 고치시오.

➡ _____

25 위 글의 내용과 일치하지 <u>않는</u> 것은?

① 진우의 가족은 저녁 식사로 파에야를 먹었다.

② 파에야는 전통적인 스페인 요리이다.

③ 진우의 가족은 바르셀로나에서 구엘 공원과 사그라다 파밀리아를 둘러보았다.

④ Antoni Gaudi는 구엘 공원과 사그라다 파밀리아의 건설 자금을 지원했다.

⑤ 구엘 공원에서 Gaudi의 창의적인 작품들을 볼 수 있다.

Lesson 6

Wonders of Nature

의사소통 기능

- 궁금증 표현하기
  I wonder what they are.
- 알고 있음 표현하기
  I heard it is the largest reed field in Korea.

언어 형식

- 'It+be동사+형용사+to+동사원형' 구문
  It is important **to understand** the roles of mudflats.

- 'not only A but also B' 구문
  Not only very small living things like plankton **but also** crabs and fish live there.

Words & Expressions

Key Words

- **air cleaner** 공기 청정기
- **appear** [əpíər] 동 나타나다
- **bloom** [blu:m] 동 (꽃이) 피다
- **cave** [keiv] 명 동굴
- **cliff** [klif] 명 절벽
- **cover** [kʌ́vər] 동 (범위가) ~에 이르다, 차지하다
- **crab** [kræb] 명 게
- **creature** [kríːtʃər] 명 생물, 생명체
- **damage** [dǽmidʒ] 명 피해
- **during** [djúəriŋ] 전 ~ 동안(에)
- **else** [els] 부 그 밖의, 그것 이외의
- **environment** [inváiərənmənt] 명 환경
- **even** [íːvən] 부 ~조차(도)
- **fall** [fɔːl] 명 (복수형으로) 폭포
- **feed** [fiːd] 동 먹이를 주다, 먹이다
- **filter** [fíltər] 동 ~을 여과하다, 거르다, 걸러 내다
- **flat** [flæt] 형 평평한
- **flood** [flʌd] 명 홍수
- **flow** [flou] 동 흐르다
- **fresh water** 민물, 담수
- **generous** [dʒénərəs] 형 관대한
- **greatly** [gréitli] 부 크게, 꽤
- **greet** [griːt] 동 인사하다
- **guess** [ges] 동 추측하다, 알아맞히다
- **heavy** [hévi] 형 (양, 정도 등이 보통보다) 많은, 심한
- **heavy rain** 호우
- **high tide** 밀물
- **information** [infərméiʃən] 명 정보
- **land** [lænd] 명 육지, 땅
- **large** [lɑːrdʒ] 형 큰, 커다란
- **low tide** 썰물
- **lung** [lʌŋ] 명 폐
- **mess** [mes] 명 엉망진창
- **mud** [mʌd] 명 진흙

- **muddy** [mʌ́di] 형 진흙투성이인, 진흙의, 질퍽한
- **mudflat** [mʌ́dflæt] 명 갯벌
- **necessary** [nésəsèri] 형 필요한
- **occur** [əkə́ːr] 동 일어나다, 발생하다
- **ocean** [óuʃən] 명 바다, 대양
- **oxygen** [áksidʒen] 명 산소
- **plain** [plein] 명 평원
- **plankton** [plǽŋktən] 명 플랑크톤
- **produce** [prədjúːs] 동 생산하다, 만들다
- **protect** [prətékt] 동 보호하다
- **provide** [prəváid] 동 제공하다, 주다
- **rain forest** 열대 우림
- **reach** [riːtʃ] 동 ~에 이르다, 도달하다
- **reason** [ríːzn] 명 이유
- **reduce** [ridjúːs] 동 줄이다
- **reed** [riːd] 명 갈대
- **regularly** [régjulərli] 부 규칙적으로
- **remove** [rimúːv] 동 제거하다
- **role** [roul] 명 역할, 임무
- **slide** [slaid] 동 미끄러지다
- **snake** [sneik] 명 뱀
- **southern** [sʌ́ðərn] 형 남쪽의, 남부의
- **stain** [stein] 명 얼룩
- **surf** [səːrf] 동 서핑하다
- **surface** [sə́ːrfis] 명 표면
- **surprising** [sərpráiziŋ] 형 놀라운
- **tide** [taid] 명 조수, 밀물과 썰물
- **trash** [træʃ] 명 쓰레기
- **truth** [truːθ] 명 진실, 사실
- **unlike** [ənláik] 전 ~와는 달리
- **various** [véəriəs] 형 각종의, 다양한
- **volume** [váljuːm] 명 ~의 양, 용량, 용적
- **wonder** [wʌ́ndər] 명 놀라움, 경이 동 ~을 궁금해 하다

Key Expressions

- **a body of water** (바다나 호수 등의) 수역
- **a large number of** 다수의, 많은 수의
- **be famous for** ~로 유명하다
- **be good for** ~에 좋다, 유익하다
- **by the way** 그런데
- **get on** (버스·열차 등을) 타다
- **look like**+명사 ~처럼 보이다
- **make a living** 생계를 유지하다

- **not only A but also B** A뿐만 아니라 B도(= B as well as A)
- **such as** ~와 같은
- **take a trip (to** 장소) (~로) 여행하다[여행가다]
- **take off** (옷 등을) 벗다, 벗기다
- **thanks to** ~ 덕분에
- **turn**+형용사 ~한 상태로 변하다, ~하게 되다
- **work out** 운동하다

Word Power

※ make를 이용한 숙어들

☐ **make a choice** (선택하다)

☐ **make a living** (생계를 꾸리다)

☐ **make a noise** (소음을 내다, 시끄럽게 하다)

☐ **make a plan** (계획을 짜다)

☐ **make an effort** (노력하다)

☐ **make a decision** (결정하다)

☐ **make a mistake** (실수하다)

☐ **make a suggestion** (제안하다)

※ 접미사 '-y'가 붙어 형용사가 되는 명사

☐ **cloud**(구름) – **cloudy**(흐린, 구름이 잔뜩 낀)

☐ **health**(건강) – **healthy**(건강한)

☐ **mess**(엉망진창) – **messy**(지저분한)

☐ **wind**(바람) – **windy**(바람이 부는)

☐ **dirt**(먼지, 때) – **dirty**(더러운)

☐ **luck**(운, 행운) – **lucky**(운이 좋은)

☐ **rain**(비) – **rainy**(비가 오는)

☐ **scare**(두려움) – **scary**(무서운, 겁나는)

English Dictionary

☐ **appear** 나타나다
→ begin to be seen suddenly
갑자기 보이기 시작하다

☐ **cliff** 절벽
→ a high steep rock, especially one facing the sea
높고 가파른 암석, 특히 바다를 향하고 있는 것

☐ **creature** 생물, 생명체
→ all living things except plants
식물을 제외한 모든 살아있는 것

☐ **else** 그 밖의, 그것 이외의
→ in addition to a person, place, or thing
어떤 사람, 장소, 물건에 더하여

☐ **filter** ~을 여과하다, 거르다
→ to pass something through a filter to remove particular things contained in it
어떤 것 안에 있는 특정한 것을 제거하기 위해, 필터(여과장치)를 통과하게 하다

☐ **flow** 흐르다
→ to move steadily without any interrupts, used to describe liquids, gas, electrical currents, etc.
액체, 기체, 전류 등을 설명할 때 사용되는 것으로, 어떠한 방해 없이 꾸준히 움직이다

☐ **generous** 관대한
→ willing to give something more than enough
어떤 것을 충분한 것 이상으로 기꺼이 주는

☐ **information** 정보
→ facts about something
어떤 것에 대한 사실들

☐ **land** 육지, 땅
→ the surface of the earth that is not water
물이 아닌 땅의 표면

☐ **large** 큰, 커다란
→ greater or bigger than usual in size, number, or amount
크기, 숫자 또는 양에서 보통보다 더 많거나 큰

☐ **lung** 폐
→ one of the two organs which you use to breathe
숨을 쉴 때 사용하는 두 개의 장기 중 하나

☐ **mud** 진흙
→ very soft wet earth 매우 부드럽고 젖은 흙

☐ **muddy** 진흙투성이인, 진흙의
→ covered with mud, or full of mud
진흙으로 덮인 또는 진흙으로 가득 찬

☐ **mudflat** 갯벌
→ a level tract lying at little depth below the surface of water or alternately covered and left bare by the tide
해수면 아래에 낮은 깊이로 펼쳐진 평평한 지역 또는 조수에 의해 번갈아 덮여지고 드러나게 되는 지역

☐ **plain** 평원
→ a large flat area of land 넓은 평평한 땅

☐ **provide** 제공하다, 주다
→ to give someone something that they need or want or make it available to them
누군가에게 그들이 필요로 하거나 원하는 것을 주거나 그들에게 이용할 수 있도록 하다

☐ **reed** 갈대
→ a tall thin plant like grass with a hollow stem that grows in or near water
물속이나 근처에서 자라는 속이 빈 줄기를 가진 풀과 같은 길고 얇은 식물

☐ **surface** 표면
→ the outer texture of anything 어떤 것의 바깥 면

☐ **tide** 조수, 밀물과 썰물
→ the periodic rise and fall of the waters of the ocean
바닷물이 주기적으로 올라가고 내려가는 것

01 짝지어진 단어의 관계가 나머지와 <u>다른</u> 하나를 고르시오.

① cloud – cloudy
② exact – exactly
③ dirt – dirty
④ luck – lucky
⑤ rain – rainy

[02~03] 다음 빈칸에 들어갈 말로 적절한 것은?

02

The earthquake causes _____ to the building.

① control
② experience
③ cost
④ effect
⑤ damage

03

Small _____ like shrimps eats these plants.

① sense
② creature
③ snake
④ place
⑤ trash

04 다음 영영풀이에 해당하는 단어를 고르시오.

a level tract lying at little depth below the surface of water or alternately covered and left bare by the tide

① wave
② storm
③ shake
④ field
⑤ mudflat

05 서답형 다음 〈보기〉의 단어를 사용하여 자연스러운 문장을 만들 수 없는 것은? (한 단어는 한 번 밖에 사용할 수 없음. 대·소문자 무시)

┌─ 보기 ─┐
by for on out

① Exercise is good _____ both body and mind.
② I used to work _____ in the gym every day.
③ _____ the way, are you free for dinner tomorrow evening?
④ Thanks _____ your help, I was able to do it.
⑤ Isn't there any way I can get _____ the next flight to Sydney?

06 주어진 문장과 의미가 같은 것을 고르시오.

He can speak not only English but also Spanish.

① He can speak either English or Spanish.
② He can speak Spanish as well as English.
③ He can't speak both English and Spanish.
④ He can't speak English but Spanish.
⑤ He can speak Spanish but he can't speak English.

01 다음 밑줄 친 부분과 의미가 가까운 것을 주어진 철자로 시작하여 쓰시오.

> I <u>got rid of</u> the mud from my shoes.

➡ r_____

[02~03] 두 문장에 공통으로 들어갈 수 있는 단어를 쓰시오.

02
> • Tom and Lisa _____ a living as teachers.
> • I'll _____ a phone call to him to ask about his tomorrow's plans.

03
> • He was famous _____ playing classical music.
> • I believe that laughing is good _____ our health.

04 다음 주어진 우리말에 맞게 빈칸을 채우시오. (철자가 주어진 경우 그 철자로 시작할 것)

(1) 우리가 제시간에 공항에 도착할 수 있겠어.

   ➡ We could r_____ the airport on time.

(2) 산소는 인간의 삶에 있어 필수적이다.

   ➡ _____ is essential to human life.

(3) 나는 규칙적으로 운동을 하고 절대로 과식을 하지 않는다.

   ➡ I _____ _____ r_____ and never eat to excess.

(4) 셔츠의 얼룩이 제거하기 어렵다.

   ➡ The shirt s_____ is very difficult to _____.

(5) 그의 방은 엉망이었다.

   ➡ His room was a _____.

05 다음 빈칸에 알맞은 단어를 〈보기〉에서 골라 쓰시오. (한 단어는 한 번 밖에 사용할 수 없음)

> ┌ 보기 ┐
> appear   bloom   cover   feed

(1) Hyenas _____ on small dead animals and birds.

(2) Forests _____ about 30 percent of the world's land area.

(3) Some colorful flowers _____ during the short summer.

(4) The moon _____ from behind the clouds.

06 다음 영영풀이에 해당하는 단어를 주어진 철자로 시작하여 쓰시오.

> facts about something

➡ i_____

Conversation

1 궁금증 표현하기

> **I wonder what they are.** 그것들이 뭔지 궁금해요.

- 궁금증을 표현할 때 '~을 궁금해 하다'라는 의미의 동사 wonder를 사용하여 'I wonder ~.'라고 말한다.

- 일반적으로 wonder 뒤에는 if절이나 의문사가 쓰인 절 등이 온다. 의문사가 쓰인 절을 사용할 때는 '의문사+주어+동사', 즉 간접의문문의 순서로 문장을 쓴다. 예를 들어, 'I wonder where was she from.'이 아니라 'I wonder where she was from.'이 옳은 문장이 된다.

- 'I wonder ~.'와 비슷한 표현으로 'I want to know ~.', 'Can you tell me ~?' 또는 'I'd like to know ~.' 등이 있다.

궁금증 표현하기

- I wonder 의문사+주어+동사. (나는 ~가 궁금해요.)
- I want to know 의문사+주어+동사. (나는 ~을 알기를 원해요.)
- Can you tell me 의문사+주어+동사? (나에게 ~을 말해 줄 수 있나요?)
- I'd like to know 의문사+주어+동사. (나는 ~을 알기를 원해요.)

핵심 Check

1. 다음 우리말과 일치하도록 빈칸에 알맞은 말을 쓰시오.

   (1) **A:** I wonder _____ now. (우리가 지금 어디에 있는지 궁금해.)

   B: It seems that we are lost. (우리는 길을 잃은 것 같아.)

   (2) **A:** I _____ late. (나는 Tom이 왜 늦는지 궁금해.)

   B: I don't know. Maybe he got up late. (몰라. 아마도 늦게 일어났나봐.)

2. 괄호 안의 단어를 순서대로 배열하여 대화를 완성하시오.

   (1) **A:** _____ (this, are, how, in, wonder, many, events, I, festival) (이 축제에 얼마나 많은 행사가 있는지 궁금해.)

   B: There are 17. (17개가 있어.)

   (2) **A:** _____ (is, I, who, she, wonder) (나는 그녀가 누군지 궁금해.)

   B: I heard that she is our new science teacher. (나는 그녀가 우리의 새로운 과학 선생님이라고 들었어.)

② 알고 있음 표현하기

I heard it is the largest reed field in Korea. 나는 그곳이 한국에서 가장 큰 갈대밭이라고 들었어.

■ 어떤 사실을 알고 있는지 말할 때 'I heard (that) ~.(나는 ~라고 들었어.)'라고 표현한다. 사실에 해당하는 내용으로 절이 나올 때는 'I heard that 주어+동사'를 사용하며, 여기서 that은 생략이 가능하다. 절이 아닌 구가 나올 경우에는 'be aware of'를 사용한다.

알고 있는 것 표현하기

- I heard (that) 주어 동사 ~. (나는 ~라는 것을 들었다.)
- I have heard (that) 주어 동사 ~. (나는 ~라는 것을 들었다.)
- I've been told (that) 주어 동사 ~. (나는 ~라는 것을 들었다.)
- I'm aware (that) 주어 동사 ~. (나는 ~라는 것을 알고 있다.)
- I'm aware of (동)명사 ~. (나는 ~을 알고 있다.)

■ 무언가에 대해 들어서 알고 있는지 물을 때는 'Did you hear about ~?(너는 ~에 대해 들었니?)'라고 말한다. 현재완료를 사용해 'Have you heard about ~?'으로 들어 본 적이 있는지 물을 수도 있다.

알고 있는지 묻기

- Did you hear (that) 주어 동사 ~? (~라는 것을 들었니?)
- Did you hear about (동)명사 ~? (~에 대해 들었니?)
- Have you heard (that) 주어 동사 ~? (~라는 것을 들었니?)
- Are you aware (that) 주어 동사 ~? (~라는 것을 알고 있니?)
- Are you aware of (동)명사 ~? (~을 알고 있니?)
- Do you know (that) 주어 동사 ~? (~라는 것을 알고 있니?)
- Do you know about (동)명사 ~? (~에 대해 알고 있니?)

핵심 Check

3. 다음 우리말과 일치하도록 빈칸에 알맞은 말을 쓰시오.

    A: I _____ the school tennis team won the match.

    (나는 학교 테니스 팀이 시합에서 이겼다는 것을 들었다.)

    B: Really? How wonderful! (정말? 멋지다!)

4. 괄호 안의 단어를 순서대로 배열하여 대화를 완성하시오.

    A: _____ today's lunch menu? (of, you, are, aware)

    (오늘의 점심 메뉴가 뭔지 알고 있니?)

    B: _____ today's lunch menu is kimchi fried rice. (heard, I, have,

    that) (나는 오늘 점심이 김치 볶음밥이라고 들었어.)

 Listen & Speak 1 A-1

> G: I ❶wonder what you did ❷during the summer vacation.
>
> B: I ❸took a trip to Kenya and ❹saw many animals on the ❺plains.
>
> G: Wonderful! ❻By the way, what are the plains?
>
> B: ❼They are large areas of flat land.
>
> G: I see.

G: 나는 네가 여름 방학 동안에 무엇을 했는지 궁금해.

B: 나는 케냐로 여행을 가서 평원에서 많은 동물들을 봤어.

G: 멋지구나! 그런데 평원이 무엇이니?

B: 그곳은 넓고 평평한 땅이야.

G: 그렇구나.

❶ wonder: ~을 궁금해 하다 wonder 다음에 궁금한 내용을 간접의문문(의문사(what)+주어(you)+동사(did))의 형식으로 사용하였다.
❷ during: ~ 동안(에) vacation: 방학
❸ take a trip (to 장소): (~로) 여행하다[여행가다]
❹ saw는 접속사 and로 동사 took a trip과 연결되어 있다.
❺ plain: 평원
❻ 'by the way'의 뜻은 '그런데'로 보통 대화의 화제를 바꿀 때 사용한다.
❼ 주어의 They는 앞 문장의 the plains를 가리키는 대명사이다. flat: 평평한

Check(√) True or False

(1) There are a lot of animals on the plains in Kenya.   T ☐ F ☐

(2) The girl already knows what the boy did during the summer vacation.   T ☐ F ☐

 Listen & Speak 2 A-1

> B: ❶Do you know how many oceans there are on the Earth?
>
> G: The answer is four, isn't it?
>
> B: No. ❷There are five oceans on the Earth. ❸They cover most of the Earth.
>
> G: How much of the Earth do they ❹cover?
>
> B: ❺I heard the oceans cover about 70% of the Earth's surface.

B: 너는 지구에 몇 개의 바다가 있는지 아니?

G: 정답은 네 개야. 그렇지 않니?

B: 아니야. 지구에는 다섯 개의 바다가 있어. 그곳은 지구의 대부분을 차지하고 있어.

G: 그곳이 지구의 얼마를 차지하고 있니?

B: 나는 바다가 지구 표면의 70%를 차지한다고 들었어.

❶ 'Do you know ~?'는 상대방이 어떠한 사실을 알고 있는지 묻는 표현이다. know의 목적어로 간접의문문(의문사+주어+동사)을 이용했다.
❷ There are ~: ~가 있다 ocean: 바다, 대양
❸ They = five oceans, most of ~: ~의 대부분
❹ cover: (범위가) ~에 이르다, 차지하다
❺ heard와 the oceans 사이에 접속사 that이 생략되어 있다. I heard (that) 주어 동사 ~: 나는 ~라는 것을 들었다 about 다음에 숫자가 나오면 '대략'의 의미이다. surface: 표면

Check(√) True or False

(3) There are four oceans on the Earth.   T ☐ F ☐

(4) Oceans on the Earth cover most of the Earth.   T ☐ F ☐

Listen & Speak 1 A-2

G: ❶Look at that lake! It's really beautiful.

B: It's not a lake. It's a ❷river.

G: ❸Is it? ❹I wonder how a river and a lake are different.

B: A river is ❺a long body of fresh water. ❻Unlike a lake, a river flows toward the ocean.

G: I got it.

❶ look at: ~을 보다 lake: 호수　❷ river: 강
❸ 'Is it' 다음에 'a lake'가 생략되어 있다.
❹ I wonder 의문사+주어+동사: 나는 ~가 궁금해요 'how a river and a lake are different'는 wonder의 목적어로 간접의문문의 순서로 사용되었다.
❺ 'a body of water'는 강이나 호수, 바다 같이 물의 큰 지역을 의미한다.
❻ unlike: ~와는 달리 flow: 흐르다 toward: ~을 향해, ~쪽으로

Listen & Speak 2 A-2

G: ❶I heard the Amazon rain forest is called the lungs of the Earth.

B: Lungs? Why?

G: ❷Because it produces about 20% of the Earth's oxygen.

B: Wow! That's a lot.

❶ heard와 the Amazon rain forest 사이에 접속사 that이 생략되어 있다. 아마존 열대 우림이 지구의 폐라고 불리는 것이므로 that절의 동사는 수동태(be+called)로 써야 한다. rain forest: 열대 우림 lung: 폐
❷ 이유를 묻는 말에 접속사 because(~ 때문에)를 이용해 설명하고 있다. produce: 생산하다, 만들다 oxygen: 산소

Conversation A

M: ❶Guess what this is! It's not a tree. It is a plant ❷that looks like tall grass. ❸In fall, it turns yellow. It grows well in wet lands. I heard Suncheon Bay ❹is famous for this plant.

❶ guess의 목적어는 'what this is'이다. 의문문이 문장의 주어, 목적어, 보어 등으로 사용될 때 '의문사+주어+동사'의 어순으로 표현한다. guess: 추측하다, 알아맞히다

❷ 여기서 that은 주격 관계대명사이므로, 'that looks like tall grass'는 앞의 a plant(식물)를 수식한다. look like+명사: ~처럼 보이다
❸ 계절 앞에는 전치사 in을 사용한다. turn+형용사: ~한 상태로 변하다, ~하게 되다
❹ be famous for: ~로 유명하다

Conversation B

Dad: Do you ❶want to see an amazing place?

Karl & Sister: Sure!

Dad: Then let's ❷get on the train.

Sister: Look at the yellow plants! ❸I wonder what they are.

Dad: They are ❹reeds. Suncheon Bay has beautiful reed fields.

Karl: Wow, the reeds are ❺even taller than you, Dad.

Sister: They really are. ❻Let me take a picture of you.

Karl: This reed field is very large.

Dad: Yes. ❼I heard it is the largest one in Korea.

Karl: Look at the sky. It's ❽turning red.

Sister: Yes, it's beautiful.

❶ want는 뒤에 to부정사(to+동사원형)를 목적어로 취할 수 있지만 동명사는 목적어로 취할 수 없다.
❷ get on: (버스·지하철 등을) 타다
❸ I wonder 의문사+주어+동사: 나는 ~가 궁금해요
❹ reed: 갈대
❺ 형용사의 비교급은 바로 앞에 much, far, even, still, a lot 등을 사용해서 강조한다.
❻ let 목적어 목적격보어(동사원형): ···가 ~하게 하다 take a picture: 사진을 찍다
❼ I heard (that) 주어 동사 ~: 나는 ~라는 것을 들었다 the largest는 large 의 최상급 표현이다. 대명사 one은 reed field를 의미한다.
❽ turn+형용사: ~한 상태로 변하다, ~하게 되다

Communication Task Step 2

A: ❶I wonder what is special about Great Plains.

B: ❷I heard it ❸is good for raising animals.

❶ I wonder 의문사+주어+동사: 나는 ~가 궁금해요 special: 특별한
❷ I heard (that) 주어 동사 ~: 나는 ~라는 것을 들었다
❸ be good for: ~에 좋다, 유익하다 raise: 키우다, 기르다

● 다음 우리말과 일치하도록 빈칸에 알맞은 말을 쓰시오. (주어진 철자가 있으면 그 철자로 시작할 것)

Listen & Speak 1 A

1. G: I _____ _____ _____ _____ the summer vacation.

   B: I _____ a _____ to Kenya and saw many animals on the plains.

   G: Wonderful! _____ the way, what are the _____?

   B: They are large areas of _____ land.

   G: I see.

2. G: Look _____ that lake! It's really beautiful.

   B: It's not a _____. It's a river.

   G: Is it? I _____ _____ a river and a lake _____ _____.

   B: A river is _____ _____ _____ _____ water.
   Unlike a lake, a river flows _____ the ocean.

   G: I _____ _____.

Listen & Speak 1 B

1. A: I wonder _____ _____ _____ _____.

   B: It is a very _____ area of land.

2. A: _____ _____ a _____ is.

   B: It is a large, _____ area of _____.

Listen & Talk 2 A

1. B: Do you know _____ _____ _____ _____ _____ _____ on the Earth?

   G: The answer is four, isn't it?

   B: No. _____ _____ five oceans on the Earth. They _____ _____ of the Earth.

   G: How _____ of the Earth do they _____?

   B: I _____ the oceans _____ _____ 70% of the Earth's _____.

2. G: I heard the Amazon _____ _____ _____ _____ the _____ of the Earth.

   B: _____? Why?

   G: Because it _____ about 20% of the Earth's _____.

   B: Wow! That's a lot.

해석

1. G: 나는 네가 여름 방학 동안에 무엇을 했는지 궁금해.
   B: 나는 케냐로 여행을 가서 평원에서 많은 동물들을 봤어.
   G: 멋지구나! 그런데 평원이 무엇이니?
   B: 그곳은 넓고 평평한 땅이야.
   G: 그렇구나.

2. G: 저 호수를 봐. 정말 아름다워.
   B: 그것은 호수가 아니야. 그것은 강이야.
   G: 그래? 나는 강과 호수가 어떻게 다른지 궁금해.
   B: 강은 민물로 된 긴 물줄기야. 호수와 다르게 강은 바다로 흘러.
   G: 알겠어.

1. A: 나는 산이 무엇인지 궁금해.
   B: 그곳은 아주 높은 지대의 땅이야.

2. A: 나는 평원이 무엇인지 궁금해.
   B: 그곳은 넓고 평평한 지대의 땅이야.

1. B: 너는 지구에 몇 개의 바다가 있는지 아니?
   G: 정답은 네 개야, 그렇지 않니?
   B: 아니야. 지구에는 다섯 개의 바다가 있어. 그곳은 지구의 대부분을 차지하고 있어.
   G: 그곳이 지구의 얼마를 차지하고 있니?
   B: 나는 바다가 지구 표면의 70%를 차지한다고 들었어.

2. G: 나는 아마존 열대 우림이 지구의 허파라고 불린다고 들었어.
   B: 허파? 왜?
   G: 왜냐하면 그곳은 지구 산소의 약 20%를 생산하기 때문이야.
   B: 우와! 엄청나구나.

Listen & Talk 2 B

1. **A:** I _____ to go to Jecheon.

   B: Why?

   A: I _____ there are beautiful _____ in Jecheon.

2. **A:** I _____ _____ _____ _____ Danyang.

   B: Why?

   A: I heard there are _____ caves in Danyang.

Conversation A

M: Guess _____ this is! It's not a tree. It is a _____ that looks like tall _____. _____ fall, it _____ yellow. It grows well in _____ lands. I _____ Suncheon Bay is famous _____ this plant.

Conversation B

Dad: Do you want to see an _____ place?

Karl & Sister: Sure!

Dad: Then let's _____ _____ the train.

Sister: Look at the yellow plants! I _____ _____ _____ _____.

Dad: They are _____. Suncheon Bay has beautiful _____ fields.

Karl: Wow, the reeds are even _____ _____ you, Dad.

Sister: They really are. Let me _____ a picture of you.

Karl: This _____ _____ is very large.

Dad: Yes. I _____ it is _____ _____ _____ in Korea.

Karl: Look at the sky. It's _____ red.

Sister: Yes, it's beautiful.

Communication Task Step 1

A: What _____ do you have?

B: I have Moraine Lake. It's in Canada.

A: What is _____ about the place?

B: The color of the water _____ light blue.

해석

1. A: 나는 제천에 가고 싶어.
   B: 왜?
   A: 나는 제천에 아름다운 호수들이 있다고 들었어.

2. A: 나는 단양에 가고 싶어.
   B: 왜?
   A: 나는 단양에 유명한 동굴들이 있다고 들었어.

M: 이것이 무엇인지 추측해 봐! 그것은 나무가 아니야. 그것은 키가 큰 풀처럼 보이는 식물이야. 가을에는 노란색으로 변해. 그것은 습지에서 잘 자라. 나는 순천만이 이 식물로 유명하다고 들었어.

아빠: 너희들 멋진 곳을 보고 싶니?
Karl, 여동생: 물론이죠!
아빠: 그러면 기차를 타자.
여동생: 저 노란색 식물들을 봐요! 저게 무엇인지 궁금해요.
아빠: 그건 갈대야. 순천만에는 아름다운 갈대밭이 있어.
Karl: 와, 갈대가 아빠보다 키가 더 커요.
여동생: 진짜 그러네요. 제가 사진을 찍어 드릴게요.
Karl: 이 갈대밭은 정말 넓네요.
아빠: 그래. 나는 이곳이 한국에서 가장 큰 갈대밭이라고 들었어.
Karl: 하늘을 보세요. 빨갛게 변하고 있어요.
여동생: 그러네, 아름다워.

A: 너는 어떤 장소를 가지고 있니?
B: 나는 모레인호를 갖고 있어. 그곳은 캐나다에 있어.
A: 그곳은 어떤 것이 특별하니?
B: 물의 색이 연한 파랑색이야.

[01~02] 대화의 밑줄 친 부분의 의도로 알맞은 것은?

01

G: Look at that lake! It's really beautiful.

B: It's not a lake. It's a river.

G: I wonder how a river and a lake are different.

B: A river is a long body of fresh water. Unlike a lake, a river flows toward the ocean.

G: I got it.

① 방법 표현하기   ② 당부하기   ③ 이유 표현하기

④ 궁금증 표현하기   ⑤ 모르는 것 말하기

02

A: I want to go to Jecheon.

B: Why?

A: I heard there are beautiful lakes in Jecheon.

① 궁금증 표현하기   ② 불확실함 말하기   ③ 놀람 표현하기

④ 충고하기   ⑤ 알고 있음 표현하기

03 밑줄 친 부분과 바꿔 쓸 수 있는 것을 모두 고르시오.

Sister: Look at the yellow plants! I wonder what they are.

Dad: They are reeds. Suncheon Bay has beautiful reed fields.

① I have learned what they are.

② I'm very sure what they are.

③ I want to know what they are.

④ I'd like to know what they are.

⑤ I already know what they are.

04 다음 대화의 빈칸에 알맞은 말은?

A: I wonder what is special about Moraine Lake.

B: _____

① I heard the color of the water is light blue.

② I hope to visit the lake.

③ I don't think the color of the water is light blue.

④ I have been to Moraine lake.

⑤ I want to visit Moraine lake.

[01~03] 다음 대화를 읽고 물음에 답하시오.

B: I just finished making a plan for my trip. (①)

G: Sure. (②) (wonder, will, do, I, you, what) (③)

B: On the first day, I'm going to go fishing on a lake. (④) The next day, I'm going to climb a mountain.

G: Is that all?

B: No. On the last day, I'm going to go swimming. (⑤)

G: Wow. You will do a lot of activities.

01 위 대화의 ①~⑤ 중 다음 주어진 말이 들어갈 알맞은 곳은?

> Do you want to hear it?

① ② ③ ④ ⑤

02 괄호 안에 주어진 단어를 배열하여 영작하시오.

➡ _____

03 위 대화를 읽고 대답할 수 있는 것을 모두 고르시오.

ⓐ For how many days will the boy take a trip?

ⓑ What will the boy do during his trip?

ⓒ Where will the boy go during his trip?

ⓓ When will the boy take a trip?

ⓔ What will the boy do on the first day of trip?

➡ _____

[04~07] 다음 대화를 읽고 물음에 답하시오.

G: I wonder what you did during the summer vacation. (①)

B: I (A)_____ a trip to Kenya and saw many animals on the plains. (②)

G: Wonderful! (③)

B: (④) They are large areas of flat land. (⑤)

G: I see.

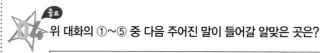

04 위 대화의 ①~⑤ 중 다음 주어진 말이 들어갈 알맞은 곳은?

> By the way, what are the plains?

① ② ③ ④ ⑤

05 빈칸 (A)에 알맞은 말을 고르시오.

① made   ② took   ③ got

④ gave   ⑤ found

06 다음 영영풀이에 해당하는 단어를 대화에서 찾아 쓰시오.

> the surface of the earth that is not water

➡ _____

07 위 대화의 내용과 일치하지 않는 것을 고르시오.

① The girl didn't know what the plains are.

② There are plains in Kenya.

③ The plains are not flat.

④ The boy went to Kenya during the summer vacation.

⑤ There are many animals in Kenya.

[08~09] 다음 대화를 읽고 물음에 답하시오.

> B: Do you know how many oceans there are on the Earth?
> G: ⓐThe answer is four, isn't it?
> B: ⓑYes. There are five oceans on the Earth. ⓒThey cover most of the Earth.
> G: ⓓHow much of the Earth do they cover?
> B: ⓔI heard the oceans cover about 70% of the Earth's surface.

08 ⓐ~ⓔ 중 흐름상 어색한 것을 고르시오.

① ⓐ　② ⓑ　③ ⓒ　④ ⓓ　⑤ ⓔ

09 위 대화의 내용과 일치하지 않는 것을 고르시오.

① The most of the Earth is covered with oceans.
② The boy knows how much of the Earth oceans cover.
③ There are 5 oceans on the Earth.
④ The girl wants to know how much of the Earth oceans cover.
⑤ The girl correctly knew how many oceans there are on the Earth.

[10~12] 다음 대화를 읽고 물음에 답하시오.

> Dad: Do you want to see an amazing place?
> Karl & Sister: Sure! (①)
> Dad: Then let's (A)＿＿＿ on the train.
> Sister: Look at the yellow plants! (②)
> Dad: They are reeds. Suncheon Bay has beautiful reed fields.
> Karl: Wow, the reeds are even taller than you, Dad. (③)
> Sister: They really are. Let me take a picture of you. (④)

> Karl: This reed field is very large.
> Dad: Yes. I heard it is the largest one in Korea. (⑤)
> Karl: Look at the sky. It's turning red.
> Sister: Yes, it's beautiful.

10 위 대화의 ①~⑤ 중 다음 주어진 말이 들어갈 알맞은 곳은?

> I wonder what they are.

① 　② 　③ 　④ 　⑤

11 빈칸 (A)에 알맞은 말을 고르시오.

① get　② give　③ take
④ pick　⑤ put

12 위 대화의 내용과 일치하지 않는 것을 고르시오.

① There are reed fields in Sunchen Bay.
② They travel by train.
③ Dad is shorter than the reeds.
④ Sunchen Bay has the second largest reed field in Korea.
⑤ They see the sunset.

13 다음 중 짝지어진 대화가 어색한 것은?

① A: I wonder where my book is.
　B: Are you talking about the math book?
② A: I want to know why you called me last night.
　B: I had a question about our English homework.
③ A: I wonder who made this hamburger.
　B: Your mom made it for you.
④ A: Can you tell me where I can buy the snacks?
　B: You can buy them over there.
⑤ A: I would like to know what you did on Sunday.
　B: I am going to take a trip to Danyang.

[01~02] 다음 대화를 읽고 물음에 답하시오.

> A: (a) 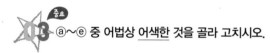나는 대평원의 특별한 점은 무엇인지 궁금해.
> (Great Plains, about, is, wonder, special, I, what)
> B: I heard it is good (A)_____ raising animals.

01 빈칸 (A)에 알맞은 전치사를 쓰시오.

➡ _____

02 (a)의 밑줄 친 우리말에 맞게 괄호 안에 주어진 단어를 배열하여 영작하시오.

➡ _____

 ⓐ~ⓔ 중 어법상 어색한 것을 골라 고치시오.

> G: ⓐI wonder what did you ⓑduring the summer vacation.
> B: ⓒI took a trip to Kenya ⓓand saw many animals on the plains.
> G: Wonderful! ⓔBy the way, what are the plains?
> B: They are large areas of flat land.
> G: I see.

➡ _____

[04~05] 다음 대화를 읽고 물음에 답하시오.

> G: Look at that lake! ⓐIt's really beautiful.
> B: ⓑIt's not a lake. It's a river.
> G: Is it? (A)I wonder how a river and a lake are different.
> B: ⓒA river is a long body of fresh water. ⓓLike a lake, ⓔa river flows toward the ocean.
> G: I got it.

04 ⓐ~ⓔ 중 흐름상 어색한 것을 바르게 고치시오.

➡ _____

05 밑줄 친 (A)와 같은 의미가 되도록 주어진 단어를 이용해서 문장을 만드시오.

➡ _____

(can, tell)

06 주어진 문장 이후에 이어질 대화의 순서를 바르게 배열하시오.

> Do you know how many oceans there are on the Earth?

> (A) I heard the oceans cover about 70% of the Earth's surface.
> (B) The answer is four, isn't it?
> (C) How much of the Earth do they cover?
> (D) No. There are five oceans on the Earth. They cover most of the Earth.

➡ _____

07 밑줄 친 우리말을 주어진 단어를 이용하여 영작하시오

> A: I want to go to Jejudo.
> B: Why?
> A: 나는 제주도에 여러 개의 오름이 있다고 들었어. (oreum, a lot of)

➡ _____

Grammar

① 'It+be동사+형용사+to+동사원형' 구문

- **It** is important **to understand** the roles of mudflats. 갯벌의 역할을 이해하는 것이 중요하다.

■ 비교적 긴 to부정사 부분이 문장의 주어로 쓰일 때 그 to부정사 부분을 일반적인 주어의 자리인 문장의 맨 앞에 두지 않고 문장 뒤에 둔다. 대신 주어 자리에는 It을 넣어주는데 그것을 가주어 It이라고 부르고 문장 뒤로 간 to부정사 부분은 진주어라고 부른다. 이때 쓰인 It은 가주어이므로 구체적인 뜻이 없으며, '…하는 것은 ~하다'로 해석한다.

- **It** is not easy **to work out**. 운동하는 것은 쉽지 않다.
  = **To work out** is not easy.

- **It** is interesting **to play** soccer. 축구하는 것은 재미있다.
  = **To play** soccer is interesting.

■ **to부정사의 의미상 주어**

'to부정사'가 행하는 동작의 주체를 to부정사의 의미상 주어라고 한다. to부정사의 의미상 주어는 to부정사 바로 앞에 'for+목적격'의 형태로 쓴다. to부정사 구문에서 to부정사의 의미상 주어가 없는 경우는 특별한 사람이 아니라 일반적인 사람이기 때문이다. 문장에 쓰인 형용사가 kind, foolish, rude, careless, wise 등과 같이 사람의 성질을 나타내는 말일 때는 'of+목적격'을 쓴다. 또한 to부정사의 부정은 to부정사 앞에 not[never]을 써서 'not[never]+to V'로 나타내며 '…하지 않는 것은 ~하다'로 해석한다.

- **It** is necessary **for** you **to save** money. 너는 돈을 저축하는 것이 필요하다.

- **It** is nice **of** him **to say** so. 그렇게 말하다니 그는 참 착하구나.

- **It** is difficult **not to be** touched by the story. 그 이야기에 감동받지 않는 것은 어렵다.

핵심 Check

1. 다음 우리말과 일치하도록 빈칸에 알맞은 말을 쓰시오.

(1) 축구를 하는 것은 재미있다.
➡ _____ is fun _____ _____ soccer.

(2) 여기서 너를 보게 되어 좋다.
➡ It's great _____ _____ you here.

(3) 당신은 돈을 저축하는 것이 필요하다.
➡ It is necessary _____ _____ _____ _____ money.

② 'not only A but also B' 구문

> **Not only** very small living things like plankton **but also** crabs and fish live there.
> 플랑크톤처럼 작은 생명체뿐만 아니라 게와 물고기도 그곳에 산다.

■ 'not only A but also B'의 형태로 'A뿐만 아니라 B도'라는 의미를 가지며 A와 B는 품사나 문장에서의 역할이 동일해야 한다. (이렇게 상호 호응 관계를 이루면서 한 쌍으로 이루어진 접속사를 상관접속사라고 한다.)

- Amy is **not only** smart **but also** friendly. Amy는 똑똑할 뿐만 아니라 다정하다. (A와 B에 해당하는 smart와 friendly는 모두 형용사이며 보어의 역할을 한다.)

■ 초점이 but also 다음의 B에 놓이며 'B as well as A'로 바꿔 쓸 수 있다.

- I like **not only** English **but also** math.
  = I like math **as well as** English. 나는 영어뿐 아니라 수학도 좋아한다.

■ 'not only A but also B'에서 A와 B 자리에는 명사(구)와 동사(구)를 비롯하여 다양한 표현이 사용될 수 있으며, but also에서 also가 생략되기도 한다.

- Laura is **not only** pretty **but also** wise. Laura는 예쁠 뿐만 아니라 현명하다.
- She **not only** wrote the text **but also** selected the pictures. 그녀는 그 본문을 썼을 뿐만 아니라 그림들을 선별하기도 했다.
- He likes **not only** pizza **but also** spaghetti.
  = He likes **not only** pizza **but** spaghetti.
  = He likes **not simply**[**merely**] pizza **but** (**also**) spaghetti.
  = He likes spaghetti **as well as** pizza. 그는 피자뿐만 아니라 스파게티도 좋아한다.

■ 'not only A but also B'와 'B as well as A'가 주어로 쓰일 경우 B에 수를 일치시킨다.

- **Not only** I **but also** my sister likes skating.
  = My sister **as well as** I likes skating. 나뿐만 아니라 내 여동생도 스케이트 타는 것을 좋아한다.

핵심 Check

2. 다음 우리말에 맞게 빈칸을 알맞게 채우시오.

(1) 그녀는 영어뿐만 아니라 불어도 한다.

➡ She speaks ＿＿＿＿＿＿ ＿＿＿＿＿＿ English but also French.

(2) 그들은 한국에서뿐만 아니라 일본에서도 인기가 있다.

➡ They are popular not only in Korea ＿＿＿＿＿＿ ＿＿＿＿＿＿ in Japan.

01 다음 빈칸에 알맞은 것을 고르시오.

> A: Is it interesting _____ ?
> B: Yes, of course.

① to draw cartoons
② to drawing cartoons
③ draws cartoons
④ you draw cartoons
⑤ of you to draw cartoons

02 다음 중 나머지와 의미가 다른 하나는?

① She is good at not only singing but also dancing.
② She is good at not only singing but dancing.
③ She is good at singing as well as dancing.
④ She is good at not simply singing but also dancing.
⑤ She is good at not merely singing but also dancing.

03 다음 문장에서 어법상 어색한 부분을 바르게 고쳐 쓰시오.

(1) Sam not only reads German but also write it.
_____ ➡ _____

(2) Mike is not only unkind but is stupid.
_____ ➡ _____

(3) Not only you but also Sophie like going shopping.
_____ ➡ _____

(4) It is impossible to crossing this river by swimming.
_____ ➡ _____

(5) That is great to cook for others.
_____ ➡ _____

(6) It is necessary of you to read the book.
_____ ➡ _____

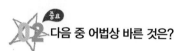

01 다음 중 어법상 바르지 <u>않은</u> 것은?

① It was fun to find the information about these places.

② It's hard to take care of children.

③ That's necessary to know when to draw the line.

④ It became common to send texts instead of sending mails between students.

⑤ It's better to speak clearly.

02 다음 중 어법상 바른 것은?

① Ezra as well as his sisters was studying in the library.

② The book is not only an expensive one but uninteresting.

③ Not only I but also David like Julie.

④ Steve is not only smart but also generously.

⑤ Bill speaks rudely not only at home but also school.

03 다음 빈칸에 알맞은 말이 바르게 짝지어진 것은?

- My dog is not only _____ but also smart.
- It is great _____ a bike in the mountains.

① cutely – ride

② cute – to ride

③ cutely – riding

④ cute – to riding

⑤ cutely – riding

04 다음 문장의 빈칸에 들어갈 알맞은 것은?

_____ is important to wear long clothes in the jungle.

① What   ② This

③ That   ④ It

⑤ One

05 다음 대화의 빈칸에 들어갈 말로 알맞은 것은?

M: Who did you meet yesterday?
W: I met not _____ Molly but Heidi.

① also   ② simple   ③ as

④ very   ⑤ merely

06 다음 괄호 안에서 알맞은 말을 고르시오.

(1) (It / That) is not difficult to use this camera.

(2) It is important (understand / to understand) other cultures.

(3) It was clever (for / of) her to come early.

(4) It not only rained but (snowy / snowed) yesterday.

(5) I like not only English (and / but) math.

(6) Not only you but also Audrey (enjoy / enjoys) going shopping.

07 다음 중 어법상 옳은 것은?

① Amy is not only smartly but also friendly.

② It is fun to going into caves.

③ It is kind for him to say so.

④ She wants not only to dance but also to sing.

⑤ Not only you but also James play the piano.

08 다음 중 밑줄 친 부분의 쓰임이 <u>다른</u> 하나는?

① <u>It</u> is fun to go on a picnic.

② <u>It</u> was not such a nice party.

③ <u>It</u>'s necessary to prepare for the worst.

④ <u>It</u> was not easy to win the race.

⑤ <u>It</u> is better to eat healthy food.

09 주어진 문장의 빈칸에 들어갈 알맞은 말을 고르시오.

> • Mike was in need of not only food but _____ clothes.

① too   ② also   ③ so

④ as well   ⑤ very

10 다음 우리말을 바르게 영작한 것을 고르시오.

> 힙합 댄스를 배우는 것은 신났었다.

① It was exciting learn hiphop dance.

② It was exciting learns hiphop dance.

③ It was exciting learned hiphop dance.

④ It was exciting to learn hiphop dance.

⑤ It was exciting to learning hiphop dance.

11 다음 두 문장을 한 문장으로 바르게 연결한 것은?

> • She is good at singing.
> • She is good at dancing, too.

① She is good at either singing or dancing.

② She is good at neither singing nor dancing.

③ She isn't good at both singing and dancing.

④ She is good at not singing but dancing.

⑤ She is good at not only singing but dancing.

12 다음 우리말과 일치하도록 빈칸에 알맞은 단어로 묶은 것은?

> • 그녀가 프랑스어를 배운 것은 아주 현명했다.
> = _____ was wise _____ her _____ French.

① It – for – learn

② It – of – to learn

③ This – for – learn

④ That – for – to learn

⑤ That – of – learning

서답형

13 주어진 어휘를 이용하여 빈칸에 알맞게 쓰시오.

> I like not only reading stories but also _____ them. (write)

서답형

14 다음 문장에서 어법상 <u>어색한</u> 것을 바르게 고쳐 다시 쓰시오.

(1) It would be really stupid for you to help them.

➡ _____

(2) This is interesting to walk in the forest.

➡ _____

(3) It is important wear a hat to block the sun.

➡ _____

(4) Not only I but also Bella were enjoying taking a walk.

➡ _____

(5) Harry is not only a great wizard but also very wise.

➡ _____

_____

중요

15 다음 중 어법상 <u>어색한</u> 것을 고르시오. (2개)

① It was a lot of fun to swim in the pond with my friends.

② It was nice for you to help the elderly woman at the bus stop.

③ It looked necessary for him to go to the dentist.

④ My brother want not only to write Spanish but also speaks it.

⑤ They can build not only muscles but also mental strength.

16 다음 우리말을 영작했을 때 <u>잘못된</u> 것을 고르시오.

> 플랑크톤뿐만 아니라 게와 물고기도 그곳에 산다.

① Not only plankton but also crabs and fish live there.

② Not only plankton but crabs and fish live there.

③ Not merely plankton but also crabs and fish live there.

④ Not only plankton but simply crabs and fish live there.

⑤ Plankton as well as crabs and fish lives there.

중요

 다음 우리말을 바르게 영작한 것을 고르시오.

> 그가 그 산에 오르는 것은 위험하다.

① It is dangerous for him climb that mountain.

② It is dangerous he climbs that mountain.

③ It is dangerous for him to climb that mountain.

④ It is dangerous of him to climb that mountain.

⑤ To climb that mountain is dangerous of you.

서답형

18 다음 두 문장을 주어진 어휘를 이용하여 한 문장으로 바꿔 쓰시오.

> Gina is pretty. She is also kind. (well)

➡ _____

01 다음 우리말을 괄호 안에 주어진 어휘를 이용하여 (a) to부정사 주어를 써서, (b) 가주어를 써서 영작하시오.

(1) 좋은 친구를 사귀는 것은 어렵다. (difficult, make)

➡ (a) _____

  (b) _____

(2) 남을 돕는 것은 중요하다. (important, others)

➡ (a) _____

  (b) _____

(3) 맛을 설명하는 것은 불가능하다. (tastes, explain)

➡ (a) _____

  (b) _____

02 다음 두 문장을 'not only A but also B' 구문을 사용하여 한 문장으로 연결하시오.

(1) Chris is friendly. He is good-looking, too.

➡ _____

(2) Marianne writes Korean well. She also speaks Korean well.

➡ _____

(3) Charlotte likes to play basketball. She enjoys watching soccer games on TV, too.

➡ _____

_____

03 그림을 보고 주어진 어휘를 이용하여 〈보기〉와 같이 쓰시오.

┤ 보기 ├
It is great to eat delicious food with friends.

(1) (exciting, watch fish swimming)

➡ _____

(2) (amazing, visit Giant's Causeway in Ireland)

➡ _____

04 두 문장의 의미가 같도록 빈칸에 알맞은 말을 쓰시오.

(1) This machine looks good. It also looks convenient.

= This machine looks not only good _____ _____ convenient.

(2) He can play the piano. He can play the violin, too.

= He can play not only the piano but the violin _____ _____ .

05 다음 우리말에 맞게 주어진 단어를 바르게 배열하시오.

(1) 나의 가족과 함께 좋은 추억을 만드는 것은 중요하다. (it, memories, family, good, important, is, make, my, with, to)

➡ _____

(2) 성공하기 위해 영어를 잘하는 것은 필요하다. (it, English, is, speak, succeed, well, necessary, to, to)

➡ _____

(3) 나는 노래 부르는 것뿐 아니라 춤추는 것도 좋아한다. (I, only, but, like, dancing, singing, not)

➡ _____

(4) 너뿐만 아니라 네 동생도 설거지를 해야 한다. (you, your brother, dishes, wash, but, should, not, also, only, the)

➡ _____

_____

06 다음 문장을 It으로 시작하여 다시 쓰시오.

(1) To eat fruit and vegetables is easy.

➡ _____

(2) To know how to greet people in different countries will be necessary.

➡ _____

_____

(3) That knowledge is power is true.

➡ _____

07 다음 중 어법상 어색한 것을 바르게 고치시오.

(1) Build a new airport in the town is a bad idea.

_____

(2) It is wise for Charles to select the book.

_____

(3) Betty should not only eat well but also working out regularly.

_____

(4) Emily as well as her sisters are good at tennis.

_____

08 다음 우리말을 괄호 안에 주어진 어휘를 이용하여 영작하시오.

(1) 적을 용서하는 것은 쉽지 않다. (forgive, an enemy, 8 단어)

➡ _____

(2) 에너지를 절약하는 것이 중요하다. (important, save, energy, 6 단어)

➡ _____

(3) 오늘은 크리스마스일 뿐만 아니라 내 생일이다. (only, Christmas, 9 단어)

➡ _____

(4) Jane뿐만 아니라 그녀의 남동생들도 친절하다. (kind, well, 8 단어)

➡ _____

Mudflats, Nature's Gift

Mudflats are large areas of muddy land at the seaside. They appear and
_{mud의 형용사형}
disappear with every tide. During low tides, they show up, and during
_{↔appear} _{~함에 따라, ~와 더불어, ~와 함께} _{썰물} _{~ 동안}
high tides, they are covered by the sea. Mudflats help sea creatures,
_{밀물} _{be동사+과거분사+by: 수동태 구문}
people, and the Earth in many ways. It is important to understand the
_{It+be동사+형용사+to부정사}
roles of mudflats. Let's see what they do.
_{간접의문문}

Mudflats are home to a lot of living things at the seaside. Not only
_{~에게} _{생물}
very small living things like plankton but also crabs and fish live there.
_{not only A but also B: A뿐만 아니라 B도, A와 B의 형태는 같아야 한다.}
Mudflats provide various types of food for them. Also, many birds eat
_{주어+provide+직접목적어+for+간접목적어: 3형식 문장}
food there.

Crab: Mudflats are my home sweet home.

---

mudflat: 갯벌	
muddy: 진흙의, 질퍽한	
appear: 나타나다, 출현하다	
tide: 조수, 밀물과 썰물	
creature: 생명체, 생물	
role: 역할, 임무	
plankton: 플랑크톤	
crab: 게	
provide: 제공하다, 주다	
various: 각종의, 다양한	

 확인문제

● 다음 문장이 본문의 내용과 일치하면 T, 일치하지 않으면 F를 쓰시오.

1 Mudflats are large areas of muddy land at the seaside. ☐

2 Mudflats disappear during low tides. ☐

3 Mudflats are home to a lot of living things at the seaside. ☐

4 Not plankton but crabs and fish live on mudflats. ☐

Mudflats are good for people, too. People who live near mudflat
areas make a living by catching fish and other sea animals nearby.
Thanks to mudflats, people can get fresh seafood. People can enjoy
fun activities, such as mud sliding and body painting on mudflats.
They can also watch a large number of birds that feed on the sea
animals there.

Boy: Mudflats are nature's gift to living things!

Mudflats help the environment greatly. Mudflats hold a lot of water,
so they can reduce damage from floods. Also, mudflats filter water
that flows from the land into the sea. They remove bad things in
the water before it enters the sea. Thanks to mudflats, the water that
reaches the sea is clean. Mudflats work as the Earth's lungs. They
produce a huge volume of oxygen that is necessary for life on the
Earth.

Earth: Mudflats keep me healthy and clean.

Mudflats are wonderful places, aren't they? They are a gift from
nature to living things on the Earth. For all these reasons, it is
necessary to protect mudflats.

---

mud: 진흙
slide: 미끄러지다
feed: 먹이를 먹다, 먹이다
make a living: 생계를 꾸리다
environment: 환경
reduce: 줄이다
damage: 피해, 손해
flood: 홍수
filter: 거르다, 걸러 내다
flow: 흐르다
remove: 제거하다
reach: ~에 이르다, 닿다, 도달하다
lung: 폐
volume: 용량, 용적
oxygen: 산소
necessary: 필요한
reason: 이유
protect: 보호하다

 확인문제

● 다음 문장이 본문의 내용과 일치하면 T, 일치하지 <u>않으면</u> F를 쓰시오.

1 Mudflats enable people to get fresh seafood. ☐

2 People can watch the sea animals that feed on birds on mudflats. ☐

3 Mudflats filter water flowing from the land into the sea. ☐

4 Thanks to mudflats, the water that arrives at the sea is clean. ☐

5 Mudflats are a gift from living things on the Earth to nature. ☐

● 우리말을 참고하여 빈칸에 알맞은 말을 쓰시오.

1 Mudflats, Nature's _____

2 Mudflats are large areas of _____ _____ at the seaside.

3 They appear and disappear _____ _____ _____.

4 During low tides, they _____ _____, and during _____ _____, they _____ _____ _____ the sea.

5 Mudflats help sea creatures, people, and the Earth _____ _____ _____.

6 It is important to understand _____ _____ _____ _____.

7 Let's see _____ _____ _____.

8 Mudflats _____ _____ _____ a lot of living things at the seaside.

9 _____ _____ very small living things like plankton _____ _____ crabs and fish live there.

10 Mudflats _____ various types of food _____ them.

11 _____, many birds eat food there.

12 Crab: Mudflats are my _____ _____ _____.

13 Mudflats _____ _____ _____ people, too.

1	갯벌, 자연의 선물
2	갯벌은 바닷가의 진흙이 있는 넓은 지역이다.
3	갯벌은 조수와 함께 나타나고 사라진다.
4	썰물일 때 갯벌이 드러나고, 밀물일 때 바다에 덮인다.
5	갯벌은 바다 생물과 사람, 지구를 많은 방면에서 돕는다.
6	갯벌의 역할을 이해하는 것이 중요하다.
7	갯벌이 무엇을 하는지 살펴보자.
8	갯벌은 바닷가에 있는 많은 생물들에게 집이다.
9	플랑크톤처럼 작은 생명체뿐만 아니라 게와 물고기도 그곳에 산다.
10	갯벌은 그들에게 다양한 종류의 먹이를 제공한다.
11	또한, 많은 새들도 그곳에서 먹이를 먹는다.
12	게: 갯벌은 나의 단란한 집이에요.
13	갯벌은 사람들에게도 유익하다.

14 People who live near mudflat areas _____ _____ _____ by catching fish and other sea animals _____.

15 _____ _____ mudflats, people can get fresh seafood.

16 People can enjoy _____ _____, _____ _____ mud sliding and body painting on mudflats.

17 They can also watch a large number of birds that _____ _____ the sea animals there.

18 Boy: Mudflats are _____ _____ to living things!

19 Mudflats _____ the environment _____.

20 Mudflats _____ a lot of water, so they can _____ _____ from floods.

21 Also, mudflats _____ water that flows _____ the land _____ the sea.

22 They _____ _____ _____ in the water before it enters the sea.

23 Thanks to mudflats, the water _____ _____ _____ _____ is clean.

24 Mudflats work _____ _____ _____ _____.

25 They produce _____ _____ _____ _____ oxygen that is necessary for life on the Earth.

26 Earth: Mudflats keep me _____ and _____.

27 Mudflats are wonderful places, _____ _____?

28 They are a gift _____ _____ _____ on the Earth.

29 For all these reasons, it is necessary _____ _____ _____.

14 갯벌 지역 인근에 사는 사람들은 근처에서 물고기와 다른 바다 동물들을 잡아 생계를 꾸린다.

15 갯벌 덕분에 사람들은 신선한 해산물을 얻을 수 있다.

16 사람들은 갯벌에서 진흙 미끄럼 타기나 보디 페인팅과 같은 즐거운 활동을 즐길 수 있다.

17 그들은 또한 그곳에서 바다 동물들을 먹는 수많은 새를 관찰할 수도 있다.

18 남자아이: 갯벌은 생명체에게 주는 자연의 선물이에요!

19 갯벌은 환경에 크게 도움이 된다.

20 갯벌은 많은 양의 물을 수용해서 홍수의 피해를 줄여 준다.

21 또한, 갯벌은 땅에서 바다로 흘러가는 물을 걸러내 준다.

22 물이 바다로 들어가기 전에 물 속에 있는 나쁜 물질을 갯벌이 제거한다.

23 갯벌 덕분에 바다에 도착한 물은 깨끗하다.

24 갯벌은 지구의 폐 역할을 한다.

25 그것들은 지구상의 생명에게 필요한 많은 양의 산소를 생산한다.

26 지구: 갯벌은 나를 건강하고 깨끗하게 지켜 줘요.

27 갯벌은 멋진 곳이다. 그렇지 않은가?

28 그곳은 자연이 지구상의 생물들에게 준 선물이다.

29 이러한 이유로, 갯벌을 보호하는 것은 필수이다.

● 우리말을 참고하여 본문을 영작하시오.

1 갯벌, 자연의 선물

➡ _____

2 갯벌은 바닷가의 진흙이 있는 넓은 지역이다.

➡ _____

3 갯벌은 조수와 함께 나타나고 사라진다.

➡ _____

4 썰물일 때 갯벌이 드러나고, 밀물일 때 바다에 덮인다.

➡ _____

5 갯벌은 바다 생물과 사람, 지구를 많은 방면에서 돕는다.

➡ _____

6 갯벌의 역할을 이해하는 것이 중요하다.

➡ _____

7 갯벌이 무엇을 하는지 살펴보자.

➡ _____

8 갯벌은 바닷가에 있는 많은 생물들에게 집이다.

➡ _____

9 플랑크톤처럼 작은 생명체뿐만 아니라 게와 물고기도 그곳에 산다.

➡ _____

10 갯벌은 그들에게 다양한 종류의 먹이를 제공한다.

➡ _____

11 또한, 많은 새들도 그곳에서 먹이를 먹는다.

➡ _____

12 게: 갯벌은 나의 단란한 집이에요.

➡ _____

13 갯벌은 사람들에게도 유익하다.

➡ _____

14 갯벌 지역 인근에 사는 사람들은 근처에서 물고기와 다른 바다 동물들을 잡아 생계를 꾸린다.

➡ _____

15 갯벌 덕분에 사람들은 신선한 해산물을 얻을 수 있다.

➡ _____

16 사람들은 갯벌에서 진흙 미끄럼 타기나 보디 페인팅과 같은 즐거운 활동을 즐길 수 있다.

➡ _____

17 그들은 또한 그곳에서 바다 동물들을 먹는 수많은 새를 관찰할 수도 있다.

➡ _____

18 남자아이: 갯벌은 생명체에게 주는 자연의 선물이에요!

➡ _____

19 갯벌은 환경에 크게 도움이 된다.

➡ _____

20 갯벌은 많은 양의 물을 수용해서 홍수의 피해를 줄여 준다.

➡ _____

21 또한, 갯벌은 땅에서 바다로 흘러가는 물을 걸러내 준다.

➡ _____

22 물이 바다로 들어가기 전에 물속에 있는 나쁜 물질을 갯벌이 제거한다.

➡ _____

23 갯벌 덕분에 바다에 도착한 물은 깨끗하다.

➡ _____

24 갯벌은 지구의 폐 역할을 한다.

➡ _____

25 그것들은 지구상의 생명에게 필요한 많은 양의 산소를 생산한다.

➡ _____

26 지구: 갯벌은 나를 건강하고 깨끗하게 지켜 줘요.

➡ _____

27 갯벌은 멋진 곳이다, 그렇지 않은가?

➡ _____

28 그곳은 자연이 지구상의 생물들에게 준 선물이다.

➡ _____

29 이러한 이유로, 갯벌을 보호하는 것은 필수이다.

➡ _____

[01~04] 다음 글을 읽고 물음에 답하시오.

　Mudflats are large areas of muddy land at the seaside. ⓐThey are appeared and disappeared with every tide. During low tides, they show up, and during high tides, they are covered by the sea. Mudflats help sea creatures, people, and the Earth in many ways. It is important to understand the roles of mudflats. Let's see what ⓑthey do.

서답형

01 위 글의 밑줄 친 ⓐ에서 어법상 틀린 부분을 찾아 고치시오.

➡ _____

_____

서답형

02 주어진 (1)과 (2)의 영영풀이에 해당하는 단어를 본문에서 찾아 각각 쓰시오.

(1) the inward flow of the tide or the time when the sea is at its highest level because the tide is in
(2) the outward flow of the tide or the time when the sea is at its lowest level because the tide is out

➡ (1) _____ (2) _____

중요

03 다음 중 갯벌에 대해 올바르게 이해하지 못한 사람을 고르시오.

① 수민: 갯벌은 바닷가의 진흙이 있는 넓은 지역이다.
② 희정: 갯벌은 조수간만이 없는 지역에서 드러난다.
③ 창수: 갯벌은 썰물일 때 드러난다.
④ 진호: 갯벌은 밀물일 때 사라진다.
⑤ 규진: 갯벌은 바다 생물과 사람, 지구를 많은 방면에서 돕는다.

04 위 글의 종류로 알맞은 것을 고르시오.

① an introduction to cultures
② geography experiment report
③ weather forecast
④ an introduction to the landform
⑤ field trip guide

[05~07] 다음 글을 읽고 물음에 답하시오.

　Mudflats help the environment greatly. (①) Mudflats hold a lot of water, so they can reduce damage from floods. (②) Also, mudflats filter water ⓐthat flows from the land into the sea. (③) They remove bad things in the water before it enters the sea. (④) Thanks to mudflats, the water that reaches the sea is clean. (⑤) They produce a huge volume of oxygen that is necessary for life on the Earth.

중요

05 위 글의 흐름으로 보아, 주어진 문장이 들어가기에 가장 적절한 곳은?

Mudflats work as the Earth's lungs.

①　　②　　③　　④　　⑤

06 위 글의 밑줄 친 ⓐthat과 문법적 쓰임이 같은 것을 모두 고르시오.

① He said that the story was interesting.
② It's the best novel that I've ever read.
③ The people that I spoke to were very helpful.
④ Ann doesn't believe the fact that Tim is older than me.
⑤ The watch that you gave me keeps good time.

서답형

07 위 글을 읽고, 바다에 도착한 물이 깨끗해지는 이유를 우리 말로 쓰시오. (40자 내외)

➡ _____

_____

[08~10] 다음 글을 읽고 물음에 답하시오.

Mudflats are good (A)[at / for] people, too. People who live near mudflat areas make a living by catching fish and (B)[another / other] sea animals nearby. Thanks to mudflats, people can get fresh seafood. People can enjoy fun activities, such as mud sliding and body painting on mudflats. They can also watch a __(a)__ number of birds that (C)[feed / food] on the sea animals there.

08 위 글의 빈칸 (a)에 들어갈 알맞은 말을 고르시오.

① many   ② much
③ high   ④ lot
⑤ large

서답형

09 위 글의 괄호 (A)~(C)에서 문맥이나 어법상 알맞은 낱말을 골라 쓰시오.

➡ (A)_____ (B)_____ (C)_____

중요

10 위 글의 앞에 올 내용으로 가장 알맞은 것을 고르시오.

① 갯벌이 유익한 다른 경우
② 갯벌의 정의
③ 갯벌의 생성 조건
④ 갯벌의 종류
⑤ 갯벌 보존의 필요성

[11~13] 다음 글을 읽고 물음에 답하시오.

All about Mudflats

Mudflats are muddy land at the seaside. ⓐ Not only plants like *hamcho* but also animals such as crabs and fish live there. They show up during low tides and are covered by the sea during high tides. If you go to mudflats, it is important to wear long clothes ⓑto protect yourself from animals that can bite you.

서답형

11 위 글의 밑줄 친 ⓐ를 다음과 같이 바꿔 쓸 때 빈칸에 들어 갈 알맞은 말을 쓰시오.

➡ Animals such as crabs and fish as well as plants like *hamcho* _____ there.

12 아래 보기에서 위 글의 밑줄 친 ⓑto protect와 to부정사의 용법이 **다른** 것의 개수를 고르시오.

┤ 보기 ├
① He cannot be rich to ask you for some money.
② Give me something to eat.
③ I got up early to catch the train.
④ I am sorry to give you trouble.
⑤ I decided to help that poor woman.

① 1개   ② 2개   ③ 3개   ④ 4개   ⑤ 5개

서답형

13 What is important if you go to mudflats? Fill in the blanks with suitable words.

➡ It is important that you should _____
_____ to protect yourself from animals that can bite you.

[14~16] 다음 글을 읽고 물음에 답하시오.

Mudflats are home ⓐ a lot of living things at the seaside. ⓑNot only very small living things like plankton but also crabs and fish live there. Mudflats provide various types of food ⓒ them. Also, many birds eat food there.

14 위 글의 빈칸 ⓐ와 ⓒ에 들어갈 전치사가 바르게 짝지어진 것은?

① to – with
② at – to
③ to – for
④ for – with
⑤ at – for

15 위 글의 밑줄 친 ⓑ와 의미가 다른 문장을 고르시오.

① Not merely very small living things like plankton but also crabs and fish live there.
② Not just very small living things like plankton but also crabs and fish live there.
③ Not simply very small living things like plankton but also crabs and fish live there.
④ Very small living things like plankton as well as crabs and fish live there.
⑤ Not only very small living things like plankton but crabs and fish live there.

16 위 글의 내용과 일치하지 않는 것은?

① 갯벌은 바닷가에 있는 많은 생물들에게 집이다.
② 플랑크톤처럼 작은 생명체는 갯벌에 살 수 없다.
③ 게와 물고기도 갯벌에 산다.
④ 갯벌은 게와 물고기 등에게 다양한 종류의 먹이를 제공한다.
⑤ 많은 새들도 갯벌에서 먹이를 먹는다.

[17~19] 다음 글을 읽고 물음에 답하시오.

Mudflats help the environment greatly. Mudflats hold a lot of water, so they can ①reduce damage from floods. (A) , mudflats filter water that flows from the land into the sea. They remove bad things in the water before it enters the sea. Thanks to mudflats, the water that ②reaches the sea is clean. Mudflats work as the Earth's lungs. They produce a ③huge volume of oxygen that is necessary for life on the Earth.
Earth: Mudflats keep me healthy and clean.
Mudflats are ④wonderful places, aren't they? They are a gift from nature to living things on the Earth. For all these reasons, it is necessary to ⑤protect mudflats.

17 위 글의 빈칸 (A)에 들어갈 알맞은 말을 고르시오.

① However
② Therefore
③ Also
④ For example
⑤ In other words

18 위 글의 밑줄 친 ①~⑤와 바꿔 쓸 수 없는 말을 고르시오.

① decrease
② gets to
③ large
④ awesome
⑤ prevent

19 본문의 내용과 일치하도록 다음 빈칸에 알맞은 단어를 쓰시오.

Mudflats can reduce damage from _____ by holding a lot of water.

➡ _____

[20~22] 다음 글을 읽고 물음에 답하시오.

Mudflats are large areas of muddy land at the seaside. They appear and disappear with every tide. During low tides, they show up, and during high tides, ⓐthey are covered by the sea. Mudflats help sea creatures, people, and the Earth in many ways. ⓑIt is important to understand the roles of mudflats. Let's see __(A)__ they do.

20 위 글의 빈칸 (A)에 들어갈 알맞은 말을 고르시오.

① how   ② when
③ where   ④ what
⑤ why

서답형
21 위 글의 밑줄 친 ⓐ를 능동태로 고치시오.

➡ _____

22 위 글의 밑줄 친 ⓑ과 문법적 쓰임이 같은 것을 고르시오. (3개)

① It is time to go to bed.
② Is it difficult for you to do the work?
③ I made it a rule to exercise every day.
④ It was necessary to go there after school.
⑤ It was dangerous to swim in the river.

[23~25] 다음 글을 읽고 물음에 답하시오.

My group made a book about the longest river, the biggest cave, the tallest falls, and the highest mountain. ⓐThat was fun to find the information about these places. ⓑThey are not only beautiful but also surprising. We felt the wonder of nature.

서답형
23 위 글의 밑줄 친 ⓐ에서 어법상 틀린 부분을 찾아 고치시오.

➡ _____

서답형
24 위 글의 밑줄 친 ⓑThey의 예를 본문에서 찾아 쓰시오.

➡ _____

_____

서답형
25 주어진 영영풀이에 해당하는 단어를 본문에서 찾아 쓰시오.

> something that is very surprising and unexpected

➡ _____

[26~27] 다음 글을 읽고 물음에 답하시오.

All about Deserts
Deserts are dry land with (A)[few / little] plants and (B)[few / little] water. Not only plants like elephant trees but also animals such as lizards and desert snakes live there. It is hot (C)[during / for] the day and cold at night. If you go to a desert, it is important to wear a hat to block the sun.

서답형
26 위 글의 괄호 (A)~(C)에서 어법상 알맞은 낱말을 골라 쓰시오.

➡ (A)_____ (B)_____ (C)_____

서답형
27 다음 문장에서 위 글의 내용과 다른 부분을 찾아서 고치시오.

> • In the deserts, it is always hot day and night.

➡ _____

_____

[01~04] 다음 글을 읽고 물음에 답하시오.

Mudflats are large areas of muddy land at the seaside. They ⓐappear and disappear with every ___(A)___ . During low tides, they show up, and during high tides, they are covered by the sea. Mudflats help sea creatures, people, and the Earth in many ways. It is important to understand the roles of mudflats. Let's see what ⓑthey do.

01 위 글의 빈칸 (A)에 들어갈 말을 본문에서 찾아 알맞은 형태로 쓰시오.

➡ _____

02 위 글의 밑줄 친 ⓐappear와 바꿔 쓸 수 있는 숙어를 본문에서 찾아 쓰시오.

➡ _____

03 다음 빈칸 (A)와 (B)에 알맞은 단어를 넣어 Mudflats에 대한 소개를 완성하시오.

> They are areas of flat empty land at the coast which appear during (A)_____ tides and (B)_____ during high tides.

04 위 글의 밑줄 친 ⓑthey가 가리키는 것을 본문에서 찾아 쓰시오.

➡ _____

[05~07] 다음 글을 읽고 물음에 답하시오.

Mudflats help the environment (A)[great / greatly]. ⓐMudflats hold a lot of water, as they can reduce damage from floods. Also, mudflats filter water that flows from the land into the sea. They (B)[generate / remove] bad things in the water before it enters the sea. ⓑ갯벌 덕분에 바다에 도착한 물은 깨끗하다. Mudflats work as the Earth's lungs. They produce a huge (C)[number / volume] of oxygen that is necessary for life on the Earth.

05 위 글의 괄호 (A)~(C)에서 문맥이나 어법상 알맞은 낱말을 골라 쓰시오.

➡ (A) _____ (B) _____ (C) _____

06 위 글의 밑줄 친 ⓐ에서 흐름상 어색한 부분을 찾아 고치시오.

➡ _____

_____

_____

07 위 글의 밑줄 친 ⓑ의 우리말에 맞게 주어진 어휘를 이용하여 11 단어로 영작하시오.

> Thanks to, that, reaches

➡ _____

[08~10] 다음 글을 읽고 물음에 답하시오.

Mudflats are home to a lot of living things at the seaside. ⓐNot only very small living things like plankton but also crabs and fish live there. ⓑMudflats provide various types of food for them. Also, many birds eat food ⓒthere.

08 위 글의 밑줄 친 ⓐ를 as well as를 사용하여 고치시오.

➡ _____

_____

09 위 글의 밑줄 친 ⓑ를 다음과 같이 바꿔 쓸 때 빈칸에 들어갈 알맞은 전치사를 쓰시오.

➡ Mudflats provide them _____ various types of food.

10 위 글의 밑줄 친 ⓒthere가 가리키는 장소를 본문에서 찾아 쓰시오.

➡ _____

[11~13] 다음 글을 읽고 물음에 답하시오.

Mudflats are good for people, too. People who live near mudflat areas make a living by (A)_____ fish and other sea animals nearby. Thanks to mudflats, people can get fresh seafood. People can enjoy ⓐfun activities, such as mud sliding and body painting (B)_____ mudflats. They can also watch a large number of birds that feed (C)_____ the sea animals there.

11 위 글의 빈칸 (A)에 catch를 알맞은 형태로 쓰시오.

➡ _____

12 위 글의 빈칸 (B)와 (C)에 공통으로 들어갈 전치사를 쓰시오.

➡ _____

13 위 글의 밑줄 친 ⓐfun activities의 예를 본문에서 찾아 쓰시오.

➡ _____

[14~17] 다음 글을 읽고 물음에 답하시오.

Mudflats help the environment greatly. Mudflats hold a lot of water, so they can reduce damage from floods. Also, mudflats filter water (A) flows from the land into the sea. They remove bad things in the water before it enters the sea. Thanks to mudflats, the water (B) reaches the sea is clean. Mudflats work as the Earth's lungs. They produce a huge volume of oxygen (C) is necessary for life on the Earth.

Earth: ⓐMudflats keep me healthily and cleanly.

Mudflats are wonderful places, (D) ? They are a gift from nature to living things on the Earth. For all these reasons, it is necessary to protect mudflats.

14 위 글의 빈칸 (A)~(C)에 공통으로 들어갈 알맞은 관계대명사를 쓰시오.

➡ _____

15 위 글의 빈칸 (D)에 들어갈 알맞은 부가의문문을 쓰시오.

➡ _____

16 위 글의 밑줄 친 ⓐ에서 어법상 틀린 부분을 찾아 고치시오.

➡ _____

17 다음 빈칸 (A)와 (B)에 알맞은 단어를 넣어 갯벌을 보호해야 하는 이유를 완성하시오.

As mudflats are a gift from (A)_____ to (B)_____ _____ on the Earth, it is necessary to protect mudflats.

해석

Enjoy Writing B

Deserts are dry land with few plants and little water. Not only plants like
elephant trees but also animals such as lizards and desert snakes live there. It
is hot during the day and cold at night. If you go to a desert, it is important to
wear a hat to block the sun.

구문해설 • **desert**: 사막 • **lizard**: 도마뱀 • **block**: 막다, 차단하다

사막은 식물과 물이 거의 없는 건조한 땅이다. 코끼리 나무 같은 식물뿐만 아니라 도마뱀이나 사막뱀 같은 동물들도 그곳에 산다. 낮에는 덥고 밤에는 춥다. 만일 사막에 간다면 햇빛을 가리기 위해 모자를 쓰는 것이 중요하다.

Enjoy Writing B

All about Mudflats

Mudflats are muddy land at the seaside. Not only plants like *hamcho* but also
animals such as crabs and fish live there. They show up during low tides and
are covered by the sea during high tides. If you go to mudflats, it is important
to wear long clothes to protect yourself from animals that can bite you.

구문해설 • **mudflat**: 갯벌 • **muddy**: 진흙의, 질퍽한 • **crab**: 게 • **show up**: 나타나다 • **low tides**: 썰물
• **high tides**: 밀물 • **bite**: (이빨로) 물다

갯벌에 관한 모든 것

갯벌은 바닷가의 진흙이 있는 지역이다. 함초와 같은 식물들뿐만 아니라 게와 물고기와 같은 동물들도 그곳에 산다. 썰물일 때 갯벌이 드러나고, 밀물일 때 바다에 덮인다. 만약 당신이 갯벌에 간다면, 당신을 물 수 있는 동물들로부터 당신을 보호하기 위해 긴 옷을 입는 것이 중요하다.

Wrap Up 1

B: I just finished making a plan for my trip. Do you want to hear it?

G: Sure. I wonder what you will do.

B: On the first day, I'm going to go fishing on a lake. The next day, I'm going
to climb a mountain.

G: Is that all?

B: No. On the last day, I'm going to go swimming.

G: Wow. You will do a lot of activities.

B: 나는 방금 여행 계획 세우는 것을 끝냈어. 그것에 대해 듣고 싶니?
G: 물론이지. 나는 네가 무엇을 할지 궁금해.
B: 첫날에 나는 호수에서 낚시를 할 거야. 다음 날에 나는 산에 오를 거야.
G: 그게 전부니?
B: 아니. 마지막 날에 나는 수영을 할 거야.
G: 우와. 너는 많은 활동들을 할 거구나.

Words & Expressions

01 다음 중 밑줄 친 단어의 쓰임이 바르지 못한 것은?

① Please clean your <u>messy</u> desk.

② I have a <u>friendy</u> pet dog.

③ It is <u>windy</u> today.

④ I am very <u>lucky</u> to have such nice friends.

⑤ She exercises every day to become <u>healthy</u>.

02 다음 중 밑줄 친 부분의 뜻풀이가 바르지 <u>않은</u> 것은?

① The tree stands on the edge of a <u>cliff</u>. (절벽)

② It <u>filters</u> the seawater to keep it clean. (거르다)

③ The water will <u>flow</u> into the rivers. (흐르다)

④ The <u>falls</u> can supply 10 percent of all the electric power for the New York State. (떨어지다)

⑤ She <u>greeted</u> me with a smile. (인사했다)

03 다음 밑줄 친 부분과 의미가 가장 가까운 것을 주어진 철자로 시작하여 쓰시오.

> This can <u>take place</u> anywhere and at any time.

➡ o _____

04 다음 빈칸에 알맞은 말을 고르시오.

> The lake is probably the most polluted _____ of water in the world.

① wave　　② tide　　③ body

④ flood　　⑤ blood

Conversation

[05~07] 다음 대화를 읽고 물음에 답하시오.

G: 나는 네가 여름 방학 동안에 무엇을 했는지 궁금해.

B: I took a trip to Kenya and (A)_____ (see) many animals on the plains.

G: Wonderful! (B)_____, what are the plains?

B: They are large areas of flat land.

G: I see.

05 빈칸 (A)에 알맞은 말을 주어진 단어를 이용해서 채우시오.

➡ _____

06 빈칸 (B)에 알맞은 말을 고르시오.

① Although

② In addition

③ On the contrary

④ Besides

⑤ By the way

07 밑줄 친 우리말을 주어진 단어를 이용하여 영작하시오. (9단어)

➡ _____

(wonder, do, during)

[08~10] 다음 대화를 읽고 물음에 답하시오.

B: Do you know how ⓐmuck oceans ⓑare there on the Earth?

G: The answer is four, ⓒisn't it?

B: No. There ⓓare five oceans on the Earth. They cover ⓔmost of the Earth.

G: (A)_____

B: I heard the oceans ⓕis covered about 70% of the Earth's surface.

08 빈칸 (A)에 들어갈 말로 알맞은 것은?

① How do five oceans cover the Earth?

② How can oceans be found?

③ How big is the biggest ocean?

④ How much of the Earth do they cover?

⑤ Why is 70% of the Earth covered by oceans?

09 위 글의 ⓐ~ⓕ 중 어법상 틀린 것만 바르게 묶은 것은?

① ⓐ, ⓑ   ② ⓒ, ⓓ

③ ⓔ, ⓕ   ④ ⓐ, ⓑ, ⓕ

⑤ ⓒ, ⓓ, ⓔ

10 다음 영영풀이에 해당하는 단어를 대화에서 찾아 쓰시오.

the flat top part of something or the outside of it

➡ _____

[11~12] 다음 대화를 읽고 물음에 답하시오.

Dad: Do you want to see an amazing place?

Karl & Sister: Sure!

Dad: Then let's get on the train.

Sister: Look at the yellow plants! I wonder what they are.

Dad: They are reeds. Suncheon Bay has beautiful reed fields.

Karl: Wow, the reeds are ___(A)___ taller than you, Dad.

Sister: They really are. Let me take a picture of you.

Karl: This reed field is very large.

Dad: Yes. (B)나는 그곳이 한국에서 가장 큰 갈대밭이라고 들었어.

Karl: Look at the sky. It's turning red.

Sister: Yes, it's beautiful.

11 빈칸 (A)에 들어가기에 어색한 것은?

① even   ② far   ③ still

④ very   ⑤ a lot

12 밑줄 친 (B)의 우리말과 의미가 같도록 주어진 단어를 이용하여 영작하시오.

➡ _____

(9단어) (in, large, it, one, heard)

Grammar

13 다음 문장을 바르게 바꿔 쓴 것이 아닌 것은?

Sam not only reads German but also writes it.

① Sam not only reads German but writes it.

② Sam not only reads German but writes it as well.

③ Sam reads German as well as writes it.

④ Sam not simply reads German but also writes it.

⑤ Sam not merely reads German but writes it.

14 다음 빈칸에 들어갈 표현이 순서대로 바르게 짝지어진 것을 고르시오.

> Hana is good at _____ math _____ art.

① not only — but
② not only — also
③ merely — also
④ simply — as well
⑤ not — too

15 밑줄 친 부분의 쓰임이 <u>다른</u> 하나는?

① It is exciting <u>to play</u> baseball.
② It's wonderful <u>to make</u> new friends.
③ It was not hard <u>to work</u> out every day.
④ He tried it several times only <u>to fail</u>.
⑤ Is it necessary <u>to buy</u> a ticket now?

16 다음 빈칸에 들어갈 말이 나머지와 <u>다른</u> 하나는?

① It is easy _____ me to learn how to ride a bike.
② It is rude _____ her to speak so loud in public.
③ It is impossible _____ Julie to work with them.
④ It is necessary _____ him to take care of others.
⑤ It is important _____ you to eat healthy food.

17 다음 ⓐ~ⓗ 중 옳은 것을 <u>모두</u> 고르면?

> ⓐ Not only you but also James play the piano.
> ⓑ Not only plants like *hamcho* but also animals such as crabs and fish live there.
> ⓒ Animals as well as plants lives in deserts.
> ⓓ They are not only beautiful but also surprising.
> ⓔ It was careless for you to break the window.
> ⓕ It will be dangerous swims in this lake.
> ⓖ That is easy for me to understand this book.
> ⓗ It is necessary for them to focus on the class.

① ⓐ, ⓒ
② ⓑ, ⓒ, ⓓ
③ ⓑ, ⓓ, ⓗ
④ ⓓ, ⓔ, ⓗ
⑤ ⓓ, ⓔ, ⓖ

18 다음 문장을 주어진 말로 시작하여 다시 쓰시오.

(1) You must be kind to other people.
➡ It is necessary _____.
(2) You should be careful when you drive a car.
➡ It is necessary _____
_____.

19 다음 중 어법상 <u>어색한</u> 문장은?

① It was foolish of him to think so.
② It was fun for us to go to an amusement park.
③ It is important to be nice to friends.
④ Not only plants like elephant trees but also animals such as lizards and desert snakes live there.
⑤ Dylan not only played computer games but also doing his homework.

Reading

[20~22] 다음 글을 읽고 물음에 답하시오.

Mudflats are large areas of muddy land at the seaside. They appear and disappear ⓐ_____ every tide. During low tides, they show up, and during high tides, they are covered by the sea. Mudflats help sea creatures, people, and the Earth ⓑ_____ many ways. ⓒIt is important to understand the roles of mudflats. Let's see what they do.

20 위 글의 빈칸 ⓐ와 ⓑ에 들어갈 알맞은 전치사를 고르시오.

① with – from ② in – by
③ in – from ④ with – in
⑤ on – through

21 위 글의 밑줄 친 ⓒ를 바르게 바꿔 쓴 문장을 <u>모두</u> 고르시오.

① Understanding the roles of mudflats are important.
② To understand the roles of mudflats is important.
③ That is important to understand the roles of mudflats.
④ To understand the roles of mudflats are important.
⑤ Understanding the roles of mudflats is important.

22 위 글을 읽고 대답할 수 <u>없는</u> 질문은?

① When do mudflats appear?
② When do mudflats disappear?
③ What are the roles of mudflats?
④ During high tides, what covers mudflats?
⑤ Are mudflats helpful to the Earth?

[23~24] 다음 글을 읽고 물음에 답하시오.

Mudflats help the environment greatly. Mudflats hold a lot of water, so they can (A)[increase / reduce] damage from floods. Also, mudflats filter water that flows from the land into the sea. They remove bad things in the water before it (B)[enters / enters into] the sea. Thanks to mudflats, the water that (C)[reaches / reaches to] the sea is clean. Mudflats work ⓐas the Earth's lungs. They produce a huge volume of oxygen that is necessary for life on the Earth.

23 위 글의 괄호 (A)~(C)에서 문맥이나 어법상 알맞은 낱말을 골라 쓰시오.

➡ (A)_____ (B)_____ (C)_____

24 위 글의 밑줄 친 ⓐas와 같은 의미로 쓰인 것을 고르시오.

① Do in Rome as the Romans do.
② He came up as I was speaking.
③ Susan is as pretty as Jane.
④ This box will serve as a table.
⑤ As we go up, the air grows colder.

[25~26] 다음 글을 읽고 물음에 답하시오.

Mudflats are good for people, too. People who live near mudflat areas make a living by ⓐcatching fish and other sea animals nearby. Thanks to mudflats, people can get fresh seafood. People can enjoy fun activities, ⓑsuch as mud sliding and body painting on mudflats. They can also watch a large number of birds that feed on the sea animals there.

25 위 글의 밑줄 친 ⓐcatching과 문법적 쓰임이 다른 것을 모두 고르시오.

① The boy sitting under the tree is my brother.
② Thank you for visiting our website.
③ I saw her walking with her boyfriend.
④ I was watching TV in the living room.
⑤ Mastering foreign languages is not easy.

26 위 글의 밑줄 친 ⓑsuch as와 바꿔 쓸 수 있는 단어를 쓰시오.

➡ _____

[27~28] 다음 글을 읽고 물음에 답하시오.

Mudflats help the environment greatly. Mudflats hold a lot of water, so they can reduce damage from floods. Also, mudflats filter water that flows from the land into the sea. They remove bad things in the water before it enters the sea. Thanks to mudflats, the water that reaches the sea is clean. Mudflats work as the Earth's ___(A)___. They produce a huge volume of oxygen that is necessary for life on the Earth.

27 위 글의 빈칸 (A)에 들어갈 알맞은 말을 고르시오.

① face   ② lungs
③ stomach   ④ head
⑤ hands and legs

28 위 글의 제목으로 알맞은 것을 고르시오.

① How to Reduce Damage from Floods
② Water Reaches the Sea through Mudflats
③ Oxygen, a Necessity for Life on the Earth
④ How Helpful Mudflats Are to the Environment!
⑤ Let's Protect the Environment

[29~31] 다음 글을 읽고 물음에 답하시오.

Mudflats are home to ①a lot of living things at the ②seaside. Not ③only very small living things ⓐlike plankton but also crabs and fish live there. Mudflats ④provide various types of food for them. ⑤Also, many birds eat food there.

29 위 글의 밑줄 친 ①~⑤와 바꿔 쓸 수 없는 말은?

① much   ② seashore
③ merely   ④ supply
⑤ In addition

30 위 글의 밑줄 친 ⓐlike와 같은 의미로 쓰인 것을 고르시오.

① I like hobbies like photography or painting.
② He is very like his father.
③ How did you like New York?
④ She responded in like manner.
⑤ Do it like this.

31 본문의 내용과 일치하도록 다음 빈칸에 알맞은 단어를 쓰시오.

Mudflats provide various types of _____ not only for living things at the seaside but also for many birds.

출제율 90%

01 다음 짝지어진 두 단어의 관계가 같도록 주어진 철자로 시작하여 빈칸에 알맞은 단어를 쓰시오.

> appear : disappear – high tide : _____

출제율 100%

02 다음 빈칸에 알맞은 단어를 〈보기〉에서 골라 쓰시오. (필요하면 대문자를 사용하고, 단어는 한 번만 사용할 것)

> ┌─ 보기 ┤
> as   during   else   unlike

(1) _____ its name, Greenland is covered with ice and snow.

(2) _____ the night, the pain sometimes wakes me up.

(3) He has many books, such _____ novels and cartoons.

(4) Nothing _____ is better than this.

[03~04] 두 문장에 공통으로 들어갈 수 있는 단어를 쓰시오.

출제율 95%

03
> • I hope to _____ a trip to Europe.
> • Could you _____ a picture of us in front of the dinosaur?

출제율 90%

04
> • I want to talk to you before I _____ a decision.
> • Don't be afraid to _____ a mistake.
> • It is rude to _____ a noise while eating.

출제율 90%

05 다음 빈칸 어디에도 들어갈 수 없는 것은?

> G: Look at that lake! It's really ⓐ _____ .
> B: It's not a lake. It's a river.
> G: Is it? I wonder ⓑ _____ a river and a lake are ⓒ _____ .
> B: A river is a ⓓ _____ body of ⓔ _____ water. Unlike a lake, a river flows toward the ocean.
> G: I got it.

① fresh   ② beautiful
③ why   ④ different
⑤ long

[06~07] 다음 대화를 읽고 물음에 답하시오.

> A: 나는 숲이 무엇인지 궁금해.
> B: It is land who covered by plants and trees.

출제율 90%

06 밑줄 친 우리말과 의미가 같도록 주어진 단어를 이용하여 영작하시오.

➡ _____ (wonder)

_____

(would, know)

출제율 90%

07 밑줄 친 문장에서 어법상 어색한 부분을 고치시오.

➡ _____

[08~09] 다음 대화를 읽고 물음에 답하시오.

> G: 나는 아마존 열대 우림이 지구의 허파라고 불린다고 들었어. (heard, Earth, I, the, the, called, Amazon, is, of, lungs, rain, the, forest)

B: Lungs? Why?

G: (A)_____ it (B)_____ about 20% of the Earth's oxygen.

B: Wow! That's a lot.

출제율 90%

08 밑줄 친 우리말을 괄호 안의 단어를 배열하여 영작하시오.

➡ _____

_____

출제율 95%

09 빈칸 (A)와 (B)에 들어갈 말로 알맞은 것끼리 짝지어진 것을 고르시오.

	(A)	(B)
①	Because	protects
②	Because	removes
③	Because	produces
④	Because of	removes
⑤	Because of	produces

[10~11] 다음 대화를 읽고 물음에 답하시오.

A: I want (A)_____ to Danyang.

B: (B)_____?

A: (C)I heard there are famous caves in Danyang.

출제율 95%

10 빈칸 (A)와 (B)에 들어갈 말로 알맞은 것끼리 짝지어진 것을 고르시오.

	(A)	(B)
①	going	Why
②	going	Where
③	to go	Why
④	to go	Where
⑤	to go	How

출제율 100%

11 밑줄 친 (C)와 바꿔 쓸 수 없는 것을 모두 고르시오.

① I have heard

② I'm aware of

③ I'm aware that

④ I'm not sure

⑤ I've been told

출제율 85%

12 빈칸 (A)~(C)에 알맞은 말을 <보기>에서 골라 쓰시오.

M: Guess what this is! It's not a tree. It is a plant that looks (A)_____ tall grass. (B)_____ fall, it turns yellow. It grows well in wet lands. I heard Suncheon Bay is famous (C)_____ this plant.

┤ 보기 ├

as   at   for   from   in   like

출제율 95%

13 다음 빈칸에 알맞은 말이 순서대로 짝지어진 것은?

• _____ is good to spend money wisely.

• It is very kind _____ you to help her.

① It – for　　② It – of

③ That – of　　④ That – for

⑤ This – for

출제율 100%

14 다음 중 어법상 적절한 문장은?

① It's important to protecting mudflats.

② It is exciting of me to play baseball.

③ Isn't it boring watch TV at home?

④ Ann felt disappointed as well as anger.

⑤ Cindy will not only go to the movies, but also meet her friends.

15 다음 우리말을 주어진 어휘를 이용하여 영작하시오.

(1) 나는 이 책을 이해하는 것이 쉽다. (this book, me, it, understand)

➡ _____

(2) 그녀를 도와주다니 너는 참 친절하구나. (you, very kind, it, to)

➡ _____

(3) 네가 밤에 여기저기 걸어다니는 것은 위험하다. (walk around, it, to)

➡ _____

(4) 고양이는 깨끗할 뿐만 아니라 영리하다. (cats, clean, well, smart)

➡ _____

(5) Junsu는 춤뿐만 아니라 노래도 잘한다. (only, also, well)

➡ _____

(6) Eric뿐 아니라 그의 형들도 빨리 달린다. (his brothers, fast runners, only, also)

➡ _____

16 다음 두 문장이 같도록 할 때 빈칸에 알맞은 것은?

> For all these reasons, to protect mudflats is necessary.
> → For all these reasons, it is necessary _____ mudflats.

① protect
② protects
③ to protecting
④ protected
⑤ to protect

[17~19] 다음 글을 읽고 물음에 답하시오.

> Mudflats are large areas of muddy land at the seaside. They appear and disappear with every tide. During low tides, they show up, and during high tides, they are covered by the sea. Mudflats help sea creatures, people, and the Earth in many ways. It is important ⓐ to understand the roles of mudflats. Let's see what they do.

17 위 글의 밑줄 친 ⓐto understand와 to부정사의 용법이 다른 것을 모두 고르시오.

① To understand the roles of mudflats is our chief concern.
② It is high time to understand the roles of mudflats.
③ It is not easy to understand the roles of mudflats.
④ This is the best way to understand the roles of mudflats.
⑤ He was wise enough to understand the roles of mudflats.

18 Why do mudflats disappear during high tides? Fill in the blank with suitable words.

➡ It's because _____ .

19 위 글의 뒤에 나올 내용으로 가장 알맞은 것을 고르시오.

① the history of mudflats
② the importance of mudflats
③ the roles of mudflats
④ the meaning of mudflats
⑤ various kinds of mudflats

[20~22] 다음 글을 읽고 물음에 답하시오.

Mudflats are home to ⓐa lot of living things at the seaside. ⓑ플랑크톤처럼 작은 생명체뿐만 아니라 게와 물고기도 그곳에 산다. Mudflats provide various types of food for them. Also, many birds eat food there.

📝 출제율 95%

20 위 글의 밑줄 친 ⓐa lot of와 바꿔 쓸 수 없는 말을 고르시오.

① lots of　　　② a number of

③ plenty of　　④ many

⑤ a great deal of

📝 출제율 100%

21 위 글의 밑줄 친 ⓑ의 우리말에 맞게 주어진 어휘를 이용하여 15 단어로 영작하시오.

> only, very small, like, also

➡ _____

_____

📝 출제율 100%

22 위 글의 제목으로 알맞은 것을 고르시오.

① Suitable Food for Many Living Things

② Mudflats, Sweet Home to Seaside Creatures

③ Various Types of Food Found at Mudflats

④ Mudflats, Paradise for Leisure

⑤ How about Going Camping at the Seaside?

[23~25] 다음 글을 읽고 물음에 답하시오.

Mudflats are good for people, too. People who live near mudflat areas make a living by catching fish and other sea animals nearby. ⓐThanks to mudflats, people can get fresh seafood. People can enjoy fun activities, such as mud sliding and body painting on mudflats. They can also watch a large number of birds that feed on the sea animals there.

📝 출제율 90%

23 위 글의 밑줄 친 ⓐ를 다음과 같이 바꿔 쓸 때 빈칸에 들어갈 알맞은 말을 쓰시오.

➡ Mudflats enable people _____ _____ fresh seafood.

📝 출제율 90%

24 How do people who live near mudflat areas make a living? Answer in English in a full sentence.

➡ _____

_____

📝 출제율 100%

25 위 글의 주제로 알맞은 것을 고르시오.

① Mudflats are large areas of muddy land at the seaside.

② Thanks to tides, mudflats appear and disappear.

③ Mudflats are nature's gift to living things.

④ Understanding the roles of mudflats is important.

⑤ We can enjoy many fun activities on mudflats.

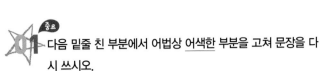

01 다음 밑줄 친 부분에서 어법상 어색한 부분을 고쳐 문장을 다시 쓰시오.

> G: I wonder what did you do while the summer vacation.
> B: I took a trip to Kenya and saw many animals on the plains.
> G: Wonderful! By the way, what are the plains?
> B: They are large areas of flat land.

➡ _____
_____

02 주어진 문장 다음에 이어질 대화의 순서를 바르게 배열하시오.

> Look at the yellow plants! I wonder what they are.

> (A) They really are. Let me take a picture of you.
> (B) Wow, the reeds are even taller than you, Dad.
> (C) They are reeds. Suncheon Bay has beautiful reed fields.

➡ _____

[03~04] 다음 대화를 읽고 물음에 답하시오.

> A: (A)_____(about, wonder, is, special, what, I, the Yangze River)
> B: (B)나는 그것이 세계에서 세 번째로 긴 강이라고 들었어.(the world, long, in, heard)

03 위 대화의 빈칸 (A)에 주어진 단어를 배열하여 알맞은 문장을 만드시오.

➡ _____

04 위 대화의 밑줄 친 (B)의 우리말을 주어진 어구를 이용하여 영어로 쓰시오.

➡ _____

05 to부정사를 진주어로 하여 주어진 문장과 같은 의미가 되도록 쓰시오.

(1) The river is dangerous to swim in.

➡ _____

(2) She was wise to decide to be a nurse.

➡ _____

06 다음 문장을 'not only A but also B' 구문을 사용하여 한 문장으로 연결하시오.

(1) Midori can speak Japanese. She can speak English, too.

➡ _____

(2) Wendy studies hard at school. She also studies hard at home.

➡ _____

07 어법상 틀린 것을 바르게 고치시오.

> Jack as well as his friends are going to climb the mountain.

_____

ⓐMudflats are good for people, too. People __(a)__ live (A)[near / nearly] mudflat areas make a living by catching fish and other sea animals (B)[nearby / nearly]. (C)[In spite of / Thanks to] mudflats, people can get fresh seafood. People can enjoy fun activities, such as mud sliding and body painting on mudflats. They can also watch a large number of birds __(b)__ feed on the sea animals there.

08 위 글의 빈칸 (a)와 (b)에 공통으로 들어갈 알맞은 관계대명사를 쓰시오.

➡ _____

09 위 글의 밑줄 친 ⓐ에 해당하는 내용을 우리말로 쓰시오. (4가지)

➡ (1) _____

_____

(2) _____

(3) _____

_____

(4) _____

_____

중요
10 위 글의 괄호 (A)~(C)에서 문맥이나 어법상 알맞은 낱말을 골라 쓰시오.

➡ (A)_____ (B)_____ (C)_____

Mudflats help the environment greatly. Mudflats hold a lot of water, so they can reduce damage from floods. Also, mudflats filter water that flows from the land into the sea. They ⓐremove bad things in the water before ⓑit enters the sea. Thanks to mudflats, the water that reaches the sea is clean. Mudflats work as the Earth's lungs. They produce a huge volume of oxygen that is necessary for life on the Earth.

Earth: Mudflats keep me healthy and clean.

Mudflats are wonderful places, aren't they? They are a gift from nature to living things on the Earth. For all these reasons, it is necessary to protect mudflats.

11 위 글의 밑줄 친 ⓐ와 바꿔 쓸 수 있는 한 단어를 본문에서 찾아 쓰시오.

➡ _____

중요
12 위 글의 밑줄 친 ⓑit이 가리키는 것을 본문에서 찾아 쓰시오.

➡ _____

13 How do mudflats help the environment? Fill in the blanks with suitable words.

➡ (1) They can reduce damage from floods by _____.

(2) They remove bad things in the water before it enters the sea by _____.

(3) They work as the Earth's lungs by

_____.

01 주어진 조건에 맞춰서 빈칸을 완성하시오.

조건
1. 주어진 질문과 정보를 활용해야 함   2. 궁금증을 나타내는 표현이 반드시 포함되어야 함.

• What time does the mall open on the opening day?
• 개점일: 5월 18일 / 오전 8시

A: Do you know the mall in the downtown?
B: Yes, I'm aware that it opens _____ .
A: _____
B: I'm aware that _____ .
A: I see. Thank you.

02 주어진 어휘와 가주어를 이용하여 3 문장 이상을 쓰시오.

| watch the soccer game | exercise regularly | see such an old house |
| use water carefully | swim in the sea | wear a helmet |

(1) _____
(2) _____
(3) _____

03 다음 조사한 내용을 바탕으로 지형을 소개하는 글을 쓰시오.

• What are deserts?
  They are dry land with few plants and little water.
• What plants live there?
  Elephant trees live there.
• What animals live there?
  Lizards, desert snakes live there.
• What is special about them?
  It is hot during the day and cold at night.

All about Deserts

Deserts are dry land with (A)_____ plants and (B)_____ water. Not only plants like elephant trees but also animals such as (C)_____ live there. It is hot during the day and (D)_____ at night.

단원별 모의고사

[01~02] 다음 빈칸에 들어갈 말로 적절한 것을 고르시오.

01

His job is not _____ interesting but also very well-paid.

① only ② well ③ so
④ as ⑤ very

02

A large _____ of people visit this museum every year.

① lots ② much ③ number
④ plenty ⑤ deal

03 〈보기〉에 주어진 단어를 이용해 빈칸을 채우시오. (형태 변화 가능)

보기
flow occur protect provide reach remove surf

(1) The road _____ down to the lake.
(2) The woman is _____ on the sea.
(3) A problem _____ during the setup.
(4) We have to _____ the environment from pollution.
(5) The river _____ into the sea.
(6) _____ your contact lenses and wear glasses.
(7) Cows _____ us with milk.

04 다음 중 영영풀이가 알맞지 <u>않은</u> 것은?

① appear: begin to be seen suddenly
② creature: all living things except plants
③ filter: to pass something through a filter to remove particular things contained in it
④ muddy: very soft wet earth
⑤ tide: the periodic rise and fall of the waters of the ocean

[05~06] 다음 대화를 읽고 물음에 답하시오.

B: I just finished making a plan for my trip. Do you want to hear it? (①)
G: Sure. I wonder <u>what did you do.</u> (②)
B: On the first day, I'm going to go fishing on a lake. (③)
G: Is that all?
B: No. On the last day, I'm going to go swimming. (④)
G: Wow. You will do a lot of activities. (⑤)

05 위 대화의 ①~⑤ 중 다음 주어진 말이 들어갈 알맞은 곳은?

The next day, I'm going to climb a mountain.

① ② ③ ④ ⑤

06 밑줄 친 부분에서 어법상 또는 문맥상 어색한 것을 찾아 바르게 고치시오.

➡ _____
_____

[07~09] 다음 대화를 읽고 물음에 답하시오.

G: Look at that lake! It's really beautiful.
B: It's not a lake. It's a river.
G: Is it? 나는 강과 호수가 어떻게 다른지 궁금해.
B: A river is a long body of fresh water. Unlike a lake, a river flows toward the ocean.
G: I got it.

07 다음 영영풀이에 해당하는 단어를 대화에서 찾아 쓰시오.

to move steadily without any interrupts, used to describe liquids, gas, electrical currents, etc.

➡ _____

08 밑줄 친 우리말을 'wonder'를 이용하여 영작하시오.

➡ _____

09 위 대화의 내용과 일치하지 않는 것을 고르시오.

① The boy knows the difference between a lake and a river.
② The lake doesn't flow toward the ocean.
③ They are looking at the lake.
④ The river is not sea water but fresh water.
⑤ The river and the lake are different.

10 다음 빈칸 어디에도 들어갈 수 없는 것은?

M: Guess ⓐ_____! It's not a tree. It is a plant that ⓑ_____ tall grass. In fall, it ⓒ_____ yellow. It ⓓ_____ well in wet lands. I heard Suncheon Bay ⓔ_____ this plant.

① turns   ② is famous for
③ grows   ④ where they are
⑤ looks like

[11~12] 다음 대화를 읽고 물음에 답하시오.

Dad: Do you want to see an amazing place?
Karl & Sister: Sure!
Dad: Then let's (A)[get / have] on the train.
Sister: Look at the yellow plants! I wonder (B) [what are they / what they are].
Dad: They are reeds. Suncheon Bay has beautiful reed fields.
Karl: Wow, the reeds are even taller (C)[as / than] you, Dad.
Sister: They really are. Let me (D)[take / taken] a picture of you.
Karl: This reed field is very large.
Dad: Yes. I heard it is the largest one in Korea.
Karl: Look at the sky. It's turning red.
Sister: Yes, it's beautiful.

11 다음 영영풀이에 해당하는 단어를 대화에서 찾아 쓰시오.

It is a tall thin plant that grows near water. Its stems can be used to make things.

➡ _____

12 (A)~(D)에 알맞은 것을 골라 쓰시오.

➡ (A)_____   (B)_____
   (C)_____   (D)_____

13 다음 중 어법상 어색한 것을 고르시오.

① It is fun to surf on sand in the desert.
② It was so foolish for Jane to do that.
③ I don't think it's a good idea to bring a smartphone to school.
④ We like not only playing soccer but also going hiking.
⑤ I as well as Sophie like to drink coffee.

14 그림을 보고 주어진 문장의 빈칸을 알맞게 채우시오. (빈칸 하나에 한 단어씩 쓸 것.)

Minhee likes to _____ _____ listen to music _____ _____ draw pictures.

15 다음 주어진 문장의 밑줄 친 부분과 쓰임이 같은 것은?

> It is a lot of fun to ride a bicycle.

① How far is it from your school to the station?

② It was three weeks later that he heard the news.

③ It was a pleasure to meet you at the party.

④ It took about 30 minutes to get to the park by bus.

⑤ I make it a rule to get up early.

16 다음 문장에서 어법상 어색한 것을 바르게 고치시오.

(1) Amy as well as her friends were looking forward to watching the movie.

_____

(2) It was foolish for him to believe such a story.

_____

17 다음 문장을 as well as를 사용하여 바꾸어 쓰시오.

(1) I saw not only *Avatar* but also *Alitar*.

➡ _____

(2) Not only his brothers but also Peter likes Minji.

➡ _____

[18~19] 다음 글을 읽고 물음에 답하시오.

Mudflats are large areas of muddy land at the seaside. They appear and disappear with every tide. During (A)[high / low] tides, they show up, and during (B)[high / low] tides, they are covered by the sea. Mudflats help sea creatures, people, and the Earth in many ways. It is important to understand the roles of mudflats. Let's see (C)[that / what] they do.

18 위 글의 괄호 (A)~(C)에서 문맥이나 어법상 알맞은 낱말을 골라 쓰시오.

➡ (A)_____ (B)_____ (C)_____

19 다음 중 위 글에 언급되어 있지 <u>않은</u> 것은?

① Mudflats appear when the tide goes out.

② Mudflats disappear when the tide comes in.

③ Mudflats help not only sea creatures but also people and the Earth.

④ It is important to protect mudflats from pollution.

⑤ Understanding the roles of mudflats is of importance.

[20~21] 다음 글을 읽고 물음에 답하시오.

Mudflats are home to a lot of living things at the seaside. ⓐNot only very small living things as plankton but also crabs and fish live there. Mudflats provide ⓑvarious types of food for them. Also, many birds eat food there.

20 위 글의 밑줄 친 ⓐ에서 어법상 틀린 부분을 찾아 고치시오.

➡ _____

21 위 글의 밑줄 친 ⓑvarious와 바꿔 쓸 수 없는 말을 고르시오.

① varied   ② diverse
③ similar   ④ different
⑤ a variety of

[22~23] 다음 글을 읽고 물음에 답하시오.

Mudflats are good for people, too. People who live near mudflat areas ⓐ생계를 꾸린다 by catching fish and other sea animals nearby. Thanks to mudflats, people can get fresh seafood. People can enjoy fun activities, such as mud sliding and body painting on mudflats. They can also watch a large number of birds that feed on the sea animals there.

22 위 글의 밑줄 친 ⓐ의 우리말을 세 단어로 쓰시오.

➡ _____

23 다음 중 갯벌에서 할 수 없는 것은?

① 물고기와 다른 바다 동물들을 잡기
② 수영을 즐기기
③ 진흙 미끄럼 타기
④ 보디 페인팅
⑤ 바다 동물들을 먹는 수많은 새를 관찰하기

[24~25] 다음 글을 읽고 물음에 답하시오.

Mudflats help the environment greatly. Mudflats hold a lot of water, so they can reduce damage from floods. Also, mudflats filter water that flows from the land into the sea. They remove bad things in the water before it enters the sea. Thanks to mudflats, the water that reaches the sea is clean. Mudflats work as the Earth's lungs. They produce a huge volume of oxygen that is necessary for life on the Earth.
Earth: Mudflats keep me healthy and clean.
Mudflats are wonderful places, aren't they? They are a gift from nature to living things on the Earth. For all these reasons, it is necessary to protect mudflats.

24 위 글의 주제로 가장 알맞은 것을 고르시오.

① Mudflats are very helpful to the environment.
② Mudflats can hold a lot of water.
③ Mudflats filter water.
④ Mudflats work as the Earth's lungs.
⑤ Oxygen is necessary for life on the Earth.

25 위 글에서 환경에 미치는 갯벌의 좋은 역할로 언급된 것을 모두 고르시오.

① 홍수로 인한 피해 축소
② 신선한 해산물 제공
③ 조류 관찰 장소 제공
④ 바다로 들어가는 물 정화
⑤ 산소 생성

Work on Your Dreams

🎙 의사소통 기능

- 강조하기

  It's important that you never give up.

- 설명 요청하기

  What do you mean by that?

🎙 언어 형식

- 'ask/want+A+to부정사 구문

  Other teams **asked** African American players **to join** them.

- 목적격 관계대명사

  I will become a player **who** people like.

Words & Expressions

Key Words

- **achieve** [ətʃíːv] 동 이루다, 달성하다
- **although** [ɔːlðóu] 접 비록 ～일지라도
- **American** [əmérikən] 명 미국인 형 미국의
- **as** [əz] 전 ～로(자격)
- **award** [əwɔ́ːrd] 명 상
- **base** [beis] 명 야구의 루
- **baseman** [béismən] 명 (1·2·3) 루수
- **bat** [bæt] 동 (공을) 치다
- **calm** [kɑːm] 형 침착한
- **classical** [klǽsikəl] 형 (음악이) 클래식의
- **color line** 인종 차별
- **difficulty** [dífikʌlti] 명 어려움, 곤경, 장애
- **earn** [əːrn] 동 얻다, 획득하다
- **effort** [éfərt] 명 노력
- **ever** [évər] 부 언젠가 한 번이라도
- **excellence** [éksələns] 명 우수, 탁월, 뛰어남
- **excellent** [éksələnt] 형 뛰어난
- **face** [feis] 동 직면하다, 직시하다
- **fail** [feil] 동 실패하다, ～하지 못하다
- **finally** [fáinəli] 부 마침내
- **gentle** [dʒéntl] 형 점잖은
- **high five** 하이파이브(기쁨의 표시로 두 사람이 팔을 들어 서로 손바닥을 마주치는 것)
- **honor** [ánər] 동 예우하다, ～을 공경하다
- **lend** [lend] 동 빌려주다
- **major** [méidʒər] 형 주요한
- **Nobel Prize** 명 노벨상
- **overcome** [óuvərkʌm] 동 극복하다
- **pain** [pein] 명 아픔, 고통
- **perfect** [pɔ́ːrfikt] 형 완벽한
- **phrase** [freiz] 명 구, 구절
- **plus** [plʌs] 전 게다가, 덧붙여
- **positive** [pázətiv] 형 긍정적인
- **present** [prizént] 동 주다, 수여하다, 증정하다
- **recognize** [rékəgnàiz] 동 인정하다, 알아보다
- **recycle** [riːsáikl] 동 재활용하다
- **respect** [rispékt] 명 존경
- **rudely** [rúːdli] 부 무례하게
- **sentence** [séntəns] 명 문장
- **skater** [skéitər] 명 스케이트 선수
- **solve** [sɑlv] 동 풀다, 해결하다
- **stadium** [stéidiəm] 명 경기장, 스타디움
- **support** [səpɔ́ːrt] 명 지지
- **talented** [tǽləntid] 형 재능이 있는
- **team** [tiːm] 명 (경기 등의) 팀
- **teammate** [tíːmeit] 명 팀 동료
- **terrible** [térəbl] 형 무서운
- **wish** [wiʃ] 동 바라다, 원하다
- **with** [wið] 전 ～와 함께, ～함에 따라

Key Expressions

- **achieve a goal** 목표를 달성하다
- **at bat** 타석에서
- **be good at** ～을 잘하다
- **by 동사ing** ～함으로써
- **cannot believe one's eyes** 눈을 의심하다(놀람)
- **earn the respect** 존경을 얻다
- **give up** 포기하다
- **help+목적어+(to) 동사원형** (목적어)가 ～하는 것을 돕다
- **keep calm** 평온을 유지하다
- **keep 동명사** ～하는 것을 계속하다
- **more than** ～보다 많이
- **no longer** 더 이상 ～ 아닌
- **one of 복수명사** ～중의 하나
- **over and over** 반복해서
- **present A with B** A에게 B를 수여하다, 증정하다
- **shout at** ～을 향해 외치다
- **take a class** 수업을 듣다
- **thanks to** ～ 덕분에
- **think to oneself** 마음속으로 생각하다
- **turn down** ～을 거절하다, 거부하다, 소리를 줄이다
- **win first place** 1등을 하다, 우승하다

Word Power

※ 형용사 – 명사
- □ **different**(다른) – **difference**(다름, 차이)
- □ **important**(중요한) – **importance**(중요성)
- □ **silent**(조용한) – **silence**(침묵)

- □ **excellent**(우수한) – **excellence**(우수, 장점)
- □ **significant**(중요한) – **significance**(중요성)

※ 비슷한 의미를 가진 어휘들
- □ **gentle**(점잖은) : **kind**(친절한)
- □ **respect**(존경) : **admiration**(존경)

- □ **finally**(마침내) : **in the end**(결국, 마침내)

English Dictionary

□ **award** 상
→ a prize or other reward that is given to someone who has achieved something
어떤 것을 달성한 사람에게 주어지는 상이나 다른 보상

□ **baseman** (1·2·3) 루수
→ a player stationed at a base 베이스에 배치된 선수

□ **bat** (공을) 치다
→ to hit the ball with a bat in a game such as baseball or cricket
야구나 크리켓 경기에서 방망이로 공을 치다

□ **calm** 침착한
→ not affected by strong emotions such as excitement, anger, shock, or fear
흥분, 화, 충격 또는 공포 같은 강한 감정에 의해 영향을 받지 않은

□ **classical** (음악이) 클래식의
→ relating to classical music 클래식 음악과 관련이 있는

□ **earn** 얻다, 획득하다
→ to get something as a result of your efforts or your behavior 노력이나 행동의 결과로 어떤 것을 얻다

□ **excellent** 뛰어난
→ unusually or extremely good 대단히 또는 극히 좋은

□ **fail** 실패하다, ~하지 못하다
→ to be unable to do something 어떤 것을 할 수 없다

□ **honor** 예우하다, ~을 공경하다
→ to show your respect or admiration for someone, especially by giving them a prize or title, or by praising them publicly
특히 상이나 타이틀을 주거나, 공적으로 칭찬함으로써 어떤 사람에게 존경이나 칭찬을 보여주다

□ **lend** 빌려주다
→ to give someone the use of something for a limited time 어떤 것을 제한된 시간 동안 사용하게 주다

□ **major** 주요한
→ greater or more important than other people or things in a group
한 그룹 안에서 다른 사람이나 사물보다 더 중요한

□ **overcome** 극복하다
→ to succeed in dealing with or controlling a problem
문제를 다루거나 통제하는 데 성공하다

□ **pain** 아픔, 고통
→ a feeling that you have in a part of your body when you are hurt or ill 아프거나 다쳤을 때 몸의 일부에서 갖는 느낌

□ **positive** 긍정적인
→ believing that good things will happen rather than bad ones 나쁜 일보다 좋은 일이 발생하리라 믿는

□ **recognize** 인정하다, 알아보다
→ to see and know what someone or something is
사람이나 사물이 무엇인지 알다

□ **rudely** 무례하게
→ in a way that shows no respect for others
다른 사람에 대한 존중을 보이지 않는 방식으로

□ **sentence** 문장
→ a sequence of words forming a meaningful grammatical structure
의미 있는 문법의 구조를 형성하는 일련의 단어들

□ **support** 지지
→ help and kindness that you give to someone who is having a difficult time
어려움을 겪고 있는 사람에게 주는 도움과 친절

□ **team** (경기 등의) 팀
→ a group of people who work together or play a game or sport together
같이 일하거나 게임이나 운동을 함께 하는 한 무리의 사람들

□ **teammate** 팀 동료
→ a person who is in the same team 같은 팀에 있는 사람

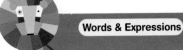

[01~02] 다음 빈칸에 들어갈 말로 적절한 것은?

01

He will _____ many difficulties in his life.

① celebrate   ② achieve
③ increase   ④ encourage
⑤ overcome

02 중요

She doesn't _____ much money, but she enjoys the work.

① earn   ② effort
③ experience   ④ respect
⑤ turn

[03~04] 다음 빈칸에 공통으로 들어갈 말로 알맞은 것은?

03

• She wanted to _____ his proposal, so she said 'no' to him.
• Could you _____ the volume? I can't concentrate on my study.

① calm down   ② break down
③ turn down   ④ pick up
⑤ take up

04 중요

• He took a deep breath and tried to _____ calm.
• I don't know what I'll do if gas prices _____ going up.

① take   ② keep   ③ get
④ hold   ⑤ have

05 중요 두 문장이 같은 의미가 되도록 빈칸에 알맞은 것을 고르시오.

• _____ he has financial problems, he has bought a new car.
= In spite of his financial problems, he has bought a new car.

① However   ② Although
③ When   ④ Therefore
⑤ Unless

[06~07] 다음 영영풀이에 해당하는 단어를 고르시오.

06

not affected by strong emotions such as excitement, anger, shock, or fear

① calm   ② nervous
③ serious   ④ comfortable
⑤ quiet

07

to show your respect or admiration for someone, especially by giving them a prize or title, or by praising them publicly

① award   ② honor
③ solution   ④ effort
⑤ contest

01 다음 밑줄 친 부분과 의미가 가장 가까운 것을 주어진 철자로 시작하여 쓰시오.

> The little boy was so <u>scared</u> that he made a lot of mistakes.

➡ a_____

02 두 문장에 공통으로 들어갈 수 있는 단어를 〈보기〉에서 골라 쓰시오.

> ┌ 보기 ┐
> as at for from in to

> • Who is the player _____ bat now?
> • I'm really poor _____ math and I want to become good _____ it.

03 괄호 안에 주어진 단어를 알맞게 배열하시오.

(1) 그들은 연습을 통해 더 빨라졌다.
  (practice, they, faster, with, became)
  ➡ _____

(2) 난 여름방학 계획을 따르는 데 실패했다.
  (to, vacation, I, plan, the, failed, follow, summer)
  ➡ _____

(3) 내가 그걸 처음 봤을 때, 내 눈을 믿을 수 없었다.
  (couldn't, when, I, my, I, that, first, believe, eyes, saw)
  ➡ _____

04 다음 빈칸에 알맞은 단어를 〈보기〉에서 골라 쓰시오. (한 단어는 한 번 밖에 사용할 수 없음)

> ┌ 보기 ┐
> excellent major positive talented

(1) He also spends a lot of time finding _____ artists.

(2) This is a _____ cause for concern.

(3) It's an _____ place to relax.

(4) Are you a _____ person or a negative person?

05 다음 우리말에 맞게 빈칸을 채우시오. (철자가 주어진 경우 그 철자로 시작할 것)

(1) 우리는 인종 차별을 하지 않는다.
  ➡ We do not draw the _____.

(2) Tony는 팀에서 1루수를 맡고 있다.
  ➡ Tony is the first _____ for the team.

(3) 비록 그들은 가난할지라도 행복하다.
  ➡ A_____ they are poor, they are happy.

(4) 그 프로젝트를 끝내는 데 많은 노력이 들었다.
  ➡ It took a lot of _____ to finish the project.

(5) 언젠가 우리 도움이 필요하면, 나한테 전화해.
  ➡ If you _____ need our help, just call me.

1 강조하기

> It's important that you never give up. 절대 포기하지 않는 것이 중요해.

■ 'It's important ~.'는 '~가 중요해'의 의미이다. important 다음에는 to부정사나 that절이 올 수 있다. 여기서 it은 가주어이며, to부정사나 that절은 진주어이다.

■ important와 비슷한 뜻인 essential, critical, significant 등을 대신 사용할 수 있다.

강조하기

- It's important that 주어 동사 ~. (~하는 것이 중요해.)
- It's important to 동사원형 ~. (~하는 것이 중요해.)
- I want to stress ~. (~을 강조하고 싶어.)

■ 'It's important to 동사원형 ~.'에서 '~하지 않는 것이 중요하다.'의 의미이면 to부정사 앞에 not을 붙여 'It's important not to 동사원형 ~.'으로 문장을 만들 수 있다.

핵심 Check

1. 다음 우리말과 일치하도록 빈칸에 알맞은 말을 쓰시오.

   A: I'm sorry, Ms. Song. (송 선생님, 죄송해요.)

   B: You're late again. _____ on time. (또 늦었구나. 시간을 지키는 것이 중요하단다.)

2. 다음 대화의 순서를 바르게 배열하시오.

   (A) It's important to stay healthy.

   (B) But I have a big test tomorrow.

   (C) You need to rest.

   ➡ _____

3. 괄호 안의 단어를 순서대로 배열하여 대화를 완성하시오.

   A: What is important when I play soccer?

   B: _____ (is, a, to, it, lot, practice, important)

   (연습을 많이 하는 것이 중요해.)

② 설명 요청하기

> **What do you mean by that?** (그게 무슨 뜻이니?)

■ 'What do you mean by that?'은 '그게 무슨 뜻이니?'라는 뜻으로 상대방과의 대화에서 이해하지 못한 부분이 있거나, 의도를 파악하지 못했을 때 부연 설명을 요청하는 의미로 쓰는 표현이다. that은 상대방이 말한 내용을 언급하는 대명사이고 by that은 '그 말로써, 그것으로'라는 뜻으로, 직역하면 '그 말로써 너는 무엇을 의미하니?'라는 뜻이다.

설명 요청하기

• What do you mean (by that)? (그게 무슨 뜻이니?)

• What is that exactly? (그게 정확히 뭐니?)

• What exactly do you mean? (정확하게 무슨 뜻이니?)

• Could you explain about that in detail? (그것을 자세히 설명해 줄 수 있나요?)

■ 설명을 할 때는 '~을 의미하다'의 뜻을 가진 'mean'을 사용해 'It means ~. (그것은 ~ 뜻이야.)'로 대답할 수 있다.

설명하기

• It means ~. (~라는 뜻이야.) • I mean ~. (~라는 뜻이야.)

핵심 Check

4. 다음 대화의 순서를 바르게 배열하시오.

(A) She's a busy worker.

(B) She's a busy bee.

(C) What do you mean by that?

➡ _____

5. 괄호 안의 단어를 순서대로 배열하여 대화를 완성하시오.

A: When it rains, it pours.

B: _____ (that, could, about, you, explain)

(그것이 무슨 뜻인지 설명해 줄래?)

A: It means "When problems come, they come together."

Listen & Speak 1 A-1

G: Hey, Minho. Did you find the answer to the math problem?

B: No. ❶It's too hard for me. ❷I'm not good at math.

G: ❸Let me see. ❹It's important that you use this math rule ❺to solve the problem.

B: Oh, I see. I'll use ❻it.

G: 이봐, 민호야. 이 수학 문제의 정답을 찾았니?

B: 아니. 그건 나에게 너무 어려워. 나는 수학을 잘하지 못 해.

G: 내가 한 번 볼게. 네가 그 문제를 풀기 위해선 이 수학 공식을 이용하는 것이 중요해.

B: 오, 알겠어. 그걸 사용해 볼게.

❶ It = The math problem, too: 너무, hard: 어려운

❷ be good at: ~을 잘하다

❸ 대화중에 질문을 받았을 때나 생각할 시간이 필요하면 'Let me think.'나 'Let me see.'라고 말할 수 있다

❹ that 이하의 내용을 강조할 때 'It's important that 주어 동사 ~.'를 사용하며, '~하는 것이 중요해.'의 의미이다.

❺ to부정사의 부사적 용법으로 '~하기 위해서'의 의미이다.

❻ it = this math rule

Check(√) True or False

(1) The math problem was too hard, so the boy didn't find the answer.   T ☐ F ☐

(2) The girl is better at math than the boy.   T ☐ F ☐

Listen & Speak 2 A-1

G: Oh, this is hard to do.

B: ❶What's the matter?

G: Can you ❷teach me how to make cookies?

B: Sure. It's a walk in the park.

G: ❸What do you mean by that?

B: ❹I mean it's easy to do.

G: 오, 이것은 하기 어렵구나.

B: 무슨 일이야?

G: 쿠키를 만드는 방법을 나에게 가르쳐 줄 수 있니?

B: 물론이지. 그건 'a walk in the park'야.

G: 그게 무슨 뜻이니?

B: 하기 쉽다는 뜻이야.

❶ 상대방의 슬픔이나 불만족, 실망의 원인에 대해 물을 때 사용되는 표현으로 What's the matter?가 쓰이며 '무슨 일[문제] 있니?'라는 뜻이다 (= What's wrong? = What's the problem? = What happened?)

❷ teach(4형식동사)+me(간접목적어,~에게)+how to make cookies(직접목적어,~을, 를), how to 동사원형: ~하는 방법

❸ 상대방에게 설명을 요청할 때 'What do you mean by that?'이라고 말한다.

❹ 설명을 요청하는 질문에 대한 대답으로 'It means ~.'나 'I mean ~.'으로 대답할 수 있다.

Check(√) True or False

(3) The boy doesn't know how to make cookies.   T ☐ F ☐

(4) "It's a walk in the park" means that it's easy to do.   T ☐ F ☐

Listen & Speak 1 A-2

G: Your poster looks great.

B: Thanks, Kate. Did you finish ❶yours?

G: Not yet. ❷I can't draw well. How can I become good at drawing?

B: It ❸takes time. ❹It's important that you draw as often as you can.

G: ❺You mean I should keep practicing?

B: That's right.

❶ yours = your poster
❷ draw: (그림을) 그리다 well은 부사로 동사인 draw를 수식하고 있다.
❸ take: (얼마의 시간이) 걸리다
❹ 강조할 때는 'It's important that 주어 동사 ~.(~가 중요해.)'를 사용한다.
❺ You mean ~?: ~라는 뜻이니? keep 동명사: ~하는 것을 계속하다

Listen & Speak 2 A-2

B: I have a singing contest tomorrow. I really ❶want to win first place.

G: I'll keep my fingers crossed for you.

B: ❷What do you mean by "keep my fingers crossed"?

G: ❸It means I wish you good luck.

B: Thank you.

❶ want는 to부정사를 목적어로 취한다. win first place: 1등을 하다, 우승하다
❷ 'What do you mean by ~?(~가 무슨 뜻이니?)'는 상대방이 말한 것을 제대로 이해하지 못하여 설명을 요청할 때 사용하는 표현이다.
❸ means와 I 사이에 접속사 that이 생략되어 있다.

Conversation A

M: ❶To achieve my dream, I went to many auditions, but I often failed. ❷However, I never gave up. I ❸took acting and dancing classes. ❹Finally, I achieved my goal. ❺It's important that you never give up.

❶ to부정사의 부사적 용법(목적)을 사용하여 '~하기 위해서'로 해석한다. achieve: 이루다, 달성하다
❷ however: 하지만 give up: 포기하다
❸ take a class: 수업을 듣다
❹ finally: 마침내 achieve a goal: 목표를 달성하다
❺ It's important that 주어 동사 ~: ~하는 것이 중요하다

Conversation B

Hana: You ❶look sad, Jiho. What's wrong?

Jiho: ❷I don't think I can achieve my dream.

Amy: ❸What do you mean by that?

Jiho: I want to be an actor, but I ❹always fail auditions. Maybe I have to give up.

Amy: Do you know this actor?

Jiho: Sure. He's a famous movie star.

Amy: He failed ❺more than 100 auditions.

Jiho: Really? Maybe I ❻should keep trying. I will practice more for my next audition.

Hana: That's right! ❼It's important that you never give up.

❶ look+형용사: ~해 보이다
❷ think와 I 사이에 접속사 that이 생략되어 있다. think의 목적어는 'I can achieve my dream'이다.
❸ What do you mean by that?: 그게 무슨 뜻이니? (= What is that exactly? = What exactly do you mean? = Could you explain about that in detail?)
❹ always(항상)는 빈도부사로 be동사나 조동사 뒤에, 일반동사 앞에 위치한다. fail: 실패하다, ~하지 못하다
❺ more than: ~ 이상
❻ should+동사원형: ~해야 한다 keep 동명사: ~하는 것을 계속하다
❼ never: 결코 ~하지 않다 give up: 포기하다

Communication Task Step 2

A: Please ❶call me "Speedy Feet."

B: ❷What do you mean by "Speedy Feet"?

A: I mean I want to be a runner.

B: What is important to do to become a runner?

A: ❸It's important that I practice running every day.

B: I'm sure you'll ❹make it.

❶ call+목적어+목적격보어: ~을 …라고 부르다
❷ What do you mean by ~?: ~가 무슨 뜻이니?
❸ It's important that 주어 동사 ~: ~하는 것이 중요하다
❹ make it: 성공하다, 해내다

● 다음 우리말과 일치하도록 빈칸에 알맞은 말을 쓰시오.

Listen & Speak 1 A

1. G: Hey, Minho. Did you _____ the answer to the math _____?

   B: No. It's _____ _____ for me. _____ _____ _____

   _____ _____.

   G: Let me see. _____ _____ _____ you use this math rule

   to _____ the problem.

   B: Oh, I see. I'll use it.

2. G: Your poster _____ great.

   B: Thanks, Kate. Did you _____ yours?

   G: Not yet. I can't _____ well. _____ can I become _____

   at drawing?

   B: It _____ time. It's _____ that you draw _____ _____

   _____ you can.

   G: You mean I should _____ _____?

   B: That's right.

Listen & Speak 1 B

1. A: It's _____ _____ _____ a good dancer. _____ should

   I do?

   B: It's _____ that you _____ give up.

   A: Okay. I will _____ _____ that.

2. A: It's _____ _____ write a good story. What should I do?

   B: _____ _____ _____ you read many books.

   A: Okay. I _____ _____ forget that.

Listen & Talk 2 A

1. G: Oh, this is _____ _____ _____.

   B: What's the matter?

   G: Can you teach me _____ _____ make cookies?

   B: Sure. It's a walk in the park.

   G: _____ _____ _____ _____ _____ that?

   B: I _____ it's easy to do.

2. **B:** I _____ a singing contest tomorrow. I really _____ _____ _____ first place.

   G: I'll keep my fingers _____ for you.

   B: _____ _____ _____ _____ _____ "keep my fingers crossed"?

   G: It _____ I wish you good _____.

   B: Thank you.

Listen & Talk 2 B

1. **A:** Two heads _____ better _____ one.

   B: _____ do you _____ _____ "Two heads are better than one"?

   A: I _____ working _____ is better _____ working _____.

2. **A:** _____ makes perfect.

   B: What do you _____ by "Practice makes perfect"?

   A: I _____ you learn something _____ _____ it _____ and over.

Conversation A

M: _____ _____ my dream, I went to many auditions, but I often _____. _____, I never gave _____. I _____ acting and dancing classes. _____, I _____ my goal. It's important that you _____ _____ up.

Conversation B

Hana: You _____ sad, Jiho. What's wrong?

Jiho: I don't think I can _____ my dream.

Amy: _____ _____ _____ _____ _____ _____?

Jiho: I want to be an actor, but I always _____ _____. Maybe I have to _____ _____.

Amy: Do you know this actor?

Jiho: Sure. He's a _____ movie star.

Amy: He failed _____ _____ 100 auditions.

Jiho: Really? Maybe I should keep _____. I will _____ more for my next audition.

Hana: That's right! It's important that _____ _____ _____ _____.

2. **B:** 나 내일 노래 경연 대회가 있어. 나는 정말 1등을 하고 싶어.
   G: 너에게 'keep my fingers crossed'할게.
   B: 'keep my fingers crossed'가 무슨 뜻이니?
   G: 그건 내가 너에게 행운을 빈다는 뜻이야.
   B: 고마워.

1. **A:** 두 개의 머리가 머리 하나보다 낫다.
   B: "두 개의 머리가 머리 하나보다 낫다."가 무슨 뜻이니?
   A: 함께 일하는 것이 혼자 일하는 것보다 낫다는 뜻이야.

2. **A:** 연습이 완벽함을 만든다.
   B: "연습이 완벽함을 만든다."가 무슨 뜻이니?
   A: 반복해서 무언가를 하면 배우게 된다는 뜻이야.

M: 내 꿈을 이루기 위해 나는 많은 오디션에 갔지만 자주 떨어졌다. 하지만 나는 절대 포기하지 않았다. 나는 연기와 춤 수업을 들었다. 마침내 나는 내 목표를 이뤘다. 절대 포기하지 않는 것이 중요하다.

하나: 너 슬퍼 보여, 지호야. 무슨 일이니?
지호: 내 생각에 나는 꿈을 이룰 수 없을 것 같아.
Amy: 그게 무슨 말이니?
지호: 나는 배우가 되고 싶지만 항상 오디션에서 떨어져. 어쩌면 나는 포기해야 할 거 같아.
Amy: 너 이 배우를 아니?
지호: 당연하지. 그는 유명한 영화배우잖아.
Amy: 그는 백 번 이상 오디션에서 떨어졌어.
지호: 정말? 그러면 나도 계속 노력해야겠구나. 나는 다음 오디션을 위해서 더 연습할 거야.
하나: 바로 그거야! 절대 포기하지 않는 것이 중요해.

Conversation 시험대비 기본평가

[01~02] 다음 대화의 빈칸에 알맞은 말은?

01

G: Hey, Minho. Did you find the answer to the math problem?

B: No. It's too hard for me. I'm not good at math.

G: Let me see. _____

B: Oh, I see. I'll use it.

① It's important to study math.

② It's important that you know many words.

③ It's important that you use this math rule to solve the problem.

④ It's important that you turn off the music when you study.

⑤ It's important that you decide what to do.

02

G: Oh, this is hard to do.

B: What's the matter?

G: Can you teach me how to make cookies?

B: Sure. It's a walk in the park.

G: _____

B: I mean it's easy to do.

① What do you mean by that?   ② Where did you walk?

③ Why do you say so?   ④ How is he doing?

⑤ What's the matter?

03 주어진 문장 다음에 이어질 대화의 순서로 알맞은 것을 고르시오.

I have a singing contest tomorrow. I really want to win first place.

(A) It means I wish you good luck.

(B) What do you mean by "keep my fingers crossed"?

(C) I'll keep my fingers crossed for you.

(D) Thank you.

① (B) – (A) – (C) – (D)   ② (B) – (C) – (A) – (D)

③ (C) – (A) – (B) – (D)   ④ (C) – (B) – (A) – (D)

⑤ (C) – (D) – (B) – (A)

[01~03] 다음 대화를 읽고 물음에 답하시오.

> G: Your poster looks great. (①)
> B: Thanks, Kate. (②)
> G: Not yet. I can't draw well. (③) How can I become good at drawing?
> B: It takes (A)_____. (④) It's important that you draw as often as you can. (⑤)
> G: You mean I should (B)_____ practicing?
> B: That's right.

01 위 대화의 ①~⑤ 중 다음 주어진 말이 들어갈 알맞은 곳은?

Did you finish yours?

①   ②   ③   ④   ⑤

02 빈칸 (A)와 (B)에 들어갈 말로 알맞은 것끼리 짝지어진 것을 고르시오.

	(A)	(B)
①	time	keep
②	time	enjoy
③	time	finish
④	money	keep
⑤	money	enjoy

03 위 대화의 내용과 일치하지 <u>않는</u> 것을 고르시오.

① The boy finished drawing his poster.
② The girl thinks the poster which the boy drew is great.
③ The boy knows how to be good at drawing.
④ The girl can draw as well as the boy.
⑤ The boy gives her some advice for drawing well.

[04~06] 다음 대화를 읽고 물음에 답하시오.

> Hana: You look sad, Jiho. What's wrong? (①)
> Jiho: I don't think I can ⓐ<u>achieve</u> my dream.
> Amy: What do you mean by that?
> Jiho: I want to be an actor, but I ⓑ<u>never fail</u> auditions. (②)
> Amy: Do you know this actor?
> Jiho: Sure. He's a famous movie star. (③)
> Amy: He failed more than 100 auditions. (④)
> Jiho: Really? Maybe I should keep ⓒ<u>trying</u>. (⑤) I will practice ⓓ<u>more</u> for my next audition.
> Hana: That's right! It's important that you ⓔ<u>never</u> give up.

04 위 대화의 ①~⑤ 중 다음 주어진 말이 들어갈 알맞은 곳은?

Maybe I have to give up.

①   ②   ③   ④   ⑤

05 위 대화의 ⓐ~ⓔ 중 흐름상 어색한 것을 고르시오.

① ⓐ   ② ⓑ   ③ ⓒ   ④ ⓓ   ⑤ ⓔ

06 위 대화의 내용과 일치하지 <u>않는</u> 것을 고르시오.

① Hana thinks it's important not to give up.
② Jiho wants to become an actor.
③ Amy told Jiho the story about the famous movie star.
④ Jiho failed auditions more than 100 times.
⑤ Jiho will keep trying for the next audition.

07 빈칸에 공통으로 들어갈 알맞은 말을 고르시오.

> A: (A)_____.
> B: What do you mean by "(B)_____"?
> A: I mean working together is better than working alone.

① keep my fingers crossed
② It's a walk in the park
③ Will is power
④ Practice makes perfect
⑤ Two heads are better than one

[08~09] 다음 짝지어진 대화가 <u>어색한</u> 것은?

08 ① A: I bought this bag at the mall. It's a steal.
　　　B: What do you mean by that?
　　　A: It's very cheap.

② A: Mina is really nice. She is all ears.
　　B: What do you mean by that?
　　A: She listens very carefully.

③ A: What is important to do to be an scientist?
　　B: It's important to study math and science.

④ A: Practice makes perfect.
　　B: What do you mean by "Practice makes perfect"?
　　A: Yes, I do. I mean you learn something by doing it over and over.

⑤ A: I have an important exam tomorrow.
　　B: I'll keep my fingers crossed for you!
　　A: Thanks for saying that. I feel much better.

09 ① A: What is important to grow taller?
　　　B: It is important to drink much milk.

② A: Is it important that I should prepare a lot for the contest?
　　B: Yes. I think practice makes perfect.

③ A: It's important to keep studying.
　　B: I'll turn off the music.

④ A: What does "No sweat, no sweet" mean?
　　B: It means "If you don't work hard, you can't achieve your goal."

⑤ A: What should we do to keep the air clean?
　　B: First of all, it's important to use public transportation.

[10~11] 다음 대화를 읽고 물음에 답하시오.

> A: It's hard to be a good dancer. (A)_____
> B: (B) 절대 포기하지 않는 것이 중요해. (is, never, important, it, give, you, that, up)
> A: Okay. I will not forget that.

10 빈칸 (A)에 알맞은 말을 고르시오.

① What are you going to do?
② What should I do?
③ What do you mean by that?
④ What are you talking about?
⑤ What do you want to be?

서답형
11 밑줄 친 (B)의 우리말에 맞게 괄호 안에 주어진 단어를 배열하여 영작하시오.

➡ _____

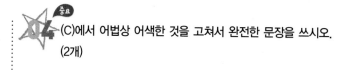

01 주어진 문장 이후에 이어질 대화의 순서를 바르게 배열하시오.

> Your poster looks great.

> (A) Not yet. I can't draw well. How can I become good at drawing?
> (B) That's right.
> (C) Thanks, Kate. Did you finish yours?
> (D) You mean I should keep practicing?
> (E) It takes time. It's important that you draw as often as you can.

➡ _____

[02~04] 다음 대화를 읽고 물음에 답하시오.

> A: Please call me "Speedy Feet."
> B: What do you mean (A)_____ "Speedy Feet"?
> A: I mean I want to be a runner.
> B: (B)달리기 선수가 되기 위해서 무엇을 하는 것이 중요하니? (to, become, runner, a, what, important, to, is, do)
> A: (C)It's important what I practice to run every day.
> B: I'm sure you'll make it.

02 빈칸 (A)에 알맞은 전치사를 쓰시오.

➡ _____

03 (B)의 밑줄 친 우리말에 맞게 괄호 안에 주어진 단어를 배열하여 영작하시오.

➡ _____

04 (C)에서 어법상 어색한 것을 고쳐서 완전한 문장을 쓰시오. (2개)

➡ _____

05 ⓐ~ⓔ 중 흐름상 어색한 것을 고치시오.

> G: Hey, Minho. ⓐDid you find the answer to the math problem?
> B: No. It's too hard for me. ⓑI'm good at math.
> G: ⓒLet me see. ⓓIt's important that you use this math rule to solve the problem.
> B: Oh, I see. ⓔI'll use it.

➡ _____
_____

06 다음 대화의 문맥상 또는 어법상 어색한 것을 고치시오. (2개)

> A: It's hard to make movies. What should I do?
> B: It's important that you think creative.
> A: Okay. I will forget that.

➡ (1) _____
_____

(2) _____

Grammar

① 'ask/want+A+to부정사' 구문

> **Other teams asked African American players to join them.**
> 다른 팀들은 아프리카계 미국인 선수들에게 자신들의 팀에 합류할 것을 요청했다.

- **'동사＋목적어＋to부정사' 구문**

  '주어＋동사＋목적어＋목적격보어'의 5형식 문장에서 want, ask, tell 등의 동사가 쓰이면 목적어와 목적격보어가 능동 관계일 때, 목적격보어로 to부정사가 온다.

  - Do you **want** me **to close** the shop? 내가 가게 문을 닫았으면 좋겠니?
  - He **asked** you **to wait** for him until 3:00. 그는 너에게 3시까지 기다려 달라고 부탁했어.

- **to부정사를 목적격보어로 취하는 동사**

  (1) 명령, 요청: tell, advise, warn, ask, request, allow 등
  - I **told** him **to do** it immediately. 나는 그에게 그것을 즉시 하라고 말했다.
  - Other players **advised** him **to stay** on the team. 다른 선수들은 그에게 팀에 남아 있으라고 충고했다.

  (2) 유도, 자극: lead, invite, encourage 등
  - He **encouraged** me **to write** poems. 그는 내게 시를 쓰도록 격려해 주었다.

  (3) 기대, 소망: like, expect, want, wish 등
  - Many people did not **expect** him **to do** well. 많은 사람들은 그가 잘하리라고 기대하지 않았다.

- **to부정사의 부정형은 'not[never]+to 동사원형'이다.**

  - He **advised** me **not to go** there. 그는 나에게 거기에 가지 말라고 충고했다.
  - I **asked** him **not to tell** anybody. 나는 그에게 누구에게도 말하지 말라고 부탁했다.
  - The doctor **ordered** me **not to smoke**. 의사는 나에게 담배를 피우지 말라고 명령했다.

핵심 Check

1. 다음 우리말과 일치하도록 빈칸에 알맞은 말을 쓰시오.

(1) 우리 부모님은 내가 그들과 함께 살기를 바라신다.
→ My parents want me ＿＿＿＿＿ ＿＿＿＿＿ with them.

(2) 나는 그에게 조심하라고 부탁했다.
→ I asked him ＿＿＿＿＿ ＿＿＿＿＿ careful.

(3) 어떻게 그런 생각을 하게 되었는가?
→ What led you ＿＿＿＿＿ ＿＿＿＿＿ so?

② 목적격 관계대명사

> • I will become a player **who** people like. 나는 사람들이 좋아하는 선수가 될 거야.

■ **목적격 관계대명사의 뜻**

관계대명사는 절과 절을 연결하는 접속사와 대명사의 기능 두 가지를 겸하는데, 관계대명사 앞의 명사(선행사)가 뒤 문장의 목적어 역할을 할 때 이 관계대명사를 '목적격 관계대명사'라고 한다.

This is the book **which** I have chosen. 이것이 내가 고른 책이다.

■ **목적격 관계대명사의 종류**

선행사가 사람일 때 'who(m),' 사물일 때 'which,' 사람과 사물 모두에 'that'을 쓸 수 있다.

선행사	사람	사물, 동물	사람, 사물, 동물
목적격 관계대명사	who(m)/that	which/that	that

That man over there is the dentist **whom** I told you about. 저기 있는 사람이 내가 너에게 얘기했던 그 치과 의사야.

■ **목적격 관계대명사의 생략**

목적격 관계대명사는 생략이 가능하다.

• I know the novelist (**who/whom/that**) he mentioned. 나는 그가 언급한 소설가를 알고 있다.

■ 목적격 관계대명사절에서는 앞에 있는 관계대명사가 동사의 목적어 역할을 하기 때문에 동사 뒤에 목적어가 없다는 것에 특히 주의해야 한다.

• I cannot find the book. I put it(=the book) on the table.
= I cannot find the book (**which/that**) I put on the table. 나는 책상 위에 두었던 책을 찾을 수 없다.

■ 목적격 관계대명사가 전치사의 목적어인 경우 전치사는 관계대명사절의 끝에 오거나 관계대명사 앞에 올 수 있다. 전치사가 관계대명사절의 끝에 올 경우에는 관계대명사를 생략할 수 있지만 전치사가 관계대명사 앞에 올 경우에는 관계대명사를 생략하지 않으며 관계대명사 that을 쓸 수 없다.

• I had some animals (**which/that**) I took care **of**. (나는 내가 돌보던 동물들을 갖고 있었다.)
= I had some animals **of which** I took care.
= I had some animals of that I took care. (×)

핵심 Check

2. 다음 괄호 안에서 알맞은 말을 고르시오.

(1) He is the man (who / which) I met yesterday.

(2) The bag (whom / which) he is carrying is very old.

01 다음 문장에서 어법상 어색한 부분을 바르게 고치시오.

(1) My mother told me bring my umbrella.

_____ ➡ _____

(2) I asked Sam borrow the book from the library

_____ ➡ _____

(3) She is an actress which I wanted to meet.

_____ ➡ _____

(4) Did you find the book who you wanted?

_____ ➡ _____

[02~03] 다음 문장의 빈칸에 들어갈 알맞은 말은?

02

Our English teacher advised us _____ harder.

① study   ② studies   ③ studied
④ studying   ⑤ to study

03

The bag _____ he is carrying is very old.

① that   ② what   ③ who
④ whom   ⑤ whose

04 다음 우리말에 맞게 빈칸에 알맞은 말을 쓰시오.

(1) 너는 내가 그 이야기를 믿으라고 기대하는 거야?
➡ Do you expect me _____ _____ the story?

(2) 그는 그들로 하여금 궁핍한 사람들을 도우라고 장려했다.
➡ He encouraged them _____ _____ the poor and needy.

(3) 소년은 한번 본 그 소녀와 사랑에 빠졌다.
➡ The boy fell in love with a girl _____ he saw once.

(4) 내가 어제 산 치마를 너에게 보여줄게.
➡ I'll show you the skirt _____ I bought yesterday.

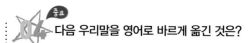

01 다음 빈칸에 알맞은 것은?

> My father told me _____ TV for an hour a day.

① watch
② watches
③ watched
④ watching
⑤ to watch

02 다음 〈보기〉의 밑줄 친 부분과 다르게 쓰인 것을 고르시오.

> ┤ 보기 ├
> Everything <u>that</u> I said was true.

① The movie <u>which</u> I saw was interesting.
② The money was returned by the boy <u>that</u> had found it.
③ Ted wants to marry the lady <u>whom</u> he loves.
④ This is the movie <u>that</u> I really wanted to watch.
⑤ I am looking for a man <u>who</u> I met at the park yesterday.

03 다음 빈칸에 들어갈 수 있는 말이 <u>다른</u> 하나는?

① The bag _____ I bought yesterday is blue.
② She is the scientist _____ I want to meet.
③ An orphan is a child _____ parents are dead.
④ This is the pen _____ was on the desk.
⑤ Kate is the writer _____ I like most.

04 다음 우리말을 영어로 바르게 옮긴 것은?

> 그의 친구들은 그가 빚을 갚을 수 있도록 해줄 것이다.

① His friends will enable him pay his debts.
② His friends will enable him pays his debts.
③ His friends will enable him paying his debts.
④ His friends will enable him to pay his debts.
⑤ His friends will enable him to paying his debts.

05 다음 중 어법상 바르지 <u>않은</u> 것은?

> Mark ①wanted ②me ③lend ④him ⑤ <u>some</u> money.

①　　②　　③　　④　　⑤

06 다음 괄호 안에서 알맞은 말을 고르시오.

(1) The people (which / that) we met were very nice.
(2) The dress (who / which) she is wearing is pretty.
(3) This is the drama about (that / which) I spoke yesterday.
(4) His support helped Robinson (play / playing) harder.
(5) I (hoped / warned) the man to keep away from my dog.

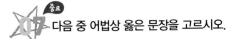

07 다음 중 어법상 옳은 문장을 고르시오.

① But she had a dream who she couldn't give up.
② This is the house in that she lives.
③ We sometimes have to eat dishes whom we don't like.
④ Another important thing which we choose is time management.
⑤ There is something who you should remember.

08 다음 빈칸에 적절하지 않은 것은?

> Sena _____ me to start studying two weeks before the test.

① watched   ② encouraged   ③ told
④ expected   ⑤ persuaded

09 다음 중 두 문장의 의미가 다른 것은?

① Mom expects that I will study hard.
  → Mom expects me to study hard.
② Sam advised her that she should not throw away the trash on the street.
  → Sam advised her not to throw away the trash on the street.
③ Ann told him that he must wear long clothes to protect himself from animals.
  → Ann told him to wear long clothes to protect himself from animals.
④ She allowed that I could eat ice cream for dessert.
  → I allowed her to eat ice cream for dessert.
⑤ Juliet told Romeo that he should come at once.
  → Juliet told Romeo to come at once.

10 다음 밑줄 친 that의 성격이 나머지 넷과 다른 것은?

① One idea is <u>that</u> a big rock from space hit the Earth.
② The phone <u>that</u> you picked up is mine.
③ An elephant is an animal <u>that</u> has a long nose.
④ Do you have some money <u>that</u> I can borrow?
⑤ The book <u>that</u> I read yesterday was very interesting.

서답형

11 괄호 안의 동사를 어법에 맞게 고쳐 쓰시오.

(1) They asked him (spend) the night in the house.
(2) Her doctors encouraged her (keep) learning Taekwondo.
(3) Why don't you help her (carry) the boxes?
(4) The teacher had the students (finish) their projects.
(5) We requested everyone in the office (assemble) in the lobby.

➡ (1) _____ (2) _____ (3) _____
   (4) _____ (5) _____

12 다음 중 어법상 어색한 부분을 찾아 바르게 고친 것은?

> He warned Cindy keep away from his dog.

① warned → has warned
② Cindy → Cindy's
③ keep → to keep
④ from → to
⑤ his → him

서답형

13 다음 문장에서 어법상 어색한 부분을 바르게 고쳐 다시 쓰시오.

(1) Sophie asked her dad help her to finish her homework.

➡ _____

(2) Mom wanted Lily coming home by 8.

➡ _____

(3) She invited me go to New York with her.

➡ _____

(4) The blue watch is the gift who I bought there for my brother.

➡ _____

_____

(5) The man which my mother is talking to is my art teacher.

➡ _____

_____

(6) The girl and her cat which I met this morning were playing in the park.

➡ _____

_____

14 괄호 안에 주어진 동사를 빈칸에 써 넣을 때 그 형태가 다른 하나는?

① The teacher wanted me _____ notes. (take)

② Jimin told me _____ a study group. (make)

③ Mom asked Rosa _____ some books to the library. (return)

④ Many people did not expect him _____ well. (do)

⑤ I feel something _____ up my back. (creep)

서답형

15 다음 문장에서 생략할 수 있는 것을 쓰시오.

(1) Mary is the girl who I met in Paris.

(2) My group thinks health is an important thing that we need for our dream.

(3) He is reading a book which is about the greenhouse gas.

➡ (1) _____ (2) _____ (3) _____

16 다음 중 어법상 어색한 것을 고르시오.

① The heavy rain caused the river overflow.

② Do not force them to agree to your opinion.

③ I warned him not to take any pictures here.

④ We want you to come and visit us.

⑤ After that season, other teams asked African American players to join them.

17 다음 두 문장을 한 문장으로 바르게 바꾸지 않은 것을 고르시오.

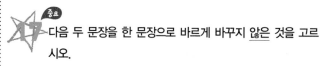

• Alice wishes to meet a boy.
• She went to the same school with him.

① Alice wishes to meet a boy she went to the same school with.

② Alice wishes to meet a boy who she went to the same school with.

③ Alice wishes to meet a boy that she went to the same school with.

④ Alice wishes to meet a boy with whom she went to the same school.

⑤ Alice wishes to meet a boy with that she went to the same school.

01 다음 문장에서 어법상 어색한 부분을 찾아 바르게 고쳐 다시 쓰시오.

(1) I want you are happy.

➡ _____

(2) Jack asked his mother woke him up at 8 o'clock.

➡ _____

(3) Tina told me finding a quiet place to study.

➡ _____

(4) Jessy got her dad drop her off at the bus stop.

➡ _____

(5) His teacher advised him not spend all his time on one subject.

➡ _____
_____

02 다음 두 문장을 관계대명사를 사용하여 한 문장으로 바꾸시오.

(1) • The man is my brother.
• You met the man on Sunday.

➡ _____
_____

(2) • That is the computer.
• I bought the computer last week.

➡ _____
_____

(3) • This is the cake.
• It was made by Ann.

➡ _____

(4) • I visited the church.
• I took some pictures of the church.

➡ _____
_____
_____

(5) • It is an experience.
• I look forward the experience.

➡ _____
_____
_____

(6) • Does Eddie have any friends?
• He can depend on them.

➡ _____
_____
_____

03 우리말에 맞게 괄호 안에 주어진 동사의 알맞은 형태를 빈칸에 쓰시오.

(1) 무엇을 가져오면 되나요?

➡ What would you like me _____? (bring)

(2) 그녀는 그들을 대회에 참가하도록 만들었다.

➡ She made them _____ part in the contest. (take)

(3) 무언가 탄내가 나는 것 같다.

➡ I think I smell something _____. (burn)

04 다음 문장에서 어법상 어색한 부분을 찾아 바르게 고쳐 다시 쓰시오.

(1) This is the bridge who my father built.

➡ _____

(2) They are the people which I met in the plane.

➡ _____

(3) I like the new computer that I bought it last week.

➡ _____

(4) Can you tell me about the church of that you took the picture last weekend?

➡ _____
_____
_____
_____

06 두 문장을 관계대명사를 사용하여 한 문장으로 썼을 때, 빈칸에 해당하는 문장을 쓰시오.

(1) • _____
• My favorite author wrote it.
→ I bought a book that my favorite author wrote.

(2) • That is the girl.
• _____
→ That is the girl whom I invited to the party.

(3) • There are three things.
• _____
_____
→ There are three things that I need to do to achieve my dream.

(4) • _____
• The famous author wrote it.
→ Is the novel which the famous author wrote fun?

05 다음 두 문장이 비슷한 의미를 갖도록 빈칸을 알맞은 말로 채우시오.

(1) Mom told me that I must come back home by tonight.
➡ Mom told me _____ back home by tonight.

(2) His boss told him that he should be more careful for the future.
➡ His boss ordered him _____ more careful for the future.

(3) The teacher told Maria that she should not give up her dream.
➡ The teacher encouraged Maria _____ _____ her dream.

07 괄호 안에 주어진 어휘를 이용하여 우리말에 맞게 영작하시오.

(1) 그녀는 너에게 자기 방 청소를 부탁했다. (ask, clean)
➡ _____

(2) 엄마는 내가 강아지를 돌볼 거라고 예상하신다. (expect, take care of)
➡ _____
_____

(3) 우리가 만났던 사람들은 매우 친절했다. (the people, nice)
➡ _____

(4) 내가 어제 산 가방은 파란색이다. (bag, buy)
➡ _____

Jackie Robinson Breaks the Color Line

It was New York City on April 15, 1947. Jackie Robinson, an African
_{날짜 앞에는 전치사 on을 쓴다.}   _{'Jackie Robinson'을 부연 설명하는 동격,}
American, went on the field as second baseman for the Brooklyn
_{동격 앞에는 콤마(,)를 쓴다.}   _{as: ~로(자격)}
Dodgers. People couldn't believe their eyes. He was the first African
              _{'~의 눈을 의심하다'라는 뜻. 놀람을 나타낼 때 쓰인다.}
American player to play on a Major League team. That day, the color
          _{to부정사의 형용사적 용법. on: 소속}
line was broken.
_{수동태(be동사+과거분사). 과거시제이므로 be동사 was가 쓰였다.}

Robinson faced many difficulties. Although Robinson was a talented
                   _{=Though}
player and a gentle person, his teammates did not want to play with
                               _{want는 to부정사를 목적어로 취하는 동사}
him. Every hotel turned the team down because Robinson was on
the team. When he was at bat, people in the stands rudely shouted at
him. Robinson thought to himself, 'I need to keep calm and focus on
                 _{재귀대명사}   _{'need to': '~해야 한다'. 뒤에 동사원형이 온다.}
baseball. I will try and become a player who people like. Then, next
                     _{목적격 관계대명사로 who 뒤의 절이 'a player'를 꾸며 준다.}
season, there will be more African American players in the league.'
Robinson put all his time and energy into baseball. With practice, he
                       _{with: ~함에 따라. ~와 더불어 with practice: 연습함에 따라서}
became great at batting and base running.
        _{at의 목적어로 동명사 batting과 'base running'이 쓰임.}

American: 미국인; 미국의
baseman: (1, 2, 3) 루수
major: 주요한, 중대한
color line: 인종 차별
although: (비록) ~이긴 하지만
talented: (타고난) 재능이 있는
teammate: 팀 동료
rudely: 무례하게, 예의 없이, 버릇없이
turn down: ~을 거절하다, 거부하다
at bat: 타석에 서서
shout at: ~에게 소리치다
think to oneself: 조용히 생각하다,
마음속으로 생각하다
keep calm: 평정을 유지하다

 확인문제

● 다음 문장이 본문의 내용과 일치하면 T, 일치하지 <u>않으면</u> F를 쓰시오.

1 Jackie Robinson was the first African American player to play on a Major League
team. ☐

2 On April 15, 1947, the color line was made. ☐

3 Robinson experienced many difficulties. ☐

4 Robinson's teammates wanted to play with him. ☐

5 When Robinson was at bat, people in the stands rudely shouted at him. ☐

6 Robinson put all his time and energy into breaking the color line. ☐

Robinson's effort moved his teammates. When people shouted at Robinson, one of his teammates walked up to Robinson and tapped him on the shoulder. "Do not listen to them. You're doing fine," he said. His support helped Robinson to play harder. Finally, Robinson earned the respect of other players and fans.

Thanks to Robinson, the Dodgers won the National League Championship in 1947. The league recognized Robinson's excellence and presented him with the Rookie of the Year Award in the same year. After that season, other teams asked African American players to join them.

Robinson's uniform number was 42. Baseball players in Major League teams no longer wear the number 42 to honor him. Every year, however, on April 15, every player wears the number that Robinson wore. The day is called "Jackie Robinson Day."

effort: 노력, 수고
support: 지지, 지원, 도움
recognize: 알아보다, 인정하다
excellence: 우수, 탁월, 뛰어남
earn the respect: 존경을 얻다
honor: 존경하다, 공경하다
no longer: 더 이상 ~ 아닌[하지 않는]

 확인문제

● 다음 문장이 본문의 내용과 일치하면 T, 일치하지 <u>않으면</u> F를 쓰시오.

1   Robinson's effort moved his teammates. ☐

2   Some of Robinson's teammates walked up to Robinson and tapped him on the shoulder. ☐

3   Thanks to Robinson, the Dodgers won the National League Championship in 1947. ☐

4   The league didn't recognize Robinson's excellence. ☐

5   Baseball players in Major League teams no longer wear the number 42 to honor Robinson. ☐

6   "Jackie Robinson Day" is April 5 of each year. ☐

● 우리말을 참고하여 빈칸에 알맞은 말을 쓰시오.

1 Jackie Robinson _____ _____ _____ _____

2 It was New York City _____ _____ _____, _____.

3 Jackie Robinson, an African American, went on the field _____ second baseman _____ the Brooklyn Dodgers.

4 People _____ _____ their eyes.

5 He was _____ _____ _____ _____ _____ to play on a Major League team.

6 That day, _____ _____ _____ _____ _____ _____.

7 Robinson _____ _____ _____.

8 _____ Robinson was a talented player and a gentle person, his teammates did not want _____ _____ _____ _____.

9 Every hotel _____ _____ _____ _____ because Robinson was on the team.

10 When he _____ _____ _____, people in the stands rudely shouted at him.

11 Robinson _____ _____ _____, 'I need to keep calm and focus on baseball.

12 I will try and become a player _____ _____ _____.

13 Then, next season, _____ _____ _____ African American players in the league.'

14 Robinson _____ all his time and energy _____ baseball.

1 Jackie Robinson 인종 차별을 깨다

2 1947년 4월 15일 뉴욕시에서였다.

3 아프리카계 미국인 Jackie Robinson은 브루클린 다저스의 2루수로 경기장에 나갔다.

4 사람들은 자신들의 눈을 의심했다.

5 그는 메이저리그 팀에서 경기한 최초의 아프리카계 미국인 선수였다.

6 그날 인종 차별이 깨졌다.

7 Robinson은 많은 어려움에 직면했다.

8 Robinson은 재능 있는 선수이고 온화한 사람이었지만 그의 팀원들은 그와 함께 경기하기를 원하지 않았다.

9 Robinson이 팀에 있었기 때문에 모든 호텔에서 그 팀을 거절했다.

10 그가 타석에 있을 때, 관중석에 있는 사람들이 그에게 무례하게 소리치기도 했다.

11 Robinson은 마음속으로 생각했다. '나는 평정심을 유지하고 야구에 집중해야 해.

12 나는 노력해서 사람들이 좋아하는 선수가 될 거야.

13 그러면 다음 시즌에는 아프리카계 미국인 선수가 리그에 더 많이 생길 거야.'

14 Robinson은 자신의 모든 시간과 에너지를 야구에 집중했다.

15 _____ _____ , he became great at _____ and _____ _____ .

16 Robinson's effort _____ his teammates.

17 When people shouted at Robinson, _____ _____ _____ walked up to Robinson and _____ _____ _____ _____ shoulder.

18 " _____ _____ _____ _____ them.

19 You're doing _____ ," he said.

20 His support helped Robinson _____ _____ harder.

21 Finally, Robinson _____ _____ _____ of other players and fans.

22 _____ _____ Robinson, the Dodgers won the National League Championship in 1947.

23 The league _____ Robinson's excellence and _____ him _____ the Rookie of the Year Award in the same year.

24 After that season, other teams _____ African American players _____ _____ them.

25 Robinson's _____ _____ was 42.

26 Baseball players in Major League teams _____ _____ wear the number 42 _____ _____ _____ .

27 Every year, _____ , on April 15, every player wears the number that Robinson _____ .

28 The day _____ _____ "Jackie Robinson Day."

---

15 연습을 함으로써 그는 타격과 주루를 잘하게 되었다.

16 Robinson의 노력은 그의 팀원들을 감동시켰다.

17 사람들이 Robinson에게 소리쳤을 때, 그의 팀 동료 중 한 명이 Robinson에게 다가가 어깨를 두드렸다.

18 "그들 말을 듣지 마.

19 너는 잘하고 있어."라고 그가 말했다.

20 그의 지지는 Robinson이 더 열심히 경기하는 데 도움이 됐다.

21 마침내, Robinson은 다른 선수들과 팬들의 존경을 받았다.

22 Robinson 덕분에 다저스는 1947년에 내셔널리그 챔피언십에서 우승하게 되었다.

23 리그에서는 Robinson의 탁월함을 인정했고, 같은 해에 그에게 신인상을 수여했다.

24 그 시즌 이후, 다른 팀들은 아프리카계 미국인 선수들에게 자신들의 팀에 합류할 것을 요청했다.

25 Robinson의 등 번호는 42번이었다.

26 메이저리그 팀의 야구 선수들은 그에 대한 존경을 보여 주기 위해 더 이상 42번을 달지 않는다.

27 하지만 매년 4월 15일, 모든 선수들은 Robinson이 달았던 번호를 단다.

28 이 날을 '재키 로빈슨 데이'라고 부른다.

● 우리말을 참고하여 본문을 영작하시오.

1 Jackie Robinson 인종 차별을 깨다

➡ _____

2 1947년 4월 15일 뉴욕시에서였다.

➡ _____

3 아프리카계 미국인 Jackie Robinson은 브루클린 다저스의 2루수로 경기장에 나갔다.

➡ _____

4 사람들은 자신들의 눈을 의심했다.

➡ _____

5 그는 메이저리그 팀에서 경기한 최초의 아프리카계 미국인 선수였다.

➡ _____

6 그날 인종 차별이 깨졌다.

➡ _____

7 Robinson은 많은 어려움에 직면했다.

➡ _____

8 Robinson은 재능 있는 선수이고 온화한 사람이었지만 그의 팀원들은 그와 함께 경기하기를 원하지 않았다.

➡ _____

9 Robinson이 팀에 있었기 때문에 모든 호텔에서 그 팀을 거절했다.

➡ _____

10 그가 타석에 있을 때, 관중석에 있는 사람들이 그에게 무례하게 소리치기도 했다.

➡ _____

11 Robinson은 마음속으로 생각했다. '나는 평정심을 유지하고 야구에 집중해야 해.

➡ _____

12 나는 노력해서 사람들이 좋아하는 선수가 될 거야.

➡ _____

13 그러면 다음 시즌에는 아프리카계 미국인 선수가 리그에 더 많이 생길 거야.'

➡ _____

14 Robinson은 자신의 모든 시간과 에너지를 야구에 집중했다.

➡ _____

15 연습을 함으로써 그는 타격과 주루를 잘하게 되었다.

➡ _____

16 Robinson의 노력은 그의 팀원들을 감동시켰다.

➡ _____

17 사람들이 Robinson에게 소리쳤을 때, 그의 팀 동료 중 한 명이 Robinson에게 다가가 어깨를 두드렸다.

➡ _____

18 "그들 말을 듣지 마.

➡ _____

19 너는 잘하고 있어."라고 그가 말했다.

➡ _____

20 그의 지지는 Robinson이 더 열심히 경기하는 데 도움이 됐다.

➡ _____

21 마침내, Robinson은 다른 선수들과 팬들의 존경을 받았다.

➡ _____

22 Robinson 덕분에 다저스는 1947년에 내셔널리그 챔피언십에서 우승하게 되었다.

➡ _____

23 리그에서는 Robinson의 탁월함을 인정했고, 같은 해에 그에게 신인상을 수여했다.

➡ _____

24 그 시즌 이후, 다른 팀들은 아프리카계 미국인 선수들에게 자신들의 팀에 합류할 것을 요청했다.

➡ _____

25 Robinson의 등 번호는 42번이었다.

➡ _____

26 메이저리그 팀의 야구 선수들은 그에 대한 존경을 보여 주기 위해 더 이상 42번을 달지 않는다.

➡ _____

27 하지만 매년 4월 15일, 모든 선수들은 Robinson이 달았던 번호를 단다.

➡ _____

28 이 날을 '재키 로빈슨 데이'라고 부른다.

➡ _____

[01~03] 다음 글을 읽고 물음에 답하시오.

It was New York City __(A)__ April 15, 1947. Jackie Robinson, an African American, went on the field ⓐas second baseman for the Brooklyn Dodgers. People couldn't believe their eyes. He was the first African American player to play __(B)__ a Major League team. That day, the color line was broken.

서답형

01 위 글의 빈칸 (A)와 (B)에 공통으로 들어갈 알맞은 전치사를 쓰시오.

➡ _____

02 위 글의 밑줄 친 ⓐas와 같은 의미로 쓰인 것을 고르시오.

① Leave it as it is.
② Yesterday he attended the meeting as a reporter.
③ Her anger grew as she talked.
④ As I was tired, I soon fell asleep.
⑤ He trembled as he spoke.

03 위 글을 읽고 Jackie Robinson에 대해 알 수 없는 것을 고르시오.

① 혈통   ② 국적
③ 수비 위치   ④ 가족 관계
⑤ 소속팀

[04~06] 다음 글을 읽고 물음에 답하시오.

Robinson faced many difficulties. Although Robinson was a talented player and a gentle person, his teammates did not want to play with him. Every hotel turned the team down (A)[because / because of] Robinson was on the team. ⓐ그가 타석에 있을 때, people in the stands rudely shouted at him.

Robinson thought to (B)[him / himself], 'I need to keep calm and focus on baseball. I will try and become a player who people like. Then, next season, there will be more African American players in the league.' Robinson put all his time and energy into baseball. With practice, he became (C)[great / greatly] at batting and base running.

서답형

04 위 글의 괄호 (A)~(C)에서 어법상 알맞은 낱말을 골라 쓰시오.

➡ (A)_____ (B)_____ (C)_____

서답형

05 위 글의 밑줄 친 ⓐ의 우리말을 5단어로 쓰시오.

➡ _____

06 위 글을 읽고 대답할 수 없는 질문은?

① Did Robinson have difficulties during his career as a major leaguer?
② Why did every hotel turn the team down?
③ When Robinson was at bat, did people in the stands welcome him?
④ Thanks to Robinson's effort, how many African American players could play on the Major League teams?
⑤ How did Robinson become a good batter and base runner?

[07~10] 다음 글을 읽고 물음에 답하시오.

Robinson's uniform number was 42. Baseball players in Major League teams no longer wear the number 42 ⓐto honor him. Every year, __(A)__, on April 15, every player wears the number that Robinson wore. ⓑThe day is called "Jackie Robinson Day."

 07 위 글의 빈칸 (A)에 들어갈 알맞은 말을 고르시오.

① therefore   ② however
③ for example   ④ in fact
⑤ in addition

08 아래 〈보기〉에서 위 글의 밑줄 친 ⓐto honor와 문법적 쓰임이 같은 것의 개수를 고르시오.

┌─── 보기 ├───
① He wept to see the sight.
② My hope is to work as a doctor in Africa.
③ I want something to write with.
④ I have nothing to do this afternoon.
⑤ I was very happy to hear the news.
└─────────────

① 1개   ② 2개   ③ 3개   ④ 4개   ⑤ 5개

서답형
09 Why do baseball players in Major League teams no longer wear the number 42? Fill in the blanks with a suitable word.

➡ They do so in order to _____ Robinson.

서답형
10 위 글의 밑줄 친 ⓑ를 능동태로 고치시오.

➡ _____

[11~13] 다음 글을 읽고 물음에 답하시오.

Robinson thought to himself, 'I need to keep calm and focus on baseball. I will try and become a player ___ⓐ___ people like. Then, next season, there will be more African American players in the league.' Robinson put all his time and energy into baseball. With practice, he became great at batting and base running.

11 위 글의 빈칸 ⓐ에 들어갈 알맞은 말을 모두 고르시오.

① what   ② who
③ whom   ④ which
⑤ that

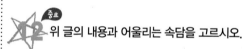 12 위 글의 내용과 어울리는 속담을 고르시오.

① Better late than never.
② A stitch in time saves nine.
③ Do to others as you would be done by.
④ Practice makes perfect.
⑤ Look before you leap.

13 위 글의 내용과 일치하지 <u>않는</u> 것은?

① Robinson은 평정심을 유지하고 야구에 집중해야 한다고 마음속으로 생각했다.
② Robinson은 노력해서 사람들이 좋아하는 선수가 되려고 결심했다.
③ Robinson 덕분에 다음 시즌에 아프리카계 미국인 선수가 리그에 더 많이 생겼다.
④ Robinson은 자신의 모든 시간과 에너지를 야구에 집중했다.
⑤ 연습을 함으로써 Robinson은 타격과 주루를 잘하게 되었다.

[14~17] 다음 글을 읽고 물음에 답하시오.

How I Will Achieve My Dream

I want to be a designer. There are ⓐthree things (A)[that / what] I need to do ⓑto achieve my dream. I need to be healthy, be creative, and never give up. Being healthy will help me (B)[keep / keeping] going for my dream. Being creative will help me do something different. Plus, I will always tell myself never ___(A)___ because it will make me (C)[try / to try] harder.

서답형

14 위 글의 빈칸 (A)에 들어갈 알맞은 말을 쓰시오.

➡ _____

서답형

15 위 글의 괄호 (A)~(C)에서 어법상 알맞은 낱말을 골라 쓰시오.

➡ (A)_____ (B)_____ (C)_____

16 위 글의 밑줄 친 ⓐ에 해당하지 않는 것은? (2개)

① to be healthy
② to work well with others
③ to be creative
④ never to give up
⑤ to help others

중요

17 위 글의 밑줄 친 ⓑ를 바꿔 쓴 것으로 옳지 않은 것을 고르시오.

① so as to achieve my dream
② in order that I can achieve my dream
③ achieving my dream
④ so that I can achieve my dream
⑤ in order to achieve my dream

[18~20] 다음 글을 읽고 물음에 답하시오.

Robinson's effort ⓐmoved ①his teammates. When people shouted at Robinson, one of ②his teammates walked up to Robinson and tapped ③him on the shoulder. "Do not listen to them. ④You're doing fine," he said. ⑤His support helped Robinson to play harder. ⓑFinally, Robinson earned the respect of other players and fans.

18 위 글의 밑줄 친 ⓐmoved와 같은 의미로 쓰인 것을 고르시오.

① He moved towards the window.
② I moved the meeting to Wednesday.
③ Their deep friendship moved us a great deal.
④ They moved into a new house.
⑤ We moved our chairs a little nearer.

중요

19 밑줄 친 ①~⑤ 중에서 가리키는 대상이 나머지 넷과 다른 것은?

①   ②   ③   ④   ⑤

20 위 글의 밑줄 친 ⓑFinally와 바꿔 쓸 수 없는 말을 고르시오.

① Lastly   ② In the long run
③ Eventually   ④ In the end
⑤ At last

[21~22] 다음 글을 읽고 물음에 답하시오.

A: It's important that I manage my time well, practice hard, and have a strong ⓐwill to achieve my dream. How about you?
B: ⓑI think being healthy, working well with others, and being creative is important.

21 위 글의 밑줄 친 ⓐwill과 같은 의미로 쓰인 것을 고르시오.

① How long will you stay in Paris?

② Her decision shows great strength of will.

③ Will you send this letter for me, please?

④ It will be fine tomorrow.

⑤ I ought to draw up my will before I die.

서답형
22 위 글의 밑줄 친 ⓑ에서 어법상 틀린 부분을 찾아 고치시오.

➡ _____

[23~24] 다음 글을 읽고 물음에 답하시오.

Robinson's effort moved his teammates. (①) When people shouted at Robinson, one of his teammates walked up to Robinson and tapped him on the shoulder. (②) "Do not listen to them. (③) You're doing fine," he said. (④) Finally, Robinson earned the respect of other players and fans. (⑤)

Thanks to Robinson, the Dodgers won the National League Championship in 1947. The league recognized Robinson's   (A)   and presented him with the Rookie of the Year Award in the same year. After that season, other teams asked African American players to join them.

서답형
23 위 글의 빈칸 (A)에 excellent를 알맞은 형태로 쓰시오.

➡ _____

중요
24 위 글의 흐름으로 보아, 주어진 문장이 들어가기에 가장 적절한 곳은?

| His support helped Robinson to play harder. |

①   ②   ③   ④   ⑤

[25~27] 다음 글을 읽고 물음에 답하시오.

How I Will Achieve My Dream

I want to be a chef. There are ⓐthree things that I need to do to achieve my dream. I need to practice hard, work well with others, and manage my time well. (A)_____ hard will help me cook well and easily. (B)_____ well with others will make ⓑit easier to work at a restaurant. Plus, I will always tell myself (C)_____ my time well because it will help me make food in time to serve.

서답형
25 위 글의 빈칸 (A)~(C)에 들어갈 말을 각각 알맞은 형태로 쓰시오.

➡ (A) _____
   (B) _____
   (C) _____

서답형
26 위 글의 밑줄 친 ⓐthree things가 가리키는 것을 본문에서 찾아 쓰시오.

➡ _____
   _____

27 위 글의 밑줄 친 ⓑit과 문법적 쓰임이 같은 것을 모두 고르시오.

① It is very hard to give up smoking.

② It is easy to get a bad habit.

③ It is quite difficult to master a foreign language.

④ I found it useless to teach him English.

⑤ I make it a rule to take a walk early in the morning.

[01~03] 다음 글을 읽고 물음에 답하시오.

It was New York City on ⓐApril 15, 1947. Jackie Robinson, an African American, went on the field as second baseman for the Brooklyn Dodgers. People couldn't believe their eyes. He was the first African American player to play on a Major League team. That day, the (A)c_____ l_____ was broken.

01 주어진 영영풀이를 참고하여 빈칸 (A)에 주어진 철자로 시작하는 단어를 쓰시오.

> barrier preventing blacks from participating in various activities with whites

➡ _____

02 위 글의 밑줄 친 ⓐ를 영어로 읽는 법을 쓰시오.

➡ _____

03 Why couldn't people believe their eyes when Jackie Robinson came out into the field? Fill in the blanks with suitable words.

➡ Because there was no _____ to play on a Major League team before him.

[04~07] 다음 글을 읽고 물음에 답하시오.

Thanks to Robinson, the Dodgers won the National League Championship in 1947. The league recognized Robinson's excellence and ⓐpresented him with the Rookie of the Year

Award in the same year. After that season, other teams asked African American players __(A)__ ⓑthem.

04 위 글의 빈칸 (A)에 join을 알맞은 형태로 쓰시오.

➡ _____

05 위 글의 밑줄 친 ⓐ를 다음과 같이 바꿔 쓸 때 빈칸에 들어갈 알맞은 말을 쓰시오.

➡ presented the Rookie of the Year Award _____ him

06 위 글의 밑줄 친 ⓑ가 가리키는 것을 본문에서 찾아 쓰시오.

➡ _____

07 When did Robinson win the Rookie of the Year Award? Answer in English in a full sentence. (5 words)

➡ _____

[08~10] 다음 글을 읽고 물음에 답하시오.

Robinson faced many difficulties. Although Robinson was a talented player and a gentle person, his teammates did not want to play with him. ⓐ모든 호텔에서 그 팀을 거절했다 because Robinson was on the team. When he was at bat, people in the stands rudely shouted at him.

08 위 글에서 'gifted'와 바꿔 쓸 수 있는 단어를 찾아 쓰시오.

➡ _____

★9 위 글의 밑줄 친 @의 우리말에 맞게 주어진 어휘를 이용하여 6단어로 영작하시오.

Every, turned

➡ _____

_____

10 본문의 내용과 일치하도록 다음 빈칸 (A)와 (B)에 알맞은 단어를 쓰시오.

In spite of his talent and (A)_____ personality, Robinson experienced many (B)_____. For example, his teammates did not want to play with him.

[11~14] 다음 글을 읽고 물음에 답하시오.

@Robinson's effort moved his teammates. When people shouted at Robinson, one of his teammates walked up to Robinson and tapped him on the shoulder. "Do not listen to ⓑthem. You're doing fine," he said. ©His support helped Robinson to play harder. Finally, ⓓ Robinson은 다른 선수들과 팬들의 존경을 받았다.

★11 위 글의 밑줄 친 @를 수동태로 고치시오.

➡ _____

_____

12 위 글의 밑줄 친 ⓑthem이 가리키는 것을 본문에서 찾아 쓰시오.

➡ _____

★13 다음 빈칸 (A)와 (B)에 알맞은 단어를 넣어 ©His support에 대한 설명을 완성하시오.

One of Robinson's (A)_____ walked up to Robinson, tapped him on the shoulder, and told him not to listen to the people who (B)_____ _____ him, adding "You're doing fine."

14 위 글의 밑줄 친 ⓓ의 우리말에 맞게 주어진 어휘를 이용하여 9단어로 영작하시오.

earn, respect, of

➡ _____

[15~17] 다음 글을 읽고 물음에 답하시오.

Robinson @마음속으로 생각했다, 'I need to keep calm and focus on baseball. ⓑI will try and become a player who people like. Then, next season, there will be more African American players in the league.' Robinson put all his time and energy into baseball. With practice, he became great at (A)_____ and (B)_____.

★15 위 글의 빈칸 (A)와 (B)에 bat와 base run을 각각 알맞은 형태로 쓰시오.

➡ (A) _____ (B) _____

16 위 글의 밑줄 친 @의 우리말을 세 단어로 쓰시오.

➡ _____

17 위 글의 밑줄 친 ⓑ에서 생략할 수 있는 단어를 생략하고 문장을 다시 쓰시오.

➡ _____

해석

Language in Use

I visited three countries last year. France was the first country which I visited.
the+서수   목적격 관계대명사(= that)

Mary is the girl who I met in Paris. The blue watch is the gift which I bought
목적격 관계대명사(= whom/that)   목적격 관계대명사(= that)

there for my brother.
= in Paris   buy A B(4형식) = buy B for A(3형식): A에게 B를 사주다

구문해설 • gift: 선물

작년에 나는 3개국을 방문했
다. 프랑스가 내가 방문한 첫
번째 국가였다. Mary는 내
가 파리에서 만났던 소녀이
다. 그 파란 시계는 그곳에서
내 동생을 위해 산 선물이다.

Enjoy Writing B

How I Will Achieve My Dream

I want to be a designer. There are three things that I need to do to achieve my
명사적 용법의 to부정사   목적격 관계대명사   부사적 용법의 to부정사

dream. I need to be healthy, be creative, and never give up. Being healthy will
동명사 주어

help me keep going for my dream. Being creative will help me do something
= to keep   help+목적어+to부정사(원형부정사)

different. Plus, I will always tell myself never to give up because it will make
주어와 목적어가 같으면 재귀대명사를 씀   tell+목적어+to부정사

me try harder.
make+목적어+원형부정사

구문해설 • achieve: 성취하다 • creative: 창의적인 • give up: ~을 포기하다 • keep going: (힘들거나 고통스
러워도) 계속 살아가다[견디다]

어떻게 나의 꿈을 성취할 것
인가

나는 디자이너가 되기를 원한
다. 나의 꿈을 성취하기 위해
내가 할 필요가 있는 세 가
지가 있다. 나는 건강해야 하
고, 창의적이어야 하고, 그리
고 결코 포기하지 말아야 한
다. 건강한 것은 나의 꿈을 계
속 유지하도록 도와줄 것이
다. 창의적인 것은 내가 무언
가 다른 것을 하도록 도와줄
것이다. 더하여, 내 스스로에
게 결코 포기하지 말라고 항
상 말할 것인데, 이는 내가 더
열심히 노력하도록 해 줄 것
이기 때문이다.

Wrap Up 2

B: It's difficult to learn English.
가주어   진주어

G: Rome was not built in a day.
be not p.p.(부정문 수동태) 하루 사이에, 하루 아침에

B: What do you mean by that?
그게 무슨 뜻이니? (= What is that exactly? = What exactly do you mean? = Could you explain about that in detail?)

G: I mean it takes time to achieve something.
take+시간: (얼마의 시간이) 걸리다   to부정사의 부사적 용법(목적): ~하기 위해서 (진주어로 쓰인 명사적 용법으로 볼 수도 있음)

B: I see.
= I understand.

B: 영어를 배우는 것은 어려
워.
G: 로마는 하루아침에 이루
어지지 않았어.
B: 그게 무슨 뜻이니?
G: 무언가를 이루는 데 시간
이 걸린다는 뜻이야.
B: 알겠어.

01 다음 빈칸에 들어갈 말이 순서대로 바르게 짝지어진 것은?

> • They gave _____ the game without scoring even one point.
> • I met a lot of nice people, thanks _____ you.

① in – to
② in – for
③ up – to
④ up – for
⑤ up – at

02 다음 중 밑줄 친 부분의 뜻풀이가 바르지 <u>않은</u> 것은?

① Sorry, we can <u>no longer</u> help you. (더 이상 ~ 아닌)
② I never expected your <u>support</u>. (지지)
③ No <u>pain</u>, no gain. (고통)
④ They will <u>present</u> him with an award for good citizenship. (선물)
⑤ She has a <u>gentle</u> heart. (점잖은)

03 다음 밑줄 친 부분과 의미가 가장 가까운 것을 주어진 철자로 시작하여 쓰시오.

> <u>In the end</u>, we all decided to organize a concert for Easter.

➡ F_____

04 다음 빈칸에 알맞은 말을 고르시오.

> One of the ways to _____ the respect is by showing responsibility for the community.

① believe
② present
③ keep
④ earn
⑤ win

[05~06] 다음 대화를 읽고 물음에 답하시오.

> B: I have a singing contest tomorrow. I really want to win first place.
> G: I'll keep my fingers crossed for you.
> B: What do you mean by "keep my fingers crossed"?
> G: It means (A)_____.
> B: Thank you.

05 빈칸 (A)에 알맞은 말을 고르시오.

① it's easy to do
② working together is better than working alone
③ you learn something by doing it over and over
④ it takes time to achieve something
⑤ I wish you good luck

06 위 대화를 읽고 대답할 수 <u>없는</u> 질문은?

① Does the girl know the meaning of "keep my fingers crossed"?
② What does the boy want at a singing contest?
③ What kind of contest is the boy going to have?
④ Where is a singing contest held?
⑤ When is there a singing contest?

[07~08] 다음 대화를 읽고 물음에 답하시오.

> A: (A)_____.
> B: What do you mean ⓐ_____ "(B)_____"?
> A: I mean you learn something ⓑ_____ doing it over and over.

07 빈칸 (A)와 (B)에 공통으로 들어갈 말을 고르시오.

① Practice makes perfect
② Rome was not built in a day
③ Will is power
④ Two heads are better than one
⑤ It's a walk in the park

08 빈칸 ⓐ와 ⓑ에 공통으로 들어갈 전치사를 쓰시오.

➡ _____

[09~10] 다음 대화를 읽고 물음에 답하시오.

G: Your poster looks great. (①)
B: Thanks, Kate. (②) Did you finish yours?
G: Not yet. I can't draw well. (③)
B: It takes time. (④) It's important that
   (A)_____. (⑤)
G: You mean I should keep practicing?
B: That's right.

09 위 대화의 ①~⑤ 중 다음 주어진 말이 들어갈 알맞은 곳은?

How can I become good at drawing?

①　　②　　③　　④　　⑤

10 빈칸 (A)에 알맞은 말을 고르시오.

① you take an art class
② you draw as often as you can
③ you see a lot of pictures
④ you go to an art gallery
⑤ you buy expensive pictures

11 다음 상황에 어울리는 말이 아닌 것을 고르시오.

You and your friend are watching a soccer game in a stadium. Your friend shouts loudly, "Way to go!" but you do not know what he means. So, you want to ask him what it means.

① What is "Way to go" exactly?
② Will you "Way to go"?
③ What exactly do you mean by "Way to go"?
④ What do you mean by "Way to go"?
⑤ Could you explain about "Way to go" in detail?

12 다음 빈칸에 들어갈 말이 순서대로 바르게 짝지어진 것은?

B: It's difficult to learn English.
G: Rome was not built in a day.
B: What do you mean by that?
G: I mean it _____ time to _____ something.
B: I see.

① takes　　　　mean
② takes　　　　achieve
③ does　　　　mean
④ does　　　　achieve
⑤ does　　　　expect

Grammar

13 다음 우리말을 주어진 어휘를 이용하여 영작하시오.

(1) 부모님이 내게 사 주신 컴퓨터가 고장 났다.
(buy, for, break)

➡ _____

_____

(2) 내가 사진을 찍어 준 남자와 그의 개가 1등을 차지했다. (the man, that, take a picture, win the first prize)

➡ _____

_____

(3) 네가 일요일에 만난 그 남자는 내 남동생이다. (meet, brother)

➡ _____

_____

(4) 그의 가족은 그가 수영 대회에 참가하기를 원했다. (take part in, the swimming competition)

➡ _____

_____

(5) 그녀는 나에게 파리에 함께 가자고 권유했다. (invite, go, her)

➡ _____

(6) 나는 그에게 시끄럽게 하지 말라고 말했다. (tell, make a noise)

➡ _____

14 다음 중 두 문장을 한 문장으로 만들었을 때 그 의미가 <u>다른</u> 하나는?

① It turned out to be a tiger shark. + It attacked her that morning.
　→ It turned out to be a tiger shark which attacked her that morning.
② Those are the flowers. + Rebecca grows them in her garden.
　→ Those are the flowers Rebecca grows in her garden.
③ Alice will send a letter to Alex. + Alice met him at the party.
　→ Alice will send a letter to Alex whom she met at the party.
④ I will become a player. + People like the player.
　→ I will become a player who people like.
⑤ The bag was sent to Wendy. + I bought the bag yesterday.
　→ Wendy sent the bag that I bought yesterday.

15 다음 중 어법상 올바른 것은?

① I didn't expect him talk to you.
② They asked John did something for them.
③ Mom wanted Sam finishing his homework.
④ It will enable Jane to complete her project.
⑤ His doctor ordered Simon to takes some rest.

16 〈보기〉의 밑줄 친 that과 용법이 <u>다른</u> 하나는?

┌─ 보기 ┐
France was the first country <u>that</u> I visited last year.
└─────┘

① The man <u>who</u> I admire the most is King Sejong.
② This is the dog <u>which</u> he often found in his garden.
③ Tom bought a backpack <u>which</u> has two side pockets.
④ You are the only person <u>that</u> I can trust.
⑤ This is the bike <u>that</u> Emily lost yesterday.

17 다음 ⓐ~ⓗ 중 옳은 것을 모두 고르면?

> ⓐ I told you to not make any noise.
> ⓑ My parents want me live with them.
> ⓒ I'll let you to go home early.
> ⓓ His wife asked him to wash the dishes.
> ⓔ His support helped Robinson to play harder.
> ⓕ He is the man which gave me a drink.
> ⓖ I didn't enjoy the movie which I saw it yesterday.
> ⓗ I will become a player that people like.

① ⓐ, ⓒ ② ⓑ, ⓒ, ⓓ
③ ⓑ, ⓓ, ⓗ ④ ⓓ, ⓔ, ⓖ
⑤ ⓓ, ⓔ, ⓗ

18 괄호 안에 주어진 어휘를 이용하여 우리말에 맞게 영작하시오.

(1) 그는 나에게 자기를 병원에 데려다 달라고 부탁했다. (ask, take, the hospital)

➡ _____

(2) 너는 그녀가 나가는 소리를 들었니? (hear, go out)

➡ _____

(3) 나는 로마에서 만난 그 여인을 잊을 수 없다. (forget, met, woman, Rome)

➡ _____
_____

Reading

[19~20] 다음 글을 읽고 물음에 답하시오.

> It was New York City on April 15, 1947. Jackie Robinson, an African American, went on the field as second baseman for the Brooklyn Dodgers. People couldn't believe their eyes. He was the first African American player ⓐto play on a Major League team. That day, the color line was broken.

19 위 글의 밑줄 친 ⓐto play와 to부정사의 용법이 다른 것을 모두 고르시오.

① He must be brave to do such a thing.
② At first, he had no friends to practice baseball together.
③ There are many African American players to play on a Major League team.
④ His dream was to be a major leaguer.
⑤ He put all his energy into baseball to become a player who people liked.

20 본문의 내용과 일치하도록 다음 빈칸 (A)와 (B)에 알맞은 단어를 쓰시오.

> On April 15, 1947, when (A)_____ _____ went on the field as second baseman for the Brooklyn Dodgers, the (B)_____ _____ was broken.

[21~23] 다음 글을 읽고 물음에 답하시오.

> Robinson faced many difficulties. ⓐ Robinson was a talented player and a gentle person, his teammates did not want to play with him. Every hotel turned the team down because Robinson was on the team. When he was at bat, people in the stands rudely shouted at him.
>
> (①) Robinson thought to himself, 'I need to keep calm and focus on baseball. (②) Then, next season, there will be more African American players in the league.' (③) Robinson put all his time and energy into baseball. (④) With practice, he became great at batting and base running. (⑤)

21 위 글의 빈칸 ⓐ에 들어갈 알맞은 말을 고르시오.

① As ② Although ③ If
④ Because ⑤ Since

22 위 글의 흐름으로 보아, 주어진 문장이 들어가기에 가장 적절한 곳은?

> I will try and become a player who people like.

①   ②   ③   ④   ⑤

23 위 글의 마지막 부분에서 알 수 있는 'Robinson'의 성격으로 가장 알맞은 것을 고르시오.

① curious   ② outgoing

③ sociable   ④ diligent

⑤ creative

[24~26] 다음 글을 읽고 물음에 답하시오.

Robinson's effort moved his teammates. When people shouted at Robinson, one of his teammates walked up to Robinson and tapped him ⓐ the shoulder. "Do not listen to them. You're doing fine," he said. His support helped Robinson to play harder. Finally, Robinson earned the respect of other players and fans.

Thanks to Robinson, the Dodgers won the National League Championship in 1947. The league recognized Robinson's excellence and presented him ⓑ the Rookie of the Year Award in the same year. After that season, ⓒ다른 팀들은 아프리카계 미국인 선수들에게 자신들의 팀에 합류할 것을 요청했다.

24 위 글의 빈칸 ⓐ와 ⓑ에 들어갈 전치사가 바르게 짝지어진 것은?

① on – with   ② by – to

③ in – for   ④ by – with

⑤ on – to

25 위 글의 밑줄 친 ⓒ의 우리말에 맞게 한 단어를 보충하여, 주어진 어휘를 알맞게 배열하시오.

> them / players / teams / asked / American / join / other / African

➡ _____

_____

26 위 글의 주제로 알맞은 것을 고르시오.

① Robinson's effort made him famous.

② Robinson earned people's recognition through his effort.

③ A teammate encouraged Robinson not to be disappointed.

④ The Dodgers won the National League Championship in 1947.

⑤ Robinson won the Rookie of the Year Award in 1947.

[27~28] 다음 글을 읽고 물음에 답하시오.

Robinson's uniform number was 42. Baseball players in Major League teams no longer wear the number 42 to honor him. Every year, however, on April 15, every player ⓐ_____ the number that Robinson ⓑ_____. The day is called "Jackie Robinson Day."

27 위 글의 빈칸 ⓐ와 ⓑ에 wear를 알맞은 형태로 쓰시오.

➡ ⓐ _____   ⓑ _____

28 다음 문장에서 위 글의 내용과 다른 부분을 찾아서 고치시오.

> Baseball players in Major League teams want to wear the number 42 to honor him.

➡ _____

출제율 90%

01 다음 짝지어진 두 단어의 관계가 <u>다른</u> 하나를 고르시오.

① different – difference
② important – importance
③ silent – silence
④ allow – allowance
⑤ excellent – excellence

출제율 95%

02 다음 중 밑줄 친 부분의 뜻풀이가 바르지 <u>않은</u> 것은?

① Writing a book requires a lot of time and <u>effort</u>. (노력)
② Everyone <u>recognized</u> his skill. (인정했다)
③ How many things do you <u>recycle</u> at your school? (재활용하다)
④ This is one of the <u>major</u> sources of energy. (주요한)
⑤ I know that they <u>face</u> lots of problems. (얼굴)

출제율 85%

03 다음 빈칸에 알맞은 단어를 고르시오.

I thought _____, "I'm in trouble."

① to me
② for me
③ to myself
④ for myself
⑤ in me

출제율 95%

04 두 문장에 공통으로 들어갈 수 있는 단어를 고르시오.

• She _____ first place in the swimming competition.
• She _____ the Best Actress award.

① won
② made
③ went
④ took
⑤ realized

출제율 100%

05 다음 대화의 빈칸에 들어갈 말을 〈보기〉에서 골라 순서대로 바르게 배열한 것은?

G: Oh, this is hard to do.
B: _____
G: _____
B: _____
G: _____
B: I mean it's easy to do.

─┤ 보기 ├─
(A) Can you teach me how to make cookies?
(B) Sure. It's a walk in the park.
(C) What's the matter?
(D) What do you mean by that?

① (B) – (A) – (C) – (D)
② (B) – (C) – (A) – (D)
③ (C) – (A) – (B) – (D)
④ (C) – (B) – (A) – (D)
⑤ (C) – (D) – (B) – (A)

[06~07] 다음 글을 읽고 물음에 답하시오.

W: Do you want to ⓐ<u>achieve</u> your dream? Remember! Great people ⓑ<u>always stop</u> learning. The best way ⓒ<u>to learn</u> is by reading. Even ⓓ<u>when</u> you are busy, you have to find time to read. However, 네가 읽을 알맞은 책을 고르는 것도 중요하다. (choose, to, it's, that, books, read, important, you, the, right) Here is ⓔ<u>what</u> to choose the right books.

06 위 글에서 문맥상 또는 어법상 어색한 것을 <u>모두</u> 고르시오.

① ⓐ ② ⓑ ③ ⓒ ④ ⓓ ⑤ ⓔ

07 다음 밑줄 친 우리말에 맞게 주어진 단어를 바르게 배열하시오.

➡ _____

08 다음 대화의 빈칸에 들어갈 수 <u>없는</u> 것은?

> B: I have a singing contest tomorrow. I really want ⓐ_____ first place.
> G: I'll ⓑ_____ my fingers ⓒ_____ for you.
> B: What do you ⓓ_____ by "ⓑ_____ my fingers ⓒ_____"?
> G: ⓔ_____ I wish you good luck.
> B: Thank you.

① lucky ② It means
③ to win ④ mean
⑤ keep

[09~11] 다음 글을 읽고 물음에 답하시오.

> M: To achieve my dream, I went to many auditions, but I often failed. (A)_____, I never gave up. I took acting and dancing classes. (B)_____, I (C)_____ my goal. (D)절대 포기하지 않는 것이 중요합니다.

09 빈칸 (A)와 (B)에 들어갈 말로 알맞은 것끼리 짝지어진 것을 고르시오.

	(A)	(B)
①	However	Though
②	Therefore	Especially
③	However	Finally
④	Therefore	Especially
⑤	In addition	Finally

10 빈칸 (C)에 알맞은 말을 위의 대화에 나온 단어를 이용해서 채우시오.

➡ _____

11 밑줄 친 (D)의 우리말을 영작하시오.

➡ _____

12 다음 대화의 순서를 바르게 배열하시오.

> (A) It's important that you never give up.
> (B) Okay. I will not forget that.
> (C) It's hard to be a good dancer. What should I do?

➡ _____

13 다음 중 어법상 올바른 것은?

① Her parents were worried and asked her stop surfing.
② He also ordered us to tell the truth and never to lie.
③ Mr. Johnson told us shook hands after the game.
④ His parents encouraged him has an interest in art.
⑤ I didn't expect you understanding me at all.

14 다음 중 어법상 어색한 문장은?

① I love the watch which my uncle bought for me.
② Paul is the boy who I often play soccer with.
③ Is this the book you were talking about it at that time?
④ I went to the office in which Anne was working.
⑤ Do you know the man your mother is talking to?

15 다음 중 밑줄 친 that과 바꿔 쓸 수 있는 것은?

> The chair that I sat on was not comfortable.

① whom　② whose　③ who
④ which　⑤ what

[16~18] 다음 글을 읽고 물음에 답하시오.

It was New York City on April 15, 1947. Jackie Robinson, an African American, went on the field as second baseman for the Brooklyn Dodgers. People couldn't believe their eyes. He was the first ⓐ아프리카계 미국인 player to play on a Major League team. ⓑThat day, the color line (A) .

16 위 글의 빈칸 (A)에 들어갈 알맞은 말을 고르시오.

① was drawn　② happened
③ was broken　④ was made
⑤ appeared

17 위 글의 밑줄 친 ⓐ의 우리말을 두 단어로 쓰시오.

➡ _____

18 위 글의 밑줄 친 ⓑThat day가 가리키는 것을 본문에서 찾아 쓰시오.

➡ _____

[19~21] 다음 글을 읽고 물음에 답하시오.

Robinson ⓐfaced many difficulties. Although Robinson was a talented player and a gentle person, his teammates did not want ⓑto play with him. Every hotel ⓒturned the team down because Robinson was on the team. When he was at bat, people in the stands rudely shouted at him.

19 위 글의 밑줄 친 ⓐfaced와 바꿔 쓸 수 있는 말을 고르시오.

① expressed　② encountered
③ accepted　④ looked into
⑤ solved

20 위 글의 밑줄 친 ⓑto play와 to부정사의 용법이 다른 것을 고르시오.

① I think it wrong to tell a lie.
② I decided to go to Madrid.
③ He wanted to buy a new smartphone.
④ This water is not good to drink.
⑤ It is necessary to finish the work now.

21 위 글의 밑줄 친 ⓒturned the team down을 다음과 같이 바꿔 쓸 때 빈칸에 들어갈 알맞은 말을 쓰시오.

➡ _____ the team

[22~24] 다음 글을 읽고 물음에 답하시오.

Robinson's effort ⓐmoved his teammates. When people shouted at Robinson, one of his teammates walked up to Robinson and tapped him on the shoulder. "Do not listen to them.

You're doing fine," he said. His support helped Robinson to play harder. Finally, Robinson earned the respect of other players and fans.

Thanks to Robinson, the Dodgers won the National League Championship in 1947. The league recognized Robinson's excellence and presented him with the Rookie of the Year Award in the same year. After that season, other teams asked African American players to join them.

출제율 100%

22 위 글의 제목으로 가장 알맞은 것을 고르시오.

① How to Earn the Respect of Others
② Robinson's Effort Bore Fruit
③ How Did the Dodgers Win the National League Championship?
④ Who Won the Rookie of the Year Award in 1947?
⑤ Many Teams Wanted African American Players.

출제율 90%

23 위 글의 밑줄 친 ⓐmoved와 바꿔 쓸 수 있는 단어를 쓰시오.

➡ _____

출제율 95%

24 위 글의 내용과 일치하지 <u>않는</u> 것은?

① When people shouted at Robinson, one of his teammates encouraged him.
② The teammate's support helped Robinson to play harder.
③ At last, other players and fans came to respect Robinson.
④ Thanks to the Dodgers, Robinson won the National League Championship in 1947.
⑤ After that season, other teams gave African American players a chance to join them.

[25~26] 다음 글을 읽고 물음에 답하시오.

Robinson's uniform number was 42. ⓐ <u>Baseball players in Major League teams no longer wear the number 42 to honor him.</u> Every year, however, on April 15, every player wears the number ⓑ<u>that</u> Robinson wore. The day is called "Jackie Robinson Day."

출제율 90%

25 위 글의 밑줄 친 ⓐ를 바르게 바꿔 쓴 문장을 <u>모두</u> 고르시오.

① Baseball players in Major League teams no more wear the number 42 to honor him.
② Baseball players in Major League teams don't wear the number 42 no longer to honor him.
③ Baseball players in Major League teams don't wear the number 42 any more to honor him.
④ Baseball players in Major League teams don't wear the number 42 no more to honor him.
⑤ Baseball players in Major League teams don't wear the number 42 any longer to honor him.

출제율 90%

26 위 글의 밑줄 친 ⓑthat과 문법적 쓰임이 같은 것을 <u>모두</u> 고르시오.

① Those are the books <u>that</u> you lent me.
② I am so tired <u>that</u> I cannot go on.
③ This is the house <u>that</u> we live in.
④ It is the movie <u>that</u> I want to see.
⑤ The trouble is <u>that</u> we have no money.

01 밑줄 친 우리말을 주어진 단어를 이용하여 영작하시오.

> A: Two heads are better than one.
> B: What do you mean by "Two heads are better than one"?
> A: 함께 일하는 것이 혼자 일하는 것보다 낫다는 뜻이야. (alone, together, working)

➡ _____

_____

04 밑줄 친 우리말을 주어진 단어를 이용하여 영작하시오.

> A: Practice makes perfect.
> B: What do you mean by "Practice makes perfect"?
> A: 반복해서 무언가를 하면 배우게 된다는 뜻이야. (over, by, I, something, learn) (11 words)

➡ _____

[02~03] 다음 대화를 읽고 물음에 답하시오.

> G: Hey, Minho. ⓐDid you find the answer to the math problem?
> B: No. ⓑIt's too easy for me. ⓒI'm not good at math.
> G: ⓓLet me see. (A)네가 그 문제를 풀기 위해선 이 수학 공식을 이용하는 것이 중요해. (it's, that, rule, solve)
> B: Oh, I see. ⓔI'll use it.

02 ⓐ~ⓔ 중 흐름상 어색한 부분을 찾아 고치시오.

➡ _____

03 밑줄 친 우리말 (A)를 주어진 단어를 이용하여 영작하시오.

➡ _____

_____

05 다음 두 문장을 관계대명사를 사용하여 한 문장으로 바꾸시오.

(1) • The Korean dishes tasted yummy.
   • We had them last night.

➡ _____

_____

(2) • I have a dog.
   • I take a walk with it every night.

➡ _____

_____

06 다음 빈칸을 알맞은 말로 채워 비슷한 뜻을 갖는 문장으로 바꾸어 쓰시오.

(1) July told her daughter that she should not go out alone at night.

➡ July ordered her daughter _____

_____.

(2) We hope that Amy will win first prize at the singing contest.

➡ We expect Amy _____

_____.

Robinson faced ⓐmany difficulties. Although Robinson was a talented player and a gentle person, his teammates did not want to play with him. Every hotel turned the team (A)[down / up] because Robinson was on the team. When he was at bat, people in the stands (B)[rude / rudely] shouted at him.

Robinson thought to himself, 'I need to keep (C)[calm / calmly] and focus on baseball. I will try and become a player who people like. ⓑThen, next season, there will be more African American players in the league.' Robinson put all his time and energy into baseball. With practice, he became great at batting and base running.

07 위 글의 밑줄 친 ⓐmany difficulties의 예를 본문에서 찾아 우리말로 쓰시오.

➡ (1) _____

(2) _____

(3) _____

_____

08 위 글의 괄호 (A)~(C)에서 문맥이나 어법상 알맞은 낱말을 골라 쓰시오.

➡ (A)_____ (B)_____ (C)_____

09 위 글의 밑줄 친 ⓑThen이 가리키는 내용을 본문에서 찾아 다음 빈칸에 알맞게 쓰시오.

➡ If _____

Robinson's effort moved his teammates. When people shouted at Robinson, one of his teammates walked up to Robinson and tapped him on the shoulder. "Do not listen to them. You're doing fine," he said. ⓐHis support helped Robinson playing harder. Finally, Robinson earned the respect of other players and fans.

ⓑThanks to Robinson, the Dodgers won the National League Championship in 1947. The league recognized Robinson's excellence and presented him with the Rookie of the Year Award in the same year. After that season, other teams asked African American players to join them.

10 위 글의 밑줄 친 ⓐ에서 어법상 틀린 부분을 찾아 고치시오.

➡ _____

11 위 글을 읽고 1947년에 Robinson과 관련하여 일어난 일 두 가지를 우리말로 쓰시오.

➡ (1) _____

_____

(2) _____

_____

12 위 글의 밑줄 친 ⓑ를 다음과 같이 바꿔 쓸 때 빈칸에 들어갈 알맞은 말을 쓰시오

➡ Robinson's effort enabled the Dodgers _____ _____ the National League Championship in 1947.

01 다음 대화의 밑줄 친 우리말을 영작하시오. (주어진 어휘를 이용할 것)

> A: Are you studying now?
> B: Yes, I am.
> A: But you're listening to music now.
> B: Yes. 음악이 공부를 더 잘할 수 있게 도와준다고 생각해요. (study, help, better)_____
> A: I don't think so. 네가 공부할 때는 집중하는 것이 중요하다. (focus, when, it)
> _____
> B: Okay. 음악 소리를 줄일게요. (I'll, the music) _____

02 〈보기〉를 참고하여 다른 사람에게 기대하는 것을 expect를 이용하여 어법에 맞게 3 문장 이상 쓰시오.

> ── 보기 ──
> I expect my friend Sora to become a scientist.

(1) _____

(2) _____

(3) _____

03 다음 내용을 바탕으로 꿈을 이루기 위한 나의 다짐을 표현하는 글을 쓰시오.

> Q1 What is your dream? My dream is to become a chef.
> Q2 How can you achieve your dream?
> ☑ practicing hard, ☑ working well with others, ☑ managing my time well
> Q3 How can things from Q2 help you?
> ☑ practicing hard
> It will help me cook well and easily.
> ☑ working well with others
> It will make it easier to work at a restaurant.
> ☑ managing my time well
> It will help me make food in time to serve.

> **How I Will Achieve My Dream**
>
> I want to be a chef. There are three things that I need to do to achieve my dream. I need (A)_____, work well with others, and manage my time well. Practicing hard will help me (B)_____. Working well with others will make it easier (C)_____. Plus, I will always tell myself to manage my time well because it will help me (D)_____.

단원별 모의고사

01 다음 빈칸에 들어갈 말로 적절한 것을 고르시오.

> Why do you always shout _____ me?

① at ② by ③ of ④ from ⑤ to

02 빈칸 (A)와 (B)에 알맞은 것끼리 짝지어진 것을 고르시오.

> • As a doctor, she (A)_____ the respect of her patients.
> • If you have a dream, never (B)_____ up and pursue your passion.

	(A)	(B)
①	earned	give
②	accepted	give
③	earned	grow
④	accepted	grow
⑤	earned	count

03 우리말 해석을 보고 주어진 단어를 이용하여 빈칸을 채우시오.

(1) I'd like to have a strong will to overcome _____ like her. (나는 그녀처럼 어려움을 극복하는 강한 의지를 갖고 싶다.) (difficult)

(2) He got a prize for _____ in B-boy dancing. (그는 B-boy 댄스 부분에서 우수상을 탔다.) (excellent)

04 주어진 영영풀이의 어휘를 빈칸에 써 넣으시오.

> help and kindness that you give to someone who is having a difficult time

> I need his help and _____.

[05~06] 다음 대화를 읽고 물음에 답하시오.

> A: (A)Will is power.
> B: What do you mean by "Will is power"?
> A: (B)강한 의지로 꿈을 이룰 수 있다는 뜻이야.
> (mean, achieve, with)

05 위 대화의 밑줄 친 (A)'Will'과 같은 의미로 사용되지 <u>않은</u> 것을 고르시오.

① The decision was made of her free will.
② He will finish the report immediately.
③ The stronger will you have, the more you will learn.
④ Humans have the freedom of the will.
⑤ Where there is a will, there is a way.

06 밑줄 친 (B)의 우리말을 주어진 단어를 이용하여 영작하시오.

➡ _____

_____

07 주어진 대화 이후에 이어질 대화의 순서를 바르게 배열하시오.

> A: Please call me "The Wizard of Goyang."
> B: What do you mean by "The Wizard of Goyang"?

> (A) What is important to do to become an inventor?
> (B) I'm sure you'll make it.
> (C) I mean I want to be an inventor.
> (D) It's important that I think creatively.

➡ _____

08 ①~⑤ 중 다음 주어진 말이 들어갈 알맞은 곳은?

> Do you want to achieve your dream? Remember! (①) Great people never stop learning. (②) The best way to learn is by reading. (③) Even when you are busy, you have to find time to read. (④) Here is how to choose the right books. (⑤)

> However, it's important that you choose the right books to read.

①   ②   ③   ④   ⑤

[09~12] 다음 대화를 읽고 물음에 답하시오.

> Hana: You look (A)_____, Jiho. What's wrong?
>
> Jiho: I don't think I can achieve my dream.
>
> Amy: (B)_____ that?
>
> Jiho: I want to be an actor, but I always fail auditions. Maybe I have to give up.
>
> Amy: Do you know this actor?
>
> Jiho: Sure. He's a famous movie star.
>
> Amy: (C)He failed much than 100 auditions.
>
> Jiho: Really? Maybe I should keep trying. I will practice more for my next audition.
>
> Hana: That's right! It's important that you never (D)_____.

09 빈칸 (A)에 알맞은 말을 고르시오.

① sleepy   ② happy   ③ sad
④ lonely   ⑤ lucky

10 빈칸 (B)에 알맞은 말을 고르시오.

① When are you going to tell me about
② Why are you telling him
③ What do you mean by
④ How do you know
⑤ Where did you hear about

11 밑줄 친 (C)에서 어법상 또는 문맥상 어색한 것을 찾아 바르게 고쳐서 완벽한 문장으로 쓰시오.

➡ _____

12 빈칸 (D)에 들어갈 말을 위의 대화에서 찾아 쓰시오.

➡ _____

13 다음 두 문장을 관계대명사를 사용하여 한 문장으로 바꾸시오.

(1) • She is the girl.
    • I love her.
    ➡ _____

(2) • Have you ever fallen in love with a lady?
    • You haven't even talked to her.
    ➡ _____
      _____
      _____

14 주어진 동사를 어법에 맞게 빈칸에 쓰시오.

(1) Mom asked David _____ the dishes. (do)

(2) Her dad allowed her _____ to the concert. (go)

(3) It caused them _____ on their freedom. (insist)

(4) I warned him _____ late. (be)

15 다음 중 어법상 어색한 문장은?

① Please allow me to stay here one more day.

② Becky asked you to clean your room.

③ He encouraged her to reveal her true feelings.

④ Everything that I said was true.

⑤ I love the jacket whom Hana is wearing.

16 다음 중 어법상 적절한 것을 고르시오.

① I will always tell myself manage my time well because it will help me to make food in time to serve.

② This is because people wanted her to become a role model for young people.

③ I like the cake who my mother made for my birthday.

④ Ryan sells oranges who he grew himself.

⑤ I will invite the friends who I met them at the party last weekend.

17 다음 문장에서 어법상 어색한 것을 바르게 고치시오.

(1) The doctor advised her drank more water.

➡ _____

(2) The teacher encouraged her trying again.

➡ _____

(3) He was not sure whether he wished her stay or go.

➡ _____

(4) What is the name of the program who he is watching?

➡ _____

[18~20] 다음 글을 읽고 물음에 답하시오.

Robinson faced many difficulties. ⓐ Although Robinson was a talented player and a gentle person, his teammates did not want to play with him. Every hotel turned the team down because Robinson was on the team. When he was at bat, people in the stands rudely shouted ①at him.

Robinson thought to himself, 'I need to keep calm and focus ②on baseball. I will try and become a player who people like. Then, next season, there will be more African American players in the league.' Robinson put all his time and energy ③into baseball. ④With practice, he became great ⑤for ⓑbatting and base running.

18 위 글의 밑줄 친 ⓐ를 다음과 같이 바꿔 쓸 때 빈칸에 들어갈 알맞은 말을 쓰시오.

➡ Robinson was a talented player and a gentle person, _____ his teammates did not want to play with him.

19 위 글의 밑줄 친 전치사 ①~⑤ 중에서 쓰임이 옳지 않은 것을 찾아 고치시오.

➡ _____

20 아래 〈보기〉에서 위 글의 밑줄 친 ⓑbatting과 문법적 쓰임이 같은 것의 개수를 고르시오.

> ┌─── 보기 ───
> ① Kids are playing on the sand.
> ② I'm proud of being Korean.
> ③ Sally's hobby is talking about entertainers.
> ④ Being on time is very important in the business world.
> ⑤ Do you know the woman standing at the gate?

① 1개   ② 2개   ③ 3개   ④ 4개   ⑤ 5개

23 위 글을 읽고 대답할 수 없는 질문은?

① Who told Robinson not to listen to people who shouted at him?
② Could Robinson earn the respect of other players and fans?
③ When did the Dodgers win the National League Championship?
④ What award did Robinson win in 1947?
⑤ How many African American players joined other teams after that season?

[21~23] 다음 글을 읽고 물음에 답하시오.

Robinson's effort moved his teammates. When people shouted at Robinson, one of his teammates walked up to Robinson and tapped him on the shoulder. "Do not listen to them. You're doing fine," he said. His support helped Robinson to play harder. Finally, Robinson earned the respect of other players and fans.

Thanks to Robinson, the Dodgers won the National League Championship in 1947. The league recognized Robinson's excellence and presented him with the Rookie of the Year Award in the same year. After that season, other teams asked African American players to ⓐjoin them.

[24~25] 다음 글을 읽고 물음에 답하시오.

Robinson's uniform number was 42. Baseball players in Major League teams no longer wear the number 42 to honor him. Every year, however, on April 15, every player wears ⓐ the number (A) Robinson wore. The day is called "Jackie Robinson Day."

24 위 글의 빈칸 (A)에 들어갈 알맞은 말을 모두 고르시오.

① who   ② what
③ that   ④ whom
⑤ which

21 위 글의 밑줄 친 ⓐjoin과 바꿔 쓸 수 있는 어구들을 쓰시오.

➡ _____

22 위 글의 내용과 어울리는 속담을 고르시오.

① Sincerity moves heaven.
② Haste makes waste.
③ Don't cry over spilt milk.
④ Everybody's business is nobody's business.
⑤ Too many cooks spoil the broth.

25 위 글의 밑줄 친 ⓐthe number가 가리키는 것을 본문에서 찾아 쓰시오.

➡ _____

INSIGHT
on the textbook
교과서 파헤치기

Lesson **5** **Different Countries, Different Cultures**

Lesson **6** **Wonders of Nature**

Lesson **7** **Work on Your Dreams**

※ 다음 영어를 우리말로 쓰시오.

01 tourist _____

02 care _____

03 abroad _____

04 wave _____

05 excuse _____

06 tour _____

07 traditional _____

08 experience _____

09 historic _____

10 column _____

11 island _____

12 roll _____

13 capital _____

14 view _____

15 cheer _____

16 work _____

17 language _____

18 unique _____

19 match _____

20 shine _____

21 careful _____

22 prefer _____

23 helpful _____

24 stadium _____

25 movement _____

26 ceiling _____

27 slide _____

28 purple _____

29 Vietnamese _____

30 design _____

31 near _____

32 theater _____

33 dish _____

34 lizard _____

35 be full of _____

36 across from _____

37 be famous for _____

38 try on _____

39 be known for _____

40 put off _____

41 on foot _____

42 cheer for _____

43 far from _____

※ 다음 우리말을 영어로 쓰시오.

01	빛나다	_____
02	역사적인	_____
03	경험; 경험하다	_____
04	섬	_____
05	전통적인	_____
06	구르다, 굴리다	_____
07	돌봄, 보살핌	_____
08	미끄러지다, 활주하다	_____
09	근처에	_____
10	도움이 되는	_____
11	~을 용서하다	_____
12	보라색	_____
13	여행객	_____
14	조심하는, 주의 깊은	_____
15	흔들다; 파도	_____
16	여행, 관광하다	_____
17	전망, 경치	_____
18	환호하다; 환호	_____
19	음식, 접시	_____
20	경기, 시합	_____
21	수도	_____

22	설계하다	_____
23	동작	_____
24	천장	_____
25	도마뱀	_____
26	기둥	_____
27	선호하다	_____
28	일하다; 작품	_____
29	언어	_____
30	외국으로(에서)	_____
31	독특한	_____
32	극장	_____
33	정거장; 멈추다	_____
34	베트남어; 베트남의	_____
35	~의 맞은편에	_____
36	~으로 가득 차다	_____
37	~의 위에, ~의 꼭대기에	_____
38	~을 응원하다	_____
39	(시간, 날짜를) 미루다	_____
40	~로부터 멀리	_____
41	~로 알려져 있다	_____
42	입어 보다	_____
43	~로 유명하다	_____

※ 다음 영영풀이에 알맞은 단어를 <보기>에서 골라 쓴 후, 우리말 뜻을 쓰시오.

1 _____ : to produce bright light: _____

2 _____ : in or to a foreign country: _____

3 _____ : to move along smoothly: _____

4 _____ : the upper inside surface of a room: _____

5 _____ : a mixture of blue and red color: _____

6 _____ : the main city of a country where its government is: _____

7 _____ : a reptile that has a rough skin and a long tail: _____

8 _____ : relating to the language, people or culture of Spain: _____

9 _____ : to give a shout out of pleasure, praise, or support: _____

10 _____ : relating to the language, people or culture of Vietnam: _____

11 _____ : a building with a big screen or stage where many people watch movies or plays: _____

12 _____ : an outlook onto, or picture of a scene: _____

13 _____ : a spicy Indian food with meat and vegetables in sauce: _____

14 _____ : to like something or someone better than another: _____

15 _____ : a journey for pleasure during which various places of interest are visited: _____

16 _____ : to forgive someone for something bad that they have done, especially something that is not very serious: _____

보기			
theater	abroad	shine	prefer
view	cheer	tour	purple
curry	lizard	capital	Vietnamese
Spanish	ceiling	slide	excuse

※ 다음 우리말과 일치하도록 빈칸에 알맞은 말을 쓰시오.

Listen & Speak 1 A

1. **B:** _____ me. _____ the Picasso Museum _____ here?

   G: Yes. It's not _____ _____ here.

   B: _____ _____ I _____ _____?

   G: _____ _____ one block and _____ _____. It's _____

   _____ _____.

2. **B:** Sally, I _____ _____ _____ some candies for Halloween.

   _____ _____ I _____ them?

   G: You can _____ _____ _____ Wendy's Candy Shop.

   B: _____ _____ _____?

   G: _____ _____two _____ and turn right. It's _____

   _____ _____.

Listen & Speak 1 B

1. **A:** _____ _____. _____ _____ _____ the park?

   B: _____ _____ _____ _____ and turn left. It's _____

   _____ _____.

2. **A:** Excuse me. _____ _____ the school?

   B: Go _____ _____ _____ and turn left. _____ _____ _____

   your right. _____ _____ _____ the restaurant.

Listen & Talk 2 A

1. **B:** _____ really hot here in Thailand. _____ _____ to the

   night market and _____ some _____ _____ _____.

   G: Sounds _____. _____ do we _____ _____?

   B: We can go _____ _____ _____ _____ _____.

   _____ _____ _____ _____ _____?

   G: I _____ the bus.

2. **G:** _____ _____ this long dress _____?

   M: It is an Ao dai, a _____ of _____ _____ from Vietnam.

   G: Can I _____ _____ _____?

   M: Sure. _____ _____ _____ _____, the purple one or the

   _____ _____?

   G: The _____ _____, please.

해석

1. **B:** 실례할게. 이 근처에 피카소 박물관이 있니?
   G: 응, 여기서 멀지 않아.
   B: 그곳에 어떻게 가니?
   G: 한 블록 직진한 후 좌회전해. 오른편에 있어.

2. **B:** Sally야, 나는 할로윈에 필요한 사탕을 사야 해. 그것들을 어디서 살 수 있니?
   G: 넌 그것들을 Wendy's 사탕 가게에서 살 수 있어.
   B: 그곳은 어디에 있니?
   G: 두 블록 직진한 후 우회전해. 도서관 맞은편에 있어.

1. **A:** 실례합니다. 공원이 어디에 있나요?
   B: 두 블록 직진한 후 좌회전하세요. 오른편에 있어요.

2. **A:** 실례합니다. 학교가 어디에 있나요?
   B: 한 블록 직진한 후 좌회전하세요. 오른편에 있어요. 식당 맞은편이에요.

1. **B:** 태국은 정말 더워. 야시장에 가서 신선한 과일 주스를 마시자.
   G: 좋아. 우리는 그곳에 어떻게 가지?
   B: 우리는 걸어가거나 버스를 탈 수 있어. 어떤 것을 선호하니?
   G: 나는 버스를 선호해.

2. **G:** 이 긴 드레스를 뭐라고 부르나요?
   M: 그것은 베트남 전통 의상의 한 종류인 아오자이야.
   G: 제가 한 번 입어볼 수 있나요?
   M: 물론이지. 너는 보라색과 노란색 중 어떤 것을 선호하니?
   G: 보라색이요.

Listen & Talk 2 B

1. A: _____ _____ _____ _____, hamburgers or spaghetti?
   B: I _____ _____.

2. A: _____ _____ _____ _____ _____, curry _____ paella?
   B: I _____ _____.

Conversation A

M: _____ _____ London City Tour. Today, _____ _____ famous places in London. Can you _____ the London Eye? It's _____ _____ _____. It's a Ferris wheel _____ the River Thames. The _____ _____ the London Eye is _____. Many people visit it _____ _____.

Conversation B

Staff: _____ _____ I _____ you?
Hana's mom: We _____ _____ _____ _____ a good _____ _____ London.
Hana: Where is the _____ _____ _____ _____ _____ _____?
Staff: We have two _____ _____. The London Eye is a Ferris wheel and the Sky Garden is a glass garden _____ _____ _____ a tall building. _____ _____ you _____?
Hana's mom: Hmm... I _____ the London Eye.
Hana: _____, _____.
Staff: Good choice. You can _____ there _____ _____.
Hana's mom: _____ is the _____ _____?
Staff: Go _____ _____ _____ and _____ _____. It's _____ _____ _____. Have a good trip!
Hana: Wow, I _____ _____ all of London. Look! _____ _____ a big clock.
Hana's mom: _____ _____ that's Big Ben. _____ _____ _____ and _____ it _____?
Hana: That _____ great.

---

1. A: 햄버거와 스파게티 중 어느 것을 선호하니?
   B: 나는 햄버거를 선호해.

2. A: 카레와 파에야 중 어느 것을 선호하니?
   B: 나는 파에야를 선호해.

M: 런던 시티 투어에 오신 걸 환영합니다. 오늘 우리는 런던에서 유명한 장소들을 방문할 거예요. 런던 아이가 보이죠? 오른편에 있어요. 그것은 템스강 근처에 있는 대관람차예요. 런던 아이에서의 전망은 놀라워요. 매년 많은 사람들이 그곳을 방문해요.

직원: 무엇을 도와드릴까요?
엄마: 우리는 런던의 멋진 경치를 즐기고 싶어요.
하나: 가기에 가장 좋은 장소는 어디인가요?
직원: 두 곳이 있습니다. 런던 아이는 대관람차이고 스카이 가든은 높은 건물 꼭대기에 있는 유리 정원이에요. 어느 것을 선호하시나요?
엄마: 흠... 저는 런던 아이가 좋아요.
하나: 저도요.
직원: 좋은 선택이에요. 그곳에 버스로 갈 수 있답니다.
엄마: 가장 가까운 버스 정거장은 어디 있나요?
직원: 여기서 한 블록 직진한 후 오른쪽으로 도세요. 왼편에 있어요. 좋은 여행하세요!
하나: 와, 런던 전체를 다 볼 수 있어요. 보세요! 커다란 시계가 있어요.
엄마: 내 생각에 저것은 빅벤 같아. 우리 나중에 가서 그곳을 방문해 볼래?
하나: 좋아요.

Step2

※ 다음 우리말에 맞도록 대화를 영어로 쓰시오.

해석

Listen & Speak 1 A

1. B: _____
   G: _____
   B: _____
   G: _____

2. B: _____
   G: _____
   B: _____
   G: _____

Listen & Speak 1 B

1. A: _____
   B: _____

2. A: _____
   B: _____

Listen & Talk 2 A

1. B: _____
   _____
   G: _____
   B: _____
   G: _____

2. G: _____
   M: _____
   G: _____
   M: _____
   G: _____

1. B: 실례할게. 이 근처에 피카소 박물관이 있니?
   G: 응, 여기서 멀지 않아.
   B: 그곳에 어떻게 가니?
   G: 한 블록 직진한 후 좌회전해. 오른편에 있어.

2. B: Sally야, 나는 할로윈에 필요한 사탕을 사야 해. 그것들을 어디서 살 수 있니?
   G: 넌 그것들을 Wendy's 사탕 가게에서 살 수 있어.
   B: 그곳은 어디에 있니?
   G: 두 블록 직진한 후 우회전해. 도서관 맞은편에 있어.

1. A: 실례합니다. 공원이 어디에 있나요?
   B: 두 블록 직진한 후 좌회전하세요. 오른편에 있어요.

2. A: 실례합니다. 학교가 어디에 있나요?
   B: 한 블록 직진한 후 좌회전하세요. 오른편에 있어요. 식당 맞은편이에요.

1. B: 태국은 정말 더워. 야시장에 가서 신선한 과일 주스를 마시자.
   G: 좋아. 우리는 그곳에 어떻게 가지?
   B: 우리는 걸어가거나 버스를 탈 수 있어. 어떤 것을 선호하니?
   G: 나는 버스를 선호해.

2. G: 이 긴 드레스를 뭐라고 부르나요?
   M: 그것은 베트남 전통 의상의 한 종류인 아오자이야.
   G: 제가 한 번 입어볼 수 있나요?
   M: 물론이지. 너는 보라색과 노란색 중 어떤 것을 선호하니?
   G: 보라색이요.

Listen & Talk 2 B

1. A: _____

   B: _____

2. A: _____

   B: _____

Conversation A

M: _____

_____

_____

_____

Conversation B

Staff: _____

Hana's mom: _____

Hana: _____

Staff: _____

_____

Hana's mom: _____

Hana: _____

Staff: _____

Hana's mom: _____

Staff: _____

Hana: _____

Hana's mom: _____

Hana: _____

1. A: 햄버거와 스파게티 중 어느 것을 선호하니?
   B: 나는 햄버거를 선호해.

2. A: 카레와 파에야 중 어느 것을 선호하니?
   B: 나는 파에야를 선호해.

M: 런던 시티 투어에 오신 걸 환영합니다. 오늘 우리는 런던에서 유명한 장소들을 방문할 거예요. 런던 아이가 보이죠? 오른편에 있어요. 그것은 템스강 근처에 있는 대관람차예요. 런던 아이에서의 전망은 놀라워요. 매년 많은 사람들이 그곳을 방문해요.

직원: 무엇을 도와드릴까요?
엄마: 우리는 런던의 멋진 경치를 즐기고 싶어요.
하나: 가기에 가장 좋은 장소는 어디인가요?
직원: 두 곳이 있습니다. 런던 아이는 대관람차이고 스카이 가든은 높은 건물 꼭대기에 있는 유리 정원이에요. 어느 것을 선호하시나요?
엄마: 흠... 저는 런던 아이가 좋아요.
하나: 저도요.
직원: 좋은 선택이에요. 그곳에 버스로 갈 수 있답니다.
엄마: 가장 가까운 버스 정거장은 어디 있나요?
직원: 여기서 한 블록 직진한 후 오른쪽으로 도세요. 왼편에 있어요. 좋은 여행하세요!
하나: 와, 런던 전체를 다 볼 수 있어요. 보세요! 커다란 시계가 있어요.
엄마: 내 생각에 저것은 빅벤 같아. 우리 나중에 가서 그곳을 방문해 볼래?
하나: 좋아요.

※ 다음 우리말과 일치하도록 빈칸에 알맞은 것을 골라 쓰시오.

1 My _____ _____ in Spain – _____ Park Jinwoo

     A. Days   B. by   C. happy

2 My family _____ _____ Spain _____ summer.

     A. to   B. traveled   C. this

3 Spain is _____ _____ lots _____ tourists.

     A. of   B. by   C. loved

4 We _____ many _____ _____.

     A. places   B. visited   C. interesting

5 _____ _____ started _____ Madrid.

     A. in   B. trip   C. our

6 Madrid is the _____ and is _____ _____ soccer.

     A. for   B. capital   C. famous

7 We _____ to a stadium to _____ a soccer _____.

     A. match   B. watch   C. went

8 My sister and I were _____ because we could watch some of the _____ _____ _____ soccer player.

     A. most   B. excited   C. famous   D. world's

9 The stadium was _____ _____ soccer _____.

     A. of   B. full   C. fans

10 As we watched the match, we cheered _____ _____ songs, _____ our hands, and _____ with the other fans.

     A. waving   B. singing   C. shouting   D. by

11 _____ we _____ Madrid, we _____ to Seville.

     A. went   B. after   C. toured

12 _____ we _____ _____ the city, we saw many historic buildings.

     A. walked   B. while   C. around

13 We _____ a flamenco _____ and _____ a flamenco dance.

     A. museum   B. watched   C. visited

14 A woman _____ a red dress was _____ the flamenco _____ wonderful _____.

     A. with   B. in   C. movements   D. dancing

---

1 스페인에서의 행복한 날들 – 박진우

2 나의 가족은 이번 여름에 스페인을 여행했다.

3 스페인은 수많은 관광객들에게 사랑받는다.

4 우리는 여러 흥미로운 장소를 방문했다.

5 우리의 여행은 마드리드에서 시작했다.

6 마드리드는 수도이며 축구로 유명하다.

7 우리는 축구 경기를 보기 위해서 경기장으로 갔다.

8 나의 여동생과 나는 세계에서 가장 유명한 축구 선수 몇몇을 볼 수 있었기 때문에 신이 났다.

9 경기장은 축구 팬들로 가득 차 있었다.

10 우리는 경기를 보는 동안 노래를 부르고, 손을 흔들고, 다른 팬들과 함께 소리를 치며 응원을 했다.

11 마드리드를 여행하고 난 후, 우리는 세비야로 갔다.

12 우리는 도시를 걸어다니는 동안, 역사상 중요한 많은 건물들을 보았다.

13 우리는 플라멩코 박물관을 방문해서 플라멩코 춤을 보았다.

14 빨간 드레스를 입은 여자가 멋진 동작으로 플라멩코를 추고 있었다.

15 _____ dinner, we _____ paella.

   A. ate   B. for

16 It is a _____ Spanish _____ _____ rice, vegetables, meat, and seafood.

   A. with   B. dish   C. traditional

17 It _____ _____ fried rice _____ Korea.

   A. in   B. like   C. tasted

18 It was _____ delicious _____ we _____ enjoyed it.

   A. that   B. so   C. all

19 In Barcelona, we _____ a _____ _____ Park Guell and Sagrada Familia.

   A. of   B. tour   C. took

20 _____ were _____ _____ Antoni Gaudi.

   A. designed   B. both   C. by

21 In Park Guell, we saw some of Gaudi's _____ works _____ a _____ lizard.

   A. like   B. colorful   C. creative

22 _____ Park Guell, we _____ Sagrada Familia.

   A. visited   B. after

23 _____ on the building started in 1883 and is still _____ _____ today.

   A. going   B. work   C. on

24 I was _____ by _____ size and _____ design.

   A. unique   B. impressed   C. its

25 The _____ inside Sagrada Familia _____ _____ the night sky _____ bright stars.

   A. with   B. shone   C. ceiling   D. like

26 Its stone _____ _____ _____ big trees.

   A. like   B. stood   C. colomns

27 At Park Guell and Sagrada Familia I could _____ Gaudi's _____ and his _____ of _____.

   A. feel   B. nature   C. love   D. creativity

28 _____ in Spain was a _____ _____.

   A. experience   B. wonderful   C. traveling

29 _____ I was there, I learned _____ _____ about Spain.

   A. lot   B. while   C. a

30 I want to _____ the _____ _____.

   A. country   B. visit   C. again

---

15 저녁 식사로 우리는 파에야를 먹었다.

16 그것은 쌀과 채소, 고기, 해산물이 들어간 전통적인 스페인 요리이다.

17 그것은 한국의 볶음밥과 같은 맛이 났다.

18 너무 맛있어서 우리 모두는 그것을 즐겼다.

19 바르셀로나에서 우리는 구엘 공원과 사그라다 파밀리아를 둘러보았다.

20 두 곳 모두 Antoni Gaudi에 의해 설계되었다.

21 구엘 공원에서 우리는 형형색색의 도마뱀과 같은 몇몇 Gaudi의 창의적인 작품들을 보았다.

22 구엘 공원을 본 다음, 우리는 사그라다 파밀리아를 방문했다.

23 건물 공사는 1883년에 시작되었고 오늘날까지도 여전히 진행 중이다.

24 나는 건물의 크기와 독특한 디자인에 감명 받았다.

25 사그라다 파밀라아 안의 천장은 밝은 별이 있는 밤하늘처럼 빛났다.

26 돌기둥은 큰 나무처럼 서 있었다.

27 구엘 공원과 사그라다 파밀리아에서 나는 Gaudi의 창의성과 자연에 대한 사랑을 느낄 수 있었다.

28 스페인 여행은 훌륭한 경험이었다.

29 나는 그곳에서 스페인에 대해 많은 것을 배웠다.

30 나는 그 나라를 다시 방문하고 싶다.

※ 다음 우리말과 일치하도록 빈칸에 알맞은 말을 쓰시오.

1 My _____ _____ in Spain – _____ Park Jinwoo

2 My family _____ _____ _____ this summer.

3 Spain _____ _____ _____ _____ _____ tourists.

4 We _____ many _____ _____.

5 _____ _____ _____ _____ Madrid.

6 Madrid is the _____ and _____ _____ _____ soccer.

7 We went to a stadium _____ _____ a _____ _____.

8 My sister and I _____ _____ _____ we could watch some of _____ _____ _____ _____ _____ _____ _____.

9 The stadium _____ _____ soccer fans.

10 As we watched the match, we _____ _____ _____ songs, _____ our hands, and _____ with the _____ _____.

11 _____ we _____ Madrid, we _____ _____ Seville.

12 _____ we _____ _____ the city, we saw _____ _____ _____.

13 We _____ a flamenco museum and _____ a flamenco dance.

14 A woman _____ _____ _____ the flamenco _____ _____ _____.

1 스페인에서의 행복한 날들 – 박진우

2 나의 가족은 이번 여름에 스페인을 여행했다.

3 스페인은 수많은 관광객들에게 사랑받는다.

4 우리는 여러 흥미로운 장소를 방문했다.

5 우리의 여행은 마드리드에서 시작했다.

6 마드리드는 수도이며 축구로 유명하다.

7 우리는 축구 경기를 보기 위해서 경기장으로 갔다.

8 나의 여동생과 나는 세계에서 가장 유명한 축구 선수 몇몇을 볼 수 있었기 때문에 신이 났다.

9 경기장은 축구 팬들로 가득 차 있었다.

10 우리는 경기를 보는 동안 노래를 부르고, 손을 흔들고, 다른 팬들과 함께 소리를 치며 응원을 했다.

11 마드리드를 여행하고 난 후, 우리는 세비야로 갔다.

12 우리는 도시를 걸어다니는 동안, 역사상 중요한 많은 건물들을 보았다.

13 우리는 플라멩코 박물관을 방문해서 플라멩코 춤을 보았다.

14 빨간 드레스를 입은 여자가 멋진 동작으로 플라멩코를 추고 있었다.

15 _____ _____, we _____ paella.

16 It is a _____ _____ _____ _____ rice, vegetables, _____, and _____.

17 It _____ _____ _____ _____ in Korea.

18 It was _____ delicious _____ we _____ _____ it.

19 In Barcelona, we _____ _____ _____ _____ Park Guell and Sagrada Familia.

20 Both _____ _____ _____ Antoni Gaudi.

21 In Park Guell, we saw some of Gaudi's _____ _____ _____ a _____ _____.

22 _____ Park Guell, we _____ Sagrada Familia.

23 _____ _____ the building started in 1883 and _____ _____ _____ _____ today.

24 I _____ _____ _____ _____ _____ _____ and unique design.

25 The ceiling inside Sagrada Familia _____ _____ the night sky _____ _____ _____.

26 Its _____ _____ _____ _____ big trees.

27 At Park Guell and Sagrada Familia I _____ _____ Gaudi's _____ and _____ _____ _____ _____.

28 _____ in Spain was _____ _____ _____.

29 _____ I was there, I learned _____ _____ about Spain.

30 I want _____ _____ the country again.

15 저녁 식사로 우리는 파에야를 먹었다.

16 그것은 쌀과 채소, 고기, 해산물이 들어간 전통적인 스페인 요리이다.

17 그것은 한국의 볶음밥과 같은 맛이 났다.

18 너무 맛있어서 우리 모두는 그것을 즐겼다.

19 바르셀로나에서 우리는 구엘 공원과 사그라다 파밀리아를 둘러보았다.

20 두 곳 모두 Antoni Gaudi에 의해 설계되었다.

21 구엘 공원에서 우리는 형형색색의 도마뱀과 같은 몇몇 Gaudi의 창의적인 작품들을 보았다.

22 구엘 공원을 본 다음, 우리는 사그라다 파밀리아를 방문했다.

23 건물 공사는 1883년에 시작되었고 오늘날까지도 여전히 진행 중이다.

24 나는 건물의 크기와 독특한 디자인에 감명 받았다.

25 사그라다 파밀라아 안의 천장은 밝은 별이 있는 밤하늘처럼 빛났다.

26 돌기둥은 큰 나무처럼 서 있었다.

27 구엘 공원과 사그라다 파밀리아에서 나는 Gaudi의 창의성과 자연에 대한 사랑을 느낄 수 있었다.

28 스페인 여행은 훌륭한 경험이었다.

29 나는 그곳에서 스페인에 대해 많은 것을 배웠다.

30 나는 그 나라를 다시 방문하고 싶다.

※ 다음 문장을 우리말로 쓰시오.

1 My Happy Days in Spain — by Park Jinwoo
➡ _____

2 My family traveled to Spain this summer.
➡ _____

3 Spain is loved by lots of tourists.
➡ _____

4 We visited many interesting places.
➡ _____

5 Our trip started in Madrid.
➡ _____

6 Madrid is the capital and is famous for soccer.
➡ _____

7 We went to a stadium to watch a soccer match.
➡ _____

8 My sister and I were excited because we could watch some of the world's most famous soccer players.
➡ _____

9 The stadium was full of soccer fans.
➡ _____

10 As we watched the match, we cheered by singing songs, waving our hands, and shouting with the other fans.
➡ _____

11 After we toured Madrid, we went to Seville.
➡ _____

12 While we walked around the city, we saw many historic buildings.
➡ _____

13 We visited a flamenco museum and watched a flamenco dance.
➡ _____

14 A woman in a red dress was dancing the flamenco with wonderful movements.
➡ _____

15 For dinner, we ate paella.
➡ _____

16 It is a traditional Spanish dish with rice, vegetables, meat, and seafood.
➡ _____

17 It tasted like fried rice in Korea.

➡ _____

18 It was so delicious that we all enjoyed it.

➡ _____

19 In Barcelona, we took a tour of Park Guell and Sagrada Familia.

➡ _____

20 Both were designed by Antoni Gaudi.

➡ _____

21 In Park Guell, we saw some of Gaudi's creative works like a colorful lizard.

➡ _____

22 After Park Guell, we visited Sagrada Familia.

➡ _____

23 Work on the building started in 1883 and is still going on today.

➡ _____

24 I was impressed by its size and unique design.

➡ _____

25 The ceiling inside Sagrada Familia shone like the night sky with bright stars.

➡ _____

26 Its stone columns stood like big trees.

➡ _____

27 At Park Guell and Sagrada Familia I could feel Gaudi's creativity and his love of nature.

➡ _____

28 Traveling in Spain was a wonderful experience.

➡ _____

29 While I was there, I learned a lot about Spain.

➡ _____

30 I want to visit the country again.

➡ _____

※ 다음 괄호 안의 단어들을 우리말에 맞도록 바르게 배열하시오.

1 (happy / my / in / Days / by / – / Spain / Jinwoo / Park)
➡ _____

2 (family / my / to / traveled / Spain / summer. / this)
➡ _____

3 (is / Spain / by / loved / lots / tourists. / of)
➡ _____

4 (visited / we / interesting / many / places.)
➡ _____

5 (trip / our / Madrid. / in / started)
➡ _____

6 (is / Madrid / capital / the / is / and / soccer. / for / famous)
➡ _____

7 (went / we / a / to / stadium / watch / to / match. / soccer / a)
➡ _____

8 (sister / my / and / were / I / excited / we / because / could / some / watch / of / world's / the / famous / most / / players. / soccer)
➡ _____
_____

9 (stadium / the / full / was / fans. / soccer / of)
➡ _____

10 (we / as / the / watched / match, / cheered / we / singing / by / songs, / waving / hands, / our / and / with / shouting / the / fans. / other)
➡ _____
_____

11 (we / after / Madrid, / toured / went / we / Seville. / to)
➡ _____

12 (we / while / walked / the / around / city, / saw / we / many / buildings. / historic)
➡ _____

13 (visited / we / flamenco / a / museum / and / a / watched / dance. / flamenco)
➡ _____

14 (woman / a / in / red / a / dress / dancing / was / flamenco / the / movements. / wonderful / with)
➡ _____

1 스페인에서의 행복한 날들 – 박진우

2 나의 가족은 이번 여름에 스페인을 여행했다.

3 스페인은 수많은 관광객들에게 사랑받는다.

4 우리는 여러 흥미로운 장소를 방문했다.

5 우리의 여행은 마드리드에서 시작했다.

6 마드리드는 수도이며 축구로 유명하다.

7 우리는 축구 경기를 보기 위해서 경기장으로 갔다.

8 나의 여동생과 나는 세계에서 가장 유명한 축구 선수 몇몇을 볼 수 있었기 때문에 신이 났다.

9 경기장은 축구 팬들로 가득 차 있었다.

10 우리는 경기를 보는 동안 노래를 부르고, 손을 흔들고, 다른 팬들과 함께 소리를 치며 응원을 했다.

11 마드리드를 여행하고 난 후, 우리는 세비야로 갔다.

12 우리는 도시를 걸어다니는 동안, 역사상 중요한 많은 건물들을 보았다.

13 우리는 플라멩코 박물관을 방문해서 플라멩코 춤을 보았다.

14 빨간 드레스를 입은 여자가 멋진 동작으로 플라멩코를 추고 있었다.

15 (dinner, / for / paella. / ate / we)

➡ _____

16 (is / it / Spanish / traditional / a / with / dish / rice, / meat, / vegetables, / seafood. / and)

➡ _____

17 (tasted / it / fried / like / Korea. / in / rice)

➡ _____

18 (was / it / delicious / so / that / all / we / it. / enjoyed)

➡ _____

19 (Barcelona, / in / took / we / tour / a / Park / of / and / Guell / Familia. / Sagrada)

➡ _____

20 (were / both / by / designed / Gaudi. / Antoni)

➡ _____

21 (Guell, / Park / in / saw / we / of / some / creative / Gaudi's / works / a / like / lizard. / colorful)

➡ _____

22 (Park / after / Guell, / visited / we / Familia. / Sagrada)

➡ _____

23 (on / work / building / the / in / started / 1883 / is / and / going / still / today. / on)

➡ _____

24 (was / I / by / impressed / size / its / and / design. / unique)

➡ _____

25 (ceiling / the / Sagrada / inside / Familia / like / shone / night / the / sky / stars. / bright / with)

➡ _____

26 (stone / its / stood / columns / trees. / big / like)

➡ _____

27 (Park / at / and / Guell / Familia / Sagrada / could / I / Gaudi's / feel / creativity / his / and / of / nature. / love)

➡ _____

28 (in / traveling / Spain / was / experiece. / wonderful / a)

➡ _____

29 (I / while / there, / was / learned / I / about / a / Spain. / lot)

➡ _____

30 (I / to / want / the / visit / again. / country)

➡ _____

15 저녁 식사로 우리는 파에야를 먹었다.

16 그것은 쌀과 채소, 고기, 해산물이 들어간 전통적인 스페인 요리이다.

17 그것은 한국의 볶음밥과 같은 맛이 났다.

18 너무 맛있어서 우리 모두는 그것을 즐겼다.

19 바르셀로나에서 우리는 구엘 공원과 사그라다 파밀리아를 둘러보았다.

20 두 곳 모두 Antoni Gaudi에 의해 설계되었다.

21 구엘 공원에서 우리는 형형색색의 도마뱀과 같은 몇몇 Gaudi의 창의적인 작품들을 보았다.

22 구엘 공원을 본 다음, 우리는 사그라다 파밀리아를 방문했다.

23 건물 공사는 1883년에 시작되었고 오늘날까지도 여전히 진행 중이다.

24 나는 건물의 크기와 독특한 디자인에 감명 받았다.

25 사그라다 파밀리아 안의 천장은 밝은 별이 있는 밤하늘처럼 빛났다.

26 돌기둥은 큰 나무처럼 서 있었다.

27 구엘 공원과 사그라다 파밀리아에서 나는 Gaudi의 창의성과 자연에 대한 사랑을 느낄 수 있었다.

28 스페인 여행은 훌륭한 경험이었다.

29 나는 그곳에서 스페인에 대해 많은 것을 배웠다.

30 나는 그 나라를 다시 방문하고 싶다.

※ 다음 우리말을 영어로 쓰시오.

1 스페인에서의 행복한 날들 – 박진우

➡ _____

2 나의 가족은 이번 여름에 스페인을 여행했다.

➡ _____

3 스페인은 수많은 관광객들에게 사랑받는다.

➡ _____

4 우리는 여러 흥미로운 장소를 방문했다.

➡ _____

5 우리의 여행은 마드리드에서 시작했다.

➡ _____

6 마드리드는 수도이며 축구로 유명하다.

➡ _____

7 우리는 축구 경기를 보기 위해서 경기장으로 갔다.

➡ _____

8 나의 여동생과 나는 세계에서 가장 유명한 축구 선수 몇몇을 볼 수 있었기 때문에 신이 났다.

➡ _____

9 경기장은 축구 팬들로 가득 차 있었다.

➡ _____

10 우리는 경기를 보는 동안 노래를 부르고, 손을 흔들고, 다른 팬들과 함께 소리를 치며 응원을 했다.

➡ _____

11 마드리드를 여행하고 난 후, 우리는 세비야로 갔다.

➡ _____

12 우리는 도시를 걸어다니는 동안, 역사상 중요한 많은 건물들을 보았다.

➡ _____

13 우리는 플라멩코 박물관을 방문해서 플라멩코 춤을 보았다.

➡ _____

14 빨간 드레스를 입은 여자가 멋진 동작으로 플라멩코를 추고 있었다.

➡ _____

15 저녁 식사로 우리는 파에야를 먹었다.

➡ _____

16 그것은 쌀과 채소, 고기, 해산물이 들어간 전통적인 스페인 요리이다.

➡ _____

17 그것은 한국의 볶음밥과 같은 맛이 났다.

➡ _____

18 너무 맛있어서 우리 모두는 그것을 즐겼다.

➡ _____

19 바르셀로나에서 우리는 구엘 공원과 사그라다 파밀리아를 둘러보았다.

➡ _____

20 두 곳 모두 Antoni Gaudi에 의해 설계되었다.

➡ _____

21 구엘 공원에서 우리는 형형색색의 도마뱀과 같은 몇몇 Gaudi의 창의적인 작품들을 보았다.

➡ _____

22 구엘 공원을 본 다음, 우리는 사그라다 파밀리아를 방문했다.

➡ _____

23 건물 공사는 1883년에 시작되었고 오늘날까지도 여전히 진행 중이다.

➡ _____

24 나는 건물의 크기와 독특한 디자인에 감명 받았다.

➡ _____

25 사그라다 파밀리아 안의 천장은 밝은 별이 있는 밤하늘처럼 빛났다.

➡ _____

26 돌기둥은 큰 나무처럼 서 있었다.

➡ _____

27 구엘 공원과 사그라다 파밀리아에서 나는 Gaudi의 창의성과 자연에 대한 사랑을 느낄 수 있었다.

➡ _____

28 스페인 여행은 훌륭한 경험이었다.

➡ _____

29 나는 그곳에서 스페인에 대해 많은 것을 배웠다.

➡ _____

30 나는 그 나라를 다시 방문하고 싶다.

➡ _____

※ 다음 우리말과 일치하도록 빈칸에 알맞은 말을 쓰시오.

Enjoy Writing

1. _____ _____ do you _____ _____ Vietnam?

2. The _____ _____ _____ is Hanoi. Vietnamese _____ _____ there.

3. Pho and banh mi _____ _____ _____ in Vietnam.

4. _____ _____ _____ _____ tourists visit Halong Bay and Nha Trang.

5. Halong Bay has 1,969 islands and Nha Trang _____ _____ _____ _____ its beautiful beaches.

6. Vietnam is _____ _____ _____ you _____ come someday.

1. 당신은 베트남에 대해서 얼마나 많이 알고 있나요?
2. 베트남의 수도는 하노이입니다. 그곳에서는 베트남어가 사용됩니다.
3. 베트남에서는 pho(퍼, 베트남 쌀국수)와 banh mi(반미, 바게트 빵으로 만든 샌드위치)가 인기 있는 요리입니다.
4. 매년 많은 관광객들이 하롱베이와 나트랑을 방문합니다.
5. 하롱베이는 1,969개의 섬을 가지고 있고 나트랑은 아름다운 해변으로 잘 알려져 있습니다.
6. 베트남은 너무 아름다워서 당신은 언젠가 꼭 오셔야 합니다.

Project Step 3

1. My group _____ Hong Kong _____ _____ _____ _____.

2. Hong Kong _____ _____ _____ many people _____ want _____ _____ fun activities.

3. We'll _____ _____ _____ _____ Mong Kok Market, Victoria Peak, and Ocean Park.

1. 우리 모둠은 여행 장소로 홍콩을 선택했다.
2. 홍콩은 재밌는 활동을 하고 싶어 하는 많은 사람들에게 사랑받는다.
3. 우리는 몽콕 시장, 빅토리아 피크 그리고 오션 파크에서 멋진 경험을 할 것이다.

Wrap Up

1. I _____ _____ _____ a book.

2. The _____ _____ _____ _____ is *The Old Man and the Sea*.

3. It _____ _____ _____ Ernest Hemingway.

4. The story was _____ great _____ I read it _____ _____.

1. 나는 어떤 책에 감동을 받았다.
2. 그 책의 제목은 '노인과 바다'이다.
3. 그것은 Ernest Hemingway에 의해 씌여졌다.
4. 그 이야기는 너무도 대단해서 나는 그것을 여러 번 읽었다.

※ 다음 우리말을 영어로 쓰시오.

Enjoy Writing

1. 당신은 베트남에 대해서 얼마나 많이 알고 있나요?

➡ _____

2. 베트남의 수도는 하노이입니다. 그곳에서는 베트남어가 사용됩니다.

➡ _____

3. 베트남에서는 pho(퍼, 베트남 쌀국수)와 banh mi(반미, 바게트 빵으로 만든 샌드위치)가 인기 있는 요리입니다.

➡ _____

4. 매년 많은 관광객들이 하롱베이와 나트랑을 방문합니다.

➡ _____

5. 하롱베이는 1,969개의 섬을 가지고 있고 나트랑은 아름다운 해변으로 잘 알려져 있습니다.

➡ _____

6. 베트남은 너무 아름다워서 당신은 언젠가 꼭 오셔야 합니다.

➡ _____

Project Step 3

1. 우리 모둠은 여행 장소로 홍콩을 선택했다.

➡ _____

2. 홍콩은 재밌는 활동을 하고 싶어 하는 많은 사람들에게 사랑받는다.

➡ _____

3. 우리는 몽콕 시장, 빅토리아 피크 그리고 오션 파크에서 멋진 경험을 할 것이다.

➡ _____

Wrap Up

1. 나는 어떤 책에 감동을 받았다.

➡ _____

2. 그 책의 제목은 '노인과 바다'이다.

➡ _____

3. 그것은 Ernest Hemingway에 의해 씌여졌다.

➡ _____

4. 그 이야기는 너무도 대단해서 나는 그것을 여러 번 읽었다.

➡ _____

※ 다음 영어를 우리말로 쓰시오.

01 bloom _____

02 reed _____

03 damage _____

04 greet _____

05 cliff _____

06 oxygen _____

07 plain _____

08 crab _____

09 trash _____

10 creature _____

11 truth _____

12 remove _____

13 surface _____

14 environment _____

15 various _____

16 appear _____

17 reason _____

18 reduce _____

19 flood _____

20 produce _____

21 generous _____

22 regularly _____

23 protect _____

24 mess _____

25 lung _____

26 stain _____

27 information _____

28 feed _____

29 muddy _____

30 necessary _____

31 occur _____

32 provide _____

33 tide _____

34 wonder _____

35 work out _____

36 such as _____

37 be good for _____

38 not only A but also B _____

39 by the way _____

40 a large number of _____

41 take off _____

42 be famous for _____

43 make a living _____

※ 다음 우리말을 영어로 쓰시오.

01 동굴	
02 나타나다	
03 피해	
04 절벽	
05 환경	
06 제거하다	
07 (꽃이) 피다	
08 ~을 여과하다	
09 각종의, 다양한	
10 표면	
11 생물, 생명체	
12 흐르다	
13 규칙적으로	
14 관대한	
15 이유	
16 홍수	
17 쓰레기	
18 생산하다, 만들다	
19 보호하다	
20 놀라움, 경이	
21 산소	

22 먹이를 주다, 먹이다	
23 진실, 사실	
24 얼룩	
25 줄이다	
26 인사하다	
27 폐	
28 엉망진창	
29 갈대	
30 진흙투성이인, 진흙의	
31 필요한	
32 일어나다, 발생하다	
33 제공하다, 주다	
34 크게, 꽤	
35 그런데	
36 생계를 유지하다	
37 ~로 유명하다	
38 ~와 같은	
39 ~에 좋다, 유익하다	
40 다수의, 많은 수의	
41 운동하다	
42 (옷 등을) 벗다, 벗기다	
43 A뿐만 아니라 B도	

※ 다음 영영풀이에 알맞은 단어를 <보기>에서 골라 쓴 후, 우리말 뜻을 쓰시오.

1 _____ : very soft wet earth: _____

2 _____ : a large flat area of land: _____

3 _____ : begin to be seen suddenly: _____

4 _____ : facts about something: _____

5 _____ : the outer texture of anything: _____

6 _____ : a high steep rock, especially one facing the sea: _____

7 _____ : the surface of the earth that is not water: _____

8 _____ : all living things except plants: _____

9 _____ : willing to give something more than enough: _____

10 _____ : one of the two organs which you use to breathe: _____

11 _____ : covered with mud, or full of mud: _____

12 _____ : a tall thin plant like grass with a hollow stem that grows in or near water
: _____

13 _____ : the periodic rise and fall of the waters of the ocean: _____

14 _____ : to pass something through a filter to remove particular things contained
in it: _____

15 _____ : to move steadily without any interrupts, used to describe liquids, gas,
electrical currents, etc.: _____

16 _____ : to give someone something that they need or want or make it available
to them: _____

보기			
provide	muddy	surface	creature
cliff	flow	reed	lung
appear	information	filter	generous
plain	tide	mud	land

※ 다음 우리말과 일치하도록 빈칸에 알맞은 말을 쓰시오.

 해석

Listen & Speak 1 A

1. G: I _____ _____ _____ _____ _____ the summer vacation.

   B: I _____ a _____ to Kenya and saw many animals on the plains.

   G: Wonderful! _____ the way, what are the _____?

   B: They are large areas of _____ _____.

   G: I see.

2. G: _____ _____ that lake! It's really _____.

   B: It's not a _____. It's a river.

   G: Is it? I _____ _____ a river and a lake _____ _____.

   B: A river is _____ _____ _____ _____ water.

   _____ a lake, a river _____ _____ the ocean.

   G: I _____ _____.

1. G: 나는 네가 여름 방학 동안에 무엇을 했는지 궁금해.
   B: 나는 케냐로 여행을 가서 평원에서 많은 동물들을 봤어.
   G: 멋지구나! 그런데 평원이 무엇이니?
   B: 그곳은 넓고 평평한 땅이야.
   G: 그렇구나.

2. G: 저 호수를 봐. 정말 아름다워.
   B: 그것은 호수가 아니야. 그것은 강이야.
   G: 그래? 나는 강과 호수가 어떻게 다른지 궁금해.
   B: 강은 민물로 된 긴 물줄기야. 호수와 다르게 강은 바다로 흘러.
   G: 알겠어.

Listen & Speak 1 B

1. A: I wonder _____ _____ _____ _____.

   B: It is a very _____ area of land.

2. A: _____ _____ _____ a _____ is.

   B: It is a _____, _____ area of _____.

1. A: 나는 산이 무엇인지 궁금해.
   B: 그곳은 아주 높은 지대의 땅이야.

2. A: 나는 평원이 무엇인지 궁금해.
   B: 그곳은 넓고 평평한 지대의 땅이야.

Listen & Talk 2 A

1. B: Do you know _____ _____ _____ _____ on the Earth?

   G: The answer is four, _____ _____?

   B: No. _____ _____ five oceans on the Earth. They _____ _____ of the Earth.

   G: _____ _____ of the Earth do they _____?

   B: I _____ the oceans _____ _____ 70% of the Earth's _____.

2. G: I _____ the Amazon _____ _____ _____ _____ the _____ of the Earth.

   B: _____? Why?

   G: _____ it _____ about 20% of the Earth's _____.

   B: Wow! That's _____ _____.

1. B: 너는 지구에 몇 개의 바다가 있는지 아니?
   G: 정답은 네 개야, 그렇지 않니?
   B: 아니야. 지구에는 다섯 개의 바다가 있어. 그곳은 지구의 대부분을 차지하고 있어.
   G: 그곳이 지구의 얼마를 차지하고 있니?
   B: 나는 바다가 지구 표면의 70%를 차지한다고 들었어.

2. G: 나는 아마존 열대 우림이 지구의 허파라고 불린다고 들었어.
   B: 허파? 왜?
   G: 왜냐하면 그곳은 지구 산소의 약 20%를 생산하기 때문이야.
   B: 우와! 엄청나구나.

Listen & Talk 2 B

1. **A:** I _____ to go to Jecheon.

   B: Why?

   A: I _____ there are beautiful _____ in Jecheon.

2. **A:** I _____ _____ _____ _____ Danyang.

   B: Why?

   A: I heard there _____ _____ _____ in Danyang.

1. A: 나는 제천에 가고 싶어.
   B: 왜?
   A: 나는 제천에 아름다운 호수들이 있다고 들었어.

2. A: 나는 단양에 가고 싶어.
   B: 왜?
   A: 나는 단양에 유명한 동굴들이 있다고 들었어.

Conversation A

M: Guess _____ this is! It's not a tree. It is a _____ that _____ _____ tall _____. _____ fall, it _____ yellow. It grows well in _____ lands. I _____ Suncheon Bay _____ _____ _____ this plant.

M: 이것이 무엇인지 추측해 봐! 그것은 나무가 아니야. 그것은 키가 큰 풀처럼 보이는 식물이야. 가을에는 노란색으로 변해. 그것은 습지에서 잘 자라. 나는 순천만이 이 식물로 유명하다고 들었어.

Conversation B

Dad: Do you want to see an _____ _____?

Karl & Sister: Sure!

Dad: Then _____ _____ _____ the train.

Sister: _____ _____ the yellow plants! I _____ _____ _____ _____.

Dad: They are _____. Suncheon Bay has beautiful _____ fields.

Karl: Wow, the reeds are even _____ _____ you, Dad.

Sister: They really are. _____ me _____ a picture _____ you.

Karl: This _____ _____ is very large.

Dad: Yes. I _____ it is _____ _____ _____ in Korea.

Karl: _____ _____ the sky. It's _____ red.

Sister: Yes, it's _____.

아빠: 너희들 멋진 곳을 보고 싶니?
Karl, 여동생: 물론이죠!
아빠: 그러면 기차를 타자.
여동생: 저 노란색 식물들을 봐요! 저게 무엇인지 궁금해요.
아빠: 그건 갈대야. 순천만에는 아름다운 갈대밭이 있어.
Karl: 와, 갈대가 아빠보다 키가 더 커요.
여동생: 진짜 그러네요. 제가 사진을 찍어 드릴게요.
Karl: 이 갈대밭은 정말 넓네요.
아빠: 그래. 나는 이곳이 한국에서 가장 큰 갈대밭이라고 들었어.
Karl: 하늘을 보세요. 빨갛게 변하고 있어요.
여동생: 그러네, 아름다워.

Communication Task Step 1

A: What _____ do you have?

B: I have Moraine Lake. It's in Canada.

A: What is _____ _____ the place?

B: The color of the water _____ _____ _____.

A: 너는 어떤 장소를 가지고 있니?
B: 나는 모레인호를 갖고 있어. 그곳은 캐나다에 있어.
A: 그곳은 어떤 것이 특별하니?
B: 물의 색이 연한 파랑색이야.

※ 다음 우리말에 맞도록 대화를 영어로 쓰시오.

Listen & Speak 1 A

1. G: _____
   B: _____
   G: _____
   B: _____
   G: _____

2. G: _____
   B: _____
   G: _____
   B: _____
   _____
   G: _____

1. G: 나는 네가 여름 방학 동안에 무엇을 했는지 궁금해.
   B: 나는 케냐로 여행을 가서 평원에서 많은 동물들을 봤어.
   G: 멋지구나! 그런데 평원이 무엇이니?
   B: 그곳은 넓고 평평한 땅이야.
   G: 그렇구나.

2. G: 저 호수를 봐. 정말 아름다워.
   B: 그것은 호수가 아니야. 그것은 강이야.
   G: 그래? 나는 강과 호수가 어떻게 다른지 궁금해.
   B: 강은 민물로 된 긴 물줄기야. 호수와 다르게 강은 바다로 흘러.
   G: 알겠어.

Listen & Speak 1 B

1. A: _____
   B: _____

2. A: _____
   B: _____

1. A: 나는 산이 무엇인지 궁금해.
   B: 그곳은 아주 높은 지대의 땅이야.

2. A: 나는 평원이 무엇인지 궁금해.
   B: 그곳은 넓고 평평한 지대의 땅이야.

Listen & Talk 2 A

1. B: _____
   G: _____
   B: _____
   G: _____
   B: _____

2. G: _____
   B: _____
   G: _____
   B: _____

1. B: 너는 지구에 몇 개의 바다가 있는지 아니?
   G: 정답은 네 개야, 그렇지 않니?
   B: 아니야. 지구에는 다섯 개의 바다가 있어. 그곳은 지구의 대부분을 차지하고 있어.
   G: 그곳이 지구의 얼마를 차지하고 있니?
   B: 나는 바다가 지구 표면의 70%를 차지한다고 들었어.

2. G: 나는 아마존 열대 우림이 지구의 허파라고 불린다고 들었어.
   B: 허파? 왜?
   G: 왜냐하면 그곳은 지구 산소의 약 20%를 생산하기 때문이야.
   B: 우와! 엄청나구나.

Listen & Talk 2 B

1. A: _____

   B: _____

   A: _____

2. A: _____

   B: _____

   A: _____

Conversation A

M: _____

_____

_____

Conversation B

Dad: _____

Karl & Sister: _____

Dad: _____

Sister: _____

Dad: _____

Karl: _____

Sister: _____

Karl: _____

Dad: _____

Karl: _____

Sister: _____

Communication Task Step 1

A: _____

B: _____

A: _____

B: _____

1. A: 나는 제천에 가고 싶어.
   B: 왜?
   A: 나는 제천에 아름다운 호수들이 있다고 들었어.

2. A: 나는 단양에 가고 싶어.
   B: 왜?
   A: 나는 단양에 유명한 동굴들이 있다고 들었어.

M: 이것이 무엇인지 추측해 봐! 그것은 나무가 아니야. 그것은 키가 큰 풀처럼 보이는 식물이야. 가을에는 노란색으로 변해. 그것은 습지에서 잘 자라. 나는 순천만이 이 식물로 유명하다고 들었어.

아빠: 너희들 멋진 곳을 보고 싶니?
Karl, 여동생: 물론이죠!
아빠: 그러면 기차를 타자.
여동생: 저 노란색 식물들을 봐요! 저게 무엇인지 궁금해요.
아빠: 그건 갈대야. 순천만에는 아름다운 갈대밭이 있어.
Karl: 와, 갈대가 아빠보다 키가 더 커요.
여동생: 진짜 그러네요. 제가 사진을 찍어 드릴게요.
Karl: 이 갈대밭은 정말 넓네요.
아빠: 그래. 나는 이곳이 한국에서 가장 큰 갈대밭이라고 들었어.
Karl: 하늘을 보세요. 빨갛게 변하고 있어요.
여동생: 그러네. 아름다워.

A: 너는 어떤 장소를 가지고 있니?
B: 나는 모레인호를 갖고 있어. 그곳은 캐나다에 있어.
A: 그곳은 어떤 것이 특별하니?
B: 물의 색이 연한 파랑색이야.

※ 다음 우리말과 일치하도록 빈칸에 알맞은 것을 골라 쓰시오.

1 Mudflats, _____ _____
A. Gift   B. Nature's

2 Mudflats are large _____ of _____ land at the _____.
A. muddy   B. areas   C. seaside

3 They _____ and disappear _____ every _____.
A. tide   B. appear   C. with

4 During low tides, they _____ _____, and during high _____, they are _____ by the sea.
A. covered   B. up   C. tides   D. show

5 Mudflats help sea _____, people, and the Earth _____ many _____.
A. ways   B. creatures   C. in

6 It is _____ to understand the _____ of _____.
A. roles   B. important   C. mudflats

7 _____ see _____ they _____.
A. what   B. let's   C. do

8 Mudflats are _____ to a lot of _____ things at the _____.
A. living   B. home   C. seaside

9 _____ _____ very small living things like plankton _____ _____ crabs and fish live there.
A. but   B. not   C. also   D. only

10 Mudflats _____ various _____ of food _____ them.
A. types   B. for   C. provide

11 _____, many birds _____ food _____.
A. there   B. also   C. eat

12 Crab: Mudflats are _____ home _____.
A. home   B. sweet   C. my

13 Mudflats are _____ _____ people, _____.
A. too   B. for   C. good

14 People who live near _____ areas _____ a _____ by catching fish and other sea animals _____.
A. make   B. nearby   C. mudflat   D. living

15 _____ _____ mudflats, people can get _____ seafood.
A. fresh   B. thanks   C. to

---

1 갯벌, 자연의 선물

2 갯벌은 바닷가의 진흙이 있는 넓은 지역이다.

3 갯벌은 조수와 함께 나타나고 사라진다.

4 썰물일 때 갯벌이 드러나고, 밀물일 때 바다에 덮인다.

5 갯벌은 바다 생물과 사람, 지구를 많은 방면에서 돕는다.

6 갯벌의 역할을 이해하는 것이 중요하다.

7 갯벌이 무엇을 하는지 살펴보자.

8 갯벌은 바닷가에 있는 많은 생물들에게 집이다.

9 플랑크톤처럼 작은 생명체뿐만 아니라 게와 물고기도 그곳에 산다.

10 갯벌은 그들에게 다양한 종류의 먹이를 제공한다.

11 또한, 많은 새들도 그곳에서 먹이를 먹는다.

12 게: 갯벌은 나의 단란한 집이에요.

13 갯벌은 사람들에게도 유익하다.

14 갯벌 지역 인근에 사는 사람들은 근처에서 물고기와 다른 바다 동물들을 잡아 생계를 꾸린다.

15 갯벌 덕분에 사람들은 신선한 해산물을 얻을 수 있다.

16 People can enjoy _____ _____, _____ _____ mud sliding and body painting on mudflats.

    A. as   B. fun   C. such   D. activities

17 They can also watch a _____ _____ of birds that _____ _____ the sea animals there.

    A. feed   B. number   C. on   D. large

18 Boy: Mudflats are _____ _____ to _____ things!

    A. living   B. gift   C. nature's

19 Mudflats _____ the environment _____.

    A. greatly   B. help

20 Mudflats _____ a lot of water, so they can _____ _____ from _____.

    A. damage   B. hold   C. floods   D. reduce

21 Also, mudflats _____ water that flows _____ the land _____ the sea.

    A. from   B. filter   C. into

22 They _____ bad _____ in the water _____ it enters the sea.

    A. before   B. things   C. remove

23 _____ to mudflats, the water that _____ the sea is _____.

    A. reaches   B. thanks   C. clean

24 Mudflats _____ _____ the Earth's _____.

    A. as   B. lungs   C. work

25 They produce a _____ volume of _____ that is _____ for life on the Earth.

    A. oxygen   B. huge   C. necessary

26 Earth: Mudflats _____ me _____ and _____.

    A. healthy   B. keep   C. clean

27 _____ are wonderful places, _____ _____?

    A. they   B. mudflats   C. aren't

28 They are a _____ from _____ to _____ things on the Earth.

    A. living   B. gift   C. nature

29 For all these _____, it is _____ to _____ mudflats.

    A. reasons   B. protect   C. necessary

---

16 사람들은 갯벌에서 진흙 미끄럼 타기나 보디 페인팅과 같은 즐거운 활동을 즐길 수 있다.

17 그들은 또한 그곳에서 바다 동물들을 먹는 수많은 새를 관찰할 수도 있다.

18 남자아이: 갯벌은 생명체에게 주는 자연의 선물이에요!

19 갯벌은 환경에 크게 도움이 된다.

20 갯벌은 많은 양의 물을 수용해서 홍수의 피해를 줄여 준다.

21 또한, 갯벌은 땅에서 바다로 흘러가는 물을 걸러내 준다.

22 물이 바다로 들어가기 전에 물 속에 있는 나쁜 물질을 갯벌이 제거한다.

23 갯벌 덕분에 바다에 도착한 물은 깨끗하다.

24 갯벌은 지구의 폐 역할을 한다.

25 그것들은 지구상의 생명에게 필요한 많은 양의 산소를 생산한다.

26 지구: 갯벌은 나를 건강하고 깨끗하게 지켜 줘요.

27 갯벌은 멋진 곳이다, 그렇지 않은가?

28 그곳은 자연이 지구상의 생물들에게 준 선물이다.

29 이러한 이유로, 갯벌을 보호하는 것은 필수이다.

※ 다음 우리말과 일치하도록 빈칸에 알맞은 말을 쓰시오.

1 Mudflats, _____ _____

2 Mudflats are large areas of _____ _____ at the seaside.

3 They appear and _____ _____ _____ _____.

4 _____ low tides, they _____ _____, and during _____ _____, they _____ _____ _____ the sea.

5 Mudflats help _____ _____, people, and the Earth _____ _____ _____.

6 It is important _____ _____ _____ _____ _____ _____.

7 _____ see _____ _____ _____.

8 Mudflats _____ _____ _____ a lot of _____ _____ at the seaside.

9 _____ _____ very small living things like plankton _____ _____ crabs and fish live there.

10 Mudflats _____ various _____ _____ food _____ them.

11 _____, many birds eat food there.

12 Crab: Mudflats are my _____ _____ _____.

13 Mudflats _____ _____ _____ people, _____.

14 People who live near mudflat areas _____ _____ _____ _____ _____ fish and other sea animals _____.

15 _____ _____ mudflats, people can get _____ _____.

1	갯벌, 자연의 선물
2	갯벌은 바닷가의 진흙이 있는 넓은 지역이다.
3	갯벌은 조수와 함께 나타나고 사라진다.
4	썰물일 때 갯벌이 드러나고, 밀물일 때 바다에 덮인다.
5	갯벌은 바다 생물과 사람, 지구를 많은 방면에서 돕는다.
6	갯벌의 역할을 이해하는 것이 중요하다.
7	갯벌이 무엇을 하는지 살펴보자.
8	갯벌은 바닷가에 있는 많은 생물들에게 집이다.
9	플랑크톤처럼 작은 생명체뿐만 아니라 게와 물고기도 그곳에 산다.
10	갯벌은 그들에게 다양한 종류의 먹이를 제공한다.
11	또한, 많은 새들도 그곳에서 먹이를 먹는다.
12	게: 갯벌은 나의 단란한 집이에요.
13	갯벌은 사람들에게도 유익하다.
14	갯벌 지역 인근에 사는 사람들은 근처에서 물고기와 다른 바다 동물들을 잡아 생계를 꾸린다.
15	갯벌 덕분에 사람들은 신선한 해산물을 얻을 수 있다.

16 People can enjoy _____ _____, _____ _____ mud sliding and body painting _____ _____.

17 They can also watch _____ _____ _____ _____ birds that _____ _____ the sea animals there.

18 Boy: Mudflats are _____ _____ to living things!

19 Mudflats _____ the _____ _____.

20 Mudflats _____ a lot of water, so they can _____ _____ _____ _____.

21 Also, mudflats _____ water that _____ _____ the land _____ the sea.

22 They _____ _____ _____ in the water before it _____ the sea.

23 _____ _____ mudflats, the water _____ _____ _____ _____ is clean.

24 Mudflats work _____ _____ _____ _____ _____.

25 They produce _____ _____ _____ _____ oxygen that is _____ for life on the Earth.

26 Earth: Mudflats _____ _____ _____ and _____.

27 Mudflats are wonderful places, _____ _____?

28 They are a gift _____ _____ _____ _____ _____ on the Earth.

29 For all these reasons, it is necessary _____ _____ _____.

16 사람들은 갯벌에서 진흙 미끄럼 타기나 보디 페인팅과 같은 즐거운 활동을 즐길 수 있다.

17 그들은 또한 그곳에서 바다 동물들을 먹는 수많은 새를 관찰할 수도 있다.

18 남자아이: 갯벌은 생명체에게 주는 자연의 선물이에요!

19 갯벌은 환경에 크게 도움이 된다.

20 갯벌은 많은 양의 물을 수용해서 홍수의 피해를 줄여 준다.

21 또한, 갯벌은 땅에서 바다로 흘러가는 물을 걸러내 준다.

22 물이 바다로 들어가기 전에 물 속에 있는 나쁜 물질을 갯벌이 제거한다.

23 갯벌 덕분에 바다에 도착한 물은 깨끗하다.

24 갯벌은 지구의 폐 역할을 한다.

25 그것들은 지구상의 생명에게 필요한 많은 양의 산소를 생산한다.

26 지구: 갯벌은 나를 건강하고 깨끗하게 지켜 줘요.

27 갯벌은 멋진 곳이다. 그렇지 않은가?

28 그곳은 자연이 지구상의 생물들에게 준 선물이다.

29 이러한 이유로, 갯벌을 보호하는 것은 필수이다.

※ 다음 문장을 우리말로 쓰시오.

1 Mudflats, Nature's Gift

➡ _____

2 Mudflats are large areas of muddy land at the seaside.

➡ _____

3 They appear and disappear with every tide.

➡ _____

4 During low tides, they show up, and during high tides, they are covered by the sea.

➡ _____

5 Mudflats help sea creatures, people, and the Earth in many ways.

➡ _____

6 It is important to understand the roles of mudflats.

➡ _____

7 Let's see what they do.

➡ _____

8 Mudflats are home to a lot of living things at the seaside.

➡ _____

9 Not only very small living things like plankton but also crabs and fish live there.

➡ _____

10 Mudflats provide various types of food for them.

➡ _____

11 Also, many birds eat food there.

➡ _____

12 Crab: Mudflats are my home sweet home.

➡ _____

13 Mudflats are good for people, too.

➡ _____

14 People who live near mudflat areas make a living by catching fish and other sea animals nearby.

➡ _____

15 Thanks to mudflats, people can get fresh seafood.

➡ _____

16 People can enjoy fun activities, such as mud sliding and body painting on mudflats.

➡ _____

17 They can also watch a large number of birds that feed on the sea animals there.

➡ _____

18 Boy: Mudflats are nature's gift to living things!

➡ _____

19 Mudflats help the environment greatly.

➡ _____

20 Mudflats hold a lot of water, so they can reduce damage from floods.

➡ _____

21 Also, mudflats filter water that flows from the land into the sea.

➡ _____

22 They remove bad things in the water before it enters the sea.

➡ _____

23 Thanks to mudflats, the water that reaches the sea is clean.

➡ _____

24 Mudflats work as the Earth's lungs.

➡ _____

25 They produce a huge volume of oxygen that is necessary for life on the Earth.

➡ _____

26 Earth: Mudflats keep me healthy and clean.

➡ _____

27 Mudflats are wonderful places, aren't they?

➡ _____

28 They are a gift from nature to living things on the Earth.

➡ _____

29 For all these reasons, it is necessary to protect mudflats.

➡ _____

※ 다음 괄호 안의 단어들을 우리말에 맞도록 바르게 배열하시오.

1 (Nature's / Gift / Mudflats,)
➡ _____

2 (are / mudflats / areas / large / muddy / of / at / land / seaside. / the)
➡ _____

3 (appear / they / and / with / disappear / tide. / every)
➡ _____

4 (low / during / tides, / show / they / up, / and / high / during / tides, / are / they / by / sea. / the / covered)
➡ _____
_____

5 (help / mudflats / creatures, / sea / people, / the / and / Earth / in / ways. / many)
➡ _____

6 (is / it / important / understand / to / roles / the / mudfalts. / of)
➡ _____

7 (see / let's / they / what / do.)
➡ _____

8 (are / mudflats / home / a / to / lot / living / of / things / the / seaside. / at)
➡ _____

9 (only / not / small / very / things / living / like / but / plankton / also / crabs / and / live / there. / fish)
➡ _____
_____

10 (provide / mudflats / types / various / food / of / them. / for)
➡ _____

11 (also, / birds / many / food / there. / eat)
➡ _____

12 (Crab: / are / mudflats / home / my / home. / sweet)
➡ _____

13 (are / mudflats / for / good / too. / people,)
➡ _____

14 (who / people / near / live / areas / mudflat / a / make / living / catching / by / fish / and / sea / other / nearby. / animals)
➡ _____
_____

15 (to / thanks / mudflats, / can / people / fresh / seafood. / get)
➡ _____

1 갯벌, 자연의 선물

2 갯벌은 바닷가의 진흙이 있는 넓은 지역이다.

3 갯벌은 조수와 함께 나타나고 사라진다.

4 썰물일 때 갯벌이 드러나고, 밀물일 때 바다에 덮인다.

5 갯벌은 바다 생물과 사람, 지구를 많은 방면에서 돕는다.

6 갯벌의 역할을 이해하는 것이 중요하다.

7 갯벌이 무엇을 하는지 살펴보자.

8 갯벌은 바닷가에 있는 많은 생물들에게 집이다.

9 플랑크톤처럼 작은 생명체뿐만 아니라 게와 물고기도 그곳에 산다.

10 갯벌은 그들에게 다양한 종류의 먹이를 제공한다.

11 또한, 많은 새들도 그곳에서 먹이를 먹는다.

12 게: 갯벌은 나의 단란한 집이에요.

13 갯벌은 사람들에게도 유익하다.

14 갯벌 지역 인근에 사는 사람들은 근처에서 물고기와 다른 바다 동물들을 잡아 생계를 꾸린다.

15 갯벌 덕분에 사람들은 신선한 해산물을 얻을 수 있다.

16 (can / people / fun / enjoy / activities, / as / such / sliding / mud / and / body / on / painting / mudflats.)

➡ _____

_____

17 (they / also / watch / can / a / number / large / birds / of / that / on / feed / sea / the / there. / animals)

➡ _____

_____

18 (Boy: / are / mudflats / gift / nature's / to / things! / living)

➡ _____

19 (help / mudflats / environment / the / greatly.)

➡ _____

20 (hold / mudflats / lot / a / of / water, / they / so / reduce / can / from / damage / floods.)

➡ _____

21 (mudflats / also, / water / filter / that / from / flows / the / into / land / sea. / the)

➡ _____

22 (remove / they / things / bad / the / in / water / before / enters / it / sea. / the)

➡ _____

23 (to / thanks / mudflats, / water / the / reaches / that / sea / the / clean. / is)

➡ _____

24 (work / mudflats / the / as / lungs. / Earth's)

➡ _____

25 (produce / they / huge / a / of / volume / oxygen / is / that / for / necessary / life / the / Earth. / on)

➡ _____

_____

26 (Earth: / keep / mudflats / me / clean. / and / healthy)

➡ _____

27 (are / mudflats / places, / wonderful / they? / aren't)

➡ _____

28 (are / they / gift / a / from / nature / living / to / things / the / Earth. / on)

➡ _____

29 (all / for / reasons, / these / is / it / necessary / protect / to / mudflats.)

➡ _____

16 사람들은 갯벌에서 진흙 미끄럼 타기나 보디 페인팅과 같은 즐거운 활동을 즐길 수 있다.

17 그들은 또한 그곳에서 바다 동물들을 먹는 수많은 새를 관찰할 수도 있다.

18 남자아이: 갯벌은 생명체에게 주는 자연의 선물이에요!

19 갯벌은 환경에 크게 도움이 된다.

20 갯벌은 많은 양의 물을 수용해서 홍수의 피해를 줄여 준다.

21 또한, 갯벌은 땅에서 바다로 흘러가는 물을 걸러내 준다.

22 물이 바다로 들어가기 전에 물 속에 있는 나쁜 물질을 갯벌이 제거한다.

23 갯벌 덕분에 바다에 도착한 물은 깨끗하다.

24 갯벌은 지구의 폐 역할을 한다.

25 그것들은 지구상의 생명에게 필요한 많은 양의 산소를 생산한다.

26 지구: 갯벌은 나를 건강하고 깨끗하게 지켜 줘요.

27 갯벌은 멋진 곳이다, 그렇지 않은가?

28 그곳은 자연이 지구상의 생물들에게 준 선물이다.

29 이러한 이유로, 갯벌을 보호하는 것은 필수이다.

※ 다음 우리말을 영어로 쓰시오.

1 갯벌, 자연의 선물

➡ _____

2 갯벌은 바닷가의 진흙이 있는 넓은 지역이다.

➡ _____

3 갯벌은 조수와 함께 나타나고 사라진다.

➡ _____

4 썰물일 때 갯벌이 드러나고, 밀물일 때 바다에 덮인다.

➡ _____

5 갯벌은 바다 생물과 사람, 지구를 많은 방면에서 돕는다.

➡ _____

6 갯벌의 역할을 이해하는 것이 중요하다.

➡ _____

7 갯벌이 무엇을 하는지 살펴보자.

➡ _____

8 갯벌은 바닷가에 있는 많은 생물들에게 집이다.

➡ _____

9 플랑크톤처럼 작은 생명체뿐만 아니라 게와 물고기도 그곳에 산다.

➡ _____

10 갯벌은 그들에게 다양한 종류의 먹이를 제공한다.

➡ _____

11 또한, 많은 새들도 그곳에서 먹이를 먹는다.

➡ _____

12 게: 갯벌은 나의 단란한 집이에요.

➡ _____

13 갯벌은 사람들에게도 유익하다.

➡ _____

14 갯벌 지역 인근에 사는 사람들은 근처에서 물고기와 다른 바다 동물들을 잡아 생계를 꾸린다.

➡ _____

15 갯벌 덕분에 사람들은 신선한 해산물을 얻을 수 있다.

➡ _____

16 사람들은 갯벌에서 진흙 미끄럼 타기나 보디 페인팅과 같은 즐거운 활동을 즐길 수 있다.

➡ _____

17 그들은 또한 그곳에서 바다 동물들을 먹는 수많은 새를 관찰할 수도 있다.

➡ _____

18 남자아이: 갯벌은 생명체에게 주는 자연의 선물이에요!

➡ _____

19 갯벌은 환경에 크게 도움이 된다.

➡ _____

20 갯벌은 많은 양의 물을 수용해서 홍수의 피해를 줄여 준다.

➡ _____

21 또한, 갯벌은 땅에서 바다로 흘러가는 물을 걸러내 준다.

➡ _____

22 물이 바다로 들어가기 전에 물속에 있는 나쁜 물질을 갯벌이 제거한다.

➡ _____

23 갯벌 덕분에 바다에 도착한 물은 깨끗하다.

➡ _____

24 갯벌은 지구의 폐 역할을 한다.

➡ _____

25 그것들은 지구상의 생명에게 필요한 많은 양의 산소를 생산한다.

➡ _____

26 지구: 갯벌은 나를 건강하고 깨끗하게 지켜 줘요.

➡ _____

27 갯벌은 멋진 곳이다, 그렇지 않은가?

➡ _____

28 그곳은 자연이 지구상의 생물들에게 준 선물이다.

➡ _____

29 이러한 이유로, 갯벌을 보호하는 것은 필수이다.

➡ _____

※ 다음 우리말과 일치하도록 빈칸에 알맞은 말을 쓰시오.

Enjoy Writing B

1. Deserts are dry land _____ _____ plants and _____ water.

2. _____ _____ plants like elephant trees _____ _____ animals _____ _____ lizards and desert snakes live there.

3. It is hot _____ _____ _____ and cold at night.

4. If you go to a desert, _____ is important _____ _____ a hat _____ _____ the sun.

1. 사막은 식물과 물이 거의 없는 건조한 땅이다.
2. 코끼리 나무 같은 식물뿐만 아니라 도마뱀이나 사막뱀 같은 동물들도 그곳에 산다.
3. 낮에는 덥고 밤에는 춥다.
4. 만일 사막에 간다면 햇빛을 가리기 위해 모자를 쓰는 것이 중요하다.

Enjoy Writing B

1. All _____ _____

2. Mudflats are _____ _____ at the _____.

3. _____ _____ plants like *hamcho* _____ _____ animals _____ _____ crabs and fish live there.

4. They _____ _____ during low tides and _____ _____ _____ the sea during high tides.

5. If you go to mudflats, it is important _____ _____ long clothes _____ _____ _____ from animals that _____ _____ you.

1. 갯벌에 관한 모든 것
2. 갯벌은 바닷가의 진흙이 있는 지역이다.
3. 함초와 같은 식물들뿐만 아니라 게와 물고기와 같은 동물들도 그곳에 산다.
4. 썰물일 때 갯벌이 드러나고, 밀물일 때 바다에 덮인다.
5. 만약 당신이 갯벌에 간다면, 당신을 물 수 있는 동물들로부터 당신을 보호하기 위해 긴 옷을 입는 것이 중요하다.

Wrap Up 1

1. B: I just _____ _____ a plan for my trip. Do you _____ _____ _____ it?

2. G: Sure. I _____ _____ _____ _____ _____.

3. B: On the first day, I'm _____ to _____ _____ on a lake. The next day, I'm going to _____ _____ _____.

4. G: _____ that _____?

5. B: No. _____ the last day, I'm _____ _____ _____ _____.

6. G: Wow. You will do _____ _____ _____ activities.

1. B: 나는 방금 여행 계획 세우는 것을 끝냈어. 그것에 대해 듣고 싶니?
2. G: 물론이지. 나는 네가 무엇을 할지 궁금해.
3. B: 첫날에 나는 호수에서 낚시를 할 거야. 다음 날에 나는 산에 오를 거야.
4. G: 그게 전부니?
5. B: 아니. 마지막 날에 나는 수영을 할 거야.
6. G: 우와. 너는 많은 활동들을 할 거구나.

※ 다음 우리말을 영어로 쓰시오.

Enjoy Writing B

1. 사막은 식물과 물이 거의 없는 건조한 땅이다.
   ➡ _____

2. 코끼리 나무 같은 식물뿐만 아니라 도마뱀이나 사막뱀 같은 동물들도 그곳에 산다.
   ➡ _____

3. 낮에는 덥고 밤에는 춥다.
   ➡ _____

4. 만일 사막에 간다면 햇빛을 가리기 위해 모자를 쓰는 것이 중요하다.
   ➡ _____

Enjoy Writing B

1. 갯벌에 관한 모든 것
   ➡ _____

2. 갯벌은 바닷가의 진흙이 있는 지역이다.
   ➡ _____

3. 함초와 같은 식물들뿐만 아니라 게와 물고기와 같은 동물들도 그곳에 산다.
   ➡ _____

4. 썰물일 때 갯벌이 드러나고, 밀물일 때 바다에 덮인다.
   ➡ _____

5. 만약 당신이 갯벌에 간다면, 당신을 물 수 있는 동물들로부터 당신을 보호하기 위해 긴 옷을 입는 것이 중요하다.
   ➡ _____
   _____

Wrap Up 1

1. B: 나는 방금 여행 계획 세우는 것을 끝냈어. 그것에 대해 듣고 싶니?
   ➡ _____

2. G: 물론이지. 나는 네가 무엇을 할지 궁금해.
   ➡ _____

3. B: 첫날에 나는 호수에서 낚시를 할 거야. 다음 날에 나는 산에 오를 거야.
   ➡ _____

4. G: 그게 전부니?
   ➡ _____

5. B: 아니. 마지막 날에 나는 수영을 할 거야.
   ➡ _____

6. G: 우와. 너는 많은 활동들을 할 거구나.
   ➡ _____

※ 다음 영어를 우리말로 쓰시오.

01 teammate	
02 perfect	
03 calm	
04 achieve	
05 difficulty	
06 face	
07 award	
08 terrible	
09 fail	
10 finally	
11 positive	
12 gentle	
13 base	
14 recognize	
15 sentence	
16 although	
17 recycle	
18 overcome	
19 earn	
20 excellence	
21 pain	

22 present	
23 effort	
24 honor	
25 lend	
26 major	
27 excellent	
28 respect	
29 solve	
30 rudely	
31 support	
32 talented	
33 phrase	
34 color line	
35 think to oneself	
36 no longer	
37 win first place	
38 turn down	
39 give up	
40 over and over	
41 present A with B	
42 at bat	
43 cannot believe one's eyes	

※ 다음 우리말을 영어로 쓰시오.

01 이루다, 달성하다 _____

02 침착한 _____

03 인정하다, 알아보다 _____

04 어려움, 곤경, 장애 _____

05 완벽한 _____

06 얻다, 획득하다 _____

07 비록 ~일지라도 _____

08 우수, 탁월, 뛰어남 _____

09 아픔, 고통 _____

10 상 _____

11 뛰어난 _____

12 긍정적인 _____

13 직면하다, 직시하다 _____

14 재활용하다 _____

15 존경 _____

16 예우하다, ~을 공경하다 _____

17 실패하다 _____

18 풀다, 해결하다 _____

19 재능이 있는 _____

20 지지 _____

21 마침내 _____

22 점잖은 _____

23 수여하다, 증정하다 _____

24 무례하게 _____

25 팀 동료 _____

26 문장 _____

27 (공을) 치다 _____

28 노력 _____

29 빌려주다 _____

30 주요한 _____

31 극복하다 _____

32 무서운 _____

33 경기장, 스타디움 _____

34 야구의 루 _____

35 포기하다 _____

36 마음속으로 생각하다 _____

37 더 이상 ~ 아닌 _____

38 ~ 덕분에 _____

39 반복해서 _____

40 1등을 하다, 우승하다 _____

41 ~을 거절하다, 소리를 줄이다 _____

42 A에게 B를 수여하다 _____

43 수업을 듣다 _____

※ 다음 영영풀이에 알맞은 단어를 <보기>에서 골라 쓴 후, 우리말 뜻을 쓰시오.

1 _____ : unusually or extremely good: _____

2 _____ : a person who is in the same team: _____

3 _____ : a player stationed at a base: _____

4 _____ : to be unable to do something: _____

5 _____ : in a way that shows no respect for others: _____

6 _____ : relating to classical music: _____

7 _____ : a feeling that you have in a part of your body when you are hurt or ill : _____

8 _____ : to give someone the use of something for a limited time: _____

9 _____ : greater or more important than other people or things in a group: _____

10 _____ : to succeed in dealing with or controlling a problem: _____

11 _____ : to hit the ball with a bat in a game such as baseball or cricket: _____

12 _____ : believing that good things will happen rather than bad ones: _____

13 _____ : to see and know what someone or something is: _____

14 _____ : a prize or other reward that is given to someone who has achieved something: _____

15 _____ : not affected by strong emotions such as excitement, anger, shock, or fear: _____

16 _____ : help and kindness that you give to someone who is having a difficult time: _____

보기			
bat	lend	baseman	teammate
support	excellent	positive	calm
fail	award	pain	overcome
recognize	classical	rudely	major

※ 다음 우리말과 일치하도록 빈칸에 알맞은 말을 쓰시오.

Listen & Speak 1 A

1. G: Hey, Minho. Did you _____ the answer to the _____ _____?

   B: No. It's _____ _____ for me. _____ _____ _____

   _____ _____.

   G: _____ me _____. _____ _____ _____ you use this

   math rule _____ _____ the problem.

   B: Oh, I see. I'll _____ it.

2. G: Your poster _____ _____.

   B: Thanks, Kate. Did you _____ _____?

   G: Not yet. I can't _____ well. _____ can I become _____

   _____ _____?

   B: It _____ time. It's _____ that you draw _____ _____

   _____ _____ _____.

   G: You _____ I should _____ _____?

   B: That's _____.

Listen & Speak 1 B

1. A: It's _____ _____ _____ a good dancer. _____ should

   I do?

   B: It's _____ that you _____ _____ _____ _____.

   A: Okay. I will _____ _____ that.

2. A: It's _____ _____ write a good story. What _____ I do?

   B: _____ _____ _____ you read many books.

   A: Okay. I _____ _____ _____ that.

Listen & Talk 2 A

1. G: Oh, this is _____ _____ _____.

   B: What's the _____?

   G: Can you teach me _____ _____ _____ cookies?

   B: Sure. It's a walk in the park.

   G: _____ _____ _____ that?

   B: I _____ it's _____ _____ _____ _____.

1. G: 이봐, 민호야. 이 수학 문제의 정답을 찾았니?
   B: 아니. 그건 나에게 너무 어려워. 나는 수학을 잘하지 못 해.
   G: 내가 한 번 볼게. 네가 그 문제를 풀기 위해선 이 수학 공식을 이용하는 것이 중요해.
   B: 오, 알겠어. 그걸 사용해 볼게.

2. G: 네 포스터가 멋져 보여.
   B: 고마워, Kate. 네 것은 끝냈니?
   G: 아직 못 끝냈어. 나는 그림을 잘 그리지 못 해. 어떻게 하면 내가 그림을 잘 그릴 수 있을까?
   B: 시간이 필요해. 네가 가능한 자주 그림을 그리는 것이 중요해.
   G: 내가 계속 연습해야 한다는 뜻이니?
   B: 맞아.

1. A: 훌륭한 댄서가 되는 것은 어려워. 내가 무엇을 해야 할까?
   B: 절대 포기하지 않는 것이 중요해.
   A: 알겠어. 그것을 잊지 않을게.

2. A: 좋은 이야기를 쓰는 것은 어려워. 내가 무엇을 해야 할까?
   B: 책을 많이 읽는 것이 중요해.
   A: 알겠어. 그것을 잊지 않을게.

1. G: 오, 이것은 하기 어렵구나.
   B: 무슨 일이야?
   G: 쿠키를 만드는 방법을 나에게 가르쳐 줄 수 있니?
   B: 물론이지. 그건 'a walk in the park'야.
   G: 그게 무슨 뜻이니?
   B: 하기 쉽다는 뜻이야.

2. **B:** I _____ a singing contest tomorrow. I really _____ _____

   _____ _____ _____ .

   G: I'll keep my fingers _____ for you.

   B: _____ _____ _____ _____ _____ "keep my fingers

   crossed"?

   G: It _____ I _____ you _____ _____ .

   B: Thank you.

Listen & Talk 2 B

1. **A:** Two heads _____ _____ _____ one.

   B: _____ do you _____ _____ "Two heads are better than

   one"?

   A: I _____ working _____ is better _____ _____ _____ _____ .

2. **A:** _____ makes _____ .

   B: What do you _____ _____ "Practice makes perfect"?

   A: I _____ you learn something _____ _____ it _____

   _____ _____ .

Conversation A

M: _____ _____ my dream, I went to many auditions, but I often

_____ . _____ , I never _____ _____ . I _____ acting

and dancing _____ . _____ , I _____ my goal. It's important

_____ you _____ _____ _____ .

Conversation B

Hana: You _____ sad, Jiho. What's _____ ?

Jiho: I _____ _____ I can _____ my dream.

Amy: _____ _____ _____ _____ _____ _____ _____ ?

Jiho: I want to be an actor, but I always _____ _____ . Maybe I

_____ _____ _____ _____ .

Amy: Do you know this _____ ?

Jiho: Sure. He's a _____ movie star.

Amy: He _____ _____ _____ _____ 100 auditions.

Jiho: Really? Maybe I _____ _____ _____ . I will

more for my next audition.

Hana: That's right! _____ _____ _____ _____ _____

_____ _____ .

44 Lesson 7. Work on Your Dreams

---

2. **B:** 나 내일 노래 경연 대회가 있어.
   나는 정말 1등을 하고 싶어.
   G: 너에게 'keep my fingers crossed'할게.
   B: 'keep my fingers crossed'가 무슨 뜻이니?
   G: 그건 내가 너에게 행운을 빈다는 뜻이야.
   B: 고마워.

1. **A:** 두 개의 머리가 머리 하나보다 낫다.
   B: "두 개의 머리가 머리 하나보다 낫다."가 무슨 뜻이니?
   A: 함께 일하는 것이 혼자 일하는 것보다 낫다는 뜻이야.

2. **A:** 연습이 완벽함을 만든다.
   B: "연습이 완벽함을 만든다."가 무슨 뜻이니?
   A: 반복해서 무언가를 하면 배우게 된다는 뜻이야.

M: 내 꿈을 이루기 위해 나는 많은 오디션에 갔지만 자주 떨어졌다. 하지만 나는 절대 포기하지 않았다. 나는 연기와 춤 수업을 들었다. 마침내 나는 내 목표를 이뤘다. 절대 포기하지 않는 것이 중요하다.

하나: 너 슬퍼 보여, 지호야. 무슨 일이니?
지호: 내 생각에 나는 꿈을 이룰 수 없을 것 같아.
Amy: 그게 무슨 말이니?
지호: 나는 배우가 되고 싶지만 항상 오디션에서 떨어져. 어쩌면 나는 포기해야 할 거 같아.
Amy: 너 이 배우를 아니?
지호: 당연하지. 그는 유명한 영화배우잖아.
Amy: 그는 백 번 이상 오디션에서 떨어졌대.
지호: 정말? 그러면 나도 계속 노력해야겠구나. 나는 다음 오디션을 위해서 더 연습할 거야.
하나: 바로 그거야! 절대 포기하지 않는 것이 중요해.

※ 다음 우리말에 맞도록 대화를 영어로 쓰시오.

Listen & Speak 1 A

1. G: _____
   B: _____
   G: _____
   B: _____

2. G: _____
   B: _____
   G: _____
   B: _____
   G: _____
   B: _____

Listen & Speak 1 B

1. A: _____
   B: _____
   A: _____

2. A: _____
   B: _____
   A: _____

Listen & Talk 2 A

1. G: _____
   B: _____
   G: _____
   B: _____
   G: _____
   B: _____

해석

1. G: 이봐, 민호야. 이 수학 문제의 정답을 찾았니?
   B: 아니. 그건 나에게 너무 어려워. 나는 수학을 잘하지 못 해.
   G: 내가 한 번 볼게. 네가 그 문제를 풀기 위해선 이 수학 공식을 이용하는 것이 중요해.
   B: 오, 알겠어. 그걸 사용해 볼게.

2. G: 네 포스터가 멋져 보여.
   B: 고마워, Kate. 네 것은 끝냈니?
   G: 아직 못 끝냈어. 나는 그림을 잘 그리지 못 해. 어떻게 하면 내가 그림을 잘 그릴 수 있을까?
   B: 시간이 필요해. 네가 가능한 자주 그림을 그리는 것이 중요해.
   G: 내가 계속 연습해야 한다는 뜻이니?
   B: 맞아.

1. A: 훌륭한 댄서가 되는 것은 어려워. 내가 무엇을 해야 할까?
   B: 절대 포기하지 않는 것이 중요해.
   A: 알겠어. 그것을 잊지 않을게.

2. A: 좋은 이야기를 쓰는 것은 어려워. 내가 무엇을 해야 할까?
   B: 책을 많이 읽는 것이 중요해.
   A: 알겠어. 그것을 잊지 않을게.

1. G: 오, 이것은 하기 어렵구나.
   B: 무슨 일이야?
   G: 쿠키를 만드는 방법을 나에게 가르쳐 줄 수 있니?
   B: 물론이지. 그건 'a walk in the park'야.
   G: 그게 무슨 뜻이니?
   B: 하기 쉽다는 뜻이야.

2. B: _____

G: _____

B: _____

G: _____

B: _____

2. B: 나 내일 노래 경연 대회가 있어. 나는 정말 1등을 하고 싶어.
G: 너에게 'keep my fingers crossed'할게.
B: 'keep my fingers crossed'가 무슨 뜻이니?
G: 그건 내가 너에게 행운을 빈다는 뜻이야.
B: 고마워.

Listen & Talk 2 B

1. A: _____

B: _____

A: _____

2. A: _____

B: _____

A: _____

1. A: 두 개의 머리가 머리 하나보다 낫다.
B: "두 개의 머리가 머리 하나보다 낫다."가 무슨 뜻이니?
A: 함께 일하는 것이 혼자 일하는 것보다 낫다는 뜻이야.

2. A: 연습이 완벽함을 만든다.
B: "연습이 완벽함을 만든다."가 무슨 뜻이니?
A: 반복해서 무언가를 하면 배우게 된다는 뜻이야.

Conversation A

M: _____

_____

_____

M: 내 꿈을 이루기 위해 나는 많은 오디션에 갔지만 자주 떨어졌다. 하지만 나는 절대 포기하지 않았다. 나는 연기와 춤 수업을 들었다. 마침내 나는 내 목표를 이뤘다. 절대 포기하지 않는 것이 중요하다.

Conversation B

Hana: _____

Jiho: _____

Amy: _____

Jiho: _____

Amy: _____

Jiho: _____

Amy: _____

Jiho: _____

Hana: _____

하나: 너 슬퍼 보여, 지호야. 무슨 일이니?
지호: 내 생각에 나는 꿈을 이룰 수 없을 것 같아.
Amy: 그게 무슨 말이니?
지호: 나는 배우가 되고 싶지만 항상 오디션에서 떨어져. 어쩌면 나는 포기해야 할 거 같아.
Amy: 너 이 배우를 아니?
지호: 당연하지. 그는 유명한 영화배우잖아.
Amy: 그는 백 번 이상 오디션에서 떨어졌대.
지호: 정말? 그러면 나도 계속 노력해야겠구나. 나는 다음 오디션을 위해서 더 연습할 거야.
하나: 바로 그거야! 절대 포기하지 않는 것이 중요해.

※ 다음 우리말과 일치하도록 빈칸에 알맞은 것을 골라 쓰시오.

1 Jackie Robinson _____ the _____ _____

    A. Color　　　　　B. Breaks　　　　　C. Line

2 _____ was New York City _____ _____ 15, 1947.

    A. April　　　　　B. it　　　　　C. on

3 Jackie Robinson, an African American, _____ _____ the field _____ second baseman _____ the Brooklyn Dodgers.

    A. on　　　　B. for　　　　C. went　　　　D. as

4 People _____ _____ their _____ .

    A. believe　　　　B. couldn't　　　　C. eyes

5 He was the _____ African _____ player to _____ _____ a Major League team.

    A. American　　　B. play　　　C. first　　　D. on

6 That day, the _____ _____ was _____ .

    A. line　　　　B. broken　　　　C. color

7 Robinson _____ _____ _____ .

    A. difficulties　　　　B. faced　　　　C. many

8 _____ Robinson was a _____ player and a _____ person, his teammates did not want to play _____ him.

    A. gentle　　　B. although　　　C. talented　　　D. with

9 _____ hotel _____ the team _____ _____ Robinson was on the team.

    A. because　　　B. turned　　　C. down　　　D. every

10 When he was at _____ , people in the stands _____ shouted _____ him.

    A. rudely　　　B. at　　　C. bat

11 Robinson _____ to _____ , 'I need to _____ calm and _____ on baseball.

    A. keep　　　B. thought　　　C. focus　　　D. himself

12 I will _____ and _____ a player who people _____ .

    A. like　　　B. try　　　C. become

13 Then, next season, _____ will _____ African American players in the _____ .'

    A. there　　　B. more　　　C. league　　　D. be

14 Robinson _____ all his time and _____ _____ baseball.

    A. into　　　B. put　　　C. energy

---

1 Jackie Robinson 인종 차별을 깨다

2 1947년 4월 15일 뉴욕시에 서였다.

3 아프리카계 미국인 Jackie Robinson은 브루클린 다저스의 2루수로 경기장에 나갔다.

4 사람들은 자신들의 눈을 의심했다.

5 그는 메이저리그 팀에서 경기한 최초의 아프리카계 미국인 선수였다.

6 그날 인종 차별이 깨졌다.

7 Robinson은 많은 어려움에 직면했다.

8 Robinson은 재능 있는 선수이고 온화한 사람이었지만 그의 팀원들은 그와 함께 경기하기를 원하지 않았다.

9 Robinson이 팀에 있었기 때문에 모든 호텔에서 그 팀을 거절했다.

10 그가 타석에 있을 때, 관중석에 있는 사람들이 그에게 무례하게 소리치기도 했다.

11 Robinson은 마음속으로 생각했다. '나는 평정심을 유지하고 야구에 집중해야 해.

12 나는 노력해서 사람들이 좋아하는 선수가 될 거야.

13 그러면 다음 시즌에는 아프리카계 미국인 선수가 리그에 더 많이 생길 거야.'

14 Robinson은 자신의 모든 시간과 에너지를 야구에 집중했다.

15 _____ _____, he became great at _____ and base _____.

    A. batting   B. with   C. running   D. practice

16 Robinson's _____ _____ his _____.

    A. moved   B. effort   C. teammates

17 When people shouted at Robinson, _____ of his teammates walked _____ to Robinson and _____ him _____ the shoulder.

    A. on   B. up   C. one   D. tapped

18 " _____ not _____ _____ them.

    A. to   B. do   C. listen

19 You're _____ _____," he said.

    A. fine   B. doing

20 His _____ _____ Robinson _____ play _____.

    A. harder   B. helped   C. support   D. to

21 _____, Robinson _____ the _____ of _____ players and fans.

    A. other   B. earned   C. finally   D. respect

22 _____ _____ Robinson, the Dodgers _____ the National League Championship _____ 1947.

    A. won   B. to   C. thanks   D. in

23 The league _____ Robinson's excellence and _____ him _____ the Rookie of the Year Award in the _____ year.

    A. presented   B. recognized   C. same   D. with

24 After that season, _____ teams _____ African American players _____ _____ them.

    A. join   B. asked   C. other   D. to

25 Robinson's _____ _____ was 42.

    A. number   B. uniform

26 Baseball players in Major League teams _____ _____ wear the number 42 _____ _____ him.

    A. honor   B. longer   C. to   D. no

27 Every year, _____, on April 15, _____ player _____ the number that Robinson _____.

    A. wears   B. however   C. wore   D. every

28 The day _____ _____ "Jackie Robinson Day."

    A. called   B. is

---

15 연습을 함으로써 그는 타격과 주루를 잘하게 되었다.

16 Robinson의 노력은 그의 팀원들을 감동시켰다.

17 사람들이 Robinson에게 소리쳤을 때, 그의 팀 동료 중 한 명이 Robinson에게 다가가 어깨를 두드렸다.

18 "그들 말을 듣지 마.

19 너는 잘하고 있어."라고 그가 말했다.

20 그의 지지는 Robinson이 더 열심히 경기하는 데 도움이 됐다.

21 마침내, Robinson은 다른 선수들과 팬들의 존경을 받았다.

22 Robinson 덕분에 다저스는 1947년에 내셔널리그 챔피언십에서 우승하게 되었다.

23 리그에서는 Robinson의 탁월함을 인정했고, 같은 해에 그에게 신인상을 수여했다.

24 그 시즌 이후, 다른 팀들은 아프리카계 미국인 선수들에게 자신들의 팀에 합류할 것을 요청했다.

25 Robinson의 등 번호는 42번이었다.

26 메이저리그 팀의 야구 선수들은 그에 대한 존경을 보여 주기 위해 더 이상 42번을 달지 않는다.

27 하지만 매년 4월 15일, 모든 선수들은 Robinson이 달았던 번호를 단다.

28 이 날을 '재키 로빈슨 데이'라고 부른다.

※ 다음 우리말과 일치하도록 빈칸에 알맞은 말을 쓰시오.

1 Jackie Robinson _____ _____ _____ _____

2 It was New York City _____ _____ _____, _____.

3 Jackie Robinson, an _____ _____, went on the field _____ second baseman _____ the Brooklyn Dodgers.

4 People _____ _____ _____ _____.

5 He was _____ _____ _____ _____ _____ to play on a Major League team.

6 That day, _____ _____ _____ _____ _____.

7 Robinson _____ _____ _____.

8 _____ Robinson was a _____ _____ and a gentle person, his teammates did not want _____ _____ _____ _____.

9 Every hotel _____ _____ _____ _____ because Robinson was on the team.

10 When he _____ _____ _____, people in the stands _____ _____ _____ him.

11 Robinson _____ _____ _____, 'I need to _____ _____ and _____ _____ baseball.

12 I will try and _____ a player _____ _____ _____.

13 Then, next season, _____ _____ _____ _____ African American players in the league.'

14 Robinson _____ all his time and energy _____ baseball.

1 Jackie Robinson 인종 차별을 깨다

2 1947년 4월 15일 뉴욕시에서였다.

3 아프리카계 미국인 Jackie Robinson은 브루클린 다저스의 2루수로 경기장에 나갔다.

4 사람들은 자신들의 눈을 의심했다.

5 그는 메이저리그 팀에서 경기한 최초의 아프리카계 미국인 선수였다.

6 그날 인종 차별이 깨졌다.

7 Robinson은 많은 어려움에 직면했다.

8 Robinson은 재능 있는 선수이고 온화한 사람이었지만 그의 팀원들은 그와 함께 경기하기를 원하지 않았다.

9 Robinson이 팀에 있었기 때문에 모든 호텔에서 그 팀을 거절했다.

10 그가 타석에 있을 때, 관중석에 있는 사람들이 그에게 무례하게 소리치기도 했다.

11 Robinson은 마음속으로 생각했다. '나는 평정심을 유지하고 야구에 집중해야 해.

12 나는 노력해서 사람들이 좋아하는 선수가 될 거야.

13 그러면 다음 시즌에는 아프리카계 미국인 선수가 리그에 더 많이 생길 거야.'

14 Robinson은 자신의 모든 시간과 에너지를 야구에 집중했다.

15 _____ _____, he became great _____ _____ and _____ _____.

16 Robinson's _____ _____ his _____.

17 When people _____ _____ Robinson, _____ _____ _____ _____ walked _____ _____ Robinson and _____ _____ _____ _____ _____.

18 "_____ _____ _____ _____ _____ them.

19 You're _____ _____," he said.

20 His support _____ Robinson _____ _____ _____.

21 Finally, Robinson _____ _____ _____ of other players and fans.

22 _____ _____ Robinson, the Dodgers _____ the National League Championship in 1947.

23 The league _____ Robinson's excellence and _____ him _____ the Rookie of the Year Award in the _____ _____.

24 After that season, _____ teams _____ African American players _____ _____ them.

25 Robinson's _____ _____ was 42.

26 Baseball players in Major League teams _____ _____ _____ the number 42 _____ _____ _____.

27 _____ year, _____, on April 15, every player _____ the number that Robinson _____.

28 The day _____ _____ "Jackie Robinson Day."

15 연습을 함으로써 그는 타격과 주루를 잘하게 되었다.

16 Robinson의 노력은 그의 팀원들을 감동시켰다.

17 사람들이 Robinson에게 소리쳤을 때, 그의 팀 동료 중 한 명이 Robinson에게 다가가 어깨를 두드렸다.

18 "그들 말을 듣지 마.

19 너는 잘하고 있어."라고 그가 말했다.

20 그의 지지는 Robinson이 더 열심히 경기하는 데 도움이 됐다.

21 마침내, Robinson은 다른 선수들과 팬들의 존경을 받았다.

22 Robinson 덕분에 다저스는 1947년에 내셔널리그 챔피언십에서 우승하게 되었다.

23 리그에서는 Robinson의 탁월함을 인정했고, 같은 해에 그에게 신인상을 수여했다.

24 그 시즌 이후, 다른 팀들은 아프리카계 미국인 선수들에게 자신들의 팀에 합류할 것을 요청했다.

25 Robinson의 등 번호는 42번이었다.

26 메이저리그 팀의 야구 선수들은 그에 대한 존경을 보여 주기 위해 더 이상 42번을 달지 않는다.

27 하지만 매년 4월 15일, 모든 선수들은 Robinson이 달았던 번호를 단다.

28 이 날을 '재키 로빈슨 데이'라고 부른다.

※ 다음 문장을 우리말로 쓰시오.

1 Jackie Robinson Breaks the Color Line

➡ _____

2 It was New York City on April 15, 1947.

➡ _____

3 Jackie Robinson, an African American, went on the field as second baseman for the Brooklyn Dodgers.

➡ _____

4 People couldn't believe their eyes.

➡ _____

5 He was the first African American player to play on a Major League team.

➡ _____

6 That day, the color line was broken.

➡ _____

7 Robinson faced many difficulties.

➡ _____

8 Although Robinson was a talented player and a gentle person, his teammates did not want to play with him.

➡ _____

9 Every hotel turned the team down because Robinson was on the team.

➡ _____

10 When he was at bat, people in the stands rudely shouted at him.

➡ _____

11 Robinson thought to himself, 'I need to keep calm and focus on baseball.

➡ _____

12 I will try and become a player who people like.

➡ _____

13 Then, next season, there will be more African American players in the league.'

➡ _____

14 Robinson put all his time and energy into baseball.

➡ _____

15 With practice, he became great at batting and base running.

➡ _____

16 Robinson's effort moved his teammates.

➡ _____

17 When people shouted at Robinson, one of his teammates walked up to Robinson and tapped him on the shoulder.

➡ _____

18 "Do not listen to them.

➡ _____

19 You're doing fine," he said.

➡ _____

20 His support helped Robinson to play harder.

➡ _____

21 Finally, Robinson earned the respect of other players and fans.

➡ _____

22 Thanks to Robinson, the Dodgers won the National League Championship in 1947.

➡ _____

23 The league recognized Robinson's excellence and presented him with the Rookie of the Year Award in the same year.

➡ _____

24 After that season, other teams asked African American players to join them.

➡ _____

25 Robinson's uniform number was 42.

➡ _____

26 Baseball players in Major League teams no longer wear the number 42 to honor him.

➡ _____

27 Every year, however, on April 15, every player wears the number that Robinson wore.

➡ _____

28 The day is called "Jackie Robinson Day."

➡ _____

※ 다음 괄호 안의 단어들을 우리말에 맞도록 바르게 배열하시오.

1 (Robinson / Jackie / Breaks / Color / the / Line)
➡ _____

2 (was / it / York / New / City / April / on / 1947. / 15,)
➡ _____

3 (Robinson, / Jackie / African / an / American, / on / went / field / the / second / as / baseman / the / for / Dodgers. / Brooklyn)
➡ _____
_____

4 (couldn't / people / their / believe / eyes.)
➡ _____

5 (was / he / first / the / American / African / to / player / on / play / a / League / Major / team.)
➡ _____

6 (day, / that / color / the / was / broken. / line)
➡ _____

7 (faced / Robinson / difficulties. / many)
➡ _____

8 (Robinson / although / a / was / player / talented / and / gentle / a / person, / teammates / his / not / did / to / want / him. / with / play)
➡ _____

9 (hotel / every / the / turned / team / down / because / was / Robinson / on / team. / the)
➡ _____

10 (he / when / at / was / bat, / in / people / the / stands / shouted / rudely / him. / at)
➡ _____

11 (thought / Robinson / himself, / to / 'I / to / need / calm / keep / and / on / focus / baseball.)
➡ _____

12 (I / try / will / and / a / become / player / people / who / like.)
➡ _____

13 (next / then, / season, / will / there / more / be / American / African / players / in / league.' / the)
➡ _____

14 (put / Robinson / all / time / his / and / into / baseball. / energy)
➡ _____

1 Jackie Robinson 인종 차별을 깨다

2 1947년 4월 15일 뉴욕시에 서였다.

3 아프리카계 미국인 Jackie Robinson은 브루클린 다저스의 2루수로 경기장에 나갔다.

4 사람들은 자신들의 눈을 의심했다.

5 그는 메이저리그 팀에서 경기한 최초의 아프리카계 미국인 선수였다.

6 그날 인종 차별이 깨졌다.

7 Robinson은 많은 어려움에 직면했다.

8 Robinson은 재능 있는 선수이고 온화한 사람이었지만 그의 팀원들은 그와 함께 경기하기를 원하지 않았다.

9 Robinson이 팀에 있었기 때문에 모든 호텔에서 그 팀을 거절했다.

10 그가 타석에 있을 때, 관중석에 있는 사람들이 그에게 무례하게 소리치기도 했다.

11 Robinson은 마음속으로 생각했다. '나는 평정심을 유지하고 야구에 집중해야 해.

12 나는 노력해서 사람들이 좋아하는 선수가 될 거야.

13 그러면 다음 시즌에는 아프리카계 미국인 선수가 리그에 더 많이 생길 거야.'

14 Robinson은 자신의 모든 시간과 에너지를 야구에 집중했다.

15 (practice, / with / became / he / at / great / batting / and / running. / base)

➡ _____

16 (effort / Robinson's / moved / teammates. / his)

➡ _____

17 (people / when / at / shouted / Robinson, / of / one / teammates / his / up / walked / to / Robinson / and / him / tapped / the / on / shoulder.)

➡ _____

_____

18 (not / "do / to / listen / them.)

➡ _____

19 (doing / you're / fine," / said. / he)

➡ _____

20 (support / his / Robinson / helped / play / harder. / to)

➡ _____

21 (Robinson / finally, / the / earned / respect / other / of / fans. / and / players)

➡ _____

22 (to / thanks / Robinson, / Dodgers / the / the / won / National / Championship / League / 1947. / in)

➡ _____

23 (league / the / Robinson's / recognized / presented / and / excellence / with / him / Rookie / the / of / the / Award / Year / the / in / year. / same)

➡ _____

_____

24 (that / after / season, / teams / other / African / asked / players / American / to / them. / join)

➡ _____

_____

25 (uniform / Robinson's / was / number / 42.)

➡ _____

26 (players / baseball / Major / in / League / no / teams / wear / longer / number / the / to / 42 / him. / honor)

➡ _____

_____

27 (year, / every / on / however, / 15, / April / player / every / the / wears / that / number / wore. / Robinson)

➡ _____

_____

28 (day / the / called / is / "Jackie / Day." / Robinson)

➡ _____

15 연습을 함으로써 그는 타격과 주루를 잘하게 되었다.

16 Robinson의 노력은 그의 팀원들을 감동시켰다.

17 사람들이 Robinson에게 소리쳤을 때, 그의 팀 동료 중 한 명이 Robinson에게 다가가 어깨를 두드렸다.

18 "그들 말을 듣지 마.

19 너는 잘하고 있어."라고 그가 말했다.

20 그의 지지는 Robinson이 더 열심히 경기하는 데 도움이 됐다.

21 마침내, Robinson은 다른 선수들과 팬들의 존경을 받았다.

22 Robinson 덕분에 다저스는 1947년에 내셔널리그 챔피언십에서 우승하게 되었다.

23 리그에서는 Robinson의 탁월함을 인정했고, 같은 해에 그에게 신인상을 수여했다.

24 그 시즌 이후, 다른 팀들은 아프리카계 미국인 선수들에게 자신들의 팀에 합류할 것을 요청했다.

25 Robinson의 등 번호는 42번이었다.

26 메이저리그 팀의 야구 선수들은 그에 대한 존경을 보여 주기 위해 더 이상 42번을 달지 않는다.

27 하지만 매년 4월 15일, 모든 선수들은 Robinson이 달았던 번호를 단다.

28 이 날을 '재키 로빈슨 데이'라고 부른다.

※ 다음 우리말을 영어로 쓰시오.

1 Jackie Robinson 인종 차별을 깨다

➡ _____

2 1947년 4월 15일 뉴욕시에서였다.

➡ _____

3 아프리카계 미국인 Jackie Robinson은 브루클린 다저스의 2루수로 경기장에 나갔다.

➡ _____

4 사람들은 자신들의 눈을 의심했다.

➡ _____

5 그는 메이저리그 팀에서 경기한 최초의 아프리카계 미국인 선수였다.

➡ _____

6 그날 인종 차별이 깨졌다.

➡ _____

7 Robinson은 많은 어려움에 직면했다.

➡ _____

8 Robinson은 재능 있는 선수이고 온화한 사람이었지만 그의 팀원들은 그와 함께 경기하기를 원하지 않았다.

➡ _____

9 Robinson이 팀에 있었기 때문에 모든 호텔에서 그 팀을 거절했다.

➡ _____

10 그가 타석에 있을 때, 관중석에 있는 사람들이 그에게 무례하게 소리치기도 했다.

➡ _____

11 Robinson은 마음속으로 생각했다. '나는 평정심을 유지하고 야구에 집중해야 해.

➡ _____

12 나는 노력해서 사람들이 좋아하는 선수가 될 거야.

➡ _____

13 그러면 다음 시즌에는 아프리카계 미국인 선수가 리그에 더 많이 생길 거야.'

➡ _____

14 Robinson은 자신의 모든 시간과 에너지를 야구에 집중했다.

➡ _____

15 연습을 함으로써 그는 타격과 주루를 잘하게 되었다.

➡ _____

16 ▶ Robinson의 노력은 그의 팀원들을 감동시켰다.

➡ _____

17 ▶ 사람들이 Robinson에게 소리쳤을 때, 그의 팀 동료 중 한 명이 Robinson에게 다가가 어깨를 두드렸다.

➡ _____

18 ▶ "그들 말을 듣지 마.

➡ _____

19 ▶ 너는 잘하고 있어."라고 그가 말했다.

➡ _____

20 ▶ 그의 지지는 Robinson이 더 열심히 경기하는 데 도움이 됐다.

➡ _____

21 ▶ 마침내, Robinson은 다른 선수들과 팬들의 존경을 받았다.

➡ _____

22 ▶ Robinson 덕분에 다저스는 1947년에 내셔널리그 챔피언십에서 우승하게 되었다.

➡ _____

23 ▶ 리그에서는 Robinson의 탁월함을 인정했고, 같은 해에 그에게 신인상을 수여했다.

➡ _____

24 ▶ 그 시즌 이후, 다른 팀들은 아프리카계 미국인 선수들에게 자신들의 팀에 합류할 것을 요청했다.

➡ _____

25 ▶ Robinson의 등 번호는 42번이었다.

➡ _____

26 ▶ 메이저리그 팀의 야구 선수들은 그에 대한 존경을 보여 주기 위해 더 이상 42번을 달지 않는다.

➡ _____

27 ▶ 하지만 매년 4월 15일, 모든 선수들은 Robinson이 달았던 번호를 단다.

➡ _____

28 ▶ 이 날을 '재키 로빈슨 데이'라고 부른다.

➡ _____

※ 다음 우리말과 일치하도록 빈칸에 알맞은 말을 쓰시오.

Language in Use

1. I visited three countries _____ _____.

2. France was _____ _____ _____ _____ I _____.

3. Mary is the girl _____ I _____ in Paris.

4. The blue watch is the _____ _____ _____ _____ there _____ my brother.

1. 작년에 나는 3개국을 방문했다.
2. 프랑스가 내가 방문한 첫 번째 국가였다.
3. Mary는 내가 파리에서 만났던 소녀이다.
4. 그 파란 시계는 그곳에서 내 동생을 위해 산 선물이다.

Enjoy Writing B

1. _____ I Will _____ My Dream

2. I _____ _____ _____ a designer.

3. There are three things _____ I _____ _____ do _____ _____ my dream.

4. I need to be _____, be _____, and never _____ _____.

5. _____ healthy will _____ me _____ for my dream.

6. Being creative will _____ _____ _____ something different.

7. Plus, I will always tell _____ never _____ _____ _____ because it will _____ _____ _____ harder.

1. 어떻게 나의 꿈을 성취할 것인가
2. 나는 디자이너가 되기를 원한다.
3. 나의 꿈을 성취하기 위해 내가 할 필요가 있는 세 가지가 있다.
4. 나는 건강해야 하고, 창의적이어야 하고, 그리고 결코 포기하지 말아야 한다.
5. 건강한 것은 나의 꿈을 계속 유지하도록 도와줄 것이다.
6. 창의적인 것은 내가 무언가 다른 것을 하도록 도와줄 것이다.
7. 더하여, 내 스스로에게 결코 포기하지 말라고 항상 말할 것인데, 이는 내가 더 열심히 노력하도록 해 줄 것이기 때문이다.

Wrap Up 2

1. B: _____ difficult _____ _____ English.

2. G: Rome _____ _____ _____ in a day.

3. B: _____ do you _____ _____ that?

4. G: I mean it _____ time _____ _____ _____.

5. B: I _____.

1. B: 영어를 배우는 것은 어려워.
2. G: 로마는 하루아침에 이루어지지 않았어.
3. B: 그게 무슨 뜻이니?
4. G: 무언가를 이루는 데 시간이 걸린다는 뜻이야.
5. B: 알겠어.

※ 다음 우리말을 영어로 쓰시오.

Language in Use

1. 작년에 나는 3개국을 방문했다.

　➡ _____

2. 프랑스가 내가 방문한 첫 번째 국가였다.

　➡ _____

3. Mary는 내가 파리에서 만났던 소녀이다.

　➡ _____

4. 그 파란 시계는 그곳에서 내 동생을 위해 산 선물이다.

　➡ _____

Enjoy Writing B

1. 어떻게 나의 꿈을 성취할 것인가

　➡ _____

2. 나는 디자이너가 되기를 원한다.

　➡ _____

3. 나의 꿈을 성취하기 위해 내가 할 필요가 있는 세 가지가 있다.

　➡ _____

4. 나는 건강해야 하고, 창의적이어야 하고, 그리고 결코 포기하지 말아야 한다.

　➡ _____

5. 건강한 것은 나의 꿈을 계속 유지하도록 도와줄 것이다.

　➡ _____

6. 창의적인 것은 내가 무언가 다른 것을 하도록 도와줄 것이다.

　➡ _____

7. 더하여, 내 스스로에게 결코 포기하지 말라고 항상 말할 것인데, 이는 내가 더 열심히 노력하도록 해 줄 것이기 때문이다.

　➡ _____

Wrap Up 2

1. B: 영어를 배우는 것은 어려워.

　➡ _____

2. G: 로마는 하루아침에 이루어지지 않았어.

　➡ _____

3. B: 그게 무슨 뜻이니?

　➡ _____

4. G: 무언가를 이루는 데 시간이 걸린다는 뜻이야.

　➡ _____

5. B: 알겠어.

　➡ _____

MEMO

MEMO

영어 기출 문제집

적중100

영어 기출 문제집

정답 및 해설

시사 | 박준언

중 2

적중100

2학기

정답 및 해설

시사 | 박준언

중 **2**

Lesson 5

Different Countries, Different Cultures

시험대비 실력평가   p.08

01 ③	02 ⑤	03 ⑤	04 ①
05 (1) capital (2) Spanish		06 ④	
07 (1) (d)ish (2) (u)nique		08 ④	

01 unique: 독특한 unusual: 특이한, 흔치 않은 / 각 등장인물은 독특한 성격을 갖고 있다.

02 Excuse me: (모르는 사람의 관심을 끌려고 할 때) 실례합니다 / 실례지만, 가장 가까운 지하철역이 어느 쪽인가요?

03 ceiling: 천장 / 방의 위쪽 내부 표면

04 shine: 빛나다 / 밝은 빛을 만들어 내다

05 (1) capital: 수도 (2) Spanish: 스페인의

06 ① coaster: (롤러) 코스터 / 그 남자는 롤러 코스터를 타고 있다. ② lizard: 도마뱀 / 도마뱀은 네 개의 다리와 긴 꼬리를 가지고 있다. ③ curry: 카레 / 그 카레는 나한테 너무 맵다. ④ view: 전망, 경치 / 나는 전망이 좋은 방을 원한다. ⑤ column: 기둥 / 그 기둥은 흰 대리석으로 만들어졌다.

07 (1) dish: 음식, 요리 / 가장 대표적인 한국 음식이 무엇이라고 생각하니? (2) unique: 독특한 / Rachel은 장미의 독특한 향기를 사랑한다.

08 ④ friend는 뒤에 ly를 붙여 형용사로 만들 수 있다. friend: 친구 friendly: 친절한 ① help: 도움 helpful: 도움이 되는 ② care: 조심 careful: 조심하는 ③ wonder: 놀라움 wonderful: 놀랄 만한, 멋진 ⑤ peace: 평화 peaceful: 평화로운

서술형 시험대비   p.09

01 (1) traditional   (2) historic[historical]

02 (1) cheers   (2) match   (3) works   (4) waves
   (5) experience

03 (1) Do you know how many tourists visit Boston
      every day?
   (2) The sun shines and the tree grows.
   (3) The crowd cheered up at the good news.
   (4) I want to study abroad.

04 (1) take   (2) turn   (3) put   (4) try

01 둘은 명사와 형용사의 관계이다. use: 사용 useful: 유용한

(1) tradition: 전통 traditional: 전통적인 (2) history: 역사 historic: 역사적인, 역사상 중요한 historical: 역사상, 역사와 관련된

02 (1) cheer: 격려하다, 환호하다, 갈채하다; 환호 (2) match: 경기, 시합; 어울리다 (3) work: 일하다, 작품 (4) wave: 흔들다; 파도 (5) experience: 경험; 경험하다

03 (1) tourist: 여행객 (2) shine: 빛나다 (3) cheer up: 기운을 내다 (4) abroad: 외국으로[에서]

04 (1) take a tour: 관광하다, 여행을 가다 / 너는 여행을 가고 싶니? (2) turn off: (전기, 가스, 수도 등을) 끄다 / TV를 꺼라. 잠잘 시간이 지났어. (3) put off: (시간, 날짜를) 미루다, 연기하다 / 다음 25일까지 여행을 미룰 수 있을까요? (4) try on: 입어 보다 / 이 재킷을 입어 봐도 돼요?

교과서
Conversation

핵심 Check   p.10~11

1 Where, bank / Go straight / next to
2 (1) Which, (p)refer / prefer, to
  (2) like better / prefer

교과서 대화문 익히기

Check(√) True or False   p.12

1 T   2 T   3 F   4 F   5 T   6 T

교과서 확인학습   p.14~15

Listen & Speak 1 A
1. Is, near / far from / How / Go straight, left, on
2. to buy, Where can / them at / Where is it / Go straight, blocks, across from

Listen & Speak 1 B
1. Where is / Go straight two blocks, on
2. Where is / straight, It's on, It's across from

Listen & Talk 2 A
1. It's, Let's go / good, How, get there / on foot or by bus , Which do you prefer / prefer
2. What is, called / type, traditional clothing / try one on / Which do you prefer

2 정답 및 해설

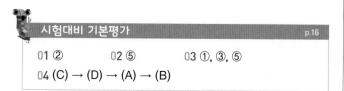

시험대비 기본평가   p.16

01 ②   02 ⑤   03 ①, ③, ⑤

04 (C) → (D) → (A) → (B)

01 'Where is ~?'는 '~가 어디에 있나요?'라는 의미로 길이나 위치를 물어볼 때 사용하는 표현이다.

02 I think hamburgers are less preferable to spaghetti. → I think hamburgers are preferable to spaghetti. less preferable은 덜 선호한다는 의미이므로, less를 빼야 햄버거를 스파게티보다 더 좋아한다는 의미가 된다.

03 ② Do you know when to go to the school? → Do you know where the school is? ④ Could I tell you where the school is? → Could you tell me where the school is?로 바꾸면 길을 물어보는 표현이 될 수 있다.

04 (C) 근처에 피카소 박물관이 있는지 묻는 질문에 (D) 그렇다고 대답한 후 여기서 멀지 않다고 언급한다. (A) 이어서 피카소 박물관을 어떻게 가는지 묻자 (B) 가는 방법을 알려준다.

시험대비 실력평가   p.17~18

01 ②   02 ②   03 ③   04 ④

05 ⑤   06 ④   07 ②

08 (A) why, (B) let's   09 ②   10 Where

11 ③   12 across from

01 far from: ~에서 먼

02 How can I get there?: 그곳에 어떻게 가니? 'Where is ~?'와 같이 'How can I get ~?'도 길이나 위치를 물어볼 때 사용하는 표현이다.

03 주어진 문장은 야시장에 어떻게 갈 수 있는지 물어보는 질문이다. 이에 대한 대답으로 가는 방법에 대한 언급이 나와야 한다. 그러므로 걸어가거나 버스를 타서 갈 수 있다는 대답 앞에 오는 것이 적절하다.

04 What do you prefer? → Which do you prefer? 걸어가거나 버스를 타는 것 중 하나를 선택하는 것이므로 의문사 Which

가 어울린다.

05 여자아이가 아니라 남자아이가 야시장에 가는 방법을 알고 있다.

06 길을 물어보는 질문에, 'I'm a stranger here, too. (저도 여기 처음이에요.)'라고 말한 후에 길을 알려 주는 것은 어울리지 않는다.

07 주어진 문장은 그것(*Best Friends*)이 언제 시작하는지 시간에 대한 정보를 묻고 있다. 그러므로 5시와 7시에 시작한다는 답이 이어지는 ②번이 적절하다.

08 (A)와 (B)에 사용된 'Why don't we ~?'와 'Let's ~'는 둘 다 '~하자'라고 제안을 할 때 사용할 수 있는 말이다. How about 다음에는 동명사가 나와야 하므로 (B)에는 let's가 적절하다.

09 ① 영화 Best Friends가 토요일 몇 시에 시작하는가? ② 어디서 그들이 토요일에 만날 것인가? ③ 여자아이는 5시나 7시 중 어떤 시간을 선호하는가? ④ 그들은 토요일 몇 시에 만날 것인가? ⑤ 그들은 토요일에 어떤 영화를 볼 것인가?

10 where: 어디서

11 Go straight two blocks: 두 블록 직진하세요. turn right: 우회전하세요.

12 across from: ~의 맞은편에

서술형 시험대비   p.19

01 'Yes, I do.'를 생략

02 Can you tell me how to get to the African Museum?

03 (A) right, (B) left, (C) across from

04 (A) on, (B) by

05 How can I get there? / Do you know how to get there? / Can you tell me how to get there?

06 or   07 to curry

01 'Which do you prefer, A or B?'는 어느 것을 선호하는지 묻는 표현으로 'Yes.'나 'No.'로 대답할 수 없다.

02 Can you tell me how to get to ~?: ~에 어떻게 가는지 말해 줄 수 있나요? / how to 동사원형: ~하는 방법 / get to 장소명사: ~에 도착하다

03 그림을 참고해 보면 ③은 두 블록 직진한 후, 우회전하면, 왼편에 있다. across from: ~의 맞은편에

04 on foot: 걸어서, by bus: 버스로

05 How can/do I get to ~?: ~에 어떻게 가나요? Do you know how to get to ~?: ~에 어떻게 가는지 아나요? Can you tell me how to get to ~?: ~에 어떻게 가는지 말해 줄 수 있나요?

06 Which do you prefer, A or B?: A와 B 중 어떤 것을 선호하니?

07 두 가지 중에서 어떤 것을 더 선호하는지 말할 때 'I prefer A to B.'를 사용한다. to B는 생략할 수 있다.

3

Grammar

1 (1) built (2) will be

2 (1) The water was so clear that you could see the bottom.

(2) He worked so hard that he became a lawyer.

(3) I'll drive fast so that you can get there in time.

시험대비 기본평가   p.22

01 (1) cleans → is cleaned

(2) is → was

(3) very → so

(4) so that → so that she

02 ④   **03** ②

04 (1) The water was so clean that we could drink it.

(2) He was injured during the soccer match.

01 (1) 방이 청소하는 것이 아니라 청소되는 것이므로 수동태가 적절하다. (2) in 1908이라는 과거를 나타내는 부사구가 있으므로 시제를 과거로 써야 한다. (3) 'so+형용사[부사]+that+주어+동사'의 형태로 원인과 결과를 나타내는 것이 적절하다. (4) so that 다음에는 '주어+동사'가 나와야 한다.

02 tomorrow가 있으므로 'will be sent'가 되어야 한다.

03 '…해서 ~하다'의 의미인 'so … that ~' 구문이다.

04 (1) 물이 깨끗해서 그 결과 마실 수 있었던 것이므로 'so … that ~' 구문으로 쓰는 것이 적절하다. (2) 부상을 입은 것이므로 수동태가 적절하다.

시험대비 실력평가   p.23~25

01 ④   **02** ③   **03** ⑤

04 weak so → so weak

05 (1) excited (2) consider (3) to (4) for (5) of

(6) so (7) that   **06** ①   **07** ①

08 ④   **09** ②   **10** ⑤

11 (1) Antoni Gaudi designed both.

(2) James took this photo.

(3) A beautiful dress was made for her by her mom.

(4) They will hold the book fair in Seoul.

(5) Who considers it to be dangerous?

12 (1) so (2) such (3) couldn't   **13** ⑤

14 ③, ⑤

15 (1) invented → was invented

(2) was happened → happened

(3) too careless → careless enough

16 ⑤   **17** ⑤   **18** ③

01 영어가 말하는 것이 아니라 말해지는 것이므로 수동태가 적절하다.

02 세차되는 것이므로 수동태가 적절하고 원인과 결과를 나타내는 'so+형용사[부사]+that+주어+동사' 구문이 적절하다.

03 The pictures drawn in France were sent to me by Jenny. sent가 능동태의 동사이므로 수동태로 바꾸면 'were sent'가 되어야 한다.

04 'so+형용사[부사]+that+주어+동사'는 원인과 결과를 나타내지만 'so that+주어+동사'는 목적을 나타낸다.

05 (1) 내가 신나게 되는 것이므로 수동태가 적절하다. (2) We가 주어이므로 능동태가 적절하다. (3) 직접목적어를 주어로 한 수동태에서 간접목적어 앞에 teach는 전치사 to를, (4) choose는 전치사 for를, (5) ask는 of를 쓴다. (6), (7) 'so+형용사[부사]+that+주어+동사' 구문이다.

06 원인과 결과를 나타내는 'so ~ that …' 구문이 적절하다.

07 by 이외의 전치사를 사용하는 수동태에 유의한다. be pleased with: ~에 기뻐하다 be satisfied with: ~에 만족하다

08 'so+형용사[부사]+that+주어+동사' 구문은 '너무 ~해서 …하다'라는 뜻으로 원인과 결과를 나타낸다.

09 'so that+주어+동사'는 목적을 나타내어 '~하기 위해서' 혹은 '~하도록'이라는 의미로 쓰인다. 부사적 용법의 '목적'과 바꿔 쓸 수 있다. 원인과 결과를 나타내는 'so ~ that …'과 혼동하지 않도록 유의한다.

10 turn off는 구동사로 하나의 단어처럼 취급하여 be turned off로 나타낸다. off를 빠뜨리지 않도록 주의한다.

11 (3) make는 직접목적어를 주어로 하는 수동태만 가능하며 간접목적어 앞에 전치사 for를 쓴다. (4) 미래 시제의 수동태는 'will be+과거분사'이며 수동태에서 일반인이 행위자일 경우 보통 'by+일반인 주어'를 생략한다. (5) 수동태의 by whom이 who로 바뀌는 것에 주의한다.

12 (1) 원인과 결과를 나타내는 'so ~ that …' 구문이다. (2) 'so ~ that …' 구문에서 that 앞에 형용사나 부사 대신 명사가 오면 so 대신 such를 쓴다. (3) so+형용사[부사]+that+주어+can't+동사원형: 너무 ~하여 …할 수 없다.

13 목적격보어가 원형부정사인 경우, 수동태 문장에서는 to부정사로 바뀐다. We were made to do our homework by our teacher.

14 ① He was seen to put the bag on the table by Ann. ② The storybook was read to him every night by his mom. ④ It was such a nice day that we went for a walk.

15 (1) WWW가 발명되는 것이므로 수동태가 적절하다. (2) happen은 자동사이므로 수동태로 쓰이지 않는다. (3) so+형용

사[부사]+that+주어+can ~ = '형용사[부사]+enough+to 동사원형', so+형용사[부사]+that+주어+can't ~ = too+형용사[부사]+to 동사원형

16 choose는 직접목적어를 주어로 한 수동태에서는 간접목적어 앞에 for를 쓴다.

17 시제가 과거이므로 was heard로 쓰고, 원형부정사인 목적격보어는 to부정사로 쓴다.

18 이유를 나타내는 Because절이므로 'so+형용사[부사]+that+주어+동사' 구문으로 원인과 결과를 나타낼 수 있다

서술형 시험대비   p.26~27

01 (1) Someone stole the painting last week.
   (2) I was impressed by its size and unique design.
   (3) Peter was heard to open the window by Eva.
   (4) A present will be given (to) me by Angie on my birthday.
   (5) The baby was taken care of by Cathy.

02 (1) so stupid that
   (2) tall enough to
   (3) too shocked to

03 (1) hard so that   (2) so hard that

04 (1) Cake is made from flour, milk, eggs and sugar.
   (2) The shirts will be ironed by John tomorrow morning.
   (3) Mike was seen to be hit by a car by Ms. Brown.
   (4) Our dog was run over by a truck.
   (5) The matter will be discussed by us tommorow.

05 (1) easy enough to   (2) so fast that

06 (1) The novel was written by Ernest Hemingway.
   (2) The first World Cup took place in Uruguay in 1930.
   (3) A fairy tale book was read to her daughter by Laura.
   (4) Kimberly was disappointed at the news.
   (5) Was Allie heard to sing by you?
   (6) It was so cold that he caught a cold.

07 (1) Claire got up too late to get on the train.
   (2) Chuck spoke so low that I could not hear him.
   (3) Bill was smart enough to solve the difficult math problems.
   (4) Juliet is so rich that she can buy the house.

08 (1) The sweater was made for me by my grandmother.
   (2) Are these rooms cleaned by her every day?
   (3) Dan was made to prepare dinner by Mariel.
   (4) Joakim was pleased with your recent success a lot.

01 (3) 목적격보어가 원형부정사인 경우 수동태에서는 to부정사로 쓴다. (4) 미래 시제의 수동태는 'will be+과거분사'이다. (5) 구동사(take care of)는 하나의 동사처럼 취급한다는 것에 주의한다.

02 (1) 'so+형용사[부사]+that+주어+동사'의 형태로 원인과 결과를 나타낸다. (2) so+형용사[부사]+that+주어+can ~ = '형용사[부사]+enough+to 동사원형' (3) so+형용사[부사]+that+주어+can't ~ = too+형용사[부사]+to 동사원형

03 (1) 목적을 나타내는 'so that'을 사용한다. (2) 원인과 결과를 나타내는 'so ~ that …'을 사용한다.

04 (1) be made of: ~로 만들어지다(물리적 변화), be made from: ~로 만들어지다(화학적 변화) (2) shirts가 다림질을 하는 것이 아니라 다림질 되는 것이므로 수동태가 적절하며 미래의 일이므로 'will be+pp' 형태가 적절하다. (3) 목적격보어가 원형부정사인 경우, 수동태 문장에서는 to부정사로 바뀐다. (4) run-ran-run (5) 'will be +pp' 형태가 되어야 한다.

05 (1) so+형용사[부사]+that+주어+can ~ = 형용사[부사]+enough+to 동사원형 (2) so+형용사[부사]+that+주어+can't ~ = too+형용사[부사]+to 동사원형

06 (1) 소설이 씌여지는 것이므로 수동태가 적절하다. (2) take place는 자동사로 쓰이므로 수동태로 쓰면 안 된다. (3) read는 직접목적어를 주어로 하는 수동태만 가능하다. fairy tale book: 동화책 (4) be disappointed at: ~에 실망하다, 낙담하다 (5) 목적격보어가 원형부정사인 경우, 수동태 문장에서는 to부정사로 바뀐다 (6) so ~ that: 너무 ~해서 …하다

07 so ~ that 주어 can't … = too ~ to …, ~ enough to부정사 = so ~ that 주어 can … 이때 to부정사 앞에 for 목적격으로 쓰인 것은 to부정사의 의미상의 주어로 that 이하의 절로 바꿀 때는 주격으로 바꿔야 하며, to부정사로 썼을 때 생략된 동사의 목적어는 써 주어야 한다.

08 (1) 직접목적어를 주어로 한 수동태에서 make는 간접목적어 앞에 전치사 for를 쓴다. (2) 의문문을 수동태로 바꿀 때는 평서문으로 바꿔서 고친 후에 다시 의문문으로 바꾸면 쉽다. (3) 목적격보어가 원형부정사인 경우, 수동태 문장에서는 to부정사로 바뀐다. (4) please는 수동태에서 by가 아니라 보통 with를 쓴다. be pleased with: ~로 기뻐하다

교과서
Reading

확인문제   p.28

1 F 2 T 3 T 4 F 5 T 6 F

1 T　2 F　3 T　4 F　5 T　6 F

교과서 확인학습 A

01 Happy Days, by
02 traveled to
03 is loved by
04 visited, interesting
05 Our trip
06 is famous for
07 to watch
08 were excited, the world's most famous soccer players
09 was full of
10 by singing, shouting
11 After
12 While, walked around
13 visited, watched
14 in a red dress, with wonderful movements
15 For
16 traditional Spanish dish with
17 tasted like
18 so, that
19 took a tour of
20 were designed by
21 creative works like
22 After
23 is still going on
24 was impressed by
25 shone like
26 stood like
27 creativity, his love of nature
28 Traveling, a wonderful experience
29 While, a lot
30 to visit

교과서 확인학습 B

1 My Happy Days in Spain by Park Jinwoo
2 My family traveled to Spain this summer.
3 Spain is loved by lots of tourists.
4 We visited many interesting places.
5 Our trip started in Madrid.
6 Madrid is the capital and is famous for soccer.
7 We went to a stadium to watch a soccer match.
8 My sister and I were excited because we could watch some of the world's most famous soccer players.
9 The stadium was full of soccer fans.
10 As we watched the match, we cheered by singing songs, waving our hands, and shouting with the other fans.
11 After we toured Madrid, we went to Seville.
12 While we walked around the city, we saw many historic buildings.
13 We visited a flamenco museum and watched a flamenco dance.
14 A woman in a red dress was dancing the flamenco with wonderful movements.
15 For dinner, we ate paella.
16 It is a traditional Spanish dish with rice, vegetables, meat, and seafood.
17 It tasted like fried rice in Korea.
18 It was so delicious that we all enjoyed it.
19 In Barcelona, we took a tour of Park Guell and Sagrada Familia.
20 Both were designed by Antoni Gaudi.
21 In Park Guell, we saw some of Gaudi's creative works like a colorful lizard.
22 After Park Guell, we visited Sagrada Familia.
23 Work on the building started in 1883 and is still going on today.
24 I was impressed by its size and unique design.
25 The ceiling inside Sagrada Familia shone like the night sky with bright stars.
26 Its stone columns stood like big trees.
27 At Park Guell and Sagrada Familia I could feel Gaudi's creativity and his love of nature.
28 Traveling in Spain was a wonderful experience.
29 While I was there, I learned a lot about Spain.
30 I want to visit the country again.

시험대비 실력평가

01 ③
02 ①, ⑤
03 ③
04 saw them in Seville
05 ②
06 ③
07 It was so delicious that we all[all of us] enjoyed it.
08 ②
09 ③
10 (A) Barcelona　(B) a colorful lizard
11 They speak Vietnamese there.
12 ②
13 ②
14 (A) ceiling　(B) there　(C) about
15 ①, ④
16 Ⓐ size, Ⓑ unique design
17 ③
18 ④
19 ②
20 ④
21 creativity
22 ①
23 ④
24 is spoken
25 Australia is so wonderful that you should visit it someday.
26 (A) the Sydney Opera House, (B) ocean roads

01 위 글은 '기행문'이다. ① (책·연극·영화 등에 대한) 논평[비평], 감상문, ② 수필, ④ 전기, ⑤ (신문·잡지의) 글, 기사

02 ① 약간의, ④ a number of: (수가) 많은, ⑤ (양이) 많은, lots of = a lot of = plenty of: (수와 양이) 많은

03 ③ 진우의 가족 여행은 마드리드에서 '시작했다.'

04 '세비야'에서 많은 역사상 중요한 건물들을 보았다.

05 ⓐ와 ②번: …하는 동안, ① …인 데 반하여(둘 사이의 대조를 나타냄), ③과 ⑤ [주절 뒤에서 반대·비교·대조를 나타내어] 그런데, 한편(으로는), ④ 잠깐, 잠시

06 ⓑ와 ②, ③, ⑤번: 현재분사, ①, ④: 동명사

07 so ~ that …: 너무 ~해서 …하다

08 ⓑ와 ②번: 작품들(명사), ① 근무하다, 취직해 있다(동사), ③ (건설) 공사[작업](명사), ④ (약 따위가) 작용하다, 듣다[on] (동사), ⑤ (기계 따위가) 움직이다, 작동하다(동사)

09 ③ 위 글은 '진우의 가족이 즐긴 요리와 장소를 소개'하는 글이다.

10 그것은 '바르셀로나'에 있고 Antoni Gaudi에 의해 설계되었다. 그곳에서 진우의 가족은 '형형색색의 도마뱀'과 같은 몇몇 Gaudi의 창의적인 작품들을 보았다.

11 일반인을 나타내는 They를 주어로 해서 바꾸는 것이 적절하다.

12 be well known for: ~으로 잘 알려져 있다

13 ② 베트남에서는 '베트남어'가 사용된다.

14 (A) 사그라다 파밀리아 안의 '천장'이라고 해야 하므로 ceiling이 적절하다. ceiling: 천장, sealing: (봉투 등을) 밀봉[밀폐]하기, (B) there는 부사이므로 전치사 없이 쓰는 것이 적절하다. (C) 스페인에 '대해' 많은 것을 배웠다고 해야 하므로 about이 적절하다. a lot of: 많은

15 ① 가주어 It을 사용하여 바꾸거나, ④ to부정사를 주어로 하여 바꾸는 것이 적절하다.

16 진우에게, 사그라다 파밀리아의 '크기'와 '독특한 디자인'은 인상적이었다. impressive: 인상적인, 인상[감명] 깊은

17 ① They visited Park Guell. ② It started in 1883. ③ 사그라다 파밀리아의 건물 공사가 오늘날까지도 여전히 진행 중인 이유는 알 수 없다. ④ Stone. ⑤ At Park Guell and Sagrada Familia.

18 주어진 문장의 Both에 주목한다. ④번 앞 문장의 Park Guell과 Sagrada Familia를 받고 있으므로 ④번이 적절하다.

19 ② paella의 조리법이 무엇인지는 대답할 수 없다. ① Rice, vegetables, meat, and seafood. ingredient: 재료, ③ They took a tour of Park Guell and Sagrada Familia. ④ Both were designed by Antoni Gaudi. ⑤ They saw some of Gaudi's creative works like a colorful lizard.

20 ④ go on = continue: 계속하다, ② remain: (처리·이행 등을 해야 할 일이) 남아 있다

21 소유격 다음에 명사를 써야 하는데, creation은 '창조, 창작'의 뜻이므로 creativity(창의성, 독창력)를 쓰는 것이 적절하다.

22 스페인 여행은 훌륭한 경험이었다며, 그 나라를 다시 방문하고 싶

다고 했으므로 '만족한' 심경이라고 하는 것이 적절하다. ① 만족한, ② 겁먹은, 무서워하는, ③ 지루한, ④ 부끄러운, ⑤ 실망한

23 ④ '사그라다 파밀리아'에서 Gaudi의 창의성과 자연에 대한 사랑을 느낄 수 있었다.

24 영어가 '사용된다'고 해야 하므로 수동태로 쓰는 것이 적절하다.

25 'so'를 보충하면 된다.

26 시드니의 관광명소는 '시드니 오페라하우스'이고 멜버른은 아름다운 '해안 도로들'로 유명하다.

🦉 서술형 시험대비 p.38~39

01 Lots of tourists love Spain.

02 (A) visited (B) to watch (C) were

03 well known

04 ⓐ singing ⓑ waving ⓒ shouting

05 After

06 Seville

07 Spanish

08 felt → tasted

09 toured

10 It tasted like fried rice in Korea.

11 paella

12 such as

13 We visited Park Guell before Sagrada Familia. 또는 Before Sagrada Familia, we visited Park Guell.

14 (A) impressed (B) shone (C) stood

15 historic

16 who[that]

17 축구 경기장에서 경기를 보며 응원했다 / 도시를 걸어다니는 동안 많은 역사상 중요한 건물들을 보았고, 플라멩코 박물관을 방문해서 플라멩코 춤을 보았다.

---

01 by 다음의 'lots of tourists'를 주어로 해서 고치는 것이 적절하다.

02 (A) visit는 타동사이므로 전치사 없이 바로 목적어를 쓰는 것이 적절하다. (B) 축구 경기를 '보기 위해서'라고 해야 하므로 to watch가 적절하다. (C) 'My sister and I'가 주어이므로 were가 적절하다.

03 be famous for = be well known for: ~로 유명하다, ~로 잘 알려져 있다

04 전치사 by 뒤에 동명사로 쓰는 것이 적절하다.

05 우리는 세비야로 가기 '전에' 마드리드를 관광했다. = 마드리드를 관광하고 난 '후', 우리는 세비야로 갔다..

06 '세비야'를 가리킨다.

07 형용사 Spanish로 쓰는 것이 적절하다. Spanish: 스페인의

08 한국의 볶음밥과 같은 '맛이 났다'고 하는 것이 적절하다. feel like: (촉감이) …하다

7

09 tour = take a tour of

10 'like'를 보충하면 된다.

11 '파에야'를 가리킨다.

12 like = such as: ~와 같은

13 '사그라다 파밀리아를 보기 전에 우리는 구엘 공원을 방문했다' 라고 고치는 것이 적절하다.

14 (A) '감명 받았다'고 해야 하므로 impressed가 적절하다. impressing: 감동시키는, (B) 밤하늘처럼 '빛났다'고 해야 하므로 shone이 적절하다. shine - shone: 빛나다, 반짝이다, shine - shined: 윤[광]을 내다, 닦다, (C) stand는 자동사라서 수동태를 만들 수 없으므로 stood가 적절하다.

15 'history'의 형용사형 historic을 쓰는 것이 적절하다. historic: 역사적으로 중요한, 역사적인, historical은 '역사에 바탕을 둔'이라는 뜻으로, 보통 과거와 관련된 것, 역사 연구와 관련된 것 또는 과거에 실제 있었던 일을 묘사할 때 사용하므로 적절하지 않다.

16 주격 관계대명사 'who'나 'that'을 쓰는 것이 적절하다.

17 마드리드의 축구 경기장에서 경기를 보며 응원했고, 세비야를 걸어 다니는 동안 많은 역사상 중요한 건물들을 보았고 플라멩코 박물관을 방문해서 플라멩코 춤을 보았다.

영역별 핵심문제

01 ②　　　　02 ④　　　　03 for　　　　04 on
05 (1) historic　(2) theater　(3) ceiling　(4) cheer for, fans
06 ⑤　　　　07 ③　　　　08 ③　　　　09 view
10 ②　　　　11 Where is the nearest bus stop?
12 (C) → (A) → (B)　　　　13 ②
14 (1) so difficult that we couldn't solve them
　　(2) too difficult for us to solve　　　　15 ①
16 ④　　　　17 so beautiful that
18 (1) was written by　(2) were built by　　19 ③
20 (1) By whom was the telephone invented?
　　(2) The roof of the house was covered with snow.
　　(3) It was so dark that nothing could be seen.
　　(4) The runner ran so fast that nobody could
　　　　catch up with him.
21 travel, tour 22 ①, ④, ⑤
23 (A) a stadium, (B) a soccer match
24 ③　　　　25 ②
26 (A) fried　(B) were　(C) creative
27 Park Guell and Sagrada Familia

01 ① cheer for: ~을 응원하다 / 우리의 국가 대표팀을 응원해요! ② get 장소 부사: ~에 도착하다 / 그곳에 어떻게 가니? ③ design: 설계하다, 디자인하다 / 나는 나의 집을 설계했다. ④ tea: 차 / 그 차는 훌륭한 맛을 지니고 있다. ⑤ title: 제목 / 이 노래의 제목이 무엇이니?

02 ① sliding, slide: 미끄러지다, 활주하다 / 아이들은 얼어붙은 호수에서 미끄럼을 타고 있다. ② waved, wave: 흔들다 / 아기는 엄마에게 손을 흔들었다. ③ rolling, roll: 구르다, 굴리다 / 그들은 큰 공을 굴리고 있다. ④ taking, take a tour: 관광하다, 여행을 가다 / 그때 시내 구경을 하시는 게 어때요? ⑤ prefer: 선호하다 / 나는 커피보다 차를 선호한다.

03 be famous for: ~로 유명하다 be well known for: ~로 잘 알려져 있다

04 get on: ~에 타다 on foot: 걸어서

06 (A) 할로윈에 필요한 사탕을 사야 하는데 그것을 어디서 살 수 있는지 물어보고, 이에 대한 대답으로 Wendy's 사탕 가게에서 살 수 있다는 대답을 들었다. (B) Wendy's 사탕 가게가 어디 있는지 질문하고 이에 대한 대답을 듣는 것이 적절하다.

07 할로윈에 필요한 사탕을 사기 위해 Wendy's 사탕 가게에 가야 할 사람은 남자아이이다.

08 ③ It's across from the school. → It's across from the cinema. 병원은 영화관 맞은편에 있다.

09 view: 전망, 경치 / 어떤 특정한 장소나 위치에서 볼 수 있는 것, 특히 아름다운 전원

10 주어진 문장은 런던 아이와 스카이 가든에 대해서 간략히 설명하고 있다. 직원이 런던의 멋진 경치를 즐기기에 좋은 장소가 두 곳 있다고 먼저 말한 후, 이에 대해 설명하는 것이 자연스러우므로 ②가 적절하다.

11 Where is ~?: ~가 어디에 있나요? the 최상급(형용사+est): 가장 ~한 stop: 정거장

12 해외 여행을 가자는 말에. (C) 어떤 도시(방콕이나 대만)를 선호하는지 묻는다. (A) 방콕을 더 좋아한다고 대답하고, 너무 화려해서 가야 한다고 말한다. (B) 그곳(방콕)에 가자고 대답한다.

13 비행기가 식당으로 바뀐 것이므로 수동태가 적절하다. The plane stopped flying and was turned into a restaurant.

14 'so+형용사[부사]+that+주어+can't ~'는 'too+형용사[부사]+to 동사원형'으로 바꿔 쓸 수 있다. 이때 to부정사의 목적어가 주어와 같을 경우 따로 써주지 않는 것에 유의한다.

15 첫 번째 문장에서는 목적격보어가 원형부정사인 경우, 수동태 문장에서는 to부정사로 바뀐다. 두 번째 문장에서는 'so+형용사[부사]+that+주어+동사'의 형태로 원인과 결과를 나타내는 것이 적절하다.

16 ① The room was so cold that David turned on the heater. ② This story was so funny that I laughed a lot. ③ Arnold got up so late that he missed the train. ⑤ John is so kind that everyone likes him.

17 'so+형용사[부사]+that+주어+동사'의 형태로 원인과 결과를 나타낸다.

18 (1) 책이 씌여진 것이고 (2) 피라미드가 건설된 것이므로

'be+pp' 형태의 수동태로 쓴다.

19 ③ write는 직접목적어를 주어로 하는 수동태만 가능하다. A long letter was written to me by my girl friend.

20 (1) 수동태의 의문문은 능동태의 평서문을 수동태로 고친 후에 다시 의문문으로 바꾸면 쉽다. (2) be covered with: ~로 덮여 있다 (3), (4) 'so+형용사[부사]+that+주어+동사' 구문은 '너무 ~해서 …하다'라는 뜻으로 원인과 결과를 나타낸다.

21 trip = travel = tour: 여행

22 ⓑ와 ②, ③번은 부사적 용법, ①, ④ 형용사적 용법 ⑤ 명사적 용법

23 진우의 가족은 스페인 여행 도중에 마드리드에 있는 '경기장'에 가서 '축구 경기'를 보았다.

24 ⓐ와 ③번: …할 때(접속사), ① …이므로, …이기 때문에(접속사), ② …하는 대로(접속사), ④ (자격·기능 등이)

25 ② 진우의 가족은 '세비야'를 걸어다녔다.

26 (A) 한국의 '볶음밥'과 같은 맛이 났다고 해야 하므로 fried가 적절하다. fried rice: 볶음밥, frying: (기름에) 굽는, 튀기는, (B) Both는 복수로 취급하므로 were가 적절하다. (C) Gaudi의 '창의적인' 작품들을 보았다고 해야 하므로 creative가 적절하다. common: 흔한, 공통의, creative: 창의적인

27 '구엘 공원'과 '사그라다 파밀리아'를 가리킨다.

단원별 예상문제
p.46~49

01 take 02 by

03 (1) cheered (2) try on (3) (f)amous for
   (4) get, on foot

04 (f)lamenco, (p)urple, (V)ietnamese
   (1) flamenco (2) Vietnamese (3) purple

05 ① 06 ② 07 ⑤

08 (A) How (B) Which (C) Where

09 Where is the best place to go to?

10 Go straight one block and turn right. It's on your left. 11 (C) → (A) → (B) → (D) 12 ②

13 (1) The shoes look so great that Sandra wants to buy them.
   (2) The stereo was so loud that it was impossible to sleep.

14 (1) so great that (2) were killed 15 ④

16 ② 17 It is well known for soccer.

18 ①, ③

19 toured of → toured 또는 took a tour of

20 ④ 21 ⑤ 22 ④

23 creative

24 They were designed by Antoni Gaudi.

---

01 take a walk: 산책하다 / 나는 나의 개와 산책하고 싶다. take a class: 수업을 받다 / 방과 후에 너는 수업을 듣거나 함께 클럽

에 가입할 수 있어. take a tour: 관광하다, 여행을 가다 / 그들은 그 성을 관광했던 것을 좋아했다.

02 수동태(be+p.p+by 행위자): …에 의해서 ~되다, by+교통수단: 교통수단으로 → by bus: 버스로

03 (1) cheer: 환호하다, 갈채하다 (2) try on: 입어 보다 (3) be famous for: ~로 유명하다 (4) on foot: 걸어서 get 장소 부사: ~에 도착하다

04 (1) flamenco: 플라멩코 (스페인 남부 Andalusia 지방 집시의 춤) / 안달루시아 집시의 격렬한 리듬을 가진 춤 / 그는 플라멩코 춤을 즐겨 춘다. (2) Vietnamese: 베트남어; 베트남의 / 베트남 언어, 사람 또는 문화와 관련된 / 그녀는 베트남에서 일자리를 구하기 위해 베트남어를 배웠다. (3) purple: 보라색 / 파란색과 빨간색을 섞은 색 / 그녀는 짙은 보라색 옷을 입었다.

05 주어진 문장은 야시장에 가서 신선한 과일 주스를 마시자고 제안하는 말이다. 날씨가 정말 덥다고 얘기하면서 이러한 제안을 하고, 이 제안에 대해서 'Sounds good.(좋아)'이라고 대답을 하고 있으므로 ①이 적절하다.

06 ② 위의 대화에서는 버스와 걷는 것 중의 선호를 물었기 때문에 버스와 택시 중에 무엇을 더 좋아하는지에 대해 대답할 수 없다. ① 그들은 야시장에 어떻게 갈 것인가? ② 남자아이는 버스와 택시 중 어떤 것을 선호하니? ③ 그들은 어디에 있는가? ④ 그들은 어디에 갈 것인가? ⑤ 그들은 무엇을 마실 것인가?

07 주어진 문장은 나중에 그곳을 방문하자고 제안하는 말이다. 여기서 그곳으로 지칭할 수 있는 장소는 런던 아이와 빅벤이며, 제안에 수락이나 거절하는 표현이 나와야 한다. 그러므로 'That sounds great.(좋아요)'라고 제안을 수락한 문장 앞에 들어가는 것이 적절하다.

08 (A) How may I help you?: 무엇을 도와드릴까요? (B) Which do you prefer(, A or B)?: (A와 B 중) 어떤 것을 선호하니? (C) Where is ~?: ~가 어디에 있나요?

09 'to go to'는 앞의 the best place를 꾸며주는 형용사적 용법으로 쓰인 to부정사이다. Where is ~?: ~가 어디에 있나요? best: 최고의, 가장 좋은

10 Go straight: 직진하세요. Turn right: 우회전하세요. It is on your left: 왼편에 있어요.

11 아프리카 박물관에 가는 방법을 물어보는 질문에 (C) 물론 가르쳐 준다고 대답하며 두 블록 직진한 후 우회전하라고 얘기한다. (A) 두 블록 직진한 후 우회전하고 그 다음에는 어떻게 하는지 질문하자. (B) 아프리카 박물관이 왼편에 있고, 신발 가게 맞은편에 있다는 추가적인 정보를 준다. (D) 길을 알려 준 것에 대해 감사를 표한다.

12 ③ 간접목적어 앞에 for 대신 to를 써야 한다.

13 (1), (2) 'so+형용사[부사]+that+주어+동사' 구문을 이용하여 원인과 결과를 나타낸다.

14 (1) 'so+형용사[부사]+that+주어+동사'로 원인과 결과를 나타낸다. (2) 누가 그 동작을 했는지 중요하지 않거나 잘 모를 때,

수동태 문장으로 표현한다.

15 ④ 세계에서 가장 유명한 축구 선수 몇몇을 볼 수 있었기 때문에 '신이 났다'고 하는 것이 적절하다. ① 재미있는, 흥미로운, ② 실망한, ③ 속상한, 마음이 상한, ⑤ 재미있는, 즐거운, amused(재미있어 하는, 즐거워하는)

16 ⓐ와 ②번: 수도, ①, ③, ④ 자본금, 자본 ⑤ 대문자

17 마드리드는 '축구'로 유명하다. be famous for = be well known for: ~로 유명하다, ~로 잘 알려져 있다

18 ⓐ와 ②, ④, ⑤번: 동명사, ①, ③번: 현재분사

19 tour = take a tour of

20 ④ 진우의 가족이 얼마나 오래 플라멩코 춤을 보았는지는 대답할 수 없다. ① At the soccer stadium. ② They sang songs, waved their hands, and shouted with the other fans. ③ They saw many historic buildings. ⑤ She was wearing a red dress.

21 ⓐ For dinner: 저녁 식사로, ⓑ with: '~로, ~이 있는'이라는 뜻의 전치사

22 파에야는 '쌀'과 '채소', '고기', '해산물'이 들어간 전통적인 스페인 요리이다.

23 뒤의 명사를 수식하는 형용사로 쓰는 것이 적절하다.

🦉 서술형 실전문제   p.50~51

01 The view from the London Eye are amazing. → The view from the London Eye is amazing.

02 Go straight two blocks and turn right.

03 (A) → (C) → (B) → (D)

04 Which do you prefer, the Roller Coaster or the Scary House?

05 (1) so colorful that   (2) so tired that, too tired to

06 (1) Many people who want to do fun activities love Hong Kong.
  (2) What was promised to do by her last weekend?
  (3) We were taught physics by Ms. Grace last year. 또는 Physics was taught (to) us by Ms. Grace last year.

07 was filled with

08 A woman in a red dress was dancing the flamenco with wonderful movements.

09 (A) Seville (B) many historic buildings

10 like

11 (A) Spanish (B) Korea (C) rice, vegetables, meat (D) seafood

12 Antoni Gaudi designed both.

01 The view가 문장의 주어로 단수형이기 때문에 are가 아니라 is가 적절하다.

02 Go straight.: 직진하세요. Turn right.: 우회전하세요.

03 지수에게 토요일에 영화를 보자고 제안한다. (A) 좋다고 대답하며 영화가 몇 시에 시작하는지 질문하자 (C) 토요일에 5시와 7시가 있다고 말하며 어떤 시간을 더 선호하는지 물어본다. (B) 7시를 더 선호한다고 대답하고 (D) 그러면 6시에 만나자고 약속 시간을 정한다.

04 Which do you prefer, A or B?: A와 B 중 어떤 것을 선호하니?

05 'so+형용사[부사]+that+주어+동사' 구문을 이용하여 원인과 결과를 나타낸다.

06 (2) 의문문의 수동태는 능동태의 의문문을 평서문으로 바꾼 후 이것을 수동태로 고치고, 다시 의문문으로 바꾸면 쉽다. (3) 4형식 문장의 수동태는 간접목적어와 직접목적어 각각을 주어로 하는 수동태가 가능하며 직접목적어를 주어로 한 수동태에서 teach 동사는 간접목적어 앞에 전치사 to를 쓴다. 이때의 to는 생각할 수도 있다.

07 be full of = be filled with: ~로 가득 차 있다

08 'in'을 보충하면 된다.

09 진우의 가족은 마드리드를 여행하고 난 후, '세비야'로 가서 도시를 걸어다니는 동안, '많은 역사상 중요한 건물들'을 보았다.

10 ⓐ tasted like: ~와 같은 맛이 났다, ⓒ like: ~와 같은

11 전통적인 '스페인' 요리인 파에야는 '한국'의 볶음밥과 같은 맛이 나고, 그것의 재료는 '쌀'과 '채소', '고기', '해산물'이다. ingredient: (특히 요리 등의) 재료[성분]

12 Antoni Gaudi를 주어로 해서 고치는 것이 적절하다.

🐰 창의사고력 서술형문제   p.52

|모범답안|

01 (A) Do you know how to get to the bank?
  (B) Go straight two blocks and turn right. / It's next to the police station. / It's across from the post office.

02 (A) capital
  (B) English
  (C) Meat pie and lamington
  (D) the Sydney Opera House
  (E) beautiful ocean roads

03 (1) He practiced dancing so hard that he became a B-boy dancer.
  (2) The thief ran away so that no one could find him.
  (3) The cartoon was so interesting that I kept reading it.

01 Do you know how to get to ~?: ~에 어떻게 가는지 아나요? Go straight: 직진하세요. Turn right: 우회전 하세요. next to: ~옆에 across from: ~의 맞은편에

01 (1) useful (2) hopeful (3) colorful
02 (1) of (2) from (3) on, of (4) on
03 (1) try on (2) (g)o on (3) across from
   (4) is well known for
04 ③
05 (1) Where / right, your left. It's next to
   (2) Where is / one block, turn left, on your right,
    across, the Flower Garden   06 abroad
07 Which city do you prefer, Bangkok or Taiwan?
08 (B) so, (C) that
09 (A) watch (B) What time (C) are
10 ②   11 called   12 on
13 Which do you prefer, the purple one or the
   yellow one?
14 (1) was heard to lock the door by me
   (2) so wonderful that
15 ②   16 ⑤
17 (1) Sharon worked hard so that she might succeed.
   (2) The box was so heavy that no one could move it.
   (3) The machine will be repaired by Mr. Kim.
18 ③
19 (A) this summer (B) interesting (C) excited
20 ②   21 ③   22 ⑤
23 traditional   24 tasted → tasted like
25 ④

01 주어진 두 단어의 관계는 명사와 형용사의 관계이다. use, hope, color는 모두 명사이고 뒤에 ful을 붙여서 형용사가 된다. (1) use: 사용 useful: 유용한 (2) hope: 희망, 기대 hopeful: 희망에 찬, 기대하는 (3) color: 색깔 colorful: 다채로운

02 (1) be full of: ~으로 가득 차다 (2) far from: ~로부터 먼 (3) on top of: ~의 위에, ~의 꼭대기에 (4) turn on: ~을 켜다

03 (1) try on: 입어 보다 (2) go on: (어떤 일이) 계속되다 (3) across from: ~의 맞은편에 (4) be well known for: ~로 잘 알려져 있다

04 ① match: 경기, 시합 / 그들은 중요한 시합을 하는 중이다. ② movement: 동작 / 그 동물은 빠른 동작으로 움직였다. ③ language: 언어 / 나는 영어, 일본어, 한국어 세 가지 언어를 할 수 있다. ④ tour: 여행 / 오늘 여행에서 우리는 많은 희귀 동물을 볼 것이다. ⑤ hamburger: 햄버거 / 그들은 어제 점심으로 햄버거를 먹었다.

05 Where is ~?: ~가 어디에 있나요? Go straight: 직진하세요. Turn left/right: 좌회전/우회전 하세요. next to: ~옆에 across from: ~의 맞은편에

06 abroad: 외국으로[에서] / 외국에서 또는 외국으로

07 Which do you prefer, A or B?: A와 B 중 어떤 것을 선호하니?

08 so 형용사/부사 that 주어 동사: 너무 ~해서 그 결과 ~하다

09 (A) Why don't we 동사원형 ~?: ~할래?(제안하기) (B) What time: 몇 시에, 질문에 대한 대답이 '토요일에는 5시와 7시 두 번 상영해.'라는 것으로 보아 시간에 대해 질문하고 있다. (C) 'There be ~'는 be동사 다음에 주어가 나온다. two showings가 주어이므로 복수동사 are가 적절하다.

10 토요일에 영화가 5시와 7시로 2개를 선택할 수 있다. 이렇게 2개가 있을 때 먼저 언급한 것은 one, 나머지는 the other로 받는다.

11 긴 드레스가 이름이 뭐라고 불리는지 묻고 있는 것이므로 수동태가 어울린다.

12 try ~ on: ~을 입어 보다

13 Which do you prefer, A or B?: A와 B 중 어느 것을 선호하니? 대명사 one은 앞서 나온 Ao dai를 의미한다.

14 (1) hear는 지각동사이므로 목적격보어로 원형부정사를 쓰지만 수동태에서는 원형부정사를 to부정사로 바꿔 주어야 한다. (2) 원인과 결과를 나타내는 'so ~ that …' 구문이 적절하다.

15 ② 직접목적어를 주어로 한 수동태에서 make는 간접목적어 앞에 전치사 for를 쓴다.

16 'so … that ~'은 '너무[매우] …해서 ~하다'의 의미로 원인과 결과를 나타낸다.

17 (1) 'so that+주어+동사' 구문은 목적을 나타내어 '~하기 위해서' 혹은 '~하도록'이라는 의미로 쓰인다. (2) 'so+형용사[부사]+that+주어+동사' 구문은 '너무 ~해서 …하다'라는 뜻으로 원인과 결과를 나타낸다. (3) 조동사가 있는 문장의 수동태는 '조동사+be+p.p.' 형식을 갖는다.

18 일반 사람이 주어인 능동태를 수동태로 바꿀 때 'by+일반 사람'은 생략 가능하다.

19 (A) 때를 나타내는 this, last, next 등의 앞에는 전치사를 붙이지 않으므로 this summer가 적절하다. (B) 감정을 나타내는 동사가 무생물을 수식할 때는 보통 현재분사를 쓰므로 interesting이 적절하다. (C) 감정을 나타내는 동사가 사람을 수식할 때는 보통 과거분사를 쓰므로 excited가 적절하다.

20 진우의 가족 여행이 왜 마드리드에서 시작했는지는 대답할 수 없다. ① This summer. ③ Madrid. ④ To watch a soccer match. ⑤ They felt excited.

21 주어진 문장의 the city에 주목한다. ③번 앞 문장의 Seville를 받고 있으므로 ③번이 적절하다.

22 ⓐ with the other fans: 다른 팬들과 함께, with wonderful movements: 멋진 동작으로, ⓑ in: '착용'을 나타내는 전치사

23 명사를 수식하므로 형용사가 되어야 한다. traditional: 전통적인

24 한국의 볶음밥과 같은 맛이 났다고 해야 하므로 tasted like로 고치는 것이 적절하다. taste like+명사: ~와 같은 맛이 나다

25 ④ Antoni Gaudi는 구엘 공원과 사그라다 파밀리아를 '설계했다.'

03 be famous for: ~로 유명하다 / 그는 클래식 음악 연주자로 유명했다. be good for: ~에 좋다, 유익하다 / 나는 웃음이 우리의 건강에 좋다고 믿는다.

04 (1) reach: ~에 이르다, 도달하다 (2) oxygen: 산소 (3) work out: 운동하다 regularly: 규칙적으로 (4) stain: 얼룩 remove: 제거하다 (5) mess: 엉망진창

05 (1) feed on: ~을 먹고 살다 / 하이에나는 죽어 있는 작은 동물과 새를 먹고 산다. (2) cover: (범위가) ~에 이르다, 차지하다 / 숲은 전세계 육지 면적의 30퍼센트를 차지하고 있다. (3) bloom: (꽃이) 피다 / 몇몇 화려한 꽃들은 짧은 여름 동안 꽃이 핀다. (4) appear: 나타나다 / 구름 뒤에서 달이 나타났다.

06 information: 정보 / 어떤 것에 대한 사실들

Lesson 6

Wonders of Nature

시험대비 실력평가 p.60

01 ② 02 ⑤ 03 ② 04 ⑤
05 ④ 06 ②

01 ②번 이외의 보기들은 명사에 접미사 '-y'가 붙어 형용사가 된 단어이지만 ②번은 형용사에 '-ly'를 붙여 부사가 되었다. exact: 정확한 exactly: 정확히 ① cloud: 구름 cloudy: 흐린, 구름이 잔뜩 낀 ③ dirt: 먼지, 때 dirty: 더러운 ④ luck: 운, 행운 lucky: 운이 좋은 ⑤ rain: 비 rainy: 비가 오는

02 damage: 피해 / 지진은 건물에 해를 가한다.

03 creature: 생물, 생명체 / 새우 같은 작은 생명체는 이 식물을 먹는다.

04 mudflat: 갯벌 / 해수면 아래에 낮은 깊이로 펼쳐진 평평한 지역 또는 조수에 의해 번갈아 덮여지고 드러나게 되는 지역

05 ① be good for: ~에 좋다, 유익하다 / 운동은 몸과 마음 둘 다에 유익하다. ② work out: 운동하다 / 나는 매일 체육관에서 운동하곤 했다. ③ by the way: 그런데 /그런데, 너 내일 저녁에 저녁식사 같이 할 시간 있니? ④ thanks to 명사: ~ 덕분에 / 네 도움 덕분에 나는 그것을 할 수 있었다. ⑤ get on: (버스·지하철 등을) 타다 / 다음 번 시드니행 비행기를 탈 수 있는 방법이 없나요?

06 not only A but also B: A뿐만 아니라 B도(= B as well as A) / 그는 영어뿐만 아니라 스페인어도 말할 수 있다.

서술형 시험대비 p.61

01 (r)emoved
02 make
03 for
04 (1) (r)each (2) Oxygen (3) work out (r)egularly
   (4) (s)tain, remove (5) mess
05 (1) feed (2) cover (3) bloom (4) appeared
06 (i)nformation

01 remove: 제거하다 get rid of: 제거하다 / 나는 내 신발의 진흙을 제거했다.

02 make a living: 생계를 꾸리다 / Tom과 Lisa는 교사로 생계를 꾸려나간다. make a phone call: 전화를 걸다 / 나는 그에게 내일 계획을 물어보기 위해서 전화를 걸 것이다.

교과서 Conversation

핵심 Check p.62~63

1 (1) where we are (2) wonder why Tom is
2 (1) I wonder how many events are in this festival.
   (2) I wonder who she is.
3 heard that
4 Are you aware of / I have heard that

교과서 대화문 익히기

Check(√) True or False p.64

1 T 2 F 3 F 4 T

교과서 확인학습 p.66~67

Listen & Speak 1 A
1. wonder what you did during / took, trip / By, plains / flat
2. at / lake / wonder how, are different / a long body of fresh, toward / got it

Listen & Speak 1 B
1. what a mountain is / high
2. I wonder what, plain / flat, land

Listen & Talk 2 A
1. how many oceans there are / There are, cover most / much, cover / heard, cover about, surface

2. rain forest is called, lungs / Lungs / produces, oxygen

Listen & Talk 2 B

1. want / heard, lakes
2. want to go to / famous

Conversation A

what, plant, grass / In, turns, wet / heard, for

Conversation B

amazing / get on / wonder what they are / reeds, reed / taller than / take / reed field / heard, the largest one / turning

Communication Task Step 1

place / special / is

시험대비 기본평가   p.68

01 ④   02 ⑤   03 ③, ④   04 ①

01 궁금증을 표현할 때 '~를 궁금해 하다'라는 의미의 동사 wonder를 사용하여 'I wonder 의문사+주어+동사 ~.'라고 말한다.

02 어떤 사실을 알고 있는지 말할 때 'I heard (that) ~.(나는 ~라고 들었어.)'라고 표현한다.

03 I want to know 의문사+주어+동사, I'd like to know 의문사+주어+동사: 나는 ~를 알기를 원해요

04 모레인호의 특별한 점을 궁금해 하는 말에, 물의 색깔이 연한 파랑색이라고 들었다고 대답해 준다. hope: 희망하다 have been to ~: ~에 가 본 경험이 있다

시험대비 실력평가   p.69~70

01 ①	02 I wonder what you will do.		
03 ⓐ, ⓑ, ⓔ	04 ③	05 ②	06 land
07 ③	08 ②	09 ⑤	10 ②
11 ①	12 ④	13 ⑤	

01 주어진 문장은 'Do you want to hear it?(그것에 대해 듣고 싶니?)'인데 내용상 it은 a plan을 의미한다. 듣고 싶은지 묻는 질문에 여자아이가 'Sure.(물론이지.)'로 대답하는 것이 어울린다.

02 I wonder 의문사+주어+동사: 나는 ~가 궁금해

03 ⓐ 남자아이는 며칠 동안 여행을 할 것인가?(3일) ⓑ 여행 기간 동안 남자아이는 무엇을 할 것인가?(첫째 날은 낚시, 둘째 날은 등산, 셋째 날은 수영) ⓒ 여행 중에 그는 어디로 갈 것인가? ⓓ 남자아이는 언제 여행을 갈 것인가? ⓔ 여행 첫 번째 날 남자아이는 무엇을 할 것인가?(호수에서 낚시)

04 주어진 문장은 평원이 무엇인지 물어보는 질문이다. 이에 대해 남자아이가 'They are large areas of flat land.(그곳은 넓고 평평한 땅이야.)'라고 대답한다.

05 take a trip (to 장소): (~로) 여행하다[여행가다]

06 land: 육지, 땅 / 물이 아닌 땅의 표면

07 평원은 넓고 평평한 땅이다. flat: 평평한

08 ⓑ Yes. → No.

09 여자아이는 4개의 바다가 있다고 생각했는데 실제로는 5개였으므로 정확하게 알고 있지 않았다.

10 주어진 문장은 그것들이(노란색 식물들이) 무엇인지 궁금증을 표현하는 문장이다. 이 궁금증을 아빠가 갈대라고 알려주는 것이 적절하므로 ②가 어울린다.

11 get on: (버스·기차 등을) 타다

12 ④ 순천만은 한국에서 2번째로 큰 갈대밭이 아니라 가장 큰 갈대밭을 가지고 있다.

13 일요일에 무엇을 했는지 묻는 질문에, 단양에 갈 계획이라고 대답하는 것은 어색하다 I am going to take a trip to Danyang. → I took a trip to Danyang.

서술형 시험대비   p.71

01 for

02 I wonder what is special about Great Plains.

03 ⓐ I wonder what did you → I wonder what you did

04 ⓓ Like a lake → Unlike a lake

05 Can you tell me how a river and a lake are different?

06 (B) → (D) → (C) → (A)

07 I heard there are a lot of *oreums* in Jejudo.

01 be good for: ~에 좋다, 유익하다

02 I wonder 의문사+주어+동사: 나는 ~가 궁금해요 special: 특별한 about: ~에 대해서

03 I wonder 의문사+주어+동사: 나는 ~가 궁금해요

04 강과 호수가 어떻게 다른지 궁금한 여자아이에게 차이점을 설명해 주고 있다. 그러므로 like(~와 같이)가 아니라 unlike(~와는 달리)의 의미인 전치사를 사용하여 차이점을 얘기하는 것을 어울린다.

05 'I wonder 의문사+주어+동사.(나는 ~가 궁금해요.)'와 'Can you tell me 의문사+주어+동사?(나에게 ~를 말해줄 수 있나요?)'의 둘 다 궁금증을 표현하는 데 사용하는 표현들이다.

06 지구에 몇 개의 바다가 있는지 아는지 물어보는 질문에 (B) 4개라고 대답하자 (D) 아니라며 지구에 5개의 바다가 있고, 지구의 대부분을 차지하고 있다고 말한다. (C) 이어서 바다가 지구의 얼마를 차지하고 있는지 질문하자 (A) 지구 표면의 70%를 바다가 차지한다고 대답한다.

07 I heard (that) 주어 동사 ~: 나는 ~라는 것을 들었다 there are 복수 명사: ~가 있다 a lot of: 많은

핵심 Check p.72~73

1 (1) It, to play (2) to see (3) for you to save

2 (1) not only (2) but also

시험대비 기본평가 p.74

01 ① **02** ③

03 (1) write → writes (2) is stupid → stupid
(3) like → likes (4) to crossing → to cross
(5) That → It (6) of → for

01 It을 가주어로 하고 to부정사를 진주어로 이용할 수 있는 ①번이 적절하다.

02 'not only A but also B'는 'B as well as A'로 바꿔 쓸 수 있다. ③번은 She is good at dancing as well as singing.으로 써야 초점이 같은 dancing에 놓인다.

03 (1) Sam을 주어로 하는 동사가 연결된 것이므로 writes가 되어야 한다. (2) 'not only A but also B' 구문에서 A와 B는 품사나 문장에서의 역할이 동일해야 한다. is의 보어로 stupid만 나와야 한다. (3) 'not only A but also B'가 주어로 쓰일 경우 B에 수를 일치시킨다. (4) 진주어로 to부정사가 적절하다. (5) 가주어로는 That이 아니라 It을 쓴다. (6) 문장에 쓰인 형용사가 사람의 성질을 나타내는 말이 아니므로 to부정사의 의미상 주어로 'for+목적격'을 써야 한다.

시험대비 실력평가 p.75~77

01 ③ **02** ① **03** ②
04 ④ **05** ⑤ **06** (1) It (2) to understand
(3) of (4) snowed (5) but (6) enjoys **07** ④
08 ② **09** ② **10** ④ **11** ⑤
12 ② **13** writing
14 (1) It would be really stupid of you to help them.
(2) It is interesting to walk in the forest.
(3) It is important to wear a hat to block the sun.
(4) Not only I but also Bella was enjoying taking a walk.
(5) Harry is not only a great wizard but also a very wise man.
15 ②, ④ **16** ⑤ **17** ③
18 Gina is kind as well as pretty.

01 가주어로는 That이 아니라 It이 적절하다.

02 ② The book is not only expensive but uninteresting. ③ Not only I but also David likes Julie. ④ Steve is not only smart but also generous. ⑤ Bill speaks rudely not only at home but also at school.

03 'not only A but also B' 구문에서 A와 B는 품사나 문장에서의 역할이 동일해야 한다. is의 보어로 형용사가 나와야 한다. It이 나와 있으므로 It을 가주어로 하고 빈칸에는 진주어로 이용할 수 있는 to부정사가 적절하다.

04 가주어로 It이 적절하다.

05 'not only A but also B'는 'not only A but B', 'not simply[merely] A but (also) B', 'B as well as A' 등으로 바꿔 쓸 수 있다.

06 (1) 가주어로 It이 적절하다. (2) 진주어로 to부정사가 적절하다. (3) 문장에 쓰인 형용사가 사람의 성질을 나타내는 말일 때 to부정사의 의미상 주어로 'of+목적격'을 쓴다. (4) 'not only A but also B' 구문에서 A와 B는 품사나 문장에서의 역할이 동일해야 한다. (5) 'not only A but also B'에서 also가 생략되기도 한다. (6) 'not only A but also B'가 주어로 쓰일 경우 B에 수를 일치시킨다.

07 ① Amy is not only smart but also friendly. ② It is fun to go into caves. ③ It is kind of him to say so. ⑤ Not only you but also James plays the piano.

08 ②번은 인칭대명사로 '그것'이라고 해석 가능하지만 나머지는 모두 가주어로 쓰인 it이다.

09 not only A but also B: A뿐만 아니라 B도

10 '힙합 댄스를 배우는 것(to learn hiphop dance)'을 진주어로 하고 가주어 It을 이용하여 'It ~ to ...' 형식으로 쓴다.

11 not only A but (also) B'의 형태로 'A뿐만 아니라 B도'라는 의미를 갖는다.

12 가주어로 it을 쓰고 진주어로 to부정사를 쓰고 문장에 쓰인 형용사가 wise로 사람의 성질을 나타내는 말이므로 to부정사의 의미상 주어로 'of+목적격'을 쓰는 것이 적절하다.

13 'not only A but also B' 구문에서 A와 B는 품사나 문장에서의 역할이 동일해야 하므로 reading에 맞추어 writing이 적절하다.

14 (1) stupid가 사람의 성질을 나타내는 형용사이므로 의미상의 주어로 'of+목적격'을 쓴다. (2) 가주어로는 this가 아니라 it을 쓴다. (3) 진주어로 to부정사를 쓴다. (4) 'not only A but also B'가 주어로 쓰일 경우 B에 수를 일치시킨다. (5) 'not only A but also B'에서 A와 B는 문법적으로 동등한 구조를 연결해야 한다.

15 문장에 쓰인 형용사가 사람의 성질을 나타내는 말일 때는 to부정사의 의미상의 주어로 'of+목적격'을 쓴다. 'not only A but also B' 구문에서 A와 B는 품사나 문장에서의 역할이 동일해야 한다.

16 'not only A but also B'는 'not only A but B', 'not simply[merely] A but (also) B', 'B as well as A' 등으로 바꿔 쓸 수 있다.

17 산에 오르는 것(to climb that mountain)'을 진주어로 하고 가주어 It을 이용하여 'It ~ to ...' 형식으로 쓴다.

18 'not only A but also B'는 'B as well as A'로 바꿔 쓸 수 있다.

서술형 시험대비   p.78~79

01 (1) (a) To make good friends is difficult.
      (b) It is difficult to make good friends.
   (2) (a) To help others is important.
      (b) It is important to help others.
   (3) (a) To explain tastes is impossible.
      (b) It is impossible to explain tastes.

02 (1) Chris is not only friendly but also good-looking.
   (2) Marianne not only writes but also speaks Korean well.
   (3) Charlotte not only likes to play basketball but also enjoys watching soccer games on TV.

03 (1) It is exciting to watch fish swimming.
   (2) It is amazing to visit Giant's Causeway in Ireland.

04 (1) but also
   (2) as well

05 (1) It is important to make good memories with my family.
   (2) It is necessary to speak English well to succeed.
   (3) I like not only singing but dancing.
   (4) Not only you but also your brother should wash the dishes.

06 (1) It is easy to eat fruit and vegetables.
   (2) It will be necessary to know how to greet people in different countries.
   (3) It is true that knowledge is power.

07 (1) Build → To build, 또는 전체 문장 → It is a bad idea to build a new airport in the town.
   (2) for → of
   (3) working → work
   (4) are → is

08 (1) It is not easy to forgive an enemy.
   (2) It is important to save energy.
   (3) Today is not only Christmas but also my birthday.
   (4) Her brothers as well as Jane are kind.

---

01 to부정사가 문장의 주어로 쓰일 때 주어 자리에 가주어 it을 두고 to부정사 부분(진주어)을 문장 뒤로 보내어 쓸 수 있다.

02 'not only A but also B' 구문에서 A와 B는 품사나 문장에서의 역할이 동일해야 한다.

03 it을 가주어로 하고 to부정사를 진주어로 하여 쓴다.

04 'not only A but also B'는 'not only A but B as well'로 바꿔 쓸 수 있다.

05 (1)~(2) '가주어(it) ~ 진주어(to부정사) …' 구문을 이용한다. (3)~(4) 'not only A but also B'를 이용하여 배열한다.

06 (1)~(2) 문장의 주어로 쓰인 to부정사를 뒤로 보내고 대신 주어 자리에 가주어 It을 쓴다. (3) 주어로 쓰인 that절의 경우에도 긴 that절을 뒤로 보내고 주어 자리에 가주어 It을 쓴다.

07 (1) to부정사를 주어로 하거나 전체 문장을 '가주어(It) ~ 진주어(to부정사) …' 구문으로 고쳐 쓴다. (2) 사람의 성질을 나타내는 wise가 쓰였으므로 to부정사의 의미상 주어 'of+목적격'을 써야 한다. (3) 'not only A but also B' 구문에서 A와 B는 품사나 문장에서의 역할이 동일해야 한다. should에 이어지는 work로 고쳐야 한다. (4) 'B as well as A'가 주어로 쓰일 경우 B에 수를 일치시킨다.

08 (1), (2) '가주어(It) ~ 진주어(to부정사) …' 구문을 이용한다. (3) 'not only A but also B' 구문을 이용한다. (4) 'B as well as A'가 주어로 쓰일 경우 B에 수를 일치시킨다.

교과서
Reading

확인문제   p.80

1 T   2 F   3 T   4 F

확인문제   p.81

1 T   2 F   3 T   4 T   5 F

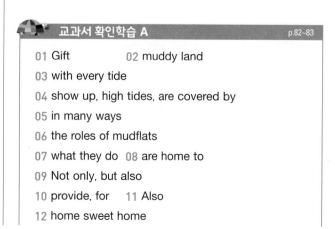

교과서 확인학습 A   p.82~83

01 Gift   02 muddy land
03 with every tide
04 show up, high tides, are covered by
05 in many ways
06 the roles of mudflats
07 what they do   08 are home to
09 Not only, but also
10 provide, for   11 Also
12 home sweet home

13 are good for

14 make a living, nearby

15 Thanks to

16 fun activities, such as   17 feed on

18 nature's gift   19 help, greatly

20 hold, reduce damage

21 filter, from, into

22 remove bad things

23 that reaches the sea

24 as the Earth's lungs

25 a huge volume of   26 healthy, clean

27 aren't they

28 from nature to living things

29 to protect mudflats

into the sea.

22 They remove bad things in the water before it enters the sea.

23 Thanks to mudflats, the water that reaches the sea is clean.

24 Mudflats work as the Earth's lungs.

25 They produce a huge volume of oxygen that is necessary for life on the Earth.

26 Earth: Mudflats keep me healthy and clean.

27 Mudflats are wonderful places, aren't they?

28 They are a gift from nature to living things on the Earth.

29 For all these reasons, it is necessary to protect mudflats.

교과서 확인학습 B
p.84~85

1 Mudflats, Nature's Gift

2 Mudflats are large areas of muddy land at the seaside.

3 They appear and disappear with every tide.

4 During low tides, they show up, and during high tides, they are covered by the sea.

5 Mudflats help sea creatures, people, and the Earth in many ways.

6 It is important to understand the roles of mudflats.

7 Let's see what they do.

8 Mudflats are home to a lot of living things at the seaside.

9 Not only very small living things like plankton but also crabs and fish live there.

10 Mudflats provide various types of food for them.

11 Also, many birds eat food there.

12 Crab: Mudflats are my home sweet home.

13 Mudflats are good for people, too.

14 People who live near mudflat areas make a living by catching fish and other sea animals nearby.

15 Thanks to mudflats, people can get fresh seafood.

16 People can enjoy fun activities, such as mud sliding and body painting on mudflats.

17 They can also watch a large number of birds that feed on the sea animals there.

18 Boy: Mudflats are nature's gift to living things!

19 Mudflats help the environment greatly.

20 Mudflats hold a lot of water, so they can reduce damage from floods.

21 Also, mudflats filter water that flows from the land

시험대비 실력평가
p.86~89

01 are appeared and disappeared → appear and disappear

02 (1) high tide (2) low tide   03 ②   04 ④

05 ⑤   06 ②, ③, ⑤

07 땅에서 바다로 물이 흘러들어가기 전에 물속에 있는 나쁜 물질을 갯벌이 제거해 주기 때문이다.

08 ⑤   09 (A) for (B) other (C) feed

10 ①   11 live   12 ②

13 wear long clothes   14 ③   15 ④

16 ②   17 ③   18 ⑤

19 floods   20 ④   21 the sea covers them

22 ②, ④, ⑤   23 That → It

24 the longest river, the biggest cave, the tallest falls, and the highest mountain

25 wonder   26 (A) few (B) little (C) during

27 it is always hot day and night → it is hot during the day and cold at night

01 appear와 disappear는 수동태로 만들 수 없는 동사들이다.

02 (1) 밀물, 조수가 안으로 들어오는 흐름 또는 조수가 들어와서 바다가 가장 높은 수위에 도달한 때, (2) 썰물, 조수가 밖으로 빠져나가는 흐름 또는 조수가 빠져나가서 바다가 가장 낮은 수위에 도달한 때

03 갯벌은 '조수와 함께' 나타나고 사라진다고 했으므로, 갯벌의 의미를 올바르게 이해하지 못한 사람은 '희정'이다.

04 위 글은 '지형을 소개하는 글'이다. ① 문화에 대한 소개서, ② 지리 실험 보고서, ③ 일기 예보, 기상 통보, ⑤ 현장학습 안내서

05 주어진 문장이 ⑤번 다음 문장의 이유에 해당하므로 ⑤번이 적절하다.

06 ⓐ와 ②, ③, ⑤번: 관계대명사, ①, ④: 접속사

07 갯벌 덕분에 바다에 도착한 물은 깨끗하다.

08 number는 'large'와 'small'을 사용하여 수량을 표현하는 명사이다.

09 (A) '유익하다'고 해야 하므로 for가 적절하다. be good at: ~을 잘하다, be good for: ~에 좋다, (B) '다른 바다 동물들'이라고 해야 하므로 other가 적절하다. another+단수명사, (C) 동사를 써야 하므로 feed가 적절하다. food: feed의 명사

10 ① 'Mudflats are good for people, too.'로 글이 시작하고 있으므로, 위 글의 앞에도 '갯벌이 유익한 다른 경우'에 대한 내용이 나왔을 것이라고 하는 것이 적절하다.

11 not only A but (also) B = B as well as A: A뿐만 아니라 B도, 'not only A but also B'나 'B as well as A'가 주어로 쓰일 경우 B에 수를 일치시킨다.

12 ⓑ와 ①, ③, ④: 부사적 용법, ② 형용사적 용법, ⑤ 명사적 용법

13 만약 당신이 갯벌에 간다면, 당신을 물 수 있는 동물들로부터 당신을 보호하기 위해 '긴 옷을 입는 것'이 중요하다.

14 ⓐ 'to'는 '~에게'라는 의미이다. ⓒ provide+사람(대상)+with 사물 = provide+사물+for[to] 사람[대상]: ~에게 …을 제공[공급]하다

15 not only[merely/just/simply] A but (also) B = B as well as A: A뿐만 아니라 B도, ④ 'Crabs and fish as well as very small living things like plankton live there.'라고 하는 것이 적절하다.

16 플랑크톤처럼 작은 생명체뿐만 아니라 게와 물고기도 갯벌에 산다.

17 앞에 나오는 내용에 추가하는 내용이 뒤에 이어지므로 Also가 가장 적절하다. ② 그러므로, ⑤ 즉, 다시 말해

18 ④ awesome: 경탄할 만한, 기막히게 좋은, 굉장한, ⑤ protect: 보호하다, prevent: 막다[예방/방지하다]

19 갯벌은 많은 양의 물을 수용해서 '홍수'의 피해를 줄여 준다.

20 앞 문장에서 갯벌의 '역할'을 이해하는 것이 중요하다고 했기 때문에, 갯벌이 '무엇을' 하는지 살펴보자고 하는 것이 적절하다. ① how는 부사이므로 do의 목적어로 쓰일 수 없고, how they do them처럼 따로 목적어를 써야 한다.

21 'the sea'를 주어로 해서 고치는 것이 적절하다.

22 ⓑ와 ②, ④, ⑤번: 가주어 , ① 비인칭 주어, ③ 가목적어

23 'That'을 가주어 'It'으로 고치는 것이 적절하다.

24 '가장 긴 강, 가장 큰 동굴, 가장 높은 폭포, 그리고 가장 높은 산'을 가리킨다.

25 wonder: 경이(로운 것), 경탄, 매우 놀라운 그리고 예상 밖의 어떤 것

26 (A) 'plants'는 셀 수 있는 명사이므로 few가 적절하다. (B) 'water'는 셀 수 없는 명사이므로 little이 적절하다. (C) during the day: 낮 동안, during+기간을 나타내는 명사, for+숫자

27 사막에서 낮에는 덥고 밤에는 춥다. day and night: 밤낮으로

01 tide

02 show up

03 (A) low   (B) disappear

04 mudflats

05 (A) greatly (B) remove (C) volume

06 as → so 또는 Mudflats hold a lot of water, as they can reduce damage from floods. → As[Because] mudflats hold a lot of water, they can reduce damage from floods.

07 Thanks to mudflats, the water that reaches the sea is clean.

08 Crabs and fish as well as very small living things like plankton live there.

09 with

10 Mudflats[mudflats]

11 catching

12 on

13 mud sliding and body painting

14 that 또는 which

15 aren't they

16 healthily and cleanly → healthy and clean

17 (A) nature (B) living things

01 every 뒤에 단수형을 쓰는 것이 적절하다. 갯벌은 '조수'와 함께 나타나고 사라진다.

02 appear = show up: 나타나다

03 갯벌은 '썰물'일 때 나타나고 밀물일 때 '사라지는' 해안의 평평하고 빈 땅의 지역이다.

04 '갯벌'을 가리킨다.

05 (A) 동사 help를 수식하므로 부사 greatly가 적절하다. (B) 나쁜 물질을 '제거한다'고 해야 하므로 remove가 적절하다. generate: 발생시키다, 만들어 내다, (C) 'oxygen'은 셀 수 없는 명사이므로 volume이 적절하다.

06 '갯벌은 많은 양의 물을 수용해서 홍수의 피해를 줄여 준다'고 해야 하므로 as를 so로 고치거나 문장을 As나 Because 등으로 시작하여 쓰는 것이 적절하다.

07 Thanks to: ~ 덕분에

08 not only A but also B = B as well as A: A뿐만 아니라 B도

09 provide+사람(대상)+with 사물 = provide+사물+for[to] 사람(대상): ~에게 …을 제공[공급]하다

10 '갯벌'을 가리킨다.

11 전치사 by 뒤에 동명사를 쓰는 것이 적절하다.

12 (B) on mudflats: 갯벌에서, (C) feed on: ~을 먹다[먹고 살다]

13 '진흙 미끄럼 타기'와 '보디 페인팅'

17

14 관계대명사 that이나 which를 쓰는 것이 적절하다.

15 문장의 동사가 be동사이므로, be동사를 사용하여 부가의문문을 만드는 것이 적절하다.

16 keep의 목적격보어이므로 형용사로 고치는 것이 적절하다.

17 갯벌은 '자연'이 지구상의 '생물들'에게 준 선물이므로, 갯벌을 보호하는 것은 필수이다.

01 ②   02 ④   03 (o)ccur   04 ③

05 saw   06 ⑤

07 I wonder what you did during the summer vacation.

08 ④   09 ④   10 surface   11 ④

12 I heard it is the largest one in Korea.

13 ③   14 ①   15 ④   16 ②

17 ③

18 (1) for you to be kind to other people

(2) for you to be careful when you drive a car

19 ⑤   20 ④   21 ②, ⑤   22 ③

23 (A) reduce (B) enters (C) reaches

24 ④   25 ①, ③, ④   26 like   27 ②

28 ④   29 ①   30 ①   31 food

01 ② 이외의 보기들은 접미사 '-y'가 붙어 형용사가 되는 명사들이다. friend는 '-ly'가 붙어 형용사가 된다. ① mess: 엉망진창 messy: 지저분한 ② friend: 친구 friendly: 친근한 ③ wind: 바람 windy: 바람이 부는 ④ luck: 운, 행운 lucky: 운이 좋은 ⑤ health: 건강 healthy: 건강한

02 fall: (복수형으로) 폭포 / 폭포는 뉴욕 주의 총 전력의 10 퍼센트를 공급할 수 있습니다.

03 take place: 일어나다, 개최되다 occur: 일어나다 / 이것은 언제 어디서든 일어날 수 있다.

04 a body of water: (바다나 호수 등의) 수역

05 took a trip과 접속사 and로 연결되어 있으므로 과거형 동사가 어울린다.

06 ① Although: ~에도 불구하고 ② In addition: 게다가 ③ On the contrary: 이와 반대로 ④ Besides: 게다가 ⑤ By the way: 그런데 (대화에서 화제를 바꿀 때 씀)

07 I wonder 의문사+주어+동사: 나는 ~가 궁금해요 during+명사: ~ 중에, ~ 동안에

08 cover: (범위가)~에 이르다, 차지하다 How much of the Earth do they cover?: 그것들이 지구의 얼마를 차지하고 있니?

09 ⓐ many, oceans는 셀 수 있는 명사이므로 much가 아니라 many의 수식을 받는다. ⓑ there are, 간접의문문의 순서는 '의문사+주어+동사'이다. ⓕ cover, 'is covered'는 수동태로 '덮여지다'의 의미이다. 바다가 지구의 표면의 70%를 차지한다는

내용이므로 능동태가 어울린다.

10 surface: 표면 / 어떤 것의 평평한 윗부분 또는 그것의 바깥쪽

11 형용사의 비교급은 바로 앞에 much, far, even, still, a lot 등을 사용해서 강조한다. very는 원급을 강조할 때 사용한다.

12 I heard (that) 주어 동사 ~: 나는 ~라는 것을 들었다 the 최상급 형용사: 가장 ~한

13 'not only A but also B'는 'B as well as A'로 바꿔 쓸 수 있다. Sam writes German as well as reads it.

14 'not only A but also B'는 'not only A but B', 'not simply[merely] A but (also) B', 'B as well as A' 등으로 바꿔 쓸 수 있다.

15 ④번은 to부정사의 부사적 용법(결과)이지만 나머지는 모두 진주어로 쓰인 명사적 용법으로 쓰였다.

16 ②에는 사람의 성격이나 성질을 나타내는 형용사(rude)가 왔으므로 의미상의 주어로 'of+목적격'을 써야 한다. 나머지는 모두 for가 들어간다.

17 ⓐ play → plays ⓒ lives → live ⓔ for → of ⓕ swims → to swim ⓖ That → It

18 '~해야 한다'는 의미를 가주어 It을 이용하여 '~할 필요가 있다'라고 쓰려면 진주어로 to부정사를 이용한다. 이때 의미상의 주어를 빠뜨리지 않도록 주의한다.

19 'not only A but also B' 구문에서 A와 B는 품사나 문장에서의 역할이 동일해야 한다. Dylan not only played computer games but also did his homework.

20 ⓐ with every tide: 조수와 '함께', ⓑ in many ways: 많은 방면에서

21 to부정사와 동명사가 주어일 때 단수 취급하는 것이 적절하다.

22 갯벌의 역할이 무엇인지는 대답할 수 없다. ① During low tides. ② During high tides. ④ The sea. ⑤ Yes.

23 (A) 홍수의 피해를 '줄여 준다'고 해야 하므로 reduce가 적절하다. (B) 물이 바다로 '들어가기 전에'라고 해야 하므로 enters가 적절하다. enter = go into, enter into: (논의·처리 등을) 시작하다, (C) reach는 타동사이므로 전치사 없이 바로 목적어를 가지는 것이 적절하다. reach = get to: ~에 도착하다

24 ⓐ와 ④번: 전치사 'as'는 자격·기능 등을 나타내어 '~로(서)'라는 뜻이다. ① (접속사) [양태] ···처럼, ···하는 대로, ···와 같이, ② (접속사) ···할 때, ③ 앞의 as가 지시부사, 뒤의 as는 접속사, ⑤ (접속사) [비례] ···함에 따라, ···할수록

25 ⓐ와 ②, ⑤: 동명사, ①, ③, ④: 현재분사

26 such as = like: ~와 같은

27 갯벌은 지구상의 생명에게 필요한 많은 양의 산소를 생산한다고 했기 때문에, 그것들은 지구의 '폐' 역할을 한다고 하는 것이 적절하다. ③ 위(胃), 복부, 배

28 이 글은 '갯벌이 환경에 크게 도움이 된다.'는 내용의 글이다.

29 ① things가 복수명사이므로 much 대신 many를 써야 한다. ② seashore: 해변, 해안, 바닷가, ③ not only A but also B = not merely[simply] A but also B ④ supply: 공급[제공]

하다, ⑤ In addition: 게다가

30 ⓐ와 ①: (전치사) …와 같은(such as), ② (전치사) …와 비슷한, ③ (동사) (…을) 좋아하다, ④ (형용사) 비슷한, ⑤ (전치사) …와 (똑)같이[마찬가지로], …처럼

31 갯벌은 바닷가에 있는 많은 생물들뿐만 아니라 많은 새들에게도 다양한 종류의 '먹이'를 제공한다.

단원별 예상문제

01 low tide   02 (1) Unlike (2) During (3) as (4) else
03 take   04 make   05 ③
06 I wonder what a forest is. /
I would like to know what a forest is.
07 who covered → that[which] is covered
08 I heard the Amazon rain forest is called the lungs of the Earth.
09 ③   10 ③   11 ②, ④
12 (A) like (B) In (C) for   13 ②   14 ⑤
15 (1) It is easy for me to understand this book.
(2) It is very kind of you to help her.
(3) It is dangerous for you to walk around at night.
(4) Cats are smart as well as clean.
(5) Junsu not only dances but also sings well.
(6) Not only Eric but also his brothers are fast runners.
16 ⑤   17 ②, ④, ⑤
18 they are covered by the sea   19 ③
20 ⑤
21 Not only very small living things like plankton but also crabs and fish live there.
22 ②   23 to get
24 They make a living by catching fish and other sea animals nearby.
25 ③

01 두 단어는 반의어 관계이다. appear: 나타나다 disappear: 사라지다 high tide: 밀물 low tide: 썰물

02 (1) unlike: ~와는 달리 / 그것의 이름과 달리, 그린랜드는 얼음과 눈으로 덮여 있습니다. (2) during: ~ 동안(에), ~ 중에 / 밤중에 통증으로 간혹 깨곤 합니다. (3) such as: ~와 같은 / 그는 소설, 만화 같은 많은 책을 갖고 있다. (4) else: 그 밖의, 그것 이외의 / 이보다 더 좋을 순 없다

03 take a trip (to 장소): (~로) 여행하다[여행가다] / 나는 유럽으로 여행 가길 희망하고 있다. take a picture: 사진을 찍다 / 저 공룡 앞에서 저희들 사진 좀 찍어 주실래요?

04 make a decision: 결정하다 / 나는 결정을 내리기 전에 너와 이야기하고 싶다. make a mistake: 실수하다 / 실수하는 것을

두려워하지 마. make a noise: 소음을 내다, 시끄럽게 하다 / 음식을 먹으면서 시끄러운 소리를 내는 것은 실례이다.

05 ③ why → how ⓐ beautiful ⓑ how ⓒ different ⓓ long ⓔ fresh. a body of water: (바다나 호수 등의) 수역 fresh water: 민물

06 I wonder 의문사+주어+동사: 나는 ~가 궁금해요 I'd like to know 의문사+주어+동사: 나는 ~을 알기를 원해요. forest: 숲

07 land는 사물이므로 주격 관계대명사 which나 that이 어울린다. '식물과 나무로 덮여진 땅'이므로 수동태(be+p.p)의 형태로 사용해야 한다.

08 I heard (that) 주어 동사 ~: 나는 ~라는 것을 들었다 rain forest: 열대 우림 lung: 폐

09 Why로 질문하였으므로 이유를 설명하는 단어가 어울리며, (A) 뒤에 주어와 동사가 나오므로 접속사 Because가 어울린다. produce: 생산하다, 만들다 protect: 보호하다 remove: 제거하다

10 want는 to부정사를 목적어로 취하는 동사이다. 단양에 가고 싶다는 말에 단양에 유명한 동굴이 있다고 들었다고 대답하므로, 단양에 왜 가고 싶은지 이유를 묻는 것이 어울린다.

11 'I heard (that) 주어 동사 ~. / I'm aware (that) 주어 동사 ~. / I'm aware of (동)명사 ~. / I have heard (that) 주어 동사 ~. / I've been told (that) 주어 동사 ~. 모두 알고 있는 것을 표현하는 말들이다. ②번은 of 다음에 (동)명사가 와야 하므로 나올 수 없다. ④ I'm not sure ~: 나는 ~을 확신하지 않는다.

12 look like+명사: ~처럼 보이다 in+계절: ~ 계절에 be famous for: ~로 유명하다

13 가주어로는 That이 아니라 It을 쓰며 문장에 쓰인 형용사가 사람의 성질을 나타내는 말일 때는 to부정사의 의미상 주어로 'of+목적격'을 쓴다.

14 ① It's important to protect mudflats. ② It is exciting for me to play baseball. ③ Isn't it boring to watch TV at home? ④ Ann felt disappointed as well as angry.

15 (1) it을 가주어로 하고 to부정사를 진주어로 이용한다. (2) 형용사 kind가 있으므로 to부정사의 의미상 주어로 'of+목적격'을 쓴다. (3) 가주어 it이 있으므로 to부정사의 의미상 주어로 'for you'를 빠뜨리면 안 된다. (4) B as well as A: A뿐만 아니라 B도 (5) not only A but also B: A뿐만 아니라 B도 (6) 'not only A but also B'나 'B as well as A'가 주어로 쓰일 경우 B에 수를 일치시킨다.

16 가주어 it을 이용하여 바꿔 쓰는 것으로 원래 문장의 to부정사를 진주어로 쓴다.

17 ⓐ와 ①, ③: 명사적 용법, ②, ④: 형용사적 용법, ⑤: 부사적 용법

18 밀물일 때 '바다에 덮이기' 때문이다.

19 갯벌의 역할을 이해하는 것이 중요하다며 갯벌이 무엇을 하는지

살펴보자고 했기 때문에, 이 글의 뒤에는 '갯벌의 역할'에 대한 내용이 이어질 것이라고 하는 것이 적절하다.

20 뒤에 복수 명사가 나오므로, (양이) 많은 것을 나타내는 ⑤는 적절하지 않다. ⓐ와 ①, ③: (수나 양이) 많은, ②, ④: (수가) 많은, ⑤ a great deal of: (양이) 많은

21 not only A but also B: A뿐만 아니라 B도

22 이 글은 '갯벌은 바닷가에 있는 많은 생물들에게 집'이라는 내용의 글이므로, 제목으로는 '갯벌, 바닷가에 있는 생물들의 집'이 적절하다.

23 enable+목적어+to부정사: ~에게 …할 수 있게 하다

24 그들은 근처에서 물고기와 다른 바다 동물들을 잡아 생계를 꾸린다.

25 이 글은 갯벌의 많은 유익한 점에 관한 글이므로, 주제로는 '갯벌은 생명체에게 주는 자연의 선물'이라고 하는 것이 적절하다.

서술형 실전문제 p.102~103

01 I wonder what you did during the summer vacation.

02 (C) → (B) → (A)

03 I wonder what is special about the Yangze River.

04 I heard it is the third longest river in the world.

05 (1) It is dangerous to swim in the river.

(2) It was wise of her to be a nurse.

06 (1) Midori can speak not only Japanese but also English.

(2) Wendy studies hard not only at school but also at home.

07 are → is

08 that

09 (1) 갯벌 지역 인근에 사는 사람은 근처에서 물고기와 다른 바다 동물들을 잡아 생계를 꾸린다.

(2) 갯벌 덕분에 사람들은 신선한 해산물을 얻을 수 있다.

(3) 사람들은 갯벌에서 진흙 미끄럼 타기나 보디 페인팅과 같은 즐거운 활동을 즐길 수 있다.

(4) 사람들은 갯벌에서 바다 동물들을 먹는 수많은 새를 관찰할 수도 있다.

10 (A) near (B) nearby (C) Thanks to

11 filter

12 the water

13 (1) holding a lot of water

(2) filtering water

(3) producing a huge volume of oxygen

01 I wonder 의문사+주어+동사 ~.: 나는 ~가 궁금해요. while과 during은 '~ 동안에'로 뜻은 같지만, 'the summer vacation'은 명사이므로 전치사인 during이 어울린다.

---

02 노란색 식물들이 무엇인지 궁금하다고 말하니까, (C) 그건 갈대라고 대답해 주며, 순천만에는 아름다운 갈대밭이 있다고 말한다. (B) 갈대가 아빠의 키보다 더 크다고 말하니까 (A) 정말 그렇다고 동의하며 사진을 찍어 준다고 말한다.

03 I wonder 의문사+주어+동사 ~.: 나는 ~가 궁금해요. special: 특별한

04 I heard (that)+주어+동사 ~.: 나는 ~라는 것을 들었다. the 서수+최상급 형용사: ~ 번째로 가장 ~한

05 (1) It을 가주어로 하고 in의 목적어로 the river를 쓴다. (2) to decide의 주어가 she이므로 of her로 의미상의 주어를 나타내야 한다.

06 'not only A but also B' 구문에서 A와 B는 품사나 문장에서의 역할이 동일해야 한다. (1) Japanese와 English를 A와 B 자리에 쓴다. (2) at school과 at home을 A와 B 자리에 쓴다.

07 'B as well as A'가 주어로 쓰일 경우 B에 수를 일치시킨다.

08 관계대명사 that은 선행사가 사람, 동물, 사물일 때 다 사용할 수 있다.

09 ⓐ 다음에 이어지는 내용을 쓰면 된다.

10 (A) 갯벌 지역 '가까이에서'라고 해야 하므로 전치사 near가 적절하다. near: (전치사) ~에서 가까이, (부사) 가까이, nearly: (부사) 거의, (B) '근처에서'라고 해야 하므로 nearby가 적절하다. (형용사) 인근의, 가까운 곳의, (부사) 인근에, 가까운 곳에, nearly: (부사) 거의, (C) 갯벌 '덕분에'라고 해야 하므로 Thanks to가 적절하다. In spite of: ~에도 불구하고

11 물속에 있는 나쁜 물질을 제거한다 = 물을 걸러내 준다 filter: 거르다, 걸러내다

12 '물'을 가리킨다.

13 (1) '많은 양의 물을 수용해서' 홍수의 피해를 줄여 준다. (2) '물을 걸러냄으로써' 물이 바다로 들어가기 전에 물속에 있는 나쁜 물질을 갯벌이 제거한다. (3) '많은 양의 산소를 생산함으로써' 지구의 폐 역할을 한다.

창의사고력 서술형 문제 p.104

|모범답안|

01 on May 18th / I wonder what time the mall opens on the opening day? / it opens at 8 a.m

02 (1) |모범답안| It is exciting to watch the soccer game. / It's necessary for you to do exercise regularly.

(2) |모범답안| It was amazing to see such an old house. / It is important to use water carefully.

(3) |모범답안| It's dangerous to swim in the sea. / It's safe to wear a helmet while riding a bike.

03 (A) |모범답안| few (B) |모범답안| little

(C) |모범답안| lizards and desert snakes

(D) |모범답안| cold

01 I heard (that) 주어 동사 ~: 나는 ~라는 것을 들었다 I wonder 의문사+주어+동사: 나는 ~가 궁금해요 날짜 앞에는 전치사 on을, 시간 앞에는 전치사 at을 사용한다.

01 ①   02 ③

03 (1) reaches (2) surfing (3) occurred (4) protect
    (5) flows (6) Remove (7) provide

04 ④   05 ③

06 I wonder what you will do. 또는 I wonder what you are going to do.

07 flow

08 I wonder how a river and a lake are different.

09 ③   10 ④   11 reed

12 (A) get (B) what they are (C) than (D) take

13 ②

14 not only[simply, merely, just] , but also

15 ③

16 (1) were → was (2) for → of

17 (1) I saw *Alitar* as well as *Avatar*.
    (2) Peter as well as his brothers likes Minji.

18 (A) low (B) high (C) what

19 ④   20 as → like 또는 such as

21 ③   22 make a living

23 ②   24 ①   25 ①, ④, ⑤

01 not only A but also B: A뿐만 아니라 B도(= B as well as A) / 그의 직업은 재미있을 뿐 아니라 보수도 매우 좋다.

02 a large number of: 다수의, 많은 수의 / 매년 많은 사람들이 이 박물관을 찾는다.

03 (1) reach: ~에 이르다, 도달하다 (2) surf: 서핑하다 (3) occur: 일어나다 (4) protect: 보호하다 (5) flow: 흐르다 (6) remove: 제거하다 (7) provide: 제공하다, 주다

04 ④의 영영풀이는 mud에 대한 설명이다. mud: 진흙, muddy: 진흙투성이인, 진흙의, 질퍽한, covered with mud, or full of mud(진흙으로 덮인 또는 진흙으로 가득 찬)

05 남자아이는 여행 계획을 말하고 있다. 주어진 문장에서 다음 날에 산에 오를 것이라고 말하고 있다. 내용상 첫날의 일정을 말하고 그 다음 날에 대해 얘기하고, 상대방이 'Is that all?(그게 전부니?)'이라고 묻고 마지막 날의 계획을 말하는 것이 자연스럽다.

06 I wonder 의문사+주어+동사: 나는 ~가 궁금해요. 여행을 가서 미래에 할 내용을 궁금해 하고 있으므로 미래 시제를 표현하는 'will+동사원형'이나 'be going to 동사원형'을 사용한다.

07 flow: 흐르다 / 액체, 기체, 전류 등을 설명할 때 사용되는 것으로, 어떠한 방해 없이 꾸준히 움직이다

08 I wonder 의문사+주어+동사: 나는 ~가 궁금해요 how: 어떻게 different: 다른

09 그들은 호수가 아니라 강을 보고 있다.

10 ⓐ what this is ⓑ looks like ⓒ turns ⓓ grows ⓔ is famous for

11 reed: 갈대 / 그것은 물 근처에서 사는 길고 얇은 식물이다. 그것의 줄기는 물건을 만들기 위해 사용될 수 있다.

12 (A) get on: (버스·지하철 등을) 타다 (B) I wonder 의문사+주어+동사: 나는 ~가 궁금해요 (C) 비교급 than: ~보다 더 ~한 (D) let+목적어+목적격보어(동사원형): ~가 …하게 하다

13 문장에 쓰인 형용사가 사람의 성질을 나타내는 말일 때 to부정사의 의미상 주어로 'of+목적격'을 쓴다. It was so foolish of Jane to do that.

14 'not only A but also B(A뿐만 아니라 B도)' 구문을 이용한다.

15 주어진 문장과 ③번은 가주어로 쓰이고 있다. ①, ④ 비인칭주어 ② It ~ that 강조 구문 ⑤ 가목적어

16 (1) 'B as well as A'가 주어로 쓰일 경우 B에 수를 일치시킨다. (2) 문장에 쓰인 형용사가 사람의 성질을 나타내는 말일 때는 to부정사의 의미상 주어로 'of+목적격'을 쓴다.

17 (1) not only A but (also) B = B as well as A 여기서 A와 B는 문법적으로 같은 성격의 것이어야 한다. (2) 'not only A but also B'나 B as well as A가 주어로 쓰일 경우 B에 수를 일치시킨다.

18 (A) '썰물'일 때 갯벌이 드러난다고 해야 하므로 'low'가 적절하다. (B) '밀물'일 때 사라진다고 해야 하므로 'high'가 적절하다. (C) 갯벌이 '무엇을' 하는지 살펴보자고 해야 하므로 what이 적절하다.

19 '갯벌을 오염으로부터 보호하는 것이 중요하다'는 내용은 언급되어 있지 않다.

20 like: (전치사) …와 같은(=such as)

21 ③ '비슷한', '유사한', ⓑ와 나머지: '다양한'

22 make a living: 생계를 꾸리다

23 갯벌에서 수영을 할 수 없다.

24 이 글은 '갯벌은 환경에 크게 도움이 된다.'는 내용의 글이다.

25 갯벌은 홍수로 인한 피해를 축소해 주고, 바다로 들어가는 물을 정화하고, 산소를 생성한다.

Work on Your Dreams

01 ⑤   02 ①   03 ③   04 ②

05 ②   06 ①   07 ②

01 overcome: 극복하다 / 그는 인생에서 많은 어려움을 극복할 것입니다.

02 earn: 얻다, 획득하다 / 그녀는 많은 돈을 벌지는 못하지만 일을 즐긴다.

03 turn down: ~을 거절하다, 거부하다, 소리를 줄이다 / • 그녀는 그의 제안을 거절하기를 원해서, 그에게 'no'라고 말했다. • 소리 좀 줄여주시겠어요? 내가 공부에 집중할 수 없어요.

04 keep calm: 평온을 유지하다 / • 그는 심호흡을 하며 평온을 유지하려고 노력했다. keep 동명사: ~하는 것을 계속하다 / • 휘발유 값이 계속 올라간다면, 어떻게 해야 할지 모르겠어요.

05 although: 비록 ~일지라도 in spite of: ~에도 불구하고 / 재정상의 문제들에도 불구하고, 그는 새 차를 구입했다.

06 calm: 침착한 / 흥분, 화, 충격 또는 공포 같은 강한 감정에 의해 영향을 받지 않은

07 honor: 예우하다, ~을 공경하다 / 특히 상이나 타이틀을 주거나, 공적으로 칭찬함으로써 어떤 사람에게 존경이나 칭찬을 보여주다

01 (a)fraid

02 at

03 (1) They became faster with practice.

    (2) I failed to follow the summer vacation plan.

    (3) I couldn't believe my eyes when I first saw that.

04 (1) talented (2) major (3) excellent (4) positive

05 (1) color line (2) baseman (3) (A)lthough

    (4) effort (5) ever

01 그 꼬마 사내아이는 너무 무서워서 많은 실수를 했다. / scared: 무서운

02 at bat: 타석에서 / 지금 타석에 있는 선수는 누구인가? be poor at: ~을 못하다 become good at: ~을 잘하게 되다 / 나는 수학을 정말 못해서 수학을 잘하고 싶어.

03   (1) with: ~함에 따라 (2) fail: 실패하다, ~하지 못하다 (3) cannot believe one's eyes: ~ 눈을 의심하다

04 (1) talented: 재능이 있는 / 그는 또한 재능 있는 예술가를 찾는 데 많은 시간을 보내고 있습니다. (2) major: 주요한 / 이것은 주요한 우려의 원인이다. (3) excellent: 뛰어난 / 그곳은 휴식을 취하기에 최적의 장소입니다. (4) positive: 긍정적인 / 당신은 긍정적인 사람인가요 아니면 부정적인 사람인가요?

05 (1) color line: 인종 차별 (2) baseman: (1·2·3) 루수 (3) although: 비록 ~일지라도 (4) effort: 노력 (5) ever: 언젠가, 한 번이라도

Conversation

1 It's important to be

2 (C) → (B) → (A)

3 It is important to practice a lot.

4 (B) → (C) → (A)

5 Could you explain about that?

교과서 대화문 익히기

1 T   2 T   3 F   4 T

Listen & Speak 1 A

1. find, problem / too hard, I'm not good at math / It's important that, solve

2. looks / finish / draw, How, good / takes, important, as often as / keep practicing

Listen & Speak 1 B

1. hard to be, What / important, never / not forget

2. hard to / It's important that / will not

Listen & Talk 2 A

1. hard to do / how to / What do you mean by / mean

2. have, want to win / crossed / What do you mean by / means, luck

Listen & Talk 2 B

1. are , than / What, mean by / mean, together, than, alone

2. Practice / mean / mean, by doing, over

Conversation A

To achieve, failed, However, up / took, Finally, achieved, never give

Conversation B

look / achieve / What do you mean by that / fail auditions, give up / famous / more than / trying, practice / you never give up

시험대비 기본평가   p.120

01 ③   02 ①   03 ④

01 It's important that 주어 동사 ~: ~하는 것이 중요해 use: 사용하다 rule: 규칙 solve: 풀다, 해결하다

02 'I mean ~.(그것은 ~ 뜻이야.)'은 설명을 요청할 때의 대답이므로 설명을 요청하는 질문이 어울린다. What do you mean by that?: 그게 무슨 뜻이니?

03 노래 경연 대회에서 1등을 하고 싶다는 말에 (C) "keep my fingers crossed"한다고 말하니까 (B) "keep my fingers crossed"가 무슨 뜻인지 물어보고 (A) 행운을 빈다는 뜻이라고 대답한다. (D) 행운을 빌어줘 고맙다고 대답한다.

시험대비 실력평가   p.121~122

01 ②   02 ①   03 ④   04 ②
05 ②   06 ④   07 ⑤   08 ④
09 ③   10 ②

11 It is important that you never give up.

01 yours는 your poster를 의미한다. 너의 포스터를 다 끝냈는지 물어보는 질문에 'Not yet.(아직 못 끝냈어.)'이 어울리므로 ②가 적절하다

02 (A) 그림을 잘 그리기 위해서 자주 그림을 그리는 것이 중요하다고 했으므로 시간이 걸린다는 말이 적절하다. (B) keep 동명사: ~하는 것을 계속하다

03 여자아이는 그림을 잘 그리지 못하고, 그림을 잘 그리기를 원한다. 남자아이의 포스터는 멋져 보였고, 그림을 잘 그리기 위한 조언을 해 주는 것을 보아 남자아이는 잘 그리는 것으로 유추할 수 있다.

04 지호는 배우가 되고 싶지만, 항상 오디션에 떨어져서 포기를 하고 싶다는 말을 하고 있다.

05 ⓑ always fail

06 지호가 아닌 유명한 영화배우가 백 번 이상 오디션에서 떨어졌다.

07 Two heads are better than one: 두 개의 머리가 머리 하나보다 낫다(= 백지장도 맞들면 낫다)

08 'What do you mean by ~?(~이 무슨 뜻이니?)'는 Yes나 No로 대답할 수 없다.

09 계속 공부하는 것이 중요하다는 말에 음악을 끌 것이라고 대답하는 것은 어색하다.

10 What should I do?: 내가 무엇을 해야 할까? 훌륭한 댄서가 되기 위해 무엇을 해야 할지 묻자, 절대 포기하지 않는 것이 중요하다고 대답한다.

11 It's important that 주어 동사 ~: ~하는 것이 중요해. give up: 포기하다

서술형 시험대비   p.123

01 (C) → (A) → (E) → (D) → (B)

02 by

03 What is important to do to become a runner?

04 It's important that I practice running every day.

05 ⓑI'm good at math. → I'm not good at math. / I'm poor at math.

06 (1) It's important that you think creative. → It's important that you think creatively.

　(2) I will forget that. → I will not[won't] forget that.

01 포스터가 멋져 보인다는 말에 (C) 고맙다고 대답하며, 상대방도 포스터를 끝냈는지 물어본다. (A) 아직 안 끝냈다고 대답하고, 그림을 잘 그리지 못 한다며 어떻게 해야 그림을 잘 그릴 수 있는지 질문한다. (E) 가능한 한 자주 그리는 것이 중요하다는 말을 하자, (D) 계속 그리는 연습을 해야 한다는 의미인지 질문하고 (B) 맞다고 대답한다.

02 What do you mean by ~?: ~이 무슨 뜻이니?

03 important: 중요한 become: ~이 되다 'to become a runner'는 to부정사의 부사적 용법(목적, ~하기 위해)으로 사용하였다.

04 'It은 가주어, that절은 진주어로 사용되었다. practice는 동명사를 목적어로 받는다.

05 남자아이는 수학 문제의 정답을 찾지 못했고, 너무 어렵다고 말하고 있으므로, 수학을 잘하지 못한다는 말과 어울린다. be good at: ~을 잘하다

06 (1) 동사를 수식할 수 있는 것은 부사이므로 creative가 아니라 creatively를 사용해야 한다. (2) 영화를 만드는 것이 어렵다는 상대방에게 창의적으로 생각하는 것이 중요하다는 말을 했는데, 이에 'I will forget that.(그것을 잊을게.)'은 어색하다.

23

1 (1) to live (2) to be (3) to think
2 (1) who (2) which

01 (1) bring → to bring (2) borrow → to borrow
    (3) which → who, whom 또는 that
    (4) who → which 또는 that
02 ⑤   03 ①
04 (1) to believe (2) to help (3) who(m)[that]
    (4) which[that]

01 (1), (2) 목적어와 목적격보어가 능동 관계일 때 tell과 ask의 목적격보어로 to부정사가 적절하다. (3) 선행사가 사람일 때 목적격 관계대명사로 which가 아니라 who, whom이나 that을 쓴다. (4) 선행사가 사물일 때 목적격 관계대명사로 who가 아니라 which나 that을 쓴다.

02 목적어와 목적격보어가 능동 관계일 때 advise의 목적격보어는 to부정사이다.

03 선행사가 사물일 때 목적격 관계대명사로 which나 that을 쓴다.

04 (1) 목적어와 목적격보어가 능동 관계일 때 expect의 목적격보어로 to부정사가 적절하다. (2) 목적어와 목적격보어가 능동 관계일 때 encourage의 목적격보어로 to부정사가 적절하다. (3) 선행사가 사람일 때 목적격 관계대명사로 who, whom이나 that을 쓴다. (4) 선행사가 사물일 때 목적격 관계대명사로 which나 that을 쓴다.

01 ⑤   02 ②   03 ③   04 ④
05 ③
06 (1) that (2) which (3) which (4) play (5) warned
07 ④   08 ①   09 ④   10 ①
11 (1) to spend (2) to keep (3) (to) carry (4) finish
    (5) to assemble   12 ③
13 (1) Sophie asked her dad to help her to finish her
       homework.
    (2) Mom wanted Lily to come home by 8.
    (3) She invited me to go to New York with her.
    (4) The blue watch is the gift which[that] I bought
       there for my brother.

---

(5) The man who[whom/that] my mother is talking
    to is my art teacher.
(6) The girl and her cat that I met this morning
    were playing in the park.
14 ⑤   15 (1) who (2) that (3) which is
16 ①   17 ⑤

01 목적어와 목적격보어가 능동 관계일 때 tell은 목적격보어로 to부정사가 나온다.

02 <보기>와 나머지는 목적격 관계대명사이지만, ②번은 주격 관계대명사이다.

03 모두 주격이나 목적격으로 사용된 관계대명사 that이 들어갈 수 있지만 ③번은 소유격 관계대명사 whose가 들어가야 한다.

04 enable은 목적격보어로 to부정사가 나온다.

05 want는 목적격보어로 동사원형이 아니라 to부정사가 나온다. to lend가 되어야 한다.

06 (1) 선행사가 사람이므로 that, (2) 선행사가 사물이므로 which, (3) 전치사 about이 있으므로 that은 쓸 수 없다. (4) 'help'는 목적격보어로 원형부사와 to부정사 둘 다 취할 수 있다. (5) to부정사를 목적격보어로 쓸 수 있는 것은 warn이다. hope는 5형식으로 쓰이지 않는다.

07 관계대명사의 선행사가 사람이면 who, whom이나 that을 쓰고 사물이면 which나 that을 쓴다. ② This is the house in which she lives. 또는 This is the house which[that] she lives in.

08 빈칸에는 to부정사를 목적격보어로 취할 수 있는 동사가 들어가야 한다. watch는 목적격보어로 동사원형이나 현재분사가 나와야 한다.

09 She allowed me to eat ice cream for dessert.

10 ①번은 접속사이지만 나머지는 모두 관계대명사이다.

11 (1), (2), (5) ask, encourage, request는 to부정사를 목적격보어로 취하는 동사이다. (3) help는 to부정사나 동사원형을 쓸 수 있다. (4) have는 사역동사로 목적격보어로 원형부사를 쓴다.

12 warn은 목적격보어로 to부정사를 쓴다.

13 (1), (2), (3) ask, want, invite는 모두 목적격보어로 to부정사가 나와야 한다. (4) 선행사가 사물일 때 목적격 관계대명사로 who가 아니라 which나 that을 쓴다. (5) 선행사가 사람일 때 목적격 관계대명사로 which가 아니라 who, whom이나 that을 쓴다. (6) 선행사가 '사람+동물'일 경우 목적격 관계대명사로 that을 쓴다.

14 feel은 지각동사로 동사원형이나 현재분사를 목적격보어로 취한다. 나머지는 모두 to부정사를 목적격보어로 취하는 동사들로 부정사의 형태가 들어가야 한다.

15 목적격 관계대명사와 '주격 관계대명사+be동사'는 생략할 수 있다.

16 cause, force, warn, want, ask는 모두 목적격보어로 to부정사를 취하는 동사이다. The heavy rain caused the river to

overflow.

17 관계대명사 that은 전치사 다음에는 쓰지 않는다. 또한 목적격 관계대명사는 생략될 수 있다.

01 (1) I want you to be happy.
   (2) Jack asked his mother to wake him up at 8 o'clock.
   (3) Tina told me to find a quiet place to study.
   (4) Jessy got her dad to drop her off at the bus stop.
   (5) His teacher advised him not to spend all his time on one subject.

02 (1) The man who[whom/that] you met on Sunday is my brother.
   (2) That is the computer which[that] I bought last week.
   (3) This is the cake which[that] was made by Ann.
   (4) I visited the church which[that] I took some pictures of. 또는 I visited the church of which I took some pictures.
   (5) It is an experience which[that] I look forward to. 또는 It is an experience to which I look forward.
   (6) Does Eddie have any friends who[whom/that] he can depend on? 또는 Does Eddie have any friends on whom he can depend?

03 (1) to bring (2) take (3) burning

04 (1) This is the bridge which[that] my father built.
   (2) They are the people who[whom/that] I met in the plane.
   (3) I like the new computer that I bought last week.
   (4) Can you tell me about the church of which you took the picture last weekend? 또는 Can you tell me about the church (which/that) you took the picture of last weekend?

05 (1) to come (2) to be (3) not to give up

06 (1) I bought a book.
   (2) I invited her to the party.
   (3) I need to do them[three things] to achieve my dream.
   (4) Is the novel fun?

07 (1) She asked you to clean her room.
   (2) Mom[My mom] expects me to take care of the puppy.
   (3) The people who(m)[that] we met were very

nice.
   (4) The bag (which/that) I bought yesterday is blue.

01 (1) want는 that절을 목적어로 하는 3형식으로 쓰이지 않으며 목적어와 목적격보어가 능동 관계일 때 목적격보어로 to부정사가 나와야 한다. (2) ask, (3) tell, (4) get (5) advise 등의 동사도 목적어와 목적격보어가 능동 관계일 때 목적격보어로 to부정사가 나와야 한다. 또한 to부정사의 부정형은 'not to 동사원형'으로 쓴다.

02 목적격 관계대명사는 수식하는 선행사가 사람이면 who나 whom, that을, 사람이나 동물이면 which나 that을 쓴다. 일반적으로 목적격 관계대명사는 생략될 수 있다. 목적격 관계대명사가 전치사의 목적어인 경우 전치사는 관계대명사절의 끝에 오거나 관계대명사 앞에 올 수 있다. 전치사가 관계대명사절의 끝에 올 경우에는 관계대명사를 생략할 수 있다. 전치사가 관계대명사 앞에 올 경우에는 관계대명사 that을 쓸 수 없으며, 관계대명사를 생략하지 않는다.

03 목적어와 목적격보어가 능동 관계일 때 (1) would like는 목적격보어로 to부정사를 쓴다. (2) make는 사역동사로 목적격보어로 원형부정사를 쓴다. (3) smell은 목적격보어로 현재분사를 쓴다.

04 (1) 선행사가 사물이므로 which나 that, (2) 선행사가 사람이므로 who, whom이나 that, (3) 관계대명사가 접속사와 대명사의 역할을 하므로 목적어로 쓰인 it을 삭제해야 한다. (4) 전치사가 관계대명사 앞에 올 경우에는 관계대명사 that을 쓸 수 없으며, 관계대명사를 생략하지 않는다.

05 (1) tell (2) order (3) encourage 모두 목적격보어로 to부정사를 쓴다.

06 목적격 관계대명사는 선행사가 사람이면 who나 whom, that, 사물이나 동물이면 which나 that을 쓰고 관계대명사절에서 목적어 역할을 한다.

07 (1), (2) ask와 expect의 목적격보어로 to부정사를 쓴다. (3), (4) 선행사가 사람이면 who, whom이나 that, 사물이나 동물이면 which나 that을 쓴다.

교과서
Reading

확인문제   p.132

1 T 2 F 3 T 4 F 5 T 6 F

25

1 T   2 F   3 T   4 F   5 T   6 F

교과서 확인학습 A   p.134~135

01 Breaks the Color Line

02 on April 15, 1947

03 as, for   04 couldn't believe

05 the first African American player

06 the color line was broken

07 faced many difficulties

08 Although, to play with him

09 turned the team down

10 was at bat   11 thought to himself

12 who people like

13 there will be more

14 put, into

15 With practice, batting, base running

16 moved

17 one of his teammates, tapped him on the

18 Do not listen to   19 fine

20 to play   21 earned the respect

22 Thanks to   23 recognized, presented, with

24 asked, to join

25 uniform number

26 no longer, to honor him

27 however, wore   28 is called

교과서 확인학습 B   p.136~137

1 Jackie Robinson Breaks the Color Line

2 It was New York City on April 15, 1947.

3 Jackie Robinson, an African American, went on the field as second baseman for the Brooklyn Dodgers.

4 People couldn't believe their eyes.

5 He was the first African American player to play on a Major League team.

6 That day, the color line was broken.

7 Robinson faced many difficulties.

8 Although Robinson was a talented player and a gentle person, his teammates did not want to play with him.

9 Every hotel turned the team down because Robinson was on the team.

10 When he was at bat, people in the stands rudely shouted at him.

11 Robinson thought to himself, 'I need to keep calm and focus on baseball.

12 I will try and become a player who people like.

13 Then, next season, there will be more African American players in the league.'

14 Robinson put all his time and energy into baseball.

15 With practice, he became great at batting and base running.

16 Robinson's effort moved his teammates.

17 When people shouted at Robinson, one of his teammates walked up to Robinson and tapped him on the shoulder.

18 "Do not listen to them.

19 You're doing fine," he said.

20 His support helped Robinson to play harder.

21 Finally, Robinson earned the respect of other players and fans.

22 Thanks to Robinson, the Dodgers won the National League Championship in 1947.

23 The league recognized Robinson's excellence and presented him with the Rookie of the Year Award in the same year.

24 After that season, other teams asked African American players to join them.

25 Robinson's uniform number was 42.

26 Baseball players in Major League teams no longer wear the number 42 to honor him.

27 Every year, however, on April 15, every player wears the number that Robinson wore.

28 The day is called "Jackie Robinson Day."

시험대비 실력평가   p.138~139

01 on   02 ②   03 ④

04 (A) because (B) himself (C) great

05 When he was at bat   06 ④

07 ②   08 ②   09 honor

10 People[They] call the day "Jackie Robinson Day."

11 ②, ③, ⑤   12 ④   13 ③

14 to give up   15 (A) that (B) keep (C) try   16 ②, ⑤

17 ③   18 ③   19 ⑤   20 ①

21 ②   22 is → are   23 excellence 24 ④

25 (A) Practicing[To Practice] (B) Working[To Work] (C) to manage

26 to practice hard, work well with others, and manage my time well   27 ④, ⑤

01 (A) 날짜 앞에 on을 쓰는 것이 적절하다. (B) '소속'을 나타내는 on을 쓰는 것이 적절하다.

02 ⓐ와 ②번: (전치사) '~로(서)'라는 뜻으로 자격을 나타낸다. ① (접속사) [상태] …인 대로, …인 채로, ③ (접속사) [비례] …함에 따라, …할수록, ④ (접속사) [이유] …이므로, …이기 때문에, ⑤ (접속사) …할 때

03 ④ 가족 관계는 알 수 없다. ① 아프리카계, ② 미국, ③ 2루수, ⑤ 브루클린 다저스

04 (A) 뒤에 절(주어+동사)이 나오므로 because가 적절하다. because of+구, (B) Robinson은 '마음속으로 생각했다'고 해야 하므로 himself가 적절하다. think to oneself: 조용히 생각하다, 마음속으로 생각하다, (C) become의 보어로 형용사를 써야 하므로 great가 적절하다.

05 at bat: 타석에 서서

06 ④ Robinson의 노력 덕분에 몇 명의 아프리카계 미국인들이 메이저리그 팀에서 경기할 수 있었는지는 대답할 수 없다. ① Yes, he did. ② Because Robinson was on the team. ③ No, they didn't. ⑤ With practice, he became great at batting and base running.

07 ② 앞에 나오는 내용과 상반되는 내용이 뒤에 이어지므로 however가 가장 적절하다. ① 그러므로, ④ 사실은, ⑤ 게다가

08 ⓐ와 ①, ⑤: 부사적 용법 ② 명사적 용법 ③, ④ 형용사적 용법

09 메이저리그 팀의 야구 선수들은 Robinson에 대한 '존경을 보여주기 위해' 더 이상 42번을 달지 않는다.

10 People[They]을 주어로 해서 고치는 것이 적절하다.

11 선행사가 사람이고 목적어 자리이므로, 목적격 관계대명사 who, whom, that을 쓰는 것이 적절하다.

12 ④ 연습이 완벽하게 만들어 준다. ① 늦어도 안 하는 것보다 낫다. ② 제때의 바늘 한 뜸이 아홉 번의 수고를 던다. (때를 놓치지 않고 신속하게 행동해야 생길 수 있는 문제를 예방할 수 있다.) ③ 남에게 받고 싶은 대로 남에게 해 주어라. ⑤ 뛰기 전에 살펴봐라. (신중하게 행동하라.)

13 Robinson은 '자신이 노력해서 사람들이 좋아하는 선수가 되면, 다음 시즌에는 아프리카계 미국인 선수가 리그에 더 많이 생길 것'이라고 마음속으로 생각했다.

14 꿈을 성취하기 위해 필요한 세 가지인 to be healthy, to be creative, and never to give up 중에서 세 번째인 never to give up을 쓰는 것이 적절하다. tell + 목적어 + to부정사

15 (A) 선행사가 있기 때문에 that이 적절하다. (B) 'help+목적어+to부정사 또는 원형부정사'이므로 keep이 적절하다. (C) 'make+목적어+원형부정사'이므로 try가 적절하다.

16 ② '남들과 잘 일하기'와 ⑤ '남들을 돕기'는 디자이너의 꿈을 성취하기 위해 필요한 요소에 속하지 않는다.

17 so as to 동사원형 = in order to 동사원형 = in order that 주어 can = so that 주어 can: ~하기 위하여

18 ⓐ와 ③번: 감동시켰다, ① (몸을) 움직였다, ② 바꿨다, ④ 이사했다, ⑤ 옮겼다

19 ⑤는 Robinson의 팀 동료 중 한 명을 가리키고, 나머지는 다 Robinson을 가리킨다.

20 ① 마지막으로, 끝으로(무엇을 열거하면서 마지막 요소 앞에 붙이는 말), ⓐ와 나머지: 마침내

21 ⓐ와 ②번: 의지(명사), ①, ④: …일[할] 것이다(조동사), ③ 무엇을 해 달라는 부탁을 할 때 씀. ⑤ 유언장(명사)

22 주어가 being, working, and being이므로 are로 고치는 것이 적절하다.

23 소유격 다음이므로 명사를 쓰는 것이 적절하다. excellence: 우수, 탁월, 뛰어남

24 주어진 문장의 His support에 주목한다. ④번 앞 문장의 내용을 받고 있으므로 ④번이 적절하다.

25 꿈을 성취하기 위해 필요한 세 가지인 to practice hard, to work well with others, and to manage my time well을 알맞은 형태로 쓰는 것이 적절하다. (A)와 (B)는 주어, (C)는 tell+목적어+to부정사

26 꿈을 성취하기 위해 필요한 세 가지인 to practice hard, to work well with others, and to manage my time well을 가리킨다.

27 ⓑ와 ④, ⑤번: 가목적어, ①, ②, ③: 가주어

🦊 서술형 시험대비 p.142~143

01 color line

02 April fifteen(th), nineteen forty-seven

03 African American player

04 to join

05 to

06 other teams

07 He won it in 1947.

08 talented

09 Every hotel turned the team down 또는 Every hotel turned down the team

10 (A) gentle (B) difficulties

11 Robinson's teammates were moved by his effort. 또는 His teammates were moved by Robinson's effort.

12 people

13 (A) teammates (B) shouted at

14 Robinson earned the respect of other players and fans.

15 (A) batting (B) base running

16 thought to himself

17 I will try and become a player people like.

01 a color line: 인종 차별, (정치적·사회적) 흑인과 백인의 차별, 흑인들이 백인과 함께 다양한 활동에 참여하는 것을 막는 장벽

02 날짜는 서수로 읽는 것이 원칙이지만 기수로도 읽는다. 그리고

April the fifteenth도 가능하다(보통 April 15th, 1947로 표기된 경우).

03 come out into the field: 출전하다, 그 이전에 메이저리그 팀에서 경기한 '아프리카계 미국인 선수'가 없었기 때문이다. (그는 메이저리그 팀에서 경기한 최초의 아프리카계 미국인 선수였다.)

04 ask+목적어+to부정사

05 present A with B = present B to A: A에게 B를 수여하다

06 '다른 팀들'을 가리킨다.

07 그는 1947년에 신인상을 수여했다.

08 talented = gifted: 재능이 있는

09 이어동사 turned down의 목적어인 'the team'을 turned down 사이에 써도 되고 뒤에 써도 된다.

10 그의 재능과 '온화한' 성격에도 불구하고, Robinson은 많은 '어려움'을 경험했다. 예를 들면, 그의 팀원들은 그와 함께 경기하기를 원하지 않았다. in spite of: ~에도 불구하고, personality: 성격

11 Robinson's teammates[his teammates]를 주어로 해서 고치는 것이 적절하다.

12 '사람들'을 가리킨다.

13 Robinson의 '팀 동료' 중 한 명이 Robinson에게 다가가 어깨를 두드리고, "너는 잘하고 있어."라고 덧붙이면서 그에게 소리치고 있는 사람들 말을 듣지 말라고 말했다.

14 earn the respect: 존경을 얻다

15 전치사 'at'의 목적어로 동명사 'batting'과 'base running'을 쓰는 것이 적절하다.

16 think to oneself: 조용히 생각하다, 마음속으로 생각하다

17 목적격 관계대명사 'whom' 대신에 쓰인 'who'를 생략할 수 있다.

영역별 핵심문제　　　　　　　　　p.145~149

01 ③	02 ④	03 (F)inally	04 ④
05 ⑤	06 ④	07 ①	08 by
09 ③	10 ②	11 ②	12 ②

13 (1) The computer (which/that) my parents bought for me is broken.
　(2) The man and his dog that I took a picture of won the first prize.
　(3) The man (who/whom/that) you met on Sunday is my brother.
　(4) His family wanted him to take part in the swimming competition.
　(5) She invited me to go to Paris with her.
　(6) I told him not to make a noise.

14 ⑤	15 ④	16 ③	17 ⑤

18 (1) He asked me to take him to the hospital.

　(2) Did you hear her go[going] out?
　(3) I can't forget the woman who[whom/that] I met in Rome.

19 ①, ④, ⑤

20 (A) Jackie Robinson　(B) color line

21 ②	22 ②	23 ④

24 ①

25 other teams asked African American players to join them

26 ②　　　　　　27 ⓐ wears ⓑ wore

28 want to wear → no longer wear

01 give up: 포기하다 / 그들은 1점도 득점하지 못하고 경기를 포기했어요. thanks to: ~ 덕분에 / 당신 덕분에, 나는 많은 좋은 사람들을 만났다.

02 present A with B: A에게 B를 수여하다 / 그들은 그에게 훌륭한 시민상을 수여할 것이다.

03 finally: 마침내 / 결국, 우리 모두는 부활절 콘서트를 조직하기로 결정했다.

04 earn the respect: 존경을 얻다 / 존경을 얻기 위한 방법들 중 하나는 사회를 위한 책임감을 보여주는 것이다.

05 'keep my fingers crossed'는 행운을 빈다는 뜻이다.

06 ① 여자아이는 "keep my fingers crossed"의 뜻을 알고 있는가? ② 남자아이는 경연 대회에서 무엇을 원하는가? ③ 남자 아이는 어떤 종류의 대회에 나갈 것인가? ④ 어디서 노래 경연 대회가 열리는가? ⑤ 언제 노래 경연 대회가 있는가?

07 반복해서 무언가를 하면 배우게 된다는 뜻을 가진 말은 'Practice makes perfect.(연습이 완벽함을 만든다.)'이다.

08 What do you mean by ~?: ~가 무슨 뜻이니? by 동사-ing: ~함으로써

09 주어진 문장은 어떻게 하면 그림을 잘 그릴 수 있는지 묻는 질문이다. 이 질문에 대한 대답으로 그림을 잘 그릴 수 있도록 하는 조언이 어울린다. 여기서는 시간이 많이 걸리고 자주 그림을 그리라고 조언했다.

10 뒤에 나오는 You mean I should keep practicing?과 어울리는 것은 가능한 한 자주 그림을 그리라는 것이다.

11 ② 이외의 보기들은 설명을 요청할 때 사용하는 표현들이다.

12 take: (얼마의 시간이) 걸리다 achieve: 이루다, 달성하다 Rome was not built in a day.: 로마는 하루아침에 이루어지지 않았다.(= 무언가를 이루는 데는 시간이 걸린다.)

13 (1) 선행사가 사물일 때 목적격 관계대명사로 which나 that을 쓰며, 생략할 수 있다. (2) 선행사가 '사람+동물'일 때 목적격 관계대명사로 that을 쓰며, 생략할 수 있다. (3) 선행사가 사람일 때 목적격 관계대명사로 who, whom이나 that을 쓴다. (4), (5), (6) want, tell, invite는 목적격보어로 to부정사가 나온다. to부정사의 부정형은 'not to 동사원형'으로 쓴다.

14 ⑤ The bag (which/that) I bought yesterday was sent

to Wendy.

15 ① I didn't expect him to talk to you. ② They asked John to do something for them. ③ Mom wanted Sam to finish his homework. ⑤ His doctor ordered Simon to take some rest.

16 ③번은 주격 관계대명사이고 나머지는 모두 목적격 관계대명사이다.

17 ⓐ to not → not to ⓑ live → to live ⓒ to go → go ⓕ which → who ⓖ it → 삭제

18 (1) ask의 목적격 보어로 to부정사가 나와야 한다. (2) 지각동사 hear의 목적격 보어로 동사원형이나 현재분사가 나와야 한다. (3) 선행사가 사람이므로 목적격 관계대명사로 who나 whom 또는 that을 쓴다.

19 ⓐ와 ②, ③: 형용사적 용법, ①, ⑤: 부사적 용법, ④ 명사적 용법, a major leaguer: 메이저 리그 선수

20 1947년 4월 15일, 'Jackie Robinson'이 브루클린 다저스의 2루수로 경기장에 나갔을 때, '인종 차별'이 깨졌다.

21 'Robinson은 재능 있는 선수이고 온화한 사람이었지만 그의 팀원들은 그와 함께 경기하길 원하지 않았다.'고 해야 하므로 'Although'를 쓰는 것이 적절하다.

22 ②번 다음 문장의 Then에 주목한다. 주어진 문장의 내용을 받고 있으므로 ②번이 적절하다.

23 ④ diligent: 근면한, 성실한, Robinson은 자신의 모든 시간과 에너지를 야구에 집중했고, 연습을 함으로써 타격과 주루를 잘하게 되었다고 했으므로 성격이 '성실하다'고 하는 것이 적절하다. ① 호기심 많은, ② 외향적인, ③ 사교적인, ⑤ 창의적인

24 ⓐ 정관사가 다른 사람의 신체의 일부를 나타내는 명사 앞에서 소유격 대명사를 대신한 구문이고, tap이나 pat과 같이 '두드리다'는 뜻일 때는 전치사 'on'을 사용하는 것이 적절하다. ⓑ present A with B = present B to A: A에게 B를 수여[제공]하다

25 'to'를 보충하면 된다. ask+목적어+to부정사

26 이 글은 Robinson이 자신의 노력을 통해 사람들의 인정을 얻었다는 내용의 글이다.

27 ⓐ every는 단수로 취급하므로 wears, ⓑ Robinson이 예전에 42번을 달았던 것이므로 wore

28 메이저리그 팀의 야구 선수들은 그에 대한 존경을 보여 주기 위해 '더 이상' 42번을 '달지 않는다.'

단원별 예상문제   p.150~153

01 ④   02 ⑤   03 ③   04 ①
05 ③   06 ②, ⑤
07 it's important that you choose the right books to read.
08 ①   09 ③   10 achieved
11 It's important that you never give up.
12 (C) → (A) → (B)   13 ②   14 ③

15 ④   16 ③   17 African American
18 April 15, 1947   19 ②   20 ④
21 refused(rejected)   22 ②
23 touched
24 ④   25 ①, ③, ⑤   26 ①, ③, ④

01 ④번은 동사와 명사의 관계이고 나머지 보기는 형용사와 명사의 관계이다. ① different: 다른 difference: 다름, 차이 ② important: 중요한 importance: 중요성 ③ silent: 조용한 silence: 침묵 ④ allow: 허락하다 allowance: 허용 ⑤ excellent: 우수한 excellence: 우수, 장점

02 face: 직면하다, 직시하다 / 나는 그들이 많은 문제들에 직면해 있다는 것을 안다.

03 think to oneself: 마음속으로 생각하다

04 win first place: 1등을 하다, 우승하다 / 그녀는 수영대회에서 1등을 했다. award: 상 win an award: 상을 타다 / 그녀는 최고의 여배우 상을 받았다.

05 이것을 하기 어렵다는 말에 (C) 무슨 일인지 물어보자 (A) 쿠키를 만드는 방법을 가르쳐 줄 수 있는지 물었다. (B) 물론이라고 대답하며, 그것이 'a walk in the park'라고 말한다. (D) 'a walk in the park'가 무슨 뜻인지 물어보자 그것은 하기 쉽다는 뜻이라고 대답한다.

06 ⓑ never stop ⓔ how

07 It's important that 주어 동사 ~: ~하는 것이 중요하다 choose: 고르다

08 ⓐ to win ⓑ keep ⓒ crossed ⓓ mean ⓔ It means

09 빈칸 (A)의 앞, 뒤의 말이 역접의 관계이므로('많은 오디션에 갔지만 자주 떨어졌다'와 '나는 절대 포기하지 않았다.') 그러므로 However(하지만)가 어울린다.

10 achieve: 이루다, 달성하다 achieve a goal: 목표를 달성하다

11 It's important that 주어 동사 ~: ~하는 것이 중요하다 give up: 포기하다

12 (C) 훌륭한 댄서가 되는 것이 어렵다고 말하면서 무엇을 해야 하는지 상대방에게 질문했다. (A) 절대로 포기하지 않는 것이 중요하다고 말하자, (B) 알았다고 잊지 않겠다고 대답한다.

13 ① Her parents were worried and asked her to stop surfing. ③ Mr. Johnson told us to shake hands after the game. ④ His parents encouraged him to have an interest in art. ⑤ I didn't expect you to understand me at all.

14 ③번은 목적격 관계대명사가 생략된 것이므로 it이 없어야 한다.

15 선행사가 사물일 때 목적격 관계대명사로 which나 that을 쓴다.

16 ③ 인종 차별이 '깨졌다'고 해야 하므로, break를 과거 수동태로 쓰는 것이 적절하다.

17 African American: 아프리카계 미국인

18 '1947년 4월 15일'을 가리킨다.

29

19 ⓐ face: 직면하다, ② encounter: 만나다, 마주치다, ① express: 표현하다, ③ accept: 수락하다, 받아들이다, ④ look into: ~을 조사하다, ⑤ solve: 해결하다

20 ④ 부사적 용법, ⓑ와 나머지: 명사적 용법

21 turn down = refuse = reject: 거절하다

22 이 글은 'Robinson이 자신의 노력을 통해 사람들의 인정을 얻었다'는 내용의 글이므로, 제목으로는 'Robinson의 노력이 결실을 맺었다'가 적절하다. bear fruit: 결실을 맺다

23 move = touch: 감동시키다

24 ④ Thanks to Robinson, the Dodgers won the National League Championship in 1947.

25 no longer = no more = not ~ any longer = not ~ any more: 더 이상 ~ 않다

26 ⓑ와 ①, ③, ④번: 관계대명사, ②, ⑤: 접속사

🦉 서술형 실전문제
p.154~155

01 I mean[It means] working together is better than working alone.

02 ⓑIt's too easy for me. → It's too hard[difficult]] for me.

03 It's important that you use this math rule to solve the problem.

04 I mean you learn something by doing it over and over.

05 (1) The Korean dishes which[that] we had last night tasted yummy.
(2) I have a dog with which I take a walk every night. 또는 I have a dog which[that] I take a walk with every night.

06 (1) not to go out alone at night
(2) to win first prize at the singing contest

07 (1) 그의 팀원들은 그와 함께 경기하기를 원하지 않았다.
(2) Robinson이 팀에 있었기 때문에 모든 호텔에서 그 팀을 거절했다.
(3) 그가 타석에 있을 때, 관중석에 있는 사람들이 그에게 무례 하게 소리치기도 했다.

08 (A) down (B) rudely (C) calm

09 I try and become a player who people like

10 playing → (to) play

11 (1) Robinson 덕분에 다저스는 1947년에 내셔널리그 챔피언십에서 우승하게 되었다.
(2) 리그에서는 Robinson의 탁월함을 인정했고, 같은 해에 그에게 신인상을 수여했다.

12 to win

---

01 설명을 할 때는 '~을 의미하다'의 뜻을 가진 'mean'을 사용해 'It means ~.'나 'I mean ~.'으로 대답할 수 있다. better than: ~보다 나은

02 ⓑ의 수학 문제가 너무 쉽다는 말과 ⓒ의 수학을 못한다는 말은 반대의 말이므로 어색하다. 여자아이가 수학 문제에 대한 조언을 해 주고 있으므로, 수학이 어렵다는 말이 어울린다.

03 It's important that 주어 동사 ~: ~하는 것이 중요하다 use: 사용하다 solve: 풀다, 해결하다

04 by 동사ing: ~함으로써 over and over: 반복해서

05 목적격 관계대명사가 수식하는 선행사가 사람이면 who나 whom, that을, 사람이 아니면 which나 that을 쓴다. 일반적으로 목적격 관계대명사는 생략될 수 있다. 목적격 관계대명사가 전치사의 목적어인 경우 전치사는 관계대명사절의 끝에 오거나 관계대명사 앞에 올 수 있다. 전치사가 관계대명사절의 끝에 올 경우에는 관계대명사를 생략할 수 있다. 전치사가 관계대명사 앞에 올 경우에는 관계대명사 that을 쓸 수 없으며, 관계대명사를 생략하지 않는다.

06 order와 expect는 목적어와 목적격보어가 능동 관계일 때 목적격보어로 to부정사를 쓴다.

07 뒤에 이어지는 내용을 쓰는 것이 적절하다.

08 (A) 'Robinson이 팀에 있었기 때문에 모든 호텔에서 그 팀을 거절했다.'고 해야 하므로 down이 적절하다. turn down: ~을 거절하다, 거부하다, turn up: 나타나다, (B) 동사 shouted를 수식하므로 부사 rudely가 적절하다. (C) keep의 보어이므로 형용사 calm이 적절하다.

09 때나 조건을 나타내는 부사절에서는 현재시제가 미래를 대신한다.

10 help+목적어+to부정사 또는 원형부정사

11 두 번째 단락의 내용을 쓰면 된다.

12 Robinson의 노력이 다저스가 1947년에 내셔널리그 챔피언십에서 우승하도록 해주었다.

🐰 창의사고력 서술형문제
p.156

|모범답안|

01 I think music helps me to study better. /
It's important to focus when you study. /
I'll turn down the music.

02 (1) I expect Mina to get good grades.
(2) I expect Luke to do exercise regularly.
(3) I expect my mom to be healthy. / I expect my dad to stop smoking.

03 (A) to practice hard (B) cook well and easily
(C) to work at a restaurant
(D) make food in time to serve

01 help+목적어+(to)동사원형: (목적어)가 ~하는 것을 돕다 It's important that 주어 동사 ~: ~하는 것이 중요해 focus: 집중하다 turn down: 소리를 줄이다

01 ①   02 ①

03 (1) difficulties (2) excellence

04 support   05 ②

06 I mean[It means] you can achieve your dream with a strong will.

07 (C) → (A) → (D) → (B)   08 ④   09 ③

10 ③   11 He failed more than 100 auditions.

12 give up

13 (1) She is the girl who[whom/that] I love.

   (2) Have you ever fallen in love with a lady to whom you haven't even talked? 또는 Have you ever fallen in love with a lady who[whom/that] you haven't even talked to?

14 (1) to do (2) to go (3) to insist (4) not to be

15 ⑤   16 ②

17 (1) drank → to drink (2) trying → to try

   (3) stay → to stay (4) who → which[that]

18 but   19 ⑤번 → at   20 ③

21 take part in 또는 participate in   22 ①

23 ⑤   24 ③, ⑤   25 42

01 shout at: ~을 향해 외치다 / 너는 왜 항상 나에게 소리를 지르니?

02 earn the respect: 존경을 얻다 / 그녀는 의사로서 환자들의 존경을 얻었다. give up: 포기하다 pursue: 추구하다 / 당신이 꿈을 갖고 있다면, 절대 포기하지 말고 당신의 열정을 추구하세요.

03 (1) difficult: 어려운 difficulty: 어려움, 곤경, 장애 (2) excellent: 뛰어난 excellence: 우수, 탁월, 뛰어남

04 support: 지지 / 어려움을 겪고 있는 사람에게 주는 도움과 친절 / 나는 그의 도움과 지지가 필요하다.

05 대화의 will은 '의지'의 뜻이다. ② ~할 것이다 / 그는 보고서를 즉시 끝낼 것이다. ① 그 결정은 그녀의 자유 의지로 되었다. ③ 의지가 강할수록 더 많이 배울 것이다. ④ 사람은 의지의 자유가 있다. ⑤ 의지가 있는 곳에 길이 있습니다.

06 achieve: 이루다, 달성하다 will: 의지

07 A가 자신을 "The Wizard of Goyang"으로 불러달라고 하자 B가 그것이 무슨 뜻인지 물어본다. (C) "The Wizard of Goyang"의 뜻이 자신이 발명가가 되고 싶다는 의미라고 설명한다. (A) 상대방에게 발명가가 되기 위해서는 무엇이 중요한지 질문하자 (D) 창의적으로 생각하는 것이 중요하다고 말하고 (B) 상대방이 성공할 것을 확신한다고 대답한다.

08 주어진 문장은 '하지만, 읽을 알맞은 책을 고르는 것이 중요하다.'란 의미이다. ④번 다음 문장에서 책을 고르는 법을 언급하고 있으므로 ④번이 적절하다. It's important that 주어 동사 ~: ~하는 것이 중요하다 right: 올바른, 알맞은

09 하나가 지호에게 무슨 일인지 묻는 질문에 꿈을 이룰 수 없을 것

같다고 대답한 것을 보았을 때 슬퍼 보인다는 것을 유추할 수 있다. ① 졸린 ② 행복한 ③ 슬픈 ④ 외로운 ⑤ 운이 좋은

10 What do you mean by ~?: ~가 무슨 뜻이니?

11 fail: 실패하다, ~하지 못하다 more than: ~보다 많이

12 give up: 포기하다

13 목적격 관계대명사는 수식하는 선행사가 사람이면 who나 whom, that을, 사람이 아니면 which나 that을 쓴다. 일반적으로 목적격 관계대명사는 생략될 수 있다. 목적격 관계대명사가 전치사의 목적어인 경우 전치사는 관계대명사절의 끝에 오거나 관계대명사 앞에 올 수 있다. 전치사가 관계대명사절의 끝에 올 경우에는 관계대명사를 생략할 수 있다. 전치사가 관계대명사 앞에 올 경우에는 관계대명사 that을 쓸 수 없으며, 관계대명사를 생략하지 않는다.

14 ask, allow, cause, warn의 목적격보어로 to부정사가 적절하다. to부정사의 부정형은 'not to 동사원형'으로 쓴다.

15 I love the jacket which[that] Hana is wearing.

16 ① tell의 목적격보어로 to부정사가 적절하다. ③, ④ 선행사가 사물일 때 목적격 관계대명사로 which나 that을 쓴다. ⑤ 목적어로 쓰인 them을 삭제해야 한다.

18 Although 대신 문장 중간에 but을 쓰는 것이 적절하다.

19 연습을 함으로써 그는 타격과 주루를 '잘하게 되었다'라고 해야 하므로, at으로 고치는 것이 적절하다. become great for: ~에 좋게 되다, become great at: ~에 잘하게 되다

20 전치사의 목적어로 동명사 'batting'과 'base running'이 쓰였다. ⓑ와 ②, ③, ④: 동명사, ①, ⑤: 현재분사

21 join = take part in = participate in: ~에 참가하다

22 ① 지성이면 감천이다. ② 서두르면 일을 그르친다. ③ 엎질러진 우유를 놓고 울어봐야 소용없다.(되돌릴 수 없는 잘못을 하고 후회해 봐야 아무 소용이 없다.) ④ 모두의 일은 어느 누구의 일도 아니다.(누군가에게 직접 책임이 지워지지 않은 일은 서로 미루다가 결국은 아무도 하지 않게 된다.) ⑤ 요리사가 너무 많으면 국을 망친다.(사공이 많으면 배가 산으로 올라간다.)

23 ⑤ 그 시즌 이후, 몇 명의 아프리카계 미국인 선수들이 다른 팀에 합류했는지는 대답할 수 없다. ① One of his teammates. ② Yes. ③ In 1947. ④ The Rookie of the Year Award.

24 목적격 관계대명사 that이나 which가 적절하다.

25 Robinson의 등 번호 '42번'을 가리킨다.

교과서 파헤치기

Lesson
5

단어 TEST Step 1   p.02

01 여행객	02 돌봄, 보살핌	03 외국으로(에서)
04 흔들다; 파도	05 ~을 용서하다, 너그러이 봐주다	
06 여행	07 전통적인	08 경험; 경험하다
09 역사적인, 역사상 중요한		10 기둥
11 섬	12 구르다, 굴리다	13 수도
14 전망, 경치	15 환호하다, 갈채하다; 환호	
16 일하다; 작품	17 언어	18 독특한
19 경기, 시합; 어울리다		20 빛나다
21 조심하는, 주의 깊은		22 선호하다
23 도움이 되는	24 경기장	25 동작
26 천장	27 미끄러지다, 활주하다	
28 보라색	29 베트남어; 베트남의	
30 설계하다, 디자인하다		31 근처에
32 극장	33 음식, 접시	34 도마뱀
35 ~으로 가득 차다	36 ~의 맞은편에	37 ~로 유명하다
38 입어 보다	39 ~로 알려져 있다	
40 (시간, 날짜를) 미루다, 연기하다		41 걸어서
42 ~을 응원하다	43 ~로부터 멀리	

단어 TEST Step 2   p.03

01 shine	02 historic	03 experience
04 island	05 traditional	06 roll
07 care	08 slide	09 near
10 helpful	11 excuse	12 purple
13 tourist	14 careful	15 wave
16 tour	17 view	18 cheer
19 dish	20 match	21 capital
22 design	23 movement	24 ceiling
25 lizard	26 column	27 prefer
28 work	29 language	30 abroad
31 unique	32 theater	33 stop
34 Vietnamese	35 across from	36 be full of
37 on top of	38 cheer for	39 put off
40 far from	41 be known for	42 try on
43 be famous for		

단어 TEST Step 3   p.04

1 shine, 빛나다   2 abroad, 외국으로(에서)
3 slide, 미끄러지다, 활주하다   4 ceiling, 천장
5 purple, 보라색   6 capital, 수도   7 lizard, 도마뱀
8 Spanish, 스페인의   9 cheer, 환호하다, 갈채하다

10 Vietnamese, 베트남의   11 theater, 극장
12 view, 전망, 경치   13 curry, 카레   14 prefer, 선호하다
15 tour, 여행   16 excuse, ~을 용서하다, 너그러이 봐주다

대화문 TEST Step 1   p.05~06

Listen & Speak 1 A

1 Excuse, Is, near / far from / How can, get there / Go straight, turn left, on your right

2 need to buy, Where can, buy / buy them at / Where is it / Go straight, blocks, across from the library

Listen & Speak 1 B

1 Excuse me, Where is / Go straight two blocks, on your right

2 Where is / straight one block, It's on, It's across from

Listen & Talk 2 A

1 It's, Let's go, have, fresh fruit juice / good, How, get there / on foot or by bus, Which do you prefer / prefer

2 What is, called / type, traditional clothing / try one on / Which do you prefer, yellow one / purple one

Listen & Talk 2 B

1 Which do you prefer / prefer hamburgers

2 Which do you prefer, or / prefer paella

Conversation A

Welcome to, we'll visit, see, on your right, near, view from, amazing, every year

Conversation B

How may, help / want to enjoy, view of / best place to go to / great places, on top of, Which do, prefer / prefer / Me, too / get, by bus / Where, nearest stop / straight one block, turn right, on your left / can see, There is / I think, Why don't we go, visit, later / sounds

대화문 TEST Step 2   p.07~08

Listen & Speak 1 A

1 B: Excuse me. Is the Picasso Museum near here?

  G: Yes. It's not far from here.

  B: How can I get there?

  G: Go straight one block and turn left. It's on your right.

2 B: Sally, I need to buy some candies for Halloween. Where can I buy them?

  G: You can buy them at Wendy's Candy Shop.

  B: Where is it?

  G: Go straight two blocks and turn right. It's across from the library.

1 A: Excuse me. Where is the park?

B: Go straight two blocks and turn left. It's on your right.

2 A: Excuse me. Where is the school?

B: Go straight one block and turn left. It's on your right. It's across from the restaurant.

1 B: It's really hot here in Thailand. Let's go to the night market and have some fresh fruit juice.

G: Sounds good. How do we get there?

B: We can go on foot or by bus. Which do you prefer?

G: I prefer the bus.

2 G: What is this long dress called?

M: It is an Ao dai, a type of traditional clothing from Vietnam.

G: Can I try one on?

M: Sure. Which do you prefer, the purple one or the yellow one?

G: The purple one, please.

1 A: Which do you prefer, hamburgers or spaghetti?

B: I prefer hamburgers.

2 A: Which do you prefer, curry or paella?

B: I prefer paella.

M: Welcome to London City Tour. Today, we'll visit famous places in London. Can you see the London Eye? It's on your right. It's a Ferris wheel near the River Thames. The view from the London Eye is amazing. Many people visit it every year.

Staff: How may I help you?

Hana's mom: We want to enjoy a good view of London.

Hana: Where is the best place to go to?

Staff: We have two great places. The London Eye is a Ferris wheel and the sky Garden is a glass garden on top of a tall building. Which do you prefer?

Hana's mom: Hmm... I prefer the London Eye.

Hana: Me, too.

Staff: Good choice. You can get there by bus.

Hana's mom: Where is the nearest stop?

Staff: Go straight one block and turn right. It's on your left. Have a good trip!

Hana: Wow, I can see all of London. Look! There is a big clock.

Hana's mom: I think that's Big Ben. Why don't we go and visit it later?

Hana: That sounds great.

01 Happy Days, by   02 traveled to, this

03 loved by, of   04 visited, interesting places

05 Our trip, in   06 capital, famous for

07 went, watch, match

08 excited, world's most famous

09 full of, fans   10 by singing, waving, shouting

11 After, toured, went

12 While, walked around

13 visited, museum, watched

14 in, dancing, with, movements   15 For, ate

16 traditional, dish with   17 tasted like, in

18 so, that, all   19 took, tour of

20 Both, designed by

21 creative, like, colorful   22 After, visited

23 Work, going on

24 impressed, its, unique

25 ceiling, shone like, with

26 columns stood like

27 feel, creativity, love, nature

28 Traveling, wonderful experience 29 While, a lot

30 visit, country again

01 Happy Days, by

02 traveled to Spain

03 is loved by lots of

04 visited, interesting places

05 Our trip started in

06 capital, is famous for

07 to watch, soccer match

08 were excited because, the world's most famous soccer players

09 was full of

10 cheered by singing, waving, shouting, other fans

11 After, toured, went to

12 While, walked around, many historic buildings

13 visited, watched

14 in a red dress was dancing, with wonderful movements

15 For dinner, ate

16 traditional Spanish dish with, meat, seafood

17 tasted like fried rice

18 so, that, all enjoyed   19 took a tour of

20 were designed by

21 creative works like, colorful lizard

22 After, visited   23 Work on, is still going on

33

24 was impressed by its size

25 shone like, with bright stars

26 stone columns stood like

27 could feel, creativity, his love of nature

28 Traveling, a wonderful experience

29 While, a lot   30 to visit

---

30 나는 그 나라를 다시 방문하고 싶다.

---

1 스페인에서의 행복한 날들 – 박진우

2 나의 가족은 이번 여름에 스페인을 여행했다.

3 스페인은 수많은 관광객들에게 사랑받는다.

4 우리는 여러 흥미로운 장소를 방문했다.

5 우리의 여행은 마드리드에서 시작했다.

6 마드리드는 수도이며 축구로 유명하다.

7 우리는 축구 경기를 보기 위해서 경기장으로 갔다.

8 나의 여동생과 나는 세계에서 가장 유명한 축구 선수 몇몇을 볼 수 있었기 때문에 신이 났다.

9 경기장은 축구 팬들로 가득 차 있었다.

10 우리는 경기를 보는 동안 노래를 부르고, 손을 흔들고, 다른 팬들과 함께 소리를 치며 응원을 했다.

11 마드리드를 여행하고 난 후, 우리는 세비야로 갔다.

12 우리는 도시를 걸어다니는 동안, 역사상 중요한 많은 건물들을 보았다.

13 우리는 플라멩코 박물관을 방문해서 플라멩코 춤을 보았다.

14 빨간 드레스를 입은 여자가 멋진 동작으로 플라멩코를 추고 있었다.

15 저녁 식사로 우리는 파에야를 먹었다.

16 그것은 쌀과 채소, 고기, 해산물이 들어간 전통적인 스페인 요리이다.

17 그것은 한국의 볶음밥과 같은 맛이 났다.

18 너무 맛있어서 우리 모두는 그것을 즐겼다.

19 바르셀로나에서 우리는 구엘 공원과 사그라다 파밀리아를 둘러보았다.

20 두 곳 모두 Antoni Gaudi에 의해 설계되었다.

21 구엘 공원에서 우리는 형형색색의 도마뱀과 같은 몇몇 Gaudi의 창의적인 작품들을 보았다.

22 구엘 공원을 본 다음, 우리는 사그라다 파밀리아를 방문했다.

23 건물 공사는 1883년에 시작되었고 오늘날까지도 여전히 진행 중이다.

24 나는 건물의 크기와 독특한 디자인에 감명 받았다.

25 사그라다 파밀라아 안의 천장은 밝은 별이 있는 밤하늘처럼 빛났다.

26 돌기둥은 큰 나무처럼 서 있었다.

27 구엘 공원과 사그라다 파밀리아에서 나는 Gaudi의 창의성과 자연에 대한 사랑을 느낄 수 있었다.

28 스페인 여행은 훌륭한 경험이었다.

29 나는 그곳에서 스페인에 대해 많은 것을 배웠다.

---

1 My Happy Days in Spain – by Park Jinwoo

2 My family traveled to Spain this summer.

3 Spain is loved by lots of tourists.

4 We visited many interesting places.

5 Our trip started in Madrid.

6 Madrid is the capital and is famous for soccer.

7 We went to a stadium to watch a soccer match.

8 My sister and I were excited because we could watch some of the world's most famous soccer players.

9 The stadium was full of soccer fans.

10 As we watched the match, we cheered by singing songs, waving our hands, and shouting with the other fans.

11 After we toured Madrid, we went to Seville.

12 While we walked around the city, we saw many historic buildings.

13 We visited a flamenco museum and watched a flamenco dance.

14 A woman in a red dress was dancing the flamenco with wonderful movements.

15 For dinner, we ate paella.

16 It is a traditional Spanish dish with rice, vegetables, meat, and seafood.

17 It tasted like fried rice in Korea.

18 It was so delicious that we all enjoyed it.

19 In Barcelona, we took a tour of Park Guell and Sagrada Familia.

20 Both were designed by Antoni Gaudi.

21 In Park Guell, we saw some of Gaudi's creative works like a colorful lizard.

22 After Park Guell, we visited Sagrada Familia.

23 Work on the building started in 1883 and is still going on today.

24 I was impressed by its size and unique design.

25 The ceiling inside Sagrada Familia shone like the night sky with bright stars.

26 Its stone columns stood like big trees.

27 At Park Guell and Sagrada Familia I could feel Gaudi's creativity and his love of nature.

28 Traveling in Spain was a wonderful experience.

29 While I was there, I learned a lot about Spain.

30 I want to visit the country again.

Enjoy Writing

1. How much, know about
2. capital of Vietnam, is spoken
3. are popular dishes
4. Every year lots of
5. is well known for
6. so beautiful that, should

Project Step 3

1. chose, for a trip
2. is loved by, who, to do
3. have great experiences at

Wrap Up

1. was moved by
2. title of the book
3. was written by
4. so, that, many times

Enjoy Writing

1. How much do you know about Vietnam?
2. The capital of Vietnam is Hanoi. Vietnamese is spoken there.
3. Pho and banh mi are popular dishes in Vietnam.
4. Every year lots of tourists visit Halong Bay and Nha Trang.
5. Halong Bay has 1,969 islands and Nha Trang is well known for its beautiful beaches.
6. Vietnam is so beautiful that you should come someday.

Project Step 3

1. My group chose Hong Kong for a trip.
2. Hong Kong is loved by many people who want to do fun activities.
3. We'll have great experiences at Mong Kok Market, Victoria Peak, and Ocean Park.

Wrap Up

1. I was moved by a book.
2. The title of the book is *The Old Man and the Sea*.
3. It was written by Ernest Hemingway.
4. The story was so great that I read it many times .

11 muddy, 진흙투성이인, 진흙의   12 reed, 갈대

13 tide, 조수, 밀물과 썰물   14 filter, ~을 여과하다, 거르다

15 flow, 흐르다   16 provide, 제공하다, 주다

단어 TEST Step 1   p.21

01 (꽃이) 피다	02 갈대	03 피해
04 인사하다	05 절벽	06 산소
07 평원	08 게	09 쓰레기
10 생물, 생명체	11 진실, 사실	12 제거하다
13 표면	14 환경	15 각종의, 다양한
16 나타나다	17 이유	18 줄이다
19 홍수	20 생산하다, 만들다	21 관대한
22 규칙적으로	23 보호하다	24 엉망진창
25 폐	26 얼룩	27 정보

28 먹이를 주다, 먹이다

29 진흙투성이인, 진흙의, 질퍽한   30 필요한

31 일어나다, 발생하다   32 제공하다, 주다

33 조수, 밀물과 썰물 34 놀라움, 경이; ~을 궁금해 하다

35 운동하다   36 ~와 같은   37 ~에 좋다, 유익하다

38 A뿐만 아니라 B도   39 그런데

40 다수의, 많은 수의 41 (옷 등을) 벗다, 벗기다

42 ~로 유명하다   43 생계를 유지하다

단어 TEST Step 2   p.22

01 cave	02 appear	03 damage
04 cliff	05 environment	06 remove
07 bloom	08 filter	09 various
10 surface	11 creature	12 flow
13 regularly	14 generous	15 reason
16 flood	17 trash	18 produce
19 protect	20 wonder	21 oxygen
22 feed	23 truth	24 stain
25 reduce	26 greet	27 lung
28 mess	29 reed	30 muddy
31 necessary	32 occur	33 provide
34 greatly	35 by the way	36 make a living
37 be famous for	38 such as	39 be good for
40 a large number of		41 work out
42 take off	43 not only A but also B	

단어 TEST Step 3   p.23

1 mud, 진흙 2 plain, 평원 3 appear, 나타나다

4 information, 정보 5 surface, 표면 6 cliff, 절벽

7 land, 육지, 땅 8 creature, 생물, 생명체

9 generous, 관대한 10 lung, 폐

대화문 TEST Step 1   p.24~25

Listen & Speak 1 A

1. wonder what you did during / took, trip / By, plains / flat land

2. Look at, beautiful / lake / wonder how, are different / a long body of fresh, Unlike, flows toward / got it

Listen & Speak 1 B

1. what a mountain is / high

2. I wonder what, plain / large, flat, land

Listen & Speak 2 A

1. how many oceans there are / isn't it / There are, cover most / How much, cover / heard, cover about, surface

2. heard, rain forest is called, lungs / Lungs / Because, produces, oxygen / a lot

Listen & Speak 2 B

1. want / heard, lakes

2. want to go to / are famous caves

Conversation A

what, plant, looks like, grass, In, turns, wet, heard, is famous for

Conversation B

amazing place / let's get on / Look at, wonder what they are / reeds, reed / taller than / Let, take, of / reed field / heard, the largest one / Look at, turning / beautiful

Communication Task Step 1

place / special about / is light blue

대화문 TEST Step 2   p.26~27

Listen & Speak 1 A

1. G: I wonder what you did during the summer vacation.

   B: I took a trip to Kenya and saw many animals on the plains.

   G: Wonderful! By the way, what are the plains?

   B: They are large areas of flat land.

   G: I see.

2. G: Look at that lake! It's really beautiful.

   B: It's not a lake. It's a river.

   G: Is it? I wonder how a river and a lake are different.

B: A river is a long body of fresh water. Unlike a lake, a river flows toward the ocean.

G: I got it.

1. A: I wonder what a mountain is.

B: It is a very high area of land.

2. A: I wonder what a plain is.

B: It is a large, flat area of land.

1. B: Do you know how many oceans there are on the Earth?

G: The answer is four, isn't it?

B: No. There are five oceans on the Earth. They cover most of the Earth.

G: How much of the Earth do they cover?

B: I heard the oceans cover about 70% of the Earth's surface.

2. G: I heard the Amazon rain forest is called the lungs of the Earth.

B: Lungs? Why?

G: Because it produces about 20% of the Earth's oxygen.

B: Wow! That's a lot.

1. A: I want to go to Jecheon.

B: Why?

A: I heard there are beautiful lakes in Jecheon.

2. A: I want to go to Danyang.

B: Why?

A: I heard there are famous caves in Danyang.

M: Guess what this is! It's not a tree. It is a plant that looks like tall grass. In fall, it turns yellow. It grows well in wet lands. I heard Suncheon Bay is famous for this plant.

Dad: Do you want to see an amazing place?

Karl & Sister: Sure!

Dad: Then let's get on the train.

Sister: Look at the yellow plants! I wonder what they are.

Dad: They are reeds. Suncheon Bay has beautiful reed fields.

Karl: Wow, the reeds are even taller than you, Dad.

Sister: They really are. Let me take a picture of you.

Karl: This reed field is very large.

Dad: Yes. I heard it is the largest one in Korea.

Karl: Look at the sky. It's turning red.

Sister: Yes, it's beautiful.

A: What place do you have?

B: I have Moraine Lake. It's in Canada.

A: What is special about the place?

B: The color of the water is light blue.

---

01 Nature's Gift   02 areas, muddy, seaside

03 appear, with, tide

04 show up, tides, covered

05 creatures, in, ways

06 important, roles, mudflats

07 Let's, what, do

08 home, living, seaside

09 Not only, but also

10 provide, types, for   11 Also, eat, there

12 my, sweet home   13 good for, too

14 mudflat, make, living, nearby

15 Thanks to, fresh

16 fun activities, such as

17 large number, feed on

18 nature's gift, living   19 help, greatly

20 hold, reduce damage, floods

21 filter, from, into

22 remove things, before

23 Thanks, reaches, clean   24 work as, lungs

25 huge, oxygen, necessary

26 keep, healthy, clean

27 Mudflats, aren't they

28 gift, nature, living

29 reasons, necessary, protect

---

01 Nature's Gift   02 muddy land

03 disappear with every tide

04 During, show up, high tides, are covered by

05 sea creatures, in many ways

06 to understand the roles of mudflats

07 Let's, what they do

08 are home to, living things

09 Not only, but also

10 provide, types of, for   11 Also

12 home sweet home

13 are good for, too

14 make a living, by catching, nearby

15 Thanks to, fresh seafood

16 fun activities, such as, on mudflats

17 a large number of, feed on

18 nature's gift

19 help, environment greatly

20 hold, reduce damage from floods

21 filter, flows from, into

22 remove bad things, enters

23 Thanks to, that reaches the sea

24 as the Earth's lungs

25 a huge volume of, necessary

26 keep me healthy, clean

27 aren't they

28 from nature to living things

29 to protect mudflats

본문 TEST Step 3   p.32~33

1 갯벌, 자연의 선물

2 갯벌은 바닷가의 진흙이 있는 넓은 지역이다.

3 갯벌은 조수와 함께 나타나고 사라진다.

4 썰물일 때 갯벌이 드러나고, 밀물일 때 바다에 덮인다.

5 갯벌은 바다 생물과 사람, 지구를 많은 방면에서 돕는다.

6 갯벌의 역할을 이해하는 것이 중요하다.

7 갯벌이 무엇을 하는지 살펴보자.

8 갯벌은 바닷가에 있는 많은 생물들에게 집이다.

9 플랑크톤처럼 작은 생명체뿐만 아니라 게와 물고기도 그곳에 산다.

10 갯벌은 그들에게 다양한 종류의 먹이를 제공한다.

11 또한, 많은 새들도 그곳에서 먹이를 먹는다.

12 게: 갯벌은 나의 단란한 집이에요.

13 갯벌은 사람들에게도 유익하다.

14 갯벌 지역 인근에 사는 사람들은 근처에서 물고기와 다른 바다 동물들을 잡아 생계를 꾸린다.

15 갯벌 덕분에 사람들은 신선한 해산물을 얻을 수 있다.

16 사람들은 갯벌에서 진흙 미끄럼 타기나 보디 페인팅과 같은 즐거운 활동을 즐길 수 있다.

17 그들은 또한 그곳에서 바다 동물들을 먹는 수많은 새를 관찰할 수도 있다.

18 남자아이: 갯벌은 생명체에게 주는 자연의 선물이에요!

19 갯벌은 환경에 크게 도움이 된다.

20 갯벌은 많은 양의 물을 수용해서 홍수의 피해를 줄여 준다.

21 또한, 갯벌은 땅에서 바다로 흘러가는 물을 걸러내 준다.

22 물이 바다로 들어가기 전에 물속에 있는 나쁜 물질을 갯벌이 제거한다.

23 갯벌 덕분에 바다에 도착한 물은 깨끗하다.

24 갯벌은 지구의 폐 역할을 한다.

25 그것들은 지구상의 생명에게 필요한 많은 양의 산소를 생산한다.

26 지구: 갯벌은 나를 건강하고 깨끗하게 지켜 줘요.

27 갯벌은 멋진 곳이다, 그렇지 않은가?

28 그곳은 자연이 지구상의 생물들에게 준 선물이다.

29 이러한 이유로, 갯벌을 보호하는것은 필수이다.

본문 TEST Step 4 - Step 5   p.34~37

1 Mudflats, Nature's Gift

2 Mudflats are large areas of muddy land at the seaside.

3 They appear and disappear with every tide.

4 During low tides, they show up, and during high tides, they are covered by the sea.

5 Mudflats help sea creatures, people, and the Earth in many ways.

6 It is important to understand the roles of mudflats.

7 Let's see what they do.

8 Mudflats are home to a lot of living things at the seaside.

9 Not only very small living things like plankton but also crabs and fish live there.

10 Mudflats provide various types of food for them.

11 Also, many birds eat food there.

12 Crab: Mudflats are my home sweet home.

13 Mudflats are good for people, too.

14 People who live near mudflat areas make a living by catching fish and other sea animals nearby.

15 Thanks to mudflats, people can get fresh seafood.

16 People can enjoy fun activities, such as mud sliding and body painting on mudflats.

17 They can also watch a large number of birds that feed on the sea animals there.

18 Boy: Mudflats are nature's gift to living things!

19 Mudflats help the environment greatly.

20 Mudflats hold a lot of water, so they can reduce damage from floods.

21 Also, mudflats filter water that flows from the land into the sea.

22 They remove bad things in the water before it enters the sea.

23 Thanks to mudflats, the water that reaches the sea is clean.

24 Mudflats work as the Earth's lungs.

25 They produce a huge volume of oxygen that is necessary for life on the Earth.

26 Earth: Mudflats keep me healthy and clean.

27 Mudflats are wonderful places, aren't they?

28 They are a gift from nature to living things on the Earth.

29 For all these reasons, it is necessary to protect mudflats.

Enjoy Writing B

1. with few, little
2. Not only, but also, such as
3. during the day
4. it, to wear, to block

Enjoy Writing B

1. about Mudflats
2. muddy land, seaside
3. Not only, but also, such as
4. show up, are covered by
5. to wear, to protect yourself, can bite

Wrap Up 1

1. finished making, want to hear
2. wonder what you will do
3. going, go fishing , climb a mountain
4. Is, all
5. On, going to go swimming
6. a lot of

Enjoy Writing B

1. Deserts are dry land with few plants and little water.
2. Not only plants like elephant trees but also animals such as lizards and desert snakes live there.
3. It is hot during the day and cold at night.
4. If you go to a desert, it is important to wear a hat to block the sun.

Enjoy Writing B

1. All about Mudflats
2. Mudflats are muddy land at the seaside.
3. Not only plants like *hamcho* but also animals such as crabs and fish live there.
4. They show up during low tides and are covered by the sea during high tides.
5. If you go to mudflats, it is important to wear long clothes to protect yourself from animals that can bite you.

Wrap Up 1

1. B: I just finished making a plan for my trip. Do you want to hear it?
2. G: Sure. I wonder what you will do.
3. B: On the first day, I'm going to go fishing on a lake. The next day, I'm going to climb a mountain.
4. G: Is that all?
5. B: No. On the last day, I'm going to go swimming.
6. G: Wow. You will do a lot of activities.

단어 TEST Step 1 p.40

01 팀 동료　02 완벽한　03 침착한
04 이루다, 달성하다　05 어려움, 곤경, 장애
06 직면하다, 직시하다　07 상
08 무서운　09 실패하다, ~하지 못하다
10 마침내　11 긍정적인　12 점잖은
13 야구의 루　14 인정하다, 알아보다
15 문장　16 비록 ~일지라도　17 재활용하다
18 극복하다　19 얻다, 획득하다　20 우수, 탁월, 뛰어남
21 아픔, 고통　22 주다, 수여하다, 증정하다
23 노력　24 예우하다, ~을 공경하다
25 빌려주다　26 주요한　27 뛰어난
28 존경　29 풀다, 해결하다　30 무례하게
31 지지　32 재능이 있는　33 구, 구절
34 인종 차별　35 마음속으로 생각하다
36 더 이상 ~ 아닌　37 1등을 하다, 우승하다
38 ~을 거절하다, 거부하다, 소리를 줄이다　39 포기하다
40 반복해서　41 A에게 B를 수여하다, 증정하다
42 타석에서　43 눈을 의심하다(놀람)

단어 TEST Step 2 p.41

01 achieve　02 calm　03 recognize
04 difficulty　05 perfect　06 earn
07 although　08 excellence　09 pain
10 award　11 excellent　12 positive
13 face　14 recycle　15 respect
16 honor　17 fail　18 solve
19 talented　20 support　21 finally
22 gentle　23 present　24 rudely
25 teammate　26 sentence　27 bat
28 effort　29 lend　30 major
31 overcome　32 terrible　33 stadium
34 base　35 give up　36 think to oneself
37 no longer　38 thanks to　39 over and over
40 win first place　41 turn down
42 present A with B　43 take a class

단어 TEST Step 3 p.42

1 excellent, 뛰어난　2 teammate, 팀 동료
3 baseman, (1, 2, 3) 루수　4 fail, 실패하다, ~하지 못하다
5 rudely, 무례하게　6 classical, (음악이) 클래식의

7 pain, 아픔, 고통　8 lend, 빌려주다
9 major, 주요한　10 overcome, 극복하다
11 bat, (공을) 치다　12 positive, 긍정적인
13 recognize, 인정하다, 알아보다
14 award, 상　15 calm, 침착한　16 support, 지지

대화문 TEST Step 1 p.43~44

Listen & Speak 1 A
1. find, math problem / too hard, I'm not good at math / Let, see, It's important that, to solve, use
2. looks great / finish yours / draw, How, good at drawing / takes, important, as often as you can / mean, keep practicing / right

Listen & Speak 1 B
1. hard to be, What / important, never give up / not forget
2. hard to, should / It's important that / will not forget

Listen & Speak 2 A
1. hard to do / matter / how to make / What do you mean by / mean, easy to do
2. have, want to win first place / crossed / What do you mean by / means, wish, good luck

Listen & Speak 2 B
1. are better than / What, mean by / mean, together, than working alone
2. Practice, perfect / mean by / mean, by doing, over and over

Conversation A
To achieve, failed, However, give up, took, classes, Finally, achieved, that, never give up

Conversation B
look, wrong / don't think, achieve / What do you mean by that / fail auditions, have to give up / actor / famous / failed more than / should keep trying, practice / It's important that you never give up

대화문 TEST Step 2 p.45~46

Listen & Speak 1 A
1. G: Hey, Minho. Did you find the answer to the math problem?
B: No. It's too hard for me. I'm not good at math.
G: Let me see. It's important that you use this math rule to solve the problem.
B: Oh, I see. I'll use it.

2. G: Your poster looks great.

B: Thanks, Kate. Did you finish yours?

G: Not yet. I can't draw well. How can I become good at drawing?

B: It takes time. It's important that you draw as often as you can.

G: You mean I should keep practicing?

B: That's right.

Listen & Speak 1 B

1. A: It's hard to be a good dancer. What should I do?

B: It's important that you never give up.

A: Okay. I will not forget that.

2. A: It's hard to write a good story. What should I do?

B: It's important that you read many books.

A: Okay. I will not forget that.

Listen & Speak 2 A

1. G: Oh, this is hard to do.

B: What's the matter?

G: Can you teach me how to make cookies?

B: Sure. It's a walk in the park.

G: What do you mean by that?

B: I mean it's easy to do.

2. B: I have a singing contest tomorrow. I really want to win first place.

G: I'll keep my fingers crossed for you.

B: What do you mean by "keep my fingers crossed"?

G: It means I wish you good luck.

B: Thank you.

Listen & Speak 2 B

1. A: Two heads are better than one.

B: What do you mean by "Two heads are better than one"?

A: I mean working together is better than working alone.

2. A: Practice makes perfect.

B: What do you mean by "Practice makes perfect"?

A: I mean you learn something by doing it over and over.

Conversation A

M: To achieve my dream, I went to many auditions, but I often failed. However, I never gave up. I took acting and dancing classes. Finally, I achieved my goal. It's important that you never give up.

Conversation B

Hana: You look sad, Jiho. What's wrong?

Jiho: I don't think I can achieve my dream.

Amy: What do you mean by that?

Jiho: I want to be an actor, but I always fail auditions.

Maybe I have to give up.

Amy: Do you know this actor?

Jiho: Sure. He's a famous movie star.

Amy: He failed more than 100 auditions.

Jiho: Really? Maybe I should keep trying. I will practice more for my next audition.

Hana: That's right! It's important that you never give up.

본문 TEST Step 1

01 Breaks, Color Line
02 It, on April

03 went on, as, for

04 couldn't believe, eyes

05 first, American, player on

06 color line, broken

07 faced many difficulties

08 Although, talented, gentle, with

09 Every, turned, down because

10 bat, rudely, at

11 thought, himself, keep, focus

12 try, become, like

13 there, be more, league

14 put, energy into

15 With practice, batting, running

16 effort moved, teammates

17 one, up, tapped, on
18 Do, listen to

19 doing fine

20 support helped, to, harder

21 Finally, earned, respect, other

22 Thanks to, won, in

23 recognized, presented, with, same

24 other, asked, to join

25 uniform number

26 no longer, to honor

27 however, every, wears, wore
28 is called

본문 TEST Step 2

01 Breaks the Color Line

02 on April 15, 1947

03 African American, as, for

04 couldn't believe their eyes

05 the first African American player

06 the color line was broken

07 faced many difficulties

08 Although, talented player, to play with him

09 turned the team down

10 was at bat, rudely shouted at

11 thought to himself, keep calm, focus on

12 become, who people like

13 there will be more

14 put, into

15 With practice, at batting, base running

16 effort moved, teammates

17 shouted at, one of his teammates, up to, tapped him on the shoulder

18 Do not listen to   19 doing fine

20 helped, to play harder

21 earned the respect

22 Thanks to, won

23 recognized, presented, with, same year

24 other, asked, to join

25 uniform number

26 no longer wear, to honor him

27 Every, however, wears, wore   28 is called

1 Jackie Robinson 인종 차별을 깨다

2 1947년 4월 15일 뉴욕시에서였다.

3 아프리카계 미국인 Jackie Robinson은 브루클린 다저스의 2루수로 경기장에 나갔다.

4 사람들은 자신들의 눈을 의심했다.

5 그는 메이저리그 팀에서 경기한 최초의 아프리카계 미국인 선수였다.

6 그날 인종 차별이 깨졌다.

7 Robinson은 많은 어려움에 직면했다.

8 Robinson은 재능 있는 선수이고 온화한 사람이었지만 그의 팀원들은 그와 함께 경기하기를 원하지 않았다.

9 Robinson이 팀에 있었기 때문에 모든 호텔에서 그 팀을 거절했다.

10 그가 타석에 있을 때, 관중석에 있는 사람들이 그에게 무례하게 소리치기도 했다.

11 Robinson은 마음속으로 생각했다. '나는 평정심을 유지하고 야구에 집중해야 해.

12 나는 노력해서 사람들이 좋아하는 선수가 될 거야.

13 그러면 다음 시즌에는 아프리카계 미국인 선수가 리그에 더 많이 생길 거야.'

14 Robinson은 자신의 모든 시간과 에너지를 야구에 집중했다.

15 연습을 함으로써 그는 타격과 주루를 잘하게 되었다.

16 Robinson의 노력은 그의 팀원들을 감동시켰다.

17 사람들이 Robinson에게 소리쳤을 때, 그의 팀 동료 중 한 명이 Robinson에게 다가가 어깨를 두드렸다.

18 "그들 말을 듣지 마.

19 너는 잘하고 있어."라고 그가 말했다.

20 그의 지지는 Robinson이 더 열심히 경기하는 데 도움이 됐다.

21 마침내, Robinson은 다른 선수들과 팬들의 존경을 받았다.

22 Robinson 덕분에 다저스는 1947년에 내셔널리그 챔피언십에서 우승하게 되었다.

23 리그에서는 Robinson의 탁월함을 인정했고, 같은 해에 그에게 신인상을 수여했다.

24 그 시즌 이후, 다른 팀들은 아프리카계 미국인 선수들에게 자신들의 팀에 합류할 것을 요청했다.

25 Robinson의 등 번호는 42번이었다.

26 메이저리그 팀의 야구 선수들은 그에 대한 존경을 보여 주기 위해 더 이상 42번을 달지 않는다.

27 하지만 매년 4월 15일, 모든 선수들은 Robinson이 달았던 번호를 단다.

28 이 날을 '재키 로빈슨 데이'라고 부른다.

1 Jackie Robinson Breaks the Color Line

2 It was New York City on April 15, 1947.

3 Jackie Robinson, an African American, went on the field as second baseman for the Brooklyn Dodgers.

4 People couldn't believe their eyes.

5 He was the first African American player to play on a Major League team.

6 That day, the color line was broken.

7 Robinson faced many difficulties.

8 Although Robinson was a talented player and a gentle person, his teammates did not want to play with him.

9 Every hotel turned the team down because Robinson was on the team.

10 When he was at bat, people in the stands rudely shouted at him.

11 Robinson thought to himself, 'I need to keep calm and focus on baseball.

12 I will try and become a player who people like.

13 Then, next season, there will be more African American players in the league.'

14 Robinson put all his time and energy into baseball.

15 With practice, he became great at batting and base running.

16 Robinson's effort moved his teammates.

17 When people shouted at Robinson, one of his

teammates walked up to Robinson and tapped him on the shoulder.

18 "Do not listen to them.

19 You're doing fine," he said.

20 His support helped Robinson to play harder.

21 Finally, Robinson earned the respect of other players and fans.

22 Thanks to Robinson, the Dodgers won the National League Championship in 1947.

23 The league recognized Robinson's excellence and presented him with the Rookie of the Year Award in the same year.

24 After that season, other teams asked African American players to join them.

25 Robinson's uniform number was 42.

26 Baseball players in Major League teams no longer wear the number 42 to honor him.

27 Every year, however, on April 15, every player wears the number that Robinson wore.

28 The day is called "Jackie Robinson Day."

2. France was the first country which I visited.

3. Mary is the girl who I met in Paris.

4. The blue watch is the gift which I bought there for my brother.

Enjoy Writing B

1. How I Will Achieve My Dream

2. I want to be a designer.

3. There are three things that I need to do to achieve my dream.

4. I need to be healthy, be creative, and never give up.

5. Being healthy will help me keep going for my dream.

6. Being creative will help me do something different.

7. Plus, I will always tell myself never to give up because it will make me try harder.

Wrap Up 2

1. B: It's difficult to learn English.

2. G: Rome was not built in a day.

3. B: What do you mean by that?

4. G: I mean it takes time to achieve something.

5. B: I see .

구석구석지문 TEST Step 1   p.57

Language in Use

1. last year

2. the first country which, visited

3. who, met

4. gift which I bought, for

Enjoy Writing B

1. How, Achieve

2. want to be

3. that, need to, to achieve

4. healthy, creative, give up

5. Being, help, keep going

6. help me do

7. myself, to give up, make me try

Wrap Up 2

1. It's, to learn

2. was not built

3. What, mean by

4. takes, to achieve something

5. see

구석구석지문 TEST Step 2   p.58

Language in Use

1. I visited three countries last year.

MEMO

적중 100

영어 기출 문제집

정답 및 해설

시사 | 박준언